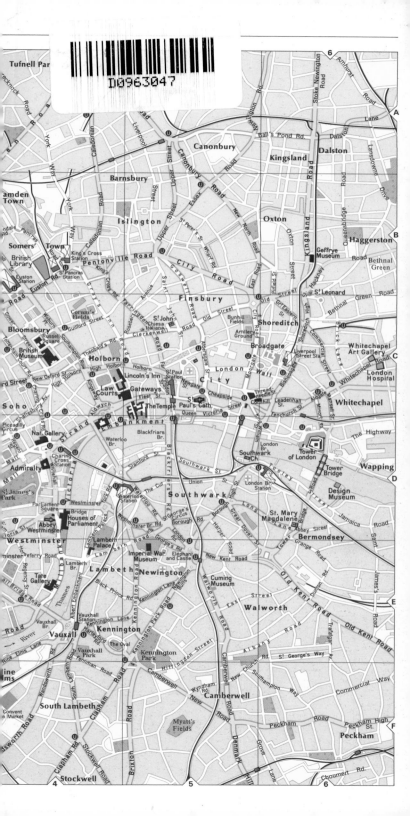

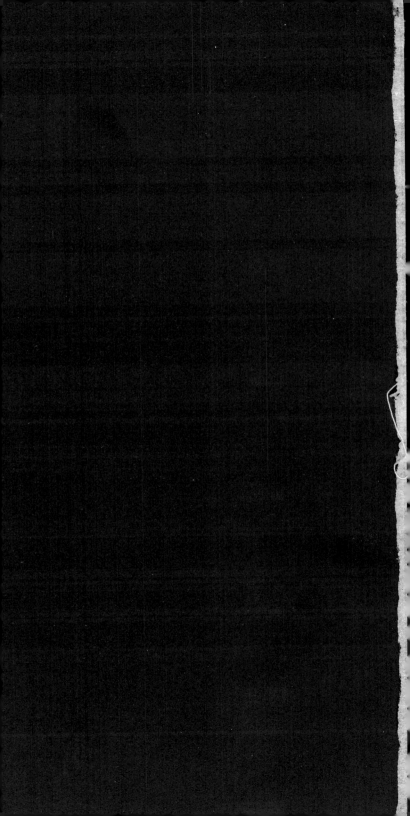

"A few customers came, chiefly for bathing-suits and hat-guards, and on Saturday night the cheapest straw hats and ties, and Mr Polly found himself more and more drawn towards the shop door and the social charm of the street." H.G. Wells

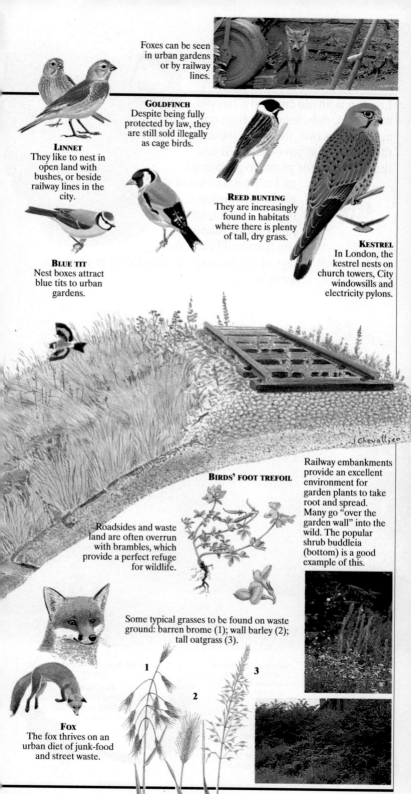

Foxes can be seen in urban gardens or by railway lines.

LINNET
They like to nest in open land with bushes, or beside railway lines in the city.

GOLDFINCH
Despite being fully protected by law, they are still sold illegally as cage birds.

REED BUNTING
They are increasingly found in habitats where there is plenty of tall, dry grass.

BLUE TIT
Nest boxes attract blue tits to urban gardens.

KESTREL
In London, the kestrel nests on church towers, City windowsills and electricity pylons.

BIRDS' FOOT TREFOIL

Railway embankments provide an excellent environment for garden plants to take root and spread. Many go "over the garden wall" into the wild. The popular shrub buddleia (bottom) is a good example of this.

Roadsides and waste land are often overrun with brambles, which provide a perfect refuge for wildlife.

Some typical grasses to be found on waste ground: barren brome (1); wall barley (2); tall oatgrass (3).

FOX
The fox thrives on an urban diet of junk-food and street waste.

GARDEN WALLS

Ivy-leaved toadflax was first introduced east of London in about 1600 and is now common on walls over most of Britain.

London is an old city and it has old walls. Sun, rain, wind and frost nag at the bricks over the years, loosening the mortar that binds them. At last there is room for plants to get a hold and a habitat of small plants and insects begins. London has many exotic plants which arrived in the great days of sea trading and now thrive in exposed, sunny walls.

HOVERFLY
Its wasp-like appearance deters would-be predators but it is actually harmless.

HOUSE SPARROW
A very common bird in London, it moves around in groups and nests in holes in walls.

STARLING
Huge flocks arrive in central London on winter evenings, drawn by the warmth.

Red valerian grows wild, mainly in the south of London.

DUNNOCK
A quiet little bird which is often seen hopping along picking for food.

Oxford ragwort thrives in the dry, dusty environment of walls and waste ground.

Canadian fleabane is very common in London.

BLACKBIRD
One of Britain's best-loved birds, the blackbird is a soulful singer.

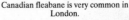

BROWN RAT
These animals flourish in sewers and on waste land. They are true urban survivors.

HISTORY

1st–10th Centuries: The Foundations

55–4 BC
The first Roman expeditions to Britain.

70–84 AD
Wales, the North and most of Scotland fall to the Romans.

Medal from the end of the 3rd century showing the Emperor Constantine.

409–10
Britain rebels and puts an end to Roman domination.

Roman mosaic excavated in the City (right).

c. 450
The Saxons invade Britain and settle in Kent.

Charles of Orleans in the Tower of London.

Londinium. The name is of Celtic origin, and was probably that of a Roman stronghold established soon after the conquest of Britain by the armies of Claudius (r. 41–54 AD). The site was chosen in 43, upstream from the Thames estuary, where the river was fordable. In approximately 50 the construction of a bridge across the river made London an important junction, which expanded to become a busy administrative and commercial settlement. This first period ended in 60–1, when the warrior-queen Boudicca from East Anglia attacked London, burned it and slaughtered up to seventy thousand Romans.

The biggest city in Britain. The important business and mercantile center of London was quickly rebuilt after the revolt had been put down. It became the seat of the garrison (inside a large fort), of the procurator (tax collector) and of the governor of Britain. It contained the only mint in the country. The city was surrounded by a wall more than 2 miles long; at its peak in the 3rd century there were almost forty thousand inhabitants. Raw materials and luxury goods from all parts of the empire arrived on the quays lining the Thames, while London exported corn, wood, silver and slaves. In the 4th century London gradually declined, thanks to British uprisings against the Romans and invasions from abroad. But when the Roman legions finally left Britain in 410, London managed to survive.

Ludenwick. Around 500 the city appeared largely deserted as the Saxons, its new conquerors, were installed outside the old Roman fortifications. In 604 the first Saxon bishop Mellitus founded St Paul's Cathedral in London, which was part of the kingdom of Essex; by the 8th century the city had recovered much of its former importance, and its troubles had diminished. In spite of Danish invasions in the 9th and 10th centuries, it continued to expand as a trading center, and took advantage of the lack of a centralized monarchy to acquire the first shoots of a civic administration, the City. Around 1050 the Anglo-Saxon King Edward the Confessor (r. 1042–66) began the construction of Westminster Abbey, consecrated in 1065. His royal residence was nearby.

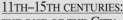

11th–15th Centuries:
The Rise of the City

The Norman Conquest reinforced the power of London. After the victory of 1066, William the Conqueror (r. 1066–87) kept guard over the City using three fortresses: the Tower, Castle Baynard and Montfichet Tower. But royal power soon became centered at Westminster, where it was to remain for the next five hundred years, separate

Henry VI (1422–71) and St Edmund.

from the power of the City. The tools of government were all concentrated in London: the royal palace, parliament and the law courts in Westminster, the law schools at the gates of the City and the Mint in the Tower.

PRIVILEGES. With commerce now flourishing, the City sought a means of keeping itself as separate from the Crown as possible. It took advantage of political difficulties in the 12th and 13th centuries to obtain greater control over its own affairs. In 1191 the future King John gave it the status of a self-governing community and in 1215 (when he was king) the right to elect its own mayor. In 1319 Edward II recognized the City's autonomy, and from 1351 it elected its own council. By the end of the 14th century London had attained such independence that the sovereign himself could go there only with the consent of the municipality.

HARD TIMES. Between 1348 and 1375 the Black Death killed half the population of London. It was followed by a period of grave social unrest, and in 1381 the imposition of a poll tax led to the Peasants' Revolt led by Wat Tyler. One hundred thousand men marched on London, sacked the town, murdered the archbishop of Canterbury and won concessions from Richard II before Tyler was seized and put to death. The badly prepared uprising then fizzled out.

THE CAPITAL CITY. During the 15th century London became the uncontested capital of England. Only the spiritual leadership lay outside, in Canterbury, but high-ranking clerics built homes in and around London in imitation of the nobility. In 1450 London was shaken by an insurrection led by Jack Cade, who entered the capital with forty thousand men from Kent and Sussex and submitted his demands. But the insurgents eventually dispersed, and Cade was killed trying to escape. The Wars of the Roses (1455–85) hardly touched London, but the accession of Henry VII (Henry Tudor) in 1485 was the beginning of England's Golden Age.

THE 16TH CENTURY: THE AGE OF THE TUDORS

THE PORT OF LONDON. London had relatively poor maritime connections with great mercantile ports such as Venice, Lisbon and Genoa. But in the 16th century the port of London expanded, forging new links with the Americas and east coast of India. Merchants evolved sophisticated trading

864–99
The start of the Danish Conquest and the reign of Alfred the Great.

1066
The Norman Conquest.

1190
Richard the Lionheart leaves for the Crusades. His brother Prince John becomes regent.

Effigy of Richard II (r. 1377–1400).

1199
Richard's brother, John Lackland, succeeds to the throne.

1215
Civil war. King John signs the Magna Carta.

1348
The Black Death.

1492
Christopher Columbus discovers America.

1517
Martin Luther and the Reformation.

View of old London Bridge before 1760.

1509–47
Reign of Henry VIII. The break with Rome, precipitated by the king's insistence on nullifying his marriage in 1533, splits the church in England.

1553–8
Reign of the Catholic Mary Tudor. Persecution of the Protestants.

1603–25
Reign of James VI of Scotland as James I of England.

Queen Elizabeth I (right).

1605
The Gunpowder Plot led by Guy Fawkes, the last important Catholic conspiracy.

Southwark Cathedral in 1647.

techniques, forming companies with shares and privileges given by royal charter. The first was the Muscovy Company of Merchant Adventurers in 1555; the Virginia Company of London was created to colonize and develop lands discovered by Sir Walter Raleigh in 1585. The East India Company was formed in 1600. It dominated the subcontinent for two hundred years and played a major role in the developing port of London. New-found prosperity brought a dramatic rise in population, which grew from 50,000 inhabitants at the start of the century to 200,000 in 1600. London spread out principally to the northwest, and to the east beyond the port as far as Wapping and Limehouse.

THE DISSOLUTION OF THE MONASTERIES. Two acts of Dissolution passed by parliament on the orders of Henry VIII in 1536 and 1539 brought in money, most of which was spent fighting the French. King and City took over the two main services provided by the monasteries, namely hospitals and education.

THE GOLDEN AGE OF QUEEN ELIZABETH. The growth of learning received a great boost when William Caxton set up the first printing press in 1477, near Westminster Abbey. The reign of Elizabeth I (1558–1603) saw great developments in the arts, particularly music, with such composers as William Byrd, John Bull and Orlando Gibbons; and also the theater, with William Shakespeare (1564–1616), Christopher Marlowe (1564–93) and many other dramatists. Even in its Golden Age, England was vulnerable to threats from abroad: in 1588 it defended itself against the Spanish Armada, which was defeated by a combination of bad weather and the navy under the command of Sir Francis Drake.

The 17th Century: Good Times and Bad

1611
Authorized Version of the Bible published.

1649
Execution of Charles I.

Great Fire of London in 1666.

THE CIVIL WARS. During the civil wars (1642–6 and 1648) London sided with the anti-royalist Puritans, who favored parliament and the Commonwealth. The City was suspicious of Charles II at the Restoration of the Stuarts in 1660, and after James II lost his throne in the revolution of 1688 it welcomed William III and Queen Mary's acceptance of the Bill of Rights.

LONDON'S MISFORTUNES. In 1665 London was ravaged by bubonic plague, which claimed 100,000 lives between April and November and led to a serious economic crisis. The capital was abandoned: the king moved to Oxford, and grass grew in the streets. The next year, the city was still recovering when it was destroyed between the September 2 and 6 by the Great Fire, which wiped out all the ancient buildings. Gradually the capital was rebuilt under the direction of Sir Christopher Wren, but many projects had to be abandoned in favor of less costly developments. The City never recovered its former density of population, for wealthier inhabitants moved to areas in west London where the aristocracy lived. To the east, new districts grew up as the docks expanded. By the end of the century London had some 600,000 inhabitants.

THE FINANCIAL CAPITAL OF THE WORLD. In the 17th century London finally overtook Amsterdam as the biggest financial and commercial center in the world. Thanks to the return of the Jewish community, authorized by Oliver Cromwell (1599–1658) in 1655, and the installation of the French Huguenot refugees at Spitalfields, London was able to ensure its supremacy. Its new status was symbolized by the founding of the Bank of England in 1694.

The coronation of George IV in 1821.

1653–8
Oliver Cromwell becomes the Lord Protector of England.

1757
Victory at Plassey in Bengal ensures British supremacy in India.

1763
The Treaty of Paris cedes Canada to the British, who had taken possession of Quebec in 1759.

1773
The Boston Tea Party. American colonists protest at the duty on imported tea which favors the East India Company.

THE 18TH CENTURY: GEORGIAN LONDON

EXPANSION. The Hanoverian period was the great age of urban development. London grew at an astonishing rate, most of all around the West End. There were three phases of development. In the first half of the century the great squares such as Hanover, Cavendish, Grosvenor and Berkeley Squares were laid out. After 1763 the West End underwent further development at the hands of two rival architects, William Chambers and Robert Adam. Between 1812 and 1830 the prince regent (the future George IV) embarked on a series of developments that gave the West End some of its finest buildings, such as those around Regent's Park. The construction of further Thames bridges between 1750 and 1819 boosted developments south of the river. The population continued to increase (though it only passed the one million mark around 1815), and social inequality became more apparent. While the West End was the center of the fashionable world, living conditions for the majority of Londoners remained precarious. A system of street lighting with oil lamps was introduced in 1750, and major renovations were carried out around Westminster in 1762. Sewers and the public water supply were extended, the streets and sidewalks were paved, statues were erected in public places, and houses were systematically numbered. But there was much unrest: the anti-Catholic Gordon Riots of 1780 and the French Revolution of 1789 brought the possibility of a bloody uprising uncomfortably close to London society.

The prince regent in 1815 (opposite).

1776
American Declaration of Independence.

1793–1815
Wars with France.

The opening of Tower Bridge in 1894.

1824
Legalization of trade unions. Opening of the first railway line in Britain, between Stockton and Darlington.

Queen Victoria
(r. 1837–1901).

1829
The Catholic Emancipation Bill grants civil rights to Roman Catholics.

1832
The Great Reform Bill extends the franchise.

Crystal Palace in 1851 (right).

1833–4
Abolition of slavery. Introduction of workhouses.

St Pancras Station after 1869.

1876
Victoria becomes Empress of India. Primary education becomes compulsory (this is free after 1891).

1899–1902
The Boer War.

1906
Birth of the Labour Party.

1918
Votes for women over the age of thirty.

Harrods, the world-famous store (right).

THE VICTORIAN ERA

THE BIGGEST CITY IN THE WORLD. From a total of 900,000 inhabitants in 1801, the population of London passed 2.4 million in 1851 to reach 6.5 million by the time Queen Victoria died in 1901. The capital attracted immigrants from all over the British Isles and Europe, in particular Jews from central Europe who settled in the East End. After 1870 births began consistently to exceed the mortality rate.

BUSINESS CAPITAL OF THE WORLD. The establishment of the great banks, the Stock Exchange, Corn Exchange and insurance companies all helped to maintain the City of London as the world center of capitalism. The port of London, which was greatly expanded by the opening of new docks between 1868 and 1905, imported raw materials and food from all over the world, and in turn exported vast quantities of manufactured goods. Much of this industry too was based in London.

THE GREAT EXHIBITION.
The brainchild of Queen Victoria's husband, Prince Albert, the Great Exhibition opened on May 1, 1851. The Crystal Palace, a glass and iron cathedral erected in Hyde Park, was designed by Joseph Paxton as a symbol of Britain's success. Six million visitors came to see the wonders on display, and there were almost 14,000 exhibitors from all over the empire.

PUBLIC TRANSPORT AND URBAN GROWTH.
The expansion of the railway system began to link London to the provinces in 1836. Then from 1863 the London underground railway (the "tube") provoked further growth of the capital. In 1820 London had an approximate radius of 3 miles: by 1914 this had tripled to 9 miles. Victorian suburbs stretched in every direction: long terraces of two-story brick houses, each with its own little patch of garden.

TWO FACES OF LONDON. The West End and the East End became the two opposite poles of London. The West End was the fashionable London of high society, with its fine houses for the rich and luxury shops that catered to their every need. The other face of London lay on the far side of the City in the East End, poor and squalid. The trade

union movement only developed seriously in London after 1880, the first big rally being held in Hyde Park in 1884; and in 1886 a mass meeting of the unemployed in Trafalgar Square sparked off a riot. The first major strike took place in the docks in 1889. The creation that same year of the London County Council, elected by the people and dominated by Fabian socialists, resulted in many reforms that improved living standards of the poor and underprivileged in the capital.

Fleet Street.

1921
Independence and partition of Ireland.

1931
Abolition of the Gold Standard, and creation of the Commonwealth.

THE 20TH CENTURY: A CITY IN RUINS

World War One hardly touched London at all, although the city did suffer its first air raid in 1915. The inter-war period that followed was marked by considerable further growth. The population of Greater London grew from 7.5 million in 1921 to 8.7 million in 1939. The suburban areas doubled in size. At the same time, the City was actually getting smaller: in 1931 it had only 11,000 residents. London also suffered from the effects of the economic depression during this period, with the General Strike of 1926, the Fascist rallies in the East End led by Sir Oswald Mosley, and hunger marches, of which the most famous was from the naval dockyards at Jarrow in 1936.

Churchill standing in the debris left by the Blitz.

WORLD WAR TWO AND THE BLITZ. London suffered two separate phases of bombardment during World War Two. After the Battle of Britain (August–September, 1940), the bombing raids in the winter of 1940–1 inflicted some terrible damage. Then, in 1944–5, the capital sustained some prolonged attacks by the V1 and V2 rockets, greatly increasing the number of casualties; and the docks, the City, the East End and Westminster were all partially destroyed. From June 1940 to December 1941 Britain was the last line of defence against Nazi Germany, and throughout the war it remained a refuge for foreign governments in exile.

1939–45
At war since 1939, Britain is led by Winston Churchill from May 1940.

1952
Accession of Queen Elizabeth II.

1969
Sectarian violence returns to Northern Ireland.

1972
Britain joins the Common Market.

1982
The Falklands War.

1989–90
Introduction of the poll tax and fall of Margaret Thatcher.

1990
John Major becomes prime minister.

POST-WAR DEVELOPMENTS. Even now, at the end of the 20th century, some of London's former grandeur still survives. But it is now the capital of a country which is no longer a great power on the world stage, though it did make a brave effort to keep up this illusion by staging the Festival of Britain in 1951. Its pride of place as the business center of the world was also hit by the closing of the docks between 1960 and 1980, and by the relocation to the provinces of much of the capital's industry. East and south London have suffered particularly from high levels of unemployment, the main victims being immigrants from former Asian and West Indian colonies who now live in the East End and the suburbs of Greater London. The physical appearance of the capital has also changed dramatically, the result of major development projects such as the recent Docklands conversion.

The Lloyd's Building in the City.

39

THE GREAT FIRE

The Great Fire of London began on Sunday, September 2, 1666, at 2 o'clock in the morning and continued burning until the following Thursday afternoon. With the exception of a small area in the northeast, the whole City center was devastated; St Paul's Cathedral was destroyed, along with 88 parish churches, 13,200 houses and countless works of art. But curiously this disaster claimed only twelve lives, and had the effect of finally ridding London of the Great Plague that had haunted it since the 14th century. Samuel Pepys, the cheerful and observant chronicler of London life, recorded the events in his *Diary*: "The wind mighty high, and driving [the fire] into the City; and everything, after so long a drought, proving combustible, even the very stones of churches."

Samuel Pepys
(1633–1703).

SAMUEL PEPYS
This great Londoner attained high government office, but the *Diary* he kept from 1660–9 was not intended for publication; written in shorthand it was not deciphered until 1825. It is a very personal record, as well as being a unique sourcebook for the events of the period, among them the Great Fire: "The fire . . . as it grew darker, appeared more and more; and in corners and upon steeples, and between churches and houses, as far as we could see up the hill of the City, in a most horrid, malicious, bloody flame. . . . We stayed till, it being darkish, we saw the fire as only one arch of fire from this to the other side of the bridge, and in a bow up the hill of above a mile long; it made me weep to see it."

Around 5p.m. on September 7, 1940, the Blitz hit London. (The word comes from the German *Blitzkrieg*, meaning "lightning war".) The attack began quite suddenly. Within twelve hours a thousand aeroplanes had bombed the capital and dropped shells with parachutes, starting more than a thousand fires: once again, London was burning. For the next two months more than two hundred bombers continued to harass and maim the capital. The Blitz finally came to an end with the most terrible raid of all on the night of May 10, 1941.

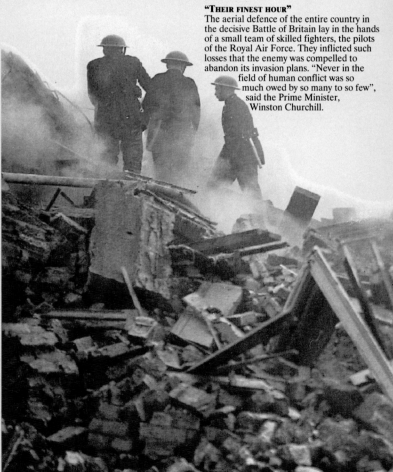

"THEIR FINEST HOUR"

The aerial defence of the entire country in the decisive Battle of Britain lay in the hands of a small team of skilled fighters, the pilots of the Royal Air Force. They inflicted such losses that the enemy was compelled to abandon its invasion plans. "Never in the field of human conflict was so much owed by so many to so few", said the Prime Minister, Winston Churchill.

THE BIGGEST TARGET IN THE WORLD

«We shall not flag or fail. We shall go on to the end... We shall defend our island whatever the cost may be. We shall fight on the beaches, we shall fight on the landing grounds, we shall fight in the fields and in the streets, we shall fight in the hills; we shall never surrender.»
Winston Churchill, 1940

BRAVING THE BOMBING

During the Blitz, in spite of the black-out, German planes dropped more than 100,000 high-explosive bombs and over one million incendiary devices. The terrible damage inflicted inspired a communal feeling of patriotic unity, and Londoners organized themselves to deal with the danger and hardship brought by the air raids. Fifteen thousand lives were lost, a relatively small figure in comparison with the 3.5 million houses that were destroyed or damaged.

"CROSS READINGS NEAR CHARING CROSS"

"To be read from top to bottom", recommends the caption to this illustration.

"A beggar works by standing out of doors in all weathers and getting varicose veins, chronic bronchitis, etc. It is a trade like any other; quite useless, of course – but many reputable trades are quite useless. And as a social type a beggar compares well with scores of others. He is honest compared with the sellers of patent medicines, high-minded compared with a newspaper proprietor, amiable compared with a hire-purchase tout – in short, a parasite, but a fairly harmless parasite."

George Orwell,
Down and Out in Paris and London

"The pre-1939 East End as a whole was rough, polyglot, noisy and in parts criminal. Courage, toughness and sometimes aggression were needed to survive. It never lacked vitality, even exuberance. Poverty undermined people but did not extinguish their spirit."

Peter Vansittart,
London, A Literary Companion

Following the Norman Conquest of 1066, French began to usurp the national language in Britain, though its influence on the different dialects was slow to take effect. The spelling of Middle English changed to resemble the spoken language rather more closely, for 11th and 12th-century scribes were strongly influenced by French models. By the 14th century, English had become a respectable written language as well as a spoken dialect; and for political, demographic and economic reasons the language spoken in London gradually evolved into the standard English which is in use today.

"COKENEY". This Middle English word originally meant "a cock's egg", a malformed egg sometimes laid by young chickens. By extension it could also be used to refer to a fool, an effeminate man, or a feeble-bodied townsman in contrast to a brawny peasant. During the course of the 17th century, *Cockney* came to be an affectionately pejorative word used to describe Londoners. By the 18th century it had become even more specific in application, meaning a working-class Londoner; in more snobbish society it was now being used in a way that was anything but affectionate. The expression "to be born within the sound of Bow Bells," means to be born within earshot of the City church of St Mary-le-Bow in Cheapside (which is not in fact all that close to the East End), and this is the one essential qualification for being a real Cockney. Formerly London grew up around two different nuclei, the commercial center of the City, and the political capital of Westminster. These two separate entities were only linked together during the 16th century. After the Great Fire, the more wealthy residents began to leave the City, whose population had formerly been drawn from all walks of life; they preferred instead the more exclusive surroundings of the

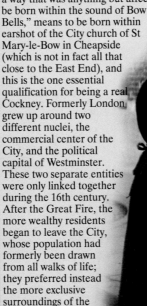

West End. The boundary beween the East End and West End in the 18th century occured around Soho Square: Regent Street was in part conceived as a *cordon sanitaire* between these two areas, a distinction that remained evident until well into the 19th century. After 1800 the construction of the docks brought a large working-class population into districts that then became collectively known as the East End. The character of the area was further defined by the increasing number of refugees and immigrants who created a class of artisans and tradesmen. The City remained as something of a little kingdom apart, retaining its own aristocracy, gentry and small businessmen. Thus, many different accents and dialects contributed towards the language of London.

STANDARD ENGLISH AND COCKNEY. The Liberal statesman WE Forster's Elementary Education Act of 1870 stressed the importance of teaching "correct English" as well as the traditional "three Rs" (reading, writing and arithmetic). It also encouraged the building of primary schools, where the children of the poor at last began to acquire some of the rudiments of an education. At the beginning of the 20th century, "Cockney" referred exclusively to a working-class Londoner, though for many the word is inseparable from the London that is described in Charles Dickens' novels. The novelist and critic JG Lockhart first coined the term "Cockney School" for some 19th-century writers (among them Keats and Shelley!) whose language in his opinion lacked the necessary classical purity. Then as now, the middle classes spoke what is known as "standard English". But a large percentage of Londoners do still talk with a mixture of accents (those of Essex and south-east London being particularly distinctive) together with a

A PUBLIC SCHOOL EDUCATION
"The low rich purr of a Great Western express is not the worst background for conversation, and the journey passed pleasantly enough. Nothing could have exceeded the kindness of the two men. They raised windows for some ladies, and lowered them for others, they rang the bell for the servant, they identified the colleges as the train slipped past Oxford, they caught books or bag-purses in the act of tumbling on to the floor. Yet there was nothing finicky about their politeness; it had the public school touch, and, though sedulous, was virile."
E.M. Forster,
Howards End

" 'My dear fellow,' said Sherlock Holmes ... 'life is infinitely stranger than anything the mind of man could invent. ... If we could fly out of that window, hover over this great city, gently remove the roofs, and peep in at the queer things going on, the strange coincidences, the plannings, the cross-purposes, the wonderful chains of events, working through generations, and leading to the most outre results, it would make all fiction with its conventionalities and foreseen conclusions most stale and unprofitable.' "
A Conan Doyle,
A Case of Identity

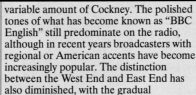

RHYMING SLANG
Market traders
evolved this curious
language as a secret
means of
communication; a
dealer could use it to
offer a low price to a
colleague, for
example, without
announcing it to his
other customers. The
rhyming tags often

contain a punning
reference to the word
they conceal, as in
"Edward Heath" for
"teeth", an allusion to
the British ex-
Premier's broad grin.

variable amount of Cockney. The polished tones of what has become known as "BBC English" still predominate on the radio, although in recent years broadcasters with regional or American accents have become increasingly popular. The distinction between the West End and East End has also diminished, with the gradual redistribution of the population. Before World War Two, the middle classes rarely set foot in the East End of London, but now many parts of the area have become "gentrified" and the 18th-century houses have become the homes of those with some money to spend. Even though the cheerful Cockney way of life is still associated with the East End, the accent has penetrated other social layers. And though the "working classes" do still predominate in the area to the east of the City, London is now a much greater mix of social groups.

THE COCKNEY REGION AND ACCENT. The present-day East End begins at Aldgate and runs the length of Commercial and Whitechapel Roads, taking in the districts of Stepney, Limehouse, Bow, Old Ford, Whitechapel and Bethnal Green in the process. One of the accent's most distinctive features is the "dropped aitch", ("half" becomes "arf"). "Th" is pronounced as "f" or "v", and sometimes even as "d"; the double t as in "butter" changes to a glottal stop or sometimes to a double d ("better" becomes "bedder"). The final t of a word can be dropped altogether ("didn'" for "didn't"). The "a" sound as in "take" changes to a long "i" ("tike"). But Cockney is also a state of mind as well as simply a London accent: its language is packed with whimsical word-plays and a cheerful disregard for the rules of grammar.

THE COCKNEY LANGUAGE. Cockney's best-known feature is its rhyming slang, which first appeared at the end of the 19th century and has been evolving ever since. Typical examples include "plates of meat" for "feet", "trouble and strife" for "wife", "bees and honey" for "money", "pleasure and pain" for "rain", and so on. To add to the confusion, half of the rhyming tag is sometimes omitted: thus "tit for tat", meaning "hat", is shortened to "titfer"; and "Lilian Gish" for "fish", becomes simply "Lilian" or "Lil". It is quite incomprehensible to the uninitiated, and, though less common now than before World War Two, remains a perfectly normal means of communication for market porters and stall-holders, who formerly used it when they didn't want their conversation to be understood by the police. Some of the most adept speakers of cockney today are traders in such places as Chapel Market in Islington, who sell china tea services or household linen at knock-down prices to the accompaniment of their own high-speed patter. These monologues, virtually incomprehensible to the tourist, rarely fail to work their good-humored magic on the gullible crowds who gather to listen.

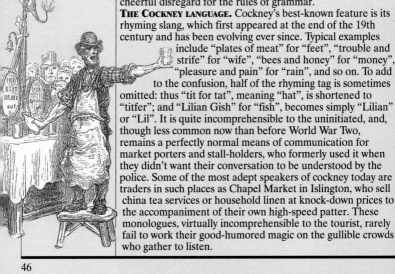

LONDON LIFE

Despite the much-publicized problems that it has recently undergone, for the vast majority of people the royal family remains the cornerstone of Britain. It is so much a part of the national life that interested visitors cannot fail to appreciate the stabilizing effect of the Crown upon the country as a whole. As head of the Anglican church, the queen has responsibilities that go beyond presiding at official ceremonies. She also has a part to play in the political life of the country. Nominally at least she chooses the prime minister and will dissolve Parliament at his request. This is a useful safety valve in times of political unrest.

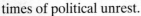

THE CORONATION OF ELIZABETH II
The elder daughter of George VI, Princess Elizabeth married Philip Mountbatten, later Duke of Edinburgh, in 1947. She was crowned on June 2, 1953.

PRINCE OF WALES
The title is reserved for the future monarch. Right: Edward, prince of Wales (later Edward VIII), stands behind his father, King George V.

QUEEN ELIZABETH II AND PRINCE PHILIP

The royal couple has four children: Charles (b. 1948), Prince of Wales; Anne (b. 1950), the Princess Royal; Andrew (b. 1960), Duke of York, and Edward (b. 1964). In 1960 the queen changed the family name from Windsor to Mountbatten-Windsor.

THE REIGN OF QUEEN VICTORIA

In 1837 the young Princess Victoria (1819–1901) succeeded her uncle William IV and became queen. In 1876 she also became empress of India. She was immensely popular for most of her long reign, a time when the British empire was at its height.

The Royal Guard consists of seven regiments: two of them are Household Cavalry (the Blues and Royals, and the Life Guards), and the other five are infantry (the Grenadier, Coldstream, Scots, Irish and Welsh Guards). The guards are equally at home on a tank or in the saddle on Horse Guards Parade riding in the ceremony of Trooping the Colour ● *53*.

THE HORSE GUARDS
1. *Blues and Royals*: blue tunic with red plume.
2. *Life Guards*: scarlet tunic and white plume.
THE FOOT GUARDS
They all wear scarlet tunic, dark blue trousers and a bearskin, but have different insignia.
3. *Grenadier Guards*: white plume on the left of the bearskin, and evenly spaced buttons.
4. *Coldstream Guards*: red plume on the right of bearskin, buttons in pairs.
5. *Irish Guards*: blue plume on the right, buttons in fours.
6. *Welsh Guards*: green and white plume on the left, buttons in fives.

Grenadier Guards entering
Ambassadors' Court in
St James's Palace
for the Changing
of the Guard.

The standard (left)
of the first battalion
of the Welsh Guards
(founded in 1915),
and that of the Life
Guards: the
sovereign's standard
(below).

THE SCOTS GUARDS

Opposite, above: The Scots
Guards bearing their standard
(regimental colors) at the Battle of
Alma (1854). The regiment of Scots Guards was
created in 1642 by Charles I. Their scarlet tunic differs
from the other Foot Guards by having buttons grouped in
threes and the thistle of Scotland on the collar. Unlike the
other regiments of the Brigade of Guards, there is no
plume on their bearskin, a helmet that came into use in
1831 and which was modeled on those of Napoleon's
Imperial Guard.

4   5   6

The London year is punctuated with ceremonies and celebrations that demonstrate the British love of tradition. Among the biggest public celebrations are Trooping the Colour, which takes place in June; the annual congregation of the Pearly Kings and Queens, at St Martin-in-the-Fields on the first Sunday in October; the Lord Mayor's Show, held on the second Saturday in November; and the Beating of the Bounds, which takes place every three years on Ascension Day.

PEARLY KINGS AND QUEENS
These costermongers wear costumes stitched with thousands of tiny pearl buttons. Every year since 1880 they have been elected by their borough, originally to help their fellow traders' relations with the police.

THE BEATING OF THE BOUNDS
The Beefeaters (Yeomen Warders of the Tower ▲ 183) escort a group of children (including choirboys), led by an almoner. The procession walks round the walls of the Tower of London, while the children strike the thirty-one ancient boundary marks with willow wands.

ROYAL BIRTHDAY
The sovereign's official birthday (not the Queen's actual birthday) is celebrated by Trooping the Colour on Horse Guards Parade, when the monarch reviews the seven regiments of the Royal Guard ● 50.

LORD MAYOR'S SHOW ▲ 146
In former times the procession used to take place on the Thames (above), with brightly decorated boats and barges. Today the incoming lord mayor reviews the troops at Mansion House before riding in his golden coach to be sworn in at the Royal Courts of Justice in the Strand.

TROOPING THE COLOUR
The "colours" are the regimental standards of the guards. The queen arrives from Buckingham Palace in a phaeton built for Queen Victoria and reviews the troops. The ceremony is a marvelous display of dazzling color and pageantry.

THE CITY CELEBRATES
The procession from the Mansion House to the Strand is magnificent, with pikemen in armor accompanying the lord mayor's coach (1757), drawn by six horses. The parade is led by the historic painted wooden effigies of Gog and Magog, the mythical giants who are supposed to have founded London.

London has some of the best theaters in the world, and theatergoing is one of the city's favorite pastimes. With plays from classical to modern, and with opera, ballet and an abundance of musical comedy, a hundred different theaters cater for all tastes: there is something for everyone. Much of its high standard and eclecticism is due to the training the actors undergo, following a system that is observed closely by other countries and is seen by many as one of the wonders of the modern theatrical world.

THE PALACE THEATRE
This enormous Victorian Gothic building opened in 1891, as the Royal English Opera House. The venture failed, so Augustus Harris took it over and opened it as a music-hall the following year as the Palace Theatre of Varieties. Pavlova and Nijinsky danced here. Too big for the produciton of straight plays, since 1924 it has been used for musical comedies, such as *Jesus Christ Superstar* (1986), *Les Miserables* (1992).

THE OLD BEDFORD
This old theater in Camden Town, was predominantly a music-hall. The upper circle (the "gods") and the boxes (above) inspired many paintings by Walter Sickert (1860–1942) ● *101*, who was the central figure in the Camden Town Group.

«I SAT IN THE DINGY BOX ABSOLUTELY ENTHRALLED. I FORGOT THAT I WAS IN LONDON AND IN THE NINETEENTH CENTURY.»

OSCAR WILDE

THE WEST END: THEATERLAND
Right, from top to bottom: Shaftesbury Avenue, the street of theaters; the front of the Albery Theatre; the Royal Opera House ▲ 274 ; the Theatre Royal Drury Lane. Like church architecture, West End theaters are mostly Victorian buildings designed for effect: imposing façades, immense pillars, and interiors decorated with statues, stucco and wrought ironwork. Inside is a wealth of fascinating history, and many theaters are open to the public during the day.

SHAKESPEAREAN FLOWERS
When Princess Elizabeth laid the foundation stone of the National Theatre in 1951, her bouquet was of flowers named in Shakespeare's plays, such as those in Perdita's garden in *The Winter's Tale.*

NATIONAL THEATRE
This is the most important theater complex in Britain. It was built on the South Bank by architect Denys Lasdun, a concrete fortress with terraces overlooking the river. It houses three separate theaters, the largest of which is named the Olivier after the company's first artistic director, Sir Laurence Olivier.

The English sport of cricket has its roots in the Middle Ages, and over the years has gradually turned into a national obsession that many Englishmen discuss endlessly all through the summer months. The name may come from *crice*, an ancient word for "stick", or from the French *cricquet*, a stick used in the game of boules. Cricket is a part of life in Commonwealth countries as well as in England, where the level of competition is extremely high and there are many important international Test matches.

THE FIELD
Two teams of eleven players meet on a large field in the center of which is the pitch, a carefully mown grass rectangle, 66 feet long and 10 feet wide and with a wicket at each end defended by a batsman.

FAIR PLAY
The behavior of players on the cricket field, like their respect for the rules of the game, is supposed to reflect the English temperament: there should be no swearing, no displays of temper and no arguments. The game itself is simple, but the rules are complicated.

HOME OF CRICKET
Lord's Cricket Ground has been the home of the MCC (Marylebone Cricket Club) since 1787.

THE EQUIPMENT
The wooden bat is 38 inches long and the blade is made of willow. The ball is covered in hard leather. The batsman wears pads and protective gloves.

THE INTERVAL
The British politician Lord Mancroft was a great lover of cricket, though he once described it as "a game which the English, not being a spiritual people, have invented in order to give themselves some conception of eternity."

HEADGEAR
A special cap completes
the cricketer's outfit, while umpires
and spectators often favor the traditional Panama.

THEY'RE OFF
Weather permitting,
the cricket season
opens in the second
week of April and
finishes in September
on the hallowed turf
of Lord's Cricket
Ground in London,
the Mecca of
cricketers
everywhere.

UNIFORM
Cricket clothes are distinctive
and elegant, in white or off-white.
Only the V-neck and waistband of
the jumper (with or without sleeves)
have bands of color. Modern protective
headgear is needed to cope with the
speed and force of today's bowling.

BEGINNING AND END OF THE GAME
The bowler sends the ball down to the opposite wicket; the batsman
tries to stop it and hit it as far as he can. In the time it takes for a
fielder to retrieve the ball, the batsmen run back and
forth between the wickets. Each "run" counts as
one point. To win, a team must score as many
runs as possible and get the opposing
team's batsmen "out" for as
few runs as possible.

PENALTIES
A batsman is "out" if the bowler
succeeds in knocking off the bails
placed horizontally on top of the wicket that the
batsman guards. He is also out if a fielder catches
the ball once he has hit it and before it touches
the ground.

THE WICKET
This consists of
three wooden
stumps 28 inches
high with the
bails resting
across the
top of
them.

LEARNING THE GAME
Cricket is taught at many English schools.

● PUBS

 One of the most characteristic features of English social life is the public house, the traditional meeting place for a pint of beer and a chat. Sport, politics and other issues of the day are freely discussed over a drink in a friendly and comfortable setting. Sadly, the large breweries that control most public houses have often introduced juke-boxes and noisy gambling machines to increase their already substantial profits in places that were once havens of calm away from the noisy streets outside.

THE LAW
Children under the age of 14 are normally not allowed in pubs. During World War I a law was passed restricting the hours of opening in an attempt to control the consumption of alcohol by workers in the munitions factories. It was repealed in 1989.

ATMOSPHERE
Pubs are cosy, designed to attract passers-by, with traditional games to play such as darts or skittles. During the Victorian era pubs also offered a more luxurious environment than the working man could hope to find at home. Left, the Queen Victoria, built around 1860. Far left, the Princess Louise.

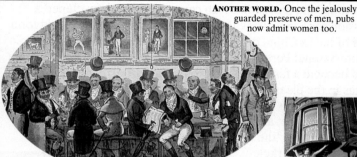

ANOTHER WORLD. Once the jealously guarded preserve of men, pubs now admit women too.

DRAFT BEER
The most common drink is bitter ale (bitter), a flat, unpressurized beer flavored with hops and served at room temperature. It is an acquired taste, and many visitors prefer lager, a pale fizzy beer, bland in flavor but sometimes deceptively strong. Dark Irish beers such as Guinness stout have greatly increased in popularity over the last twenty years.

PUB NAMES
Many pubs have names linked to local history or trades: the Carpenters' Arms, the Coach and Horses, the Ferry-boat Inn, the Waggoners and the Narrow-boat all evoke the character of a city now irrevocably changed by the invention of the motor car.

In the second half of the 17th century England developed a passion for a new drink that came from China. "I did send for a cup of tee (a China drink) of which I had never drank before," wrote Samuel Pepys in his diary in 1660. By the 18th century tea had become a fashionable refreshment, drunk in public by both sexes in the pleasure gardens of London such as Vauxhall and Ranelagh. It was celebrated in verse by Edmund Waller, Alexander Pope, and William Cowper, who borrowed his famous phrase, "the cups that cheer but not inebriate", from Bishop Berkeley.

THE TEA PLANT
Camellia sinensis is an Asiatic evergreen shrub, pruned for several years before being harvested to obtain the maximum number of buds. Different varieties, such as green teas (China), black fermented teas (India and Ceylon) or semi-fermented oolong (Taiwan), all come

from the same plant: the difference between them lies in the way the leaves are treated after picking. Each tea has a distinctive color and aroma, determined by the climate (ideally hot and humid), the altitude (6,500 feet) and the season in which it is harvested (spring is best). Quality also varies according to the leaves: the smallest and youngest leaves nearest the tip of the plant produce the finest teas, while the oldest and biggest leaves are used for teas of an inferior quality.

VITAL INGREDIENTS
Like wine, tea has regions renowned for producing leaves of outstanding flavor and fragrance. Darjeeling produces a fruity brew that goes well with cake, while Ceylon is excellent at breakfast. The teapot is silver, pewter, china or earthenware. Water must be free of lime and iron (which precipitates tannin).

TEA TIME

Some time in the 19th century Anna, Duchess of Bedford, began to serve tea and cake between luncheon and dinner in order to stave off what she called "that sinking feeling". Subsequently the ritual of afternoon tea was popularized, if not initiated, by Queen Victoria. It soon became a favorite British institution, conventionally presided over by the lady of the house and ideally situated at the fireside in winter or in the garden in summertime. The ritual establishes "tea time" as a time to relax and make civilized conversation. Henry James thought the day held no more pleasant period than the hour given over to afternoon tea. Small sandwiches, perhaps filled with thinly sliced cucumber, buttered scones with strawberry jam and thick or "clotted" cream, and a range of different cakes are traditional teatime accompaniments.

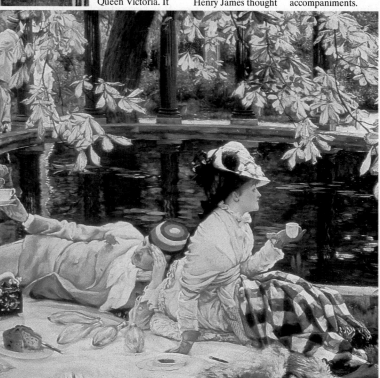

MAKING TEA

Care taken in the preparation will result in a brew which is bright and fragrant. Use freshly boiling water. Warm the teapot beforehand, and put in one teaspoon of leaves for each person plus what the British call "one for the pot". Carefully pour the boiling water onto the leaves, stir, cover and leave to stand for five minutes (a minute or two less for tea-bags, which easily become bitter). Pour and serve with milk or lemon and sugar. Some maintain that the milk should be put in the cup before the tea, claiming it makes a richer brew; but milk is generally handed round with the sugar after the tea has been poured.

61

CHRISTMAS PUDDING

Christmas pudding is the traditional way of rounding off the festive dinner on December 25. It is usually made several weeks in advance, and then stored in a cool place, in order to give the flavor plenty of time to mature. The quantities of dried fruit and sugar used in its preparation allow it to keep for a long time, perhaps up to a year or more. It is served hot, usually with brandy butter.

2. Finely chop ½ cup blanched almonds.

3. Mix in 1 cup plain flour, sifted with a teaspoon of powdered ginger.

6. Add the chopped almonds and one grated carrot. Stir again.

7. Beat six eggs with a whisk.

10. Put the bowl in boiling water, which should come half-way up the side.

11. Cover and simmer for 8 hours. Allow to cool, remove and store in a cool, dry place. Reheat in the same way for 2 hours to serve.

Making Christmas Pudding is a lengthy process. First assemble all the ingredients, before mixing them together in successive stages.

1. Into a large bowl put 2 cups stale breadcrumbs, 1 cup soft brown sugar, a teaspoon of chopped preserved ginger and a teaspoon of grated nutmeg. Then mix well.

4. Add the following chopped crystallized fruit, well mixed together: ½ cup cherries, ¼ cup lemon peel, ½ cup orange peel and 2 tablespoons lime.

5. To this add 1 cup currants, 1 cup sultanas and 1 cup raisins, mixing thoroughly.

8. Add the eggs to the mixture, stirring continuously, then add 2 tablespoons of molasses, mix in 1 cup grated beef suet, and stir in ¾ cup dark beer (Guinness is ideal).

9. Turn the mixture into a buttered ovenproof bowl, cover with greaseproof paper and seal with aluminium foil or a cloth, tied firmly around beneath the rim with string.

12. To make brandy butter, cream together 1 cup granulated sugar and ¾ cup unsalted butter, then gradually stir in ½ cup of brandy.

● ENGLISH SPECIALTIES

COOKIES
The English may have a cookie (or biscuit) whenever it is time for a cup of tea. Among the most popular are Digestive Biscuits (sometimes with chocolate on one side), and Ginger Snaps (above).

DESSERTS
Gelatine (English jelly) is a very popular dessert with the young: it comes in a variety of colors and flavors, such as lime (above), and is also used in making trifle. Also popular is Treacle Tart, an open pastry case baked with a filling of golden syrup and breadcrumbs.

Potato chips (crisps) are sold in pubs: they are an ideal snack with a pint of beer. There are many flavors, such as Salt and Vinegar, Cheese and Onion, or Smoky Bacon.

London would not be London without its famous red double-decker buses: above, a miniature version to take home as a souvenir of your visit.

NEWSPAPERS
The British national press has a worldwide reputation for excellence. The quality broadsheet papers (*The Times*, the *Guardian*, the *Independent*, the *Financial Times* and the *Daily Telegraph*) are side by side on news-stands with the popular tabloids, such as the *Sun* and the *Daily Mirror*. The *Evening Standard* is the only daily evening paper in London. The British press pioneered weekend color supplements, now standard in many countries.

BEER
Even in the 14th century Chaucer's Canterbury pilgrims sang the praises of London ale. Among the great breweries are Fuller, Smith & Turner at Chiswick, Young's of Wandsworth (whose beers are still delivered by horse and dray), and Courage's Anchor Brewery in Southwark. The traditional product is unpasteurized, drawn from a cask without carbon dioxide pressure.

ARCHITECTURE

Londinium was the name given by the Romans in the 1st century AD to the settlement that originally consisted of a Thames crossing – later a bridge – and a garrison. It was surrounded with a stout wall ● 34. Devastated in the 5th century by Anglo-Saxon invaders, it was gradually rebuilt to become the capital of the kingdom of Essex in the 7th century. On a piece of land to the west the Anglo-Saxons built a palace and an abbey of Westminster (the abbey in the west) as the nucleus of another town. Houses for high-ranking clerics, shops and taverns occupied the space between these two buildings. London also extended south of its bridge, but in a haphazard fashion.

The wall was raised and strengthened in the Middle Ages when the upper part of the Roman wall was replaced by brick fortifications.

LONDON WALL ▲ 178
The wall enclosing London, built by the Romans between 190 and 220 AD.

The original wall ran round the Tower to Cripplegate ▲ 181, under the Old Bailey and back down to the Thames. The ground level was constantly rising (see above); this was the reason for the medieval additions to the wall and explains why much of it is now buried beneath the ground.

GUILDHALL ▲ 148
Of the original medieval building constructed between 1411 and 1440, the vaulted crypt and porch plus much of the masonry remain to show the city's pride in its commercial success.

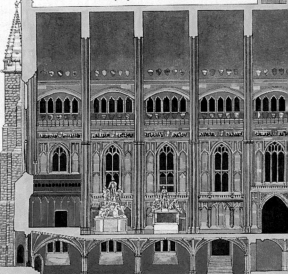

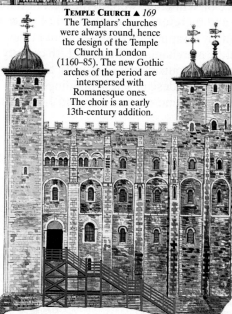

TEMPLE CHURCH ▲ *169*
The Templars' churches were always round, hence the design of the Temple Church in London (1160–85). The new Gothic arches of the period are interspersed with Romanesque ones. The choir is an early 13th-century addition.

WHITE TOWER ▲ *182*
Part of the Tower of London, this was built to keep a wary eye on Londoners, and not for their protection. It was constructed on the orders of William the Conqueror between 1077 and 1097, and is the most important Norman fortified building in Britain. Built of Caen stone with walls 12 feet thick at the base, its heavy Norman solidity contrasts with the charming pepper-pot cupolas, which are a later addition.

ST BARTHOLOMEW THE GREAT ▲ *176*
St Bartholomew's was part of an Augustinian Priory founded in 1123. It is the most impressive Romanesque survival in London.

The Guildhall was beautified in the 18th century.

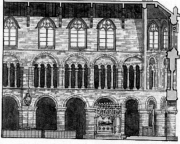

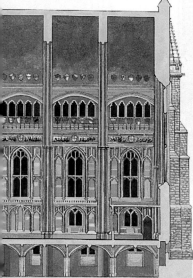

WESTMINSTER HALL ▲ *133*
Its hammer-beam roof was constructed by Henry Yevele in the late 14th century. Never before had such a framework been built on so large a scale.

MIDDLE TEMPLE HALL
▲ *162*. The rose window is an example of the Gothic style surviving into the 16th century.

QUEEN'S CHAPEL, ST JAMES'S PALACE
▲ *241*
Inigo Jones' elegant Italianate design adapts well to the sober formality of this Catholic chapel, built in 1625 for Charles I's French wife, Henrietta Maria.

There are surprisingly few surviving buildings from the period 1500–1666 in London. The most important Tudor buildings, such as the Palace of Whitehall, were to the west of the City and therefore missed the Great Fire ● *40*, but many disappeared in subsequent blazes. Wealthy merchants of the early 17th century built houses outside the City walls, and took pride in their design. These buildings are a fascinating blend of classicism and Jacobean Mannerism.

LINCOLN'S INN ▲ *165*
One of the entrance gates (1518), showing the unusual decoration of blue brickwork on a red background.

CHARLTON HOUSE, GREENWICH
Sir Adam Newton was tutor to Prince Henry, the eldest son of James I. His house, built between 1607 and 1612, has the finest Jacobean façade in London. This detail shows the ornate entrance to the substantial E-shaped building, which has an unusually large window on the top floor.

STAPLE INN, HIGH HOLBORN
These houses are the only surviving examples of 16th-century domestic architecture in central London. Their half-timbered frames, projecting upper stories and strip windows are typical Elizabethan features. They were heavily restored in 1937.

QUEEN'S HOUSE ▲ *327*
Inigo Jones' earliest
building (1616–37) was
also England's first house
in the Palladian style.

MIDDLE TEMPLE HALL
▲ *162*
Built between 1560 and
1570, Middle Temple has
many medieval elements
in its Elizabethan design.
The hall has a spectacular
double hammer-beam
roof. The magnificent
carved oak screen at the
east end was carefully
re-assembled after
being hit by a
German bomb during
the Second World
War

THE BANQUETING
HOUSE ▲ *144*
Built between 1619
and 1622, this was
Inigo Jones' second
royal commission. Its
façade was
remarkable for its
dignity, further
enhanced in 1829–30
when Sir John Soane
recovered it in
Portland stone.

ST JAMES'S PALACE
▲ *240.* Henry VIII
commissioned this
building as a "goodly
manor" for one of his
illegitimate children,
the Duke of Richmond.
The apartments, chapel
and tall gatehouse form
a continuous sequence
of Tudor building in
red brick with a blue
diaper pattern.

PRINCE HENRY'S ROOM
FLEET STREET
(1610–11) The Prince
of Wales' three feathers
and the letters PH are
on the ceiling.

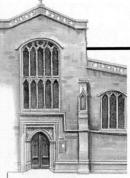

ST MARY ALDERMARY ▲ 157
Completed in 1682 in Gothic style; Wren may have copied the early-17th-century church destroyed in the fire but probably felt free to take liberties with the design of the original.

In the Middle Ages London had more than a hundred churches, eighty-eight of which were destroyed or damaged in the Great Fire of 1666 ● 40, along with Old St Paul's Cathedral. Sir Christopher Wren (1632–1723) set out to redesign the entire City after the fire. This grand scheme was never entirely realized, but he rebuilt St Paul's ▲ 171, 174 and designed fifty-one new London churches.

ST MARY LE BOW ▲ 157
The elegant spire of Wren's church (1670–83) projects forward of the main building. The interior was largely rebuilt after wartime bomb damage.

**VAULTING OF
ST MARY ALDERMARY
▲ 157**
Wren's superb plaster rosettes and fan vaulting of the interior roof seem more Baroque than Gothic.

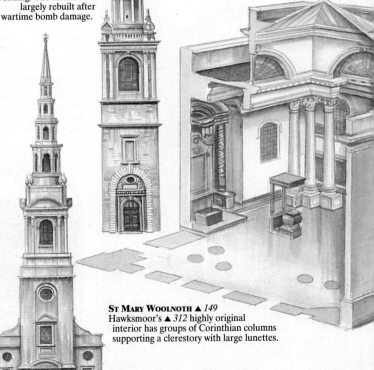

ST MARY WOOLNOTH ▲ 149
Hawksmoor's ▲ 312 highly original interior has groups of Corinthian columns supporting a clerestory with large lunettes.

ST BRIDE'S, FLEET STREET
The tower composed of successively diminishing octagonal figures is Wren's tallest spire (226 feet). A City baker of the time copied the new spire for a wedding cake, and the tradition has stuck.

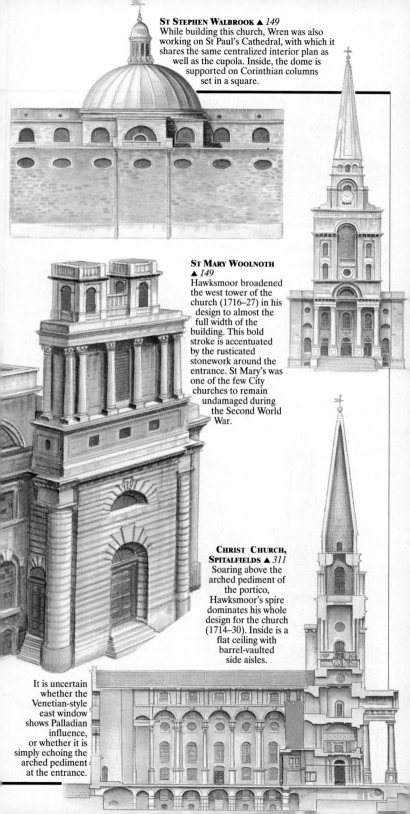

ST STEPHEN WALBROOK ▲ *149*
While building this church, Wren was also working on St Paul's Cathedral, with which it shares the same centralized interior plan as well as the cupola. Inside, the dome is supported on Corinthian columns set in a square.

ST MARY WOOLNOTH
▲ *149*
Hawksmoor broadened the west tower of the church (1716–27) in his design to almost the full width of the building. This bold stroke is accentuated by the rusticated stonework around the entrance. St Mary's was one of the few City churches to remain undamaged during the Second World War.

CHRIST CHURCH, SPITALFIELDS ▲ *311*
Soaring above the arched pediment of the portico, Hawksmoor's spire dominates his whole design for the church (1714–30). Inside is a flat ceiling with barrel-vaulted side aisles.

It is uncertain whether the Venetian-style east window shows Palladian influence, or whether it is simply echoing the arched pediment at the entrance.

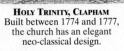

HOLY TRINITY, CLAPHAM
Built between 1774 and 1777,
the church has an elegant
neo-classical design.

Much of London's distinctive character
derives from the fact that it is quite visibly a
collection of separate villages. Some of its
parish churches are medieval buildings,
although the majority have been
rebuilt in more recent times. They
display a rich variety of styles, and
some of them
are still
surrounded by ancient graveyards. Most
are little known to the general public.

**ST JOHN,
HAMPSTEAD ▲ 261**
The 14th-century
church was rebuilt
1744–7 by John
Sanderson when
Hampstead was
becoming a
popular spa. In
1872 it was
enlarged by F.P.
Cockerell to make
room for the
rapidly increasing
population of the
borough. John
Constable is buried
within the
tree-shaded
churchyard.

ST MARY, ISLINGTON
The graceful slim
steeple is all that
remains of the
original church
(1751–4) in Upper
Street. The porch
was added in 1903.

ST MARY THE VIRGIN, WANSTEAD
Built in 1790 by Thomas Hardwick, the
church has an exceptionally fine interior,
with slender Corinthian columns, box

pews and a pulpit with columns modeled as palm
trees. In the churchyard is the "Watcher's Box", a
safeguard against grave robbers.

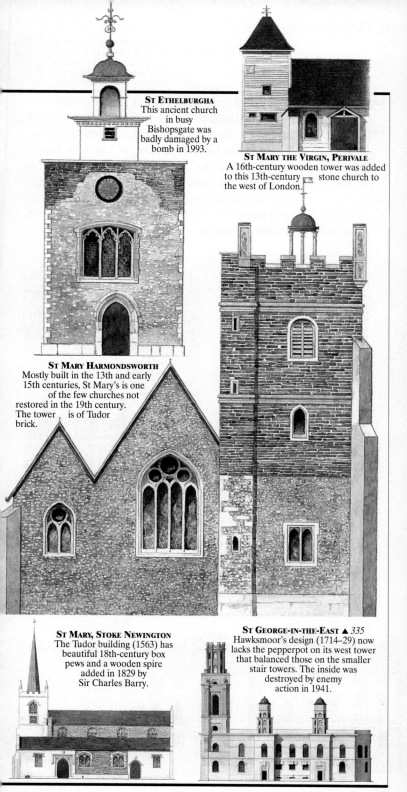

St Ethelburgha
This ancient church in busy Bishopsgate was badly damaged by a bomb in 1993.

St Mary the Virgin, Perivale
A 16th-century wooden tower was added to this 13th-century stone church to the west of London.

St Mary Harmondsworth
Mostly built in the 13th and early 15th centuries, St Mary's is one of the few churches not restored in the 19th century. The tower is of Tudor brick.

St Mary, Stoke Newington
The Tudor building (1563) has beautiful 18th-century box pews and a wooden spire added in 1829 by Sir Charles Barry.

St George-in-the-East ▲ *335*
Hawksmoor's design (1714–29) now lacks the pepperpot on its west tower that balanced those on the smaller stair towers. The inside was destroyed by enemy action in 1941.

73

● GEORGIAN HOUSES

ALBURY STREET, DEPTFORD
Built by a local mason between 1706 and
1714 in a district inhabited by wealthy
shipowners, Albury Street has some
splendid ornamental carved doorways.

After the Great Fire of 1666 legislation
was passed in the Georgian period requiring
houses to be built in terraces, which served as
models for the later expansion of London. New
features introduced in the late 17th century included the
widespread use of brick, and sash windows with a metal
counterbalance suspended over a pulley. As a precaution
against fire, laws passed in 1707 and 1709 restricted the use
of wood on building façades.

FENTON HOUSE, HAMPSTEAD ▲ 262
This magnificent residence was built in
1693. Its graceful hipped roof was a popular
feature of the time. The colonnade on the
side facing the street was added later.

NEWINGTON GREEN, ISLINGTON
Numbers 52–5 (1658) are among the oldest
surviving houses
in London.

39–43 OLD TOWN, CLAPHAM
The high roof and busy façade of the Queen Anne terrace
seem old-fashioned for its date (1707). Top-heavy doorways
and cornices under the eaves fell out of use after 1709.

QUEEN ANNE'S GATE
This superb group of
regular houses was begun
in 1704 near St James's
Park.

**57–60 LINCOLN'S INN
FIELDS ▲ 165**
No. 57–8 (far left)
was built in 1730
to com-
plement
its 17th-
century neighbor
Lindsey House (left,
1640). Both houses
were later divided
into two separate
dwellings.

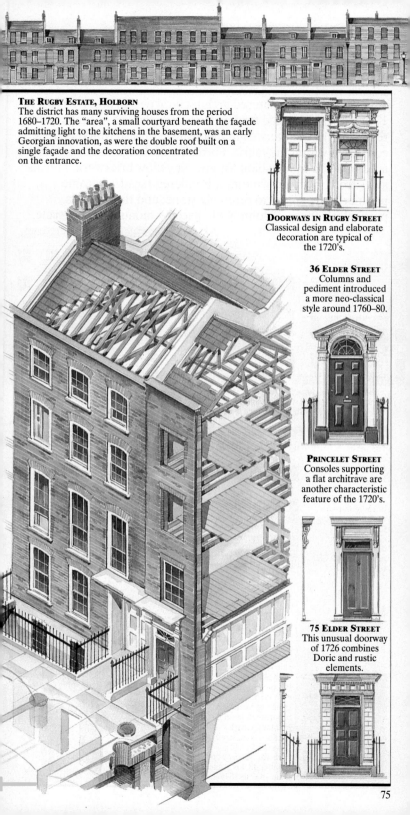

THE RUGBY ESTATE, HOLBORN

The district has many surviving houses from the period 1680–1720. The "area", a small courtyard beneath the façade admitting light to the kitchens in the basement, was an early Georgian innovation, as were the double roof built on a single façade and the decoration concentrated on the entrance.

DOORWAYS IN RUGBY STREET
Classical design and elaborate decoration are typical of the 1720's.

36 ELDER STREET
Columns and pediment introduced a more neo-classical style around 1760–80.

PRINCELET STREET
Consoles supporting a flat architrave are another characteristic feature of the 1720's.

75 ELDER STREET
This unusual doorway of 1726 combines Doric and rustic elements.

A note of austerity entered architectural design around 1760. In 1774 a law was passed further restricting the use of timber and requiring the counterweight mechanism of sash windows to be concealed within the fabric. Formality of design was accompanied by a fashion for grey or yellow brickwork, moving away from warm brown tones. Rendered façades became popular too, painted to resemble stone; and the terraces, particularly those of John Nash, became monumental in scale.

BEDFORD SQUARE ▲ *300* (c. 1775) The center house on each side is stuccoed, and doorways are decorated with Coade stone ● *82*.

FITZROY SQUARE ▲ *308* Designed by R. Adam in 1792.

CUMBERLAND TERRACE ▲ *256* The most magnificent of John Nash's Regent's Park terraces was built in 1826–7 in three linked groups, the center one having Corinthian columns and a decorated pediment. It is 800 feet long.

DOUGHTY STREET ▲ *298* Late Georgian terraces line either side of the street. They are of simple but pleasing design with brick façades (some of them have unfortunately been painted). Charles Dickens completed *Oliver Twist* and *Nicholas Nickleby* at number 48, his home from 1837 to 1839.

THE PARAGON, BLACKHEATH
The English custom of building semi-detached

houses dates back at least to the 18th century. The fourteen huge houses that make up this group, designed by Michael Searles around 1790, are linked by Tuscan colonnades. It is one of the finest Georgian housing developments in London.

CHESTER TERRACE (1825) ▲ *258*
Wings at either end of John Nash's longest Regent's Park terrace (940 feet) are connected to the main building by graceful arches.

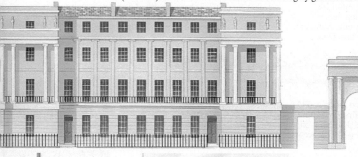

LONSDALE SQUARE
In the 1840's many architects and builders abandoned the neo-classical style, and under the influence of the Romantic movement began to favor mock-Tudor design. R.C. Carpenter was one who adapted the Tudor style to this charming square, designed for the Drapers' Company.

MILNER SQUARE
The unique design of this Islington square dates from about 1843. The houses are now apartments. Each has three bays separated by thin pilasters which, with the continuous attic floor at the top, give the houses a curiously elongated appearance. Like other squares in the borough, its entrances are in the middle of the sides rather than at the corners.

● THE DOCKS

BUTLER'S WHARF AND COURAGE'S BREWERY
The immense riverside façade of Butler's
Wharf adjoins the distinctive outline of
the Courage Brewery.

In 1799 a law was passed which set in motion
the expansion and development of the docks.
The first new one was built in the following
year, and 19th-century London became the
biggest port in the country. This expansion was
assisted by the facility of storing goods in
bonded warehouses without having to pay duty.
In spite of their closure around 1970, these
gaunt, tall buildings still present a spectacular
industrial landscape.

SHAD THAMES
At the back of
Butler's Wharf on the
western side are the
remains of an
18th-century brewery.
The street has
preserved much of its
character, with high
gabled roofs and the
latticed ironwork of
its footbridges
evoking the 19th-
century engravings of
Gustave Doré.

WEST INDIA DOCK ▲ 330, 337
Severely functional in appearance, the façade of these bonded
warehouses (1802–3) has a wealth of detail, with stair towers for
shifting goods between floors, lunettes on the top floor and round
windows in the central bays.

TOBACCO DOCK ▲ 335
Of the first docks built in London by D.A. Alexander,
from 1811 to 1814, only this remarkable warehouse for
the storage of tobacco now remains.

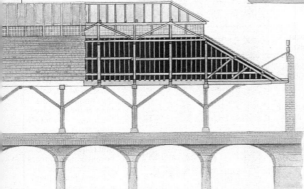

**STONE, IRON AND
WOOD**
The complex
structure using all
three materials is also
known as the "Skin
Floor": imported furs
were stored here too.
The sophisticated
cast-iron framework
of Tobacco Dock,
which supports a
timber-framed roof,
is set on a brick
and stone system
of wine cellars.

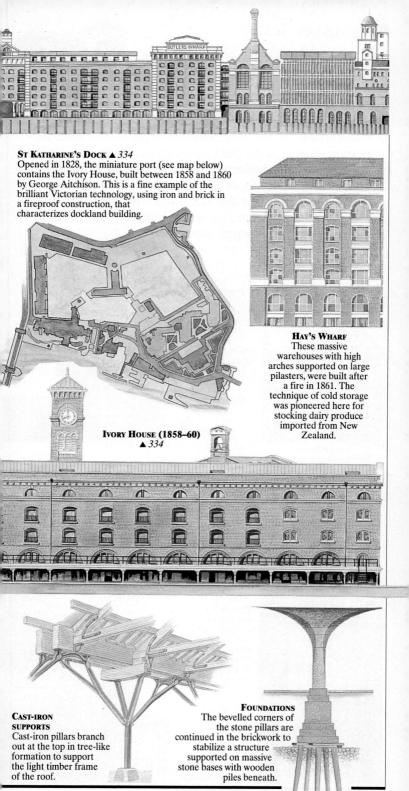

St Katharine's Dock ▲ 334

Opened in 1828, the miniature port (see map below) contains the Ivory House, built between 1858 and 1860 by George Aitchison. This is a fine example of the brilliant Victorian technology, using iron and brick in a fireproof construction, that characterizes dockland building.

Hay's Wharf

These massive warehouses with high arches supported on large pilasters, were built after a fire in 1861. The technique of cold storage was pioneered here for stocking dairy produce imported from New Zealand.

Ivory House (1858–60) ▲ 334

Cast-iron supports

Cast-iron pillars branch out at the top in tree-like formation to support the light timber frame of the roof.

Foundations

The bevelled corners of the stone pillars are continued in the brickwork to stabilize a structure supported on massive stone bases with wooden piles beneath.

79

Railway motif on the
capital of a column at
St Pancras Station.

Around 1820 there was a revival of interest in medieval
architecture. But it was the religious revival of the 1840's that
was responsible for the reintroduction of the Gothic style. An
important pioneer in the field was Augustus Pugin (1812–52),
a Catholic architect, writer and propagandist. He worked with
Barry on the new Houses of Parliament. Anglican architects
such as Butterfield, Scott and Street went on to adapt his ideas
using the medium of brick. Before long, mock-Gothic factories
and houses were springing up everywhere.

NEW RIVER PUMPING STATION
With its tower-shaped chimney, battlements, and windows like loopholes, this industrial building in Green Lanes looks like a medieval castle. Built 1854–6 by W. Chadwell Mylne, it has been replaced by a miniscule plant alongside.

TOWER HOUSE
The neo-Gothic architect William Burges built himself this house in Kensington 1876–81. In the tower is a circular staircase.

ST PANCRAS STATION
George Gilbert Scott designed this splendid fantasy (1866–8) for the Midland Railway at the same time as he was working on the Albert Memorial.

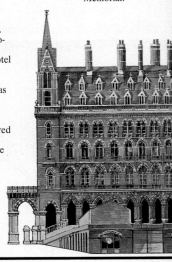

ST PANCRAS HOTEL
The ultimate in neo-Gothic design, the Midland Grand Hotel (1868–74) at St Pancras is as extravagant inside as out, although it closed in 1935. Its colorful façade is made up of bright red Nottingham brick, red and grey granite and beige stone. Scott's huge building was considered by many to be the finest hotel in England (it boasted the first ever Ladies' Smoking Room).

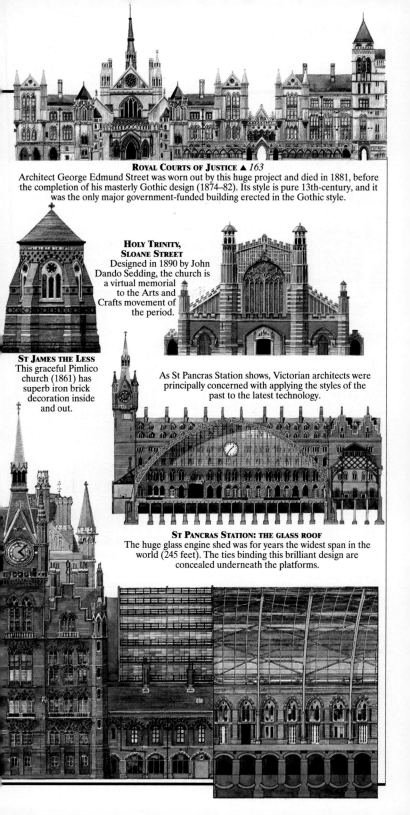

ROYAL COURTS OF JUSTICE ▲ *163*
Architect George Edmund Street was worn out by this huge project and died in 1881, before the completion of his masterly Gothic design (1874–82). Its style is pure 13th-century, and it was the only major government-funded building erected in the Gothic style.

HOLY TRINITY, SLOANE STREET
Designed in 1890 by John Dando Sedding, the church is a virtual memorial to the Arts and Crafts movement of the period.

ST JAMES THE LESS
This graceful Pimlico church (1861) has superb iron brick decoration inside and out.

As St Pancras Station shows, Victorian architects were principally concerned with applying the styles of the past to the latest technology.

ST PANCRAS STATION: THE GLASS ROOF
The huge glass engine shed was for years the widest span in the world (245 feet). The ties binding this brilliant design are concealed underneath the platforms.

● TERRACOTTA AND ARTIFICIAL STONE

GALLIPOLI BATHS
A decorated oriental-style kiosk (1895) provides the entrance to these sumptuous public baths.

In the 1770's the fashion emerged for decorating brick façades with moulded ceramics. London has no stone quarries of its own, so encouraged the manufacture of interesting artificial materials like Coade stone. Terracotta manufactured by such firms as Doulton and Company became a distinctive feature on Victorian buildings. Ceramics were much used for creating historical designs, while in the early 20th century these clean bright surfaces were popular for decorating the exteriors of theaters and picture palaces.

MOUNT STREET
Pink terracotta virtually covers this delightful 1893 terrace.

THE PALACE THEATRE, CAMBRIDGE CIRCUS ● 54–5
Thomas Collcutt built this enormous theater on an imposing corner site in 1890. Its extravagant decoration features bands of pale faience separating the red brick of the façade.

HACKNEY EMPIRE
Frank Matcham's dignified façade for this famous variety hall (1901) features a pair of remarkable terracotta domes.

NATURAL HISTORY MUSEUM ▲ 234
Architect Alfred Waterhouse covered his palatial design in decorative patterns of terracotta. The museum took almost nine years to build, and opened in 1881. Its inspiration is Romanesque rather than Gothic, and the interior resembles a giant cathedral. The huge façade is 675 feet wide.

ROYAL ALBERT HALL ▲ *235*
The huge domed concert hall (1867–71) is a
memorial to Prince Albert, who worked so
hard at making South Kensington a center
for the advancement of learning. The
fundamental design is simple: it is the
intricate terracotta ornamentation that gives
the building its festive air.

DEBENHAM HOUSE, 8 ADDISON ROAD
Architect Halsey Ricardo covered the exterior
of this millionaire's residence (1905–7) with
ceramic tiles.

DOULTON FACTORY
The building was expressly
designed by architect R. Stark
Wilkinson to show the range
of building products
manufactured by Doulton
and Co., which explains its
curious polychrome
appearance.

CARLTON CINEMA
George Coles designed this 1929 cinema in the
Egyptian style, using luridly colored tiles
known as Hathernware. The result is
novel and arresting, ideal for a
picture palace.

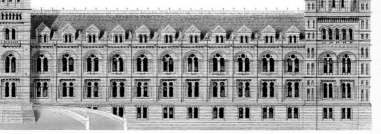

London needed many markets to provision its enormous population and to supply its commercial needs. Smithfield for meat, Billingsgate for fish, Covent Garden, Spitalfields and Borough for fruit and vegetables, and numerous others were established in the Middle Ages and enlarged in more recent times. The elegant West End arcades cater predominantly for luxury goods.

SMITHFIELD MARKET ▲ *177.* The monumental Victorian market buildings were designed by Sir Horace Jones in 1866–8. Broad aisles between the market stalls have cast-iron arched roofs, while the redbrick exterior has decorative stone cladding and domed towers at the corners.

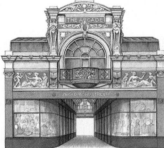

FAÇADE OF THE ROYAL ARCADE
This was modeled on the nearby Burlington Arcade.

BURLINGTON ARCADE ▲ *281*
Inspired by Continental models, Burlington Arcade was opened in 1819. Two lines of elegant small shopfronts run north from Piccadilly beneath a graceful glass roof; the ponderous façades at either end are an early 20th-century addition.

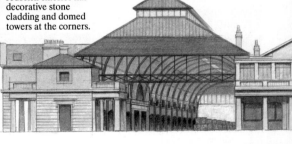

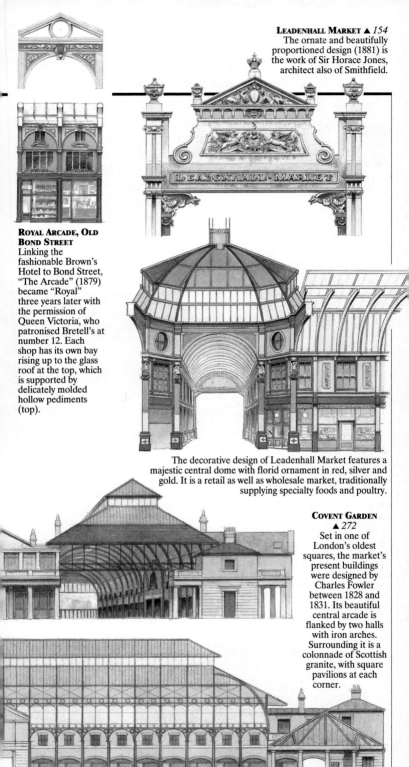

LEADENHALL MARKET ▲ *154*
The ornate and beautifully proportioned design (1881) is the work of Sir Horace Jones, architect also of Smithfield.

ROYAL ARCADE, OLD BOND STREET
Linking the fashionable Brown's Hotel to Bond Street, "The Arcade" (1879) became "Royal" three years later with the permission of Queen Victoria, who patronised Bretell's at number 12. Each shop has its own bay rising up to the glass roof at the top, which is supported by delicately molded hollow pediments (top).

The decorative design of Leadenhall Market features a majestic central dome with florid ornament in red, silver and gold. It is a retail as well as wholesale market, traditionally supplying specialty foods and poultry.

COVENT GARDEN ▲ *272*
Set in one of London's oldest squares, the market's present buildings were designed by Charles Fowler between 1828 and 1831. Its beautiful central arcade is flanked by two halls with iron arches. Surrounding it is a colonnade of Scottish granite, with square pavilions at each corner.

THE MAYFLOWER INN
This Rotherhithe pub celebrates the ship of the Pilgrim Fathers, moored nearby in 1620.

In the late 19th century competition from the large breweries proved too much for their smaller, less prosperous rivals and led to the construction of immense and palatial pubs. Just about every London street has one of these garish façades, with ornate frosted-glass windows and gilded calligraphy extolling the quality of the drink inside. The rich brewers spared no expense to attract the custom of the working man, making him comfortable in a setting much more luxurious than he could find at home.

THE GEORGE, BOROUGH HIGH STREET
Last London coach stop on the road to Canterbury, the George is the only surviving galleried inn in London. Built in 1676, it is little altered, though missing one side of the courtyard.

THE SALISBURY, GREEN LANES
The center of a property development by the builder J.C. Hill, this grandiose "gin palace" opened in 1899. Inside is a concert hall and billiard room, as well as a suite of comfortable drinking parlors. The Art Nouveau decorations in glass, carved wood and wrought iron are a delight.

THE PRINCE ALFRED
A notable feature of this pub built around 1890, is its series of tiny bars or 'snugs', now a rare survivor from times when pubs were not always 'fit' places to be seen in.

CROCKERS, ABERDEEN PLACE
Formerly called the Crown, it was built by the successful publican, Frank Crocker, in 1898. It combined the facilities of a bar and lounge with a billiard hall and suite of meeting rooms. The interior decor remains a masterpiece of late Victorian fantasy.

THE PRINCESS LOUISE
The interior of this pub was redesigned in 1891 by the firm of Simpson and Son, who decorated it with ornamental panels and friezes. Morris and Son supplied the gilded and engraved mirrors, creating a sumptuous design which has been well preserved.

THE BLACK FRIAR, BLACKFRIARS BRIDGE
Built around 1875, the pub interior was created in 1904, with its cheerful friezes of merry friars in marble, brass, copper, wood and mosaic.

THE GROTTO OF THE BLACK FRIAR
In 1917 a grotto-like addition was built into the vaults of the neighboring railway, and moral inscriptions such as "industry is all" were at odds with the jocular pub atmosphere.

THE EDWARDIAN WEST END

BUSH HOUSE
The huge building (1925–35) at the Aldwych is in the style known as American Corinthian.

At the beginning of the 20th century the Crown and the Grosvenor Estate, which between them owned most of the West End, redeveloped much of the land in order to exploit their property to the maximum. At about the same time less prestigious areas were also opened up with new streets that soon became popular. Department stores and office blocks were built on a grand scale, completely transforming London's shopping streets.

27–30 WIGMORE STREET, FORMERLY DEBENHAMS
Opened in 1909, this old department store was covered with Carrara tiling.

INVERESK HOUSE
At the west entry to the Aldwych is one of London's first steel-framed buildings (1906–7), built in the French style and clad with granite. Its original appearance is marred by the addition of two extra top floors. Inveresk House was formerly the home of the now defunct daily, the *Morning Post*.

SELFRIDGES ▲ *297*
Built between 1907 and 1928, this giant among department stores has a steel frame, with massive Ionic columns along its immense façade.

REGENT STREET ▲ *283*

John Nash's original Regency design was considered inadequate at the turn of the century, and was rebuilt on a monumental scale by Sir Reginald Blomfield in the French Baroque style.

LIBERTY'S ▲ *283*

The father and son team of architects E.T. and E.S. Hall designed this new Marlborough Street building in 1924 in mock Tudor style, complete with hand-made roof tiles and oak timbers from two old British warships.

HARRODS, KNIGHTSBRIDGE ▲ *225*

London's most exclusive department store is also the biggest in Europe. The façade is covered in red terracotta tiles that give the building its distinctive appearance. It was designed by C.W. Stephens and built 1894–1911.

THE COTY FACTORY
One of the great Art Deco designs was built for the Coty cosmetics company on the Great West Road around 1932.

London more than doubled in size between 1914 and 1938. The slump of the period hit heavy industry that relied on coal but, with the recovery, industries powered by electricity sprang up to replace them along the arterial roads out of London. New suburbs developed to house skilled workers for these factories, and extensions to the underground railway assisted the growth of these so-called dormitory towns. The new Art Deco style was reflected in pubs, cinemas, apartment blocks and even churches.

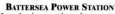

ODEON, WOOLWICH
George Coles' 1937 design for this cinema is a particularly fine example of a style derived from German models, composed of white rectangular shapes.

BATTERSEA POWER STATION
One of London's most loved monuments, this magnificent industrial building was constructed between 1929 and 1955 by Sir Giles Gilbert Scott. Affectionately described as an upside-down billiard table, it was closed in 1983 and is now in a sorry half-demolished condition.

GROSVENOR CINEMA, RAYNERS LANE
F.E. Bromige's 1936 design explores convex and concave spaces centered around a sinuous projecting fin. Its architect also built many other cinemas in the new suburbs.

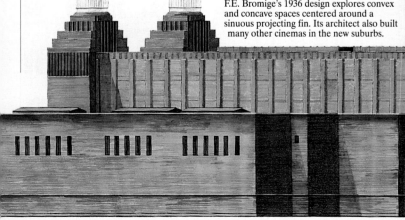

SOUTHGATE STATION
The same clarity is applied to a
circular volume, with very
refined lines, in this impressive
1933 design showing strong
Swedish influence.

OSTERLEY STATION
The eccentric tower
designed for London
Transport by Adams, Holden
and Pearson in 1934 strives
to state the distant suburb's
links with modernity and
with London.

UNDERGROUND STATIONS
Charles Holden, an architect much
appreciated for his revolutionary classical
designs on the Underground, had been
powerfully influenced by a visit to Sweden
and the Netherlands in 1931. The extension
of the Piccadilly line allowed him to put his
new ideas into practice. His first station,
Sudbury Town (1932), is an uncluttered
light design of brick and glass with a flat
concrete roof.

HOOVER BUILDING, WESTERN AVENUE
Wallis, Gilbert and Partners were famous for their factory
designs in the 1930's. Their 1932 design for Hoover, with
green windows and stripes of red and blue faience, was an
expression of the desire for a factory to be a "palace of
work". In 1992 the plain rear factory block was rebuilt as
a supermarket.

ST SAVIOUR'S CHURCH, ELTHAM
Built in 1932 by Welch, Cachemaille-
Day and Lander, the church was
extremely modernistic with brick ribs
and tall slits for windows. Its design
resembles those of the Odeon chain of
cinemas later in the decade.

MODERN AND POST-MODERN LONDON

DAILY EXPRESS BUILDING, FLEET STREET
Completed in 1932, this gleaming black-glass block has gracefully curved corners.

Few cities have suffered as much as London at the hands of property speculators, resulting in a great many office blocks of no architectural interest whatever. But there are some buildings, mostly private commissions, which show great originality and imagination. In the late 1980's came some impressive high-tech constructions and American post-modernist buildings (a style much appreciated in London).

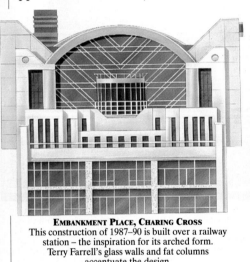

EMBANKMENT PLACE, CHARING CROSS
This construction of 1987–90 is built over a railway station – the inspiration for its arched form. Terry Farrell's glass walls and fat columns accentuate the design.

THE ARK, HAMMERSMITH
Completed in 1992 by Ralph Erskine, this extraordinary building resembles a gigantic liner. Its curved outline is dictated by the shape of a raised trunk road.

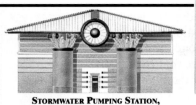

STORMWATER PUMPING STATION, ISLE OF DOGS ▲ *336*
Between 1986 and 1988 John Outram built this eclectic, brightly colored construction incorporating Hollywood-style Egyptian columns.

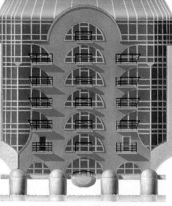

CHINA WHARF, MILL STREET
The partnership of Campbell, Zogolovich, Wilkinson and Gough were among the first to introduce post-modernism to London. This concrete, brick and glass building with mock-oriental arches (1986–8) is a housing development of seventeen apartments.

LLOYD'S BUILDING ▲ *153*
Richard Rogers is the best known and most controversial architect in Britain. The dramatic building he designed for Lloyd's (1978–86) is his biggest project in London. Lifts, lavatories and other services are installed on the outside, with the twelve-story glass atrium supported on columns in the center, giving the building a fortified appearance.

CANARY WHARF TOWER, ISLE OF DOGS ▲ *338*
At 800 feet, this is Britain's tallest building, its distinct pyramidal top visible even from the distant Kent countryside.

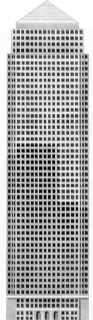

CANARY WHARF TOWER
Completed in 1991, the clean, unfussy outline of Cesar Pelli's monumental tower is the centerpiece of a new commercial district. Very high buildings such as this make the greatest impact with minimum decoration.

● BRIDGES

THE CLATTERN BRIDGE, KINGSTON
Built in the 12th century, this is the oldest bridge in the London area.

BLACKFRIARS RAILWAY BRIDGE
Built 1862–4, the bridge is supported on massive red granite columns. The railway's insignia are on the monumental stone piers.

Until 1738 London Bridge was the only one spanning the Thames in the city itself, which helped to ensure that river traffic was a lot busier then than it is now, with crowds of ferryboats. Today London has thirty-one bridges (including railway bridges), some of the most elegant being 19th-century iron constructions.

COLUMN FROM BLACKFRIARS RAILWAY BRIDGE

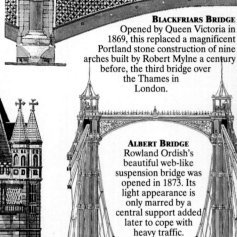

BLACKFRIARS BRIDGE
Opened by Queen Victoria in 1869, this replaced a magnificent Portland stone construction of nine arches built by Robert Mylne a century before, the third bridge over the Thames in London.

ALBERT BRIDGE
Rowland Ordish's beautiful web-like suspension bridge was opened in 1873. Its light appearance is only marred by a central support added later to cope with heavy traffic.

TOWER BRIDGE ▲ 190:
The world-famous outline of Tower Bridge shows its two functions: the lower span opens in the center to let tall ships through, while pedestrians climb the stairs in the towers to cross the river by the high walkway.

LONDON AS SEEN BY PAINTERS

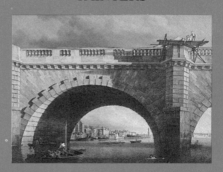

The Houses of Parliament had just been built when Claude Monet (1840–1926), taking refuge in London from the war of 1870 and the Commune which followed it, painted his famous picture of 1871, *The Thames at Westminster* (2). The way Monet treats the misty atmosphere with subtle gradations of color is typical of his visual preoccupations at this time. When he came back to London, in 1899, he painted a series of views of the Houses of Parliament from the balcony of his room in the Savoy Hotel. In the 18th century Canaletto (1697–1768) had likewise drawn inspiration from the banks of the Thames. In his picture *The Thames and the City of London from Richmond House* (1747) (1, detail) he captures the majestic sweep of the Thames toward St Paul's Cathedral with the magical lightness we recognize from his views of Venice. His style was to influence many English artists: Samuel Scott, for example, adapted it in his painting *An Arch of Old Westminster Bridge* (1750) ● 95, in which the human figures are eclipsed by the immense scale of the bridge.

1

2

97

I n his picture *Saint
Pancras Hotel and
Station from
Pentonville Road:
Sunset* (1884) (4) the
Irish painter John
O'Connor (1830–89)
selected one of the
most characteristic
sights of Victorian
London. The station,
with its vast glass roof
(ultra-modern and
quite without
precedent when it was
built) looks more like
some Gothic palace
from the distant past.
In this view of St
Pancras, looking
down from the hill
above, O'Connor has
contrasted the
romantic sunset and
foggy landscape with
the busy street in the
foreground. The *View
of Greenwich* (2) by
Henry Pethers
(1828–65) has a
disturbing, almost
surrealist, quality. Its
grandiose scale
suggests one of
Claude Lorrain's
harbor scenes at
sunset. Atkinson
Grimshaw (1836–93)
specialized in
nocturnal river
landscapes. His views
of the Thames (1 &
3) have a rather
sinister air about
them, recalling the
writer Arthur Conan
Doyle's more
mysterious tales.

	1
2	3
4	

Walter Greaves (1846–1930), in his picture *Hammersmith Bridge on Boat Race Day* (c. 1862), has filled the canvas with a forceful throng of figures. The Boat Race between Oxford and Cambridge Universities has been an annual event since 1829, held on the Thames between Putney and Mortlake. Greaves' naïve style, with its exaggerated perspective, is a highly original view of a crowd waiting to watch the race. Scenes portraying daily life became more common in the 20th century with the emergence of schools like the Camden Town Group, whose members shared the influence of French Impressionism and a fascination with the commonplace details of everyday events.

Malcolm Drummond (1880–1945) peopled his painting *St James' Park* (1912) (3) with Londoners in an extraordinary variety of poses that comes close to caricature. In *Piccadilly Circus* (1912) (4) by Charles Ginner (1878–1952), the technique of composition recalls photography, as well as the influence of Degas and Sickert. The density of the painting's surface, composed of a mosaic of tiny brush spots, intensifies the frantic activity of this busy intersection. The same air of hustle and bustle infects *The Strand by Night* (1, detail) by Christopher Nevinson (1889–1946) with figures hurrying through the rain. The influence of the Futurists is clearly apparent in the jagged geometrical shapes.

1
2

3	4

In his watercolor *The White House at Chelsea* (1800) (2) Thomas Girtin (1775–1802) shows a rural view of the Thames, at a time when Chelsea was still a country village. Girtin evolved a distinctive style very early in his career, his talent being widely acclaimed in his short life. The lyrical atmosphere which dominates Girtin's picture is recalled a century and a half later in *The Quiet River: The Thames at Chiswick* (1943–4) by Victor Pasmore (b. 1908) (1, detail). An altogether more eventful day on the river was captured by J.M.W. Turner (1775–1851) in his painting of the *Houses of Parliament on Fire* in 1834 (3), which he watched from a boat on the Thames. The dramatic effect of this watercolor is heightened by the orange reflections in the water, which add an extra dimension to this awesome, historic moment. Watercolor is the perfect medium for capturing the immediacy of this kind of scene, where buildings, water and fire merge into a whirl of color. Turner later exhibited two much more characteristic oil canvases of the same event, and neither of them captured the vivid drama of this little sketch.

| 1 |
| 2 |
| 3 |

The American James Abbott McNeill Whistler (1834–1903) settled in London in 1859 and painted a series of pictures featuring misty twilight scenes of the Thames. *Nocturne in Blue and Gold: Old Battersea Bridge* (1872) is heavily influenced by Japanese art, and the work's abstract quality is underlined by its title, which relegates the actual subject of the painting to second place in favor of music and color.

LONDON AS SEEN BY WRITERS

● LONDON AS SEEN BY WRITERS

A COLLECTION OF VILLAGES

WHERE WILL IT ALL END?

Daniel Defoe (1660–1731) was a prolific writer of novels, poetry, satire, journals and political pamphlets and he produced 560 books in his lifetime. He was a particularly good observer of the tiny detail that sums up a scene and this skill, along with his plain, unadorned prose, made him an excellent reporter. His three-volume guidebook to the British Isles is an account of the state of the country and in the passage below he bemoans the steady growth of London.

❝ London, as a city only, and as its walls and liberties line it out, might, indeed, be viewed in a small compass; but when I speak of London, now in the modern acceptation, you expect I shall take in all that vast mass of buildings, reaching from Black-wall in the east, to Tot-Hill Fields in the west; and extended in an unusual breadth, from the bridge, or river, in the south, to Islington north; and from Peterburgh House on the bank side in Westminster, to Cavendish Square, and all the new buildings by, and beyond, Hannover Square, by which the city of London, for so it is still to be called, is extended to Hide Park Corner in the Brentford Road, and almost to Marybone in the Acton Road, and how much further it may spread, who knows? ... We see several villages, formerly standing, as it were, in the country, and at a great distance, now joined to the streets by continued buildings, and more making haste to meet in the like manner; for example, Deptford, this town was formerly reckoned, at least two miles off from Redriff, and that over the marshes too, a place unlikely ever to be inhabited; and yet now, by the increase of buildings in that town itself, and the many streets erected at Redriff, and by the docks and building-yards on the riverside, which stand between both, the town of Deptford, and the streets of Redriff, or Rotherhith (as they write it) are effactually joined.... The town of Islington, on the north side of the city, is in like manner joined to the streets of London, excepting one small field, and which is in itself so small, that there is no doubt, but in a very few years, they will be entirely joined, and the same may be said of Mile-End, on the east end of the town.... That Westminster is in a fair way to shake hands with Chelsea, as St Gyles's is with Marybone; and Great Russel Street by Montague House, with Tottenham-Court: all this is very evident, and yet all these put together, are still to be called London. Whither will this monstrous city then extend? and where must a circumvallation or communication line of it be placed? ❞

DANIEL DEFOE,
A TOUR THROUGH THE WHOLE ISLAND OF GREAT BRITAIN, 1724–6

ANONYMITY

Henry James (1843–1916)lived in London for more than twenty years, during which he wrote most of his novels.He also wrote several volumes of travel sketches. His impressions of London, although written from the point of view of a foreigner, would probably strike a chord with many born and bred Londoners.

❝ It is, no doubt, not the taste of every one, but for the real London-lover the mere immensity of the place is a large part of its savour. A small London would be an abomination, as it fortunately is an impossibility, for the idea and the name are beyond everything an expression of extent and number. Practically, of course, one lives in a quarter, in a plot; but in imagination and by a constant mental act of reference the accommodated haunter enjoys the whole – and it is only of him that I deem it

worth while to speak. He fancies himself, as they say, for being a particle in so unequalled an aggregation; and its immeasurable circumference, even though unvisited and lost in smoke, gives him the sense of a social, an intellectual margin. There is a luxury in the knowledge that he may come and go without being noticed, even when his comings and goings have no nefarious end. I don't mean by this that the tongue of London is not a very active member; the tongue of London would indeed be worthy of a chapter by itself. But the eyes which at least in some measure feed its activity are ... solicited at any moment by a thousand different objects. If the place is big, everything it contains is certainly not so; but this may at least be said, that if small questions play a part there, they play it without illusions about its importance. There are too many questions, small or great; and each day, as it arrives, leads its children, like a kind of mendicant mother, by the hand. Therefore perhaps the most general characteristic is the absence of insistence. Habits and inclinations flourish and fall, but intensity is never one of them. **99**

HENRY JAMES,
ENGLISH HOURS, 1905

A CHANGING NEIGHBORHOOD

Evelyn Waugh (1903–66) was born in Hampstead, the son of a publisher; his autobiographical "A Little Learning" covers this period. As a novelist, he became famous for his satirical digs at the frivolity of the inter-war generation.

66 I was four years old when my father built his house in what was then the village of North End, Hampstead. He was, in fact, the first of its spoliators. When we settled there the tube reached no further than Hampstead. Golders Green was a grassy cross-road with a sign pointing to London, Finchley and Hendon; such a place as where "the Woman in White" was encountered. All round us lay dairy farms, market gardens and a few handsome old houses of brick or stucco standing in twenty acres or more; not far off there survived woods where we picked bluebells, and streams beside which we opened our picnic baskets. North End Road was a steep, dusty lane with white posts and rails bordering its footways. North End, the reader may remember, was the place where Bill Sikes spent the first night of his flight after the murder of Nancy.... Soon after ours other new houses sprang up alongside us. Opposite us stood a large late Victorian villa named Ivy House (whrer Pavlova spent her last years) with wooded grounds. Soon these were built on, leaving only the garden and a pond for the ballerina's privacy. Then the tube emerged into the open at Golders Green and round the station grew shops, a theatre, a cinema and a dense spread of new brick and rough cast dwellings not unlike our own. Eventually (I think soon after the first war) our postal address was altered from Hampstead to Golders Green. My father deplored the change. and, as far as was possible, ignored it, because Hampstead had historic associations, with Keats and Blake and Constable, while Golders Green meant, to him, merely a tube station. **99**

EVELYN WAUGH, *A LITTLE LEARNING*, 1964

THE BLITZ

London suffered its worst damage since the Great Fire of 1666 in the Blitz of World War II. The great 20th-century English novelist Graham Greene (1904-91) used it as the setting for one of his finest thrillers "The Ministry of Fear". In the excerpt below Greene describes how the very real threat of the terrifying bombing raids changed Londoners' lives.

❝Rowe had breakfast in an A.B.C. in Clapham High Street. Boards had taken the place of windows and the top floor had gone; it was like a shack put up in an earthquake town for relief work. For the enemy had done a lot of damage in Clapham. London was no longer one great city: it was a collection of small towns. People went to Hampstead or St John's Wood for a quiet week-end, and if you lived in Holborn you hadn't time between the sirens to visit friends as far away as Kensington. So special characteristics developed, and in Clapham where day raids were frequent there was a hunted look which was absent from Westminster, where the night raids were heavier but the shelters were better. The waitress who brought Rowe's toast and coffee looked jumpy and pallid, as if she had lived too much on the run; she had an air of listening whenever gears shrieked. Gray's Inn and Russell Square were noted for a more reckless spirit, but only because they had the day to recover in.❞

GRAHAM GREENE,
THE MINISTRY OF FEAR, 1943

WAPPING

William Wymark Jacobs (1863-1943) is best remembered as a writer of short stories. These were of two basic types: the macabre, exemplified by his gruesome tale "The Monkey's Paw"; and an altogether jollier type of yarn, comic adventures set among the seafaring community of the Port of London at the turn of the century.

❝ As a residential neighbourhood Wapping is perhaps undesirable, though a considerable population contrives to exist in the narrow streets hemmed in between the dock walls and the warehouses bordering the river. For the river itself is completely hidden, except where the swing-bridges, which give entrance to the docks, afford a passing glimpse. From a picturesque point of view Wapping was no doubt much better in the days when docks and swing-bridges were unknown; when the bow-windows of its ancient taverns projected quaintly over the river and the waterman's stairs inspired the muse of the songwriter. Then the raucous bellowings of the hurrying steamers were unheard, and sailing craft thoughtfully waited for tides, while master mariners sat drinking in the bow-windows aforesaid. The old church and the charity school, with the overgrown graveyard opposite, with its rank grass and dingy trees, are the remains of those days. The green of the churchyard is a relief to the bricks and mortar, for trees are scarce in Wapping, though there are a few others in front of the old-fashioned houses on the breezy pier-head hard by – trees which, having been coaxed to grow in that uncongenial spot, conscientiously endeavour to indicate the seasons, and make very few mistakes considering. High Street, Wapping, the principal thoroughfare, realising, possibly, that High Streets are apt to adhere too slavishly to one pattern, appears to have determined to be original. It sternly eschews the drapers and hatters, the bootmakers and tailors of other High Streets.... One window is much like another – herrings, rejoicing in their strength, competing for favour with bacon of guaranteed mildness and eggs of blameless exterior. ❞

W.W. JACOBS,
WAPPING ON THAMES, 1926

LONDON BRIDGE

Thomas Stearns Eliot (1888–1965) was born in St Louis but moved to London in 1914. The following excerpt is from "The Waste Land", a poem which quickly came to be seen as representing the inter-war frustrations of his generation. Eliot claimed that it was not so much a piece of social criticism as "a piece of rhythmical grumbling". This section describes City clerks unwillingly traveling to work.

Unreal City,
Under the brown fog of a winter dawn,
A crowd flowed over London Bridge, so many,
I had not thought death had undone so many.
Sighs, short and infrequent, were exhaled,
And each man fixed his eyes before his feet,
Flowed up the hill and down King William Street,
To where Saint Mary Woolnoth kept the hours
With a dead sound on the final stroke of nine.

T.S. ELIOT, *THE WASTE LAND*, 1922

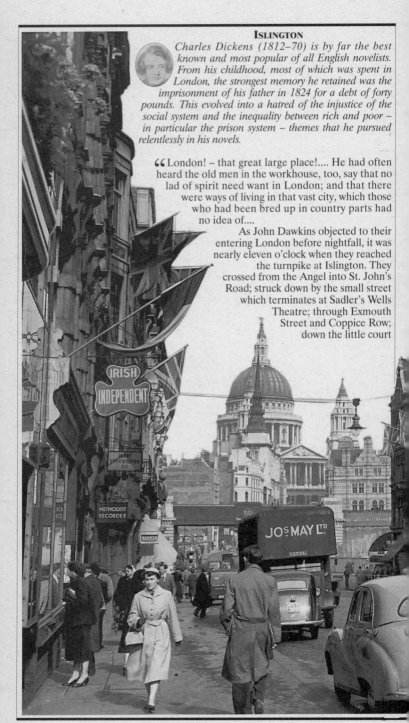

ISLINGTON

Charles Dickens (1812–70) is by far the best known and most popular of all English novelists. From his childhood, most of which was spent in London, the strongest memory he retained was the imprisonment of his father in 1824 for a debt of forty pounds. This evolved into a hatred of the injustice of the social system and the inequality between rich and poor – in particular the prison system – themes that he pursued relentlessly in his novels.

66 London! – that great large place!.... He had often heard the old men in the workhouse, too, say that no lad of spirit need want in London; and that there were ways of living in that vast city, which those who had been bred up in country parts had no idea of....
    As John Dawkins objected to their entering London before nightfall, it was nearly eleven o'clock when they reached the turnpike at Islington. They crossed from the Angel into St. John's Road; struck down by the small street which terminates at Sadler's Wells Theatre; through Exmouth Street and Coppice Row; down the little court

by the side of the workhouse; across the classic ground which once bore the name of Hockley-in-the-Hole; thence into Little Saffron Hill; and so into Saffron Hill the Great: along which the Dodger scudded at a rapid pace, directing Oliver to follow close at his heels.

Although Oliver had enough to occupy his attention in keeping sight of his leader, he could not help bestowing a few hasty glances on either side of the way, as he passed along. A dirtier or more wretched place he had never seen. The street was very narrow and muddy, and the air was impregnated with filthy odours. There were a good many small shops; but the only stock in trade appeared to be heaps of children, who, even at that time of night, were crawling in and out of the doors, or screaming from the inside. The sole places that seemed to prosper amid the general blight of the place, were the public-houses; and in them, the lowest orders of Irish were wrangling with might and main. Covered ways and yards, which here and there diverged from the main street, disclosed little knots of houses, where drunken men and women were positively wallowing in filth; and from several of the door-ways, great ill-looking fellows were cautiously emerging, bound, to all appearance, on no very well-disposed or harmless errands.

Oliver was just considering whether he hadn't better run away, when they reached the bottom of the hill. His conductor, catching him by the arm, pushed open the door of a house near Field Lane; and, drawing him into the passage, closed it behind them. **"**

CHARLES DICKENS,
OLIVER TWIST, 1837

COVENT GARDEN

Oscar Wilde (1854–1900) is best known for his society comedies and for his homosexuality. In 1895 he was sentenced to two years' hard labour for having homosexual relations with the son of the Marquis of Queensberry. While in prison he was made bankrupt and on his release he moved to France and lived out the rest of his life in exile. In his one novel "The Picture of Dorian Gray", against a London setting he recounts the adventures of a beautiful young man in search of pleasure but haunted by the effects of the passage of time.

" As the dawn was just breaking he found himself close to Covent Garden. The darkness lifted, and, flushed with faint fires, the sky hollowed itself into a perfect pearl. Huge carts filled with nodding lilies rumbled slowly down the polished empty street. The air was heavy with the perfume of the flowers, and their beauty seemed to bring him an anodyne for his pain. He followed into the market, and watched the men unloading their waggons. A white-smocked carter offered him some cherries. He thanked him, and wondered why he refused to accept any money for them, and began to eat them listlessly. They had been plucked at midnight, and the coldness of the moon had entered into them. A long line of boys carrying crates of striped tulips, and of yellow and red roses, defiled in front of him, threading their way through the huge jade-green piles of vegetables. Under the portico, with its grey sun-bleached pillars, loitered a troop of draggled bare-headed girls, waiting for the auction to be over. Others crowded round the swinging doors of the coffee-house in the Piazza. The heavy cart-horses slipped and stamped upon the rough stones, shaking their bells and trappings. Some of the drivers were lying asleep on a pile of sacks. Iris-necked, and pink-footed, the pigeons ran about picking up seeds. **"**

OSCAR WILDE, *THE PICTURE OF DORIAN GRAY,* 1890

HYDE PARK

At the age of seventeen Joseph Conrad (1857-1924) left his native Poland to go to sea. Before getting his master's certificate he worked on British coasters, using his spare time to learn English and read Shakespeare. He wrote his first novel "Almayer's Folly" in English, and in 1896 settled in England where in spite of indifferent health he devoted himself to writing. Of "The Secret Agent" he remarked, "I have just finished a novel without a single drop of water in it (except for the rain); this is natural enough because all of it is set in London."

❝Through the park railings these glances beheld men and women riding in the Row, couples cantering past harmoniously, others advancing sedately at a walk, loitering groups of three or four, solitary horsemen looking unsociable, and solitary women followed at a long distance by a groom with a cockade to his hat and a leather belt over his tight-fitting coat. Carriages went bowling by, mostly two-horse broughams, with here and there a victoria with the skin of some wild beast inside and a woman's face and hat emerging above the folded hood. And a peculiarly London sun – against which nothing could be said except that it looked bloodshot – glorified all this by its stare. It hung at a moderate elevation above Hyde Park Corner with an air of punctual and benign vigilance. The very pavement under Mr. Verloc's feet had an old-gold tinge in that diffused light, in which neither wall, nor tree, nor beast, nor man cast a shadow. Mr. Verloc was going westward through a town without shadows in an atmosphere of powdered old gold. There were red, coppery gleams on the roofs of houses, on the corners of walls, on the panels of carriages, on the very coats of the horses, and on the broad back of Mr. Verloc's overcoat, where they produced a dull effect of rustiness. But Mr. Verloc was not in the least conscious of having got rusty. He surveyed through the park railings the evidences of the town's opulence and luxury with an approving eye.❞

JOSEPH CONRAD,
THE SECRET AGENT, 1907

CHELSEA

Thomas Carlyle (1795–1881), the English scholar and historian, moved to Cheyne Row in 1834 with his wife Jane. While still house-hunting, he described Chelsea in a letter to Jane, obviously attracted by the peace and quiet.

❝A broad highway with huge shady trees, boats lying moored, and a smell of shipping and tar. Battersea Bridge (of wood) a few yards off; the broad river with white-trowsered, white-shirted Cockneys dashing by like arrows in their long canoes of boats; beyond the green beautiful knolls of Surrey with their villages – on the whole a most artificial green-painted, yet lively, fresh, almost opera-looking business, such as you can fancy. Chelsea is a single heterogeneous kind of spot, very dirty and confused in some places, quite beautiful in others, abounding in antiquities and the traces of great men – Sir Thomas More, Steele, Smollett, etc.❞

THOMAS CARLYLE,
LETTER, 1834

LONDON TRANSPORT

THE HANSOM CAB

Jerome Klapka Jerome (1859-1927) achieved a kind of immortality with his comic novel "Three Men in a Boat", a hilarious chronicle of a boating holiday on the Thames at the turn of the century. Jerome was a prolific journalist, and joint editor of a humorous magazine, "The Idler", for some years. The excerpt below is from his autobiography.

❝It was a picturesque vehicle, the old hansom: there was that to be said for it....But to ride in, they were the most uncomfortable contrivances ever invented. To get into them, you grabbed at two handles, one jutting out from the splash board and the other just over the wheel, and hauled yourself up on to a small iron step. If the horse made a start before you got further, you were carried down the street in this position, looking like a monkey on a stick. If you had not secured a firm hold, you were jerked back into the gutter: which was safer, but even less dignified. Getting out was more difficult. A false step landed you on all fours, and your aunt or your sister, or whatever it might happen to be, stepped on you. To enter or alight without getting your hat knocked off by the reins was an art in itself. The seat was just big enough for two. It was high, and only long ladies could reach the floor. The others bobbed up and down with their feet dangling. The world always thought the worst, but as often as not, one put one's arm round her purely to prevent her from slipping off. There was a trap-door in the roof. Along dim-lit roads, one noticed the cabman holding it open, and driving with his head bent down... I have no regrets for the passing of the hansom.

The old two-horse bus, one is glad had disappeared, if only for the sake of the horses. It had straw inside and a little oil lamp that made up in smell what it lacked in illuminating power... There was no bell. Passengers stopped the bus by prodding the conductor with their umbrellas. The driver wore a mighty coat with flapping capes, and wrapped a rug round his legs before strapping himself to his seat. He was a genial soul, not above accepting a cigar, and had a tongue as clever as his hands. Wit and sarcasm dropped from him as he drove. The motor has silenced the humour of the streets.❞

JEROME K. JEROME,
MY LIFE AND TIMES, 1926

RAILWAY STATIONS

Edward Morgan Forster (1879–1970) born in Tonbridge, England, went to Cambridge University before devoting himself to a life of journalism, literary criticism and fiction. In his books, which generally deal with characters drawn from genteel society, Forster explores social differences set against the different environments of urban and country life. This is particularly true of "Howards End", for example in this passage about the great London termini, which are described as necessary evils to be endured in effecting the transition from town to the country house.

❝Like many others who have lived long in a great capital, she had strong feelings about the various railway termini. They are our gates to the glorious and the unknown. Through them we pass out into adventure and sunshine, to them, alas! we return. In Paddington all Cornwall is latent and the remoter west; down the inclines of Liverpool Street lie fenlands and the illimitable Broads; Scotland is through the pylons of Euston; Wessex behind the poised chaos of Waterloo. Italians realise this, as is natural; those of them who are so unfortunate as to serve as waiters in Berlin call the Anhalt Bahnhof the Stazione d'Italia, because by it they must return to their homes. And he is a chilly Londoner who does not endow his stations with some personality, and extend to them, however shyly, the emotions of fear and love.

To Margaret – I hope that it will not set the reader against her – the station of King's Cross had always suggested Infinity. Its very situation – withdrawn a little behind the facile splendours of St. Pancras – implied a comment on the materialism of life. Those two great arches, colourless, indifferent, shouldering between them an unlovely clock, were fit portals for some eternal adventure, whose issue might be prosperous, but would certainly not be expressed in the ordinary language of prosperity. If you think this is ridiculous, remember that it is not Margaret who is telling you about it; and let me hasten to add that they were in plenty of time for the train....**99**

EDWARD MORGAN FORSTER,
HOWARDS END, 1910

TRAMS

Born in Bradford, John Boynton Priestley (1894–1984) settled in London in 1922 and quickly made a name for himself as a journalist and critic. He wrote stories of ordinary, unremarkable men and women with remarkably sharp and humorous observation. "Angel Pavement", a saga of clerical staff in a dreary City office was a grim "Realist" novel of London life which became an instant best-seller when it appeared.

66 Before he reached the High Street and his tram, the bottom of his trousers were unpleasantly heavy, his boots gave out a squelching sound, and the newspaper he carried was being rapidly reconverted to its original pulp. The tram, its windows steaming and streaming, was more crowded than usual, of course, and carried its maximum cargo of wet clothes, the wearers of which were simply so many irritable ghosts. After enormous difficulty, Mr. Smeeth succeeded in filling and lighting his morning pipe of T. Benenden's Own, and then – so stubborn is the spirit of man – succeeded in unfolding and examining his pulpy newspaper. Before he had

reached the end of City Road, he had learned that the cost of a public school education was too high, that the night clubs on Broadway were not doing the business they had done, that a man in Birmingham had cut his wife's throat, that students in Cairo were again on strike, that an old woman in Hammersmith had died of starvation, that a policeman in Suffolk had found six pound notes in the prisoner's right sock, and that bubonic plague is conveyed to human beings by fleas from infected rats.**99**

J.B. PRIESTLEY,
ANGEL PAVEMENT, 1930

A NIGHT IN WESTMINSTER ABBEY

When the French writer and politician Chateaubriand (1768-1848) arrived in London on May 21, 1793, it was as an exile from revolutionary France. There he became familiar with poverty and hunger, keeping body and soul together with some private teaching and translating. But it was in London that he wrote his first book "An Historical, Political and Moral Essay on Ancient and Modern Revolutions, and Their Relation to the French Revolution" (1797), which brought him to the attention of other refugees in exile. During his years in London, dealt with in volume 10 of his "Memoirs from Beyond the Grave", he relates the extraordinary episode when, accidentally locked in Westminster Abbey, he was compelled to spend the night there.

❝On one occasion it happened that towards the end of day, having wished to view the Abbey at dusk, I completely lost myself in admiration of such lofty and fanciful architecture. Awed by the 'dark immensity of Christian churches' (Montaigne), I wandered slowly about till I found myself overtaken by the night: the doors were closed. I tried to find a way out; I shouted for the usher, I banged on the doors: but all the noise I made was scattered and lost in the silence, so I resigned myself to settle down and sleep with the dead. After some deliberation in the choice of my lodging I stopped by the tomb of the Earl of Chatham, at the foot of the rood screen and by the two floors of the Knights' Chapel and that of Henry VII. At the foot of these stairs, the shelter they offered barred by metal gates, a tomb set into the wall opposite a marble figure of the Grim Reaper offered some refuge. A draped marble shroud formed a little niche, and like Charles Quint before me I resigned myself to my entombment.

It was the perfect place from which to see the world for what it really is. What glories are enclosed within these vaults! But what remains? Vain are their sorrows, vain are their joys; the wretched Lady Jane Grey is no different now from the once happy Adela of Salisbury (only her skeleton is less ghastly because it lacks the skull: her mortal remains are the lovelier thanks to her fate and the absence of all that once made her beautiful. The tournament of the victor at Crecy, or Henry VIII's Field of Cloth of Gold will never be seen again in this mausoleum. Bacon, Newton, Milton too are all deeply buried, gone just as surely as all their unknown contemporaries. And I, an exile, outcast and poor, would I wish to cease from being the small, forgotten, miserable creature that I am, to have been one of these dead souls, famous, powerful and sated with pleasures? But that's not what life is! Should we be surprised when we peer into the beyond that we glimpse no sign of divinity? Time is a veil that separates us from God just as an eyelid will shut out the light from an eye.

Crouching on my marble coverlet I come down from these lofty thoughts to find my anxiety tinged with a certain pleasure at my predicament. When the wind used to howl round my tower-house at Combourg it was much the same: a shrieking gale and a disembodied spirit have much in common.

As my eyes got used to the darkness, I began to make out the shapes of figures on top of the tombs. Gazing at the gothic corbelling round the tomb of the English St Denis it seemed to me that all the past years and all that has happened hung from it like ancient lanterns: the whole edifice was a monument of petrified history.

I heard the clock strike ten and then eleven. The hammer that rose and fell upon the bell was the only other living thing there with me. Outside now and then I could hear a passing carriage or the call of a watchman, nothing more. These far-off sounds seemed part of another world. Mist from the river mingled with smoke had penetrated the Abbey, adding to the Stygian gloom inside.

At length the faint sign of dawn began to grow in a distant corner: I stared at this slowly growing light that seemed to emanate from the two little sons of Edward IV, murdered by their uncle. 'Thus lay the gentle babes,' says the Bard, 'Girdling one another within their alabaster innocent arms: Their lips were four red roses on a stalk, Which in their summer beauty kissed each other.' But God wasn't sending me these sweet, sad litle souls, instead I could make out the faint apparition of a young girl carrying a lantern shaded with a twist of paper; it was the little bell-ringer. I heard the sound of a kiss, and the bell tolled daybreak. The poor girl was scared out of her wits when I emerged to leave through the cloister door with her. I told her of my adventure, and she told me she was standing in for her father who was sick; neither of us mentioned the little kiss I had heard. **,,**

CHATEAUBRIAND,
MEMOIRS FROM BEYOND THE GRAVE, 1849–50

THE QUEEN IN BOND STREET

London, where Virginia Woolf (1882-1941) was born, played a prominent role in her life and her novels. In fact it was in her London house behind the British Museum that the so-called Bloomsbury Group was founded, bringing together writers, historians, economists and critics in one of the key movements of modern English thought. In London too, together with her husband Leonard Woolf, she founded the Hogarth Press, taking on the duties of a publisher as well as an author. In the novel "Mrs Dalloway" we follow society hostess Clarissa through the streets of London getting ready for a large party at her house that evening.

,, The motor car with its blinds drawn and an air of inscrutable reserve proceeded towards Piccadilly, still gazed at, still ruffling the faces on both sides of the street with the same dark breath of veneration whether for Queen, Prince, or Prime Minister nobody knew. The face itself had been seen only once by three people for a few seconds. Even the sex was now in dispute. But there could be no doubt that greatness was seated within; greatness was passing, hidden, down Bond Street, removed only by a hand's-breadth from ordinary people who might now, for the first and last time, be within speaking distance of the majesty of England, of the enduring symbol of the state which will be known to curious antiquaries, sifting the ruins of time, when London is a grass-grown path and all those hurrying along the pavement this Wednesday morning are but bones with a few wedding rings mixed up in their dust and the gold stoppings of innumerable decayed teeth. The face in the motor car will then be known.

It is probably the Queen, thought Mrs. Dalloway, coming out of Mulberry's with her flowers; the Queen. And for a second she wore a look of extreme dignity standing by the flower shop in the sunlight while the car passed at a foot's pace, with its blinds drawn. The Queen going to some hospital; the Queen opening some bazaar, thought Clarissa.

The crush was terrific for the time of day. Lords, Ascot, Hurlingham, what was it? she wondered, for the street was blocked. The British middle classes sitting sideways on the tops of omnibuses with parcels and umbrellas, yes, even furs on a day like this, were, she thought, more ridiculous, more unlike anything there has ever been than one could conceive; and the Queen herself held up; the Queen herself unable to pass. Clarissa was suspended on one side of Brook Street; Sir John Buckhurst, the old Judge on the other, with the car between them (Sir John had laid down the law for years and liked a well-dressed woman) when the chauffeur, leaning ever so slightly, said or showed something to the policeman, who saluted and raised his arm and jerked his head and moved the omnibus to the side and the car passed through. Slowly and very silently it took its way.

Clarissa guessed; Clarissa knew of course; she had seen something white, magical, circular, in the footman's hand, a disc inscribed with a name, – the Queen's, the Prince of Wales's, the Prime Minister's? – which, by force of its own lustre, burnt its way through (Clarissa saw the car diminishing, disappearing), to blaze among the candelabras, glittering stars, breasts stiff with oak leaves, Hugh Whitbread and all his colleagues, the gentlemen of England, that night in Buckingham Palace. And Clarissa too, gave a party. She stiffened a little; so she would stand at the top of her stairs. **"**

VIRGINIA WOOLF,
MRS DALLOWAY, 1925

MORMONS IN WHITECHAPEL

George Orwell (1903–50) worked in a series of ill-paid jobs in London and Paris while struggling to have his writing accepted by a publisher. He describes this period in "Down and Out in Paris and London", published in 1933, from which the following description of London street life is taken.

"All day I loafed in the streets, east as far as Wapping, west as far as Whitechapel. It was queer after Paris; everything was so much cleaner and quieter and drearier. One missed the scream of the trams, and the noisy, festering life of the back streets, and the armed men clattering through the squares. The crowds were better dressed and the faces comelier and milder and more alike, without that fierce individuality and malice of the French. There was less drunkenness, and less dirt, and less quarrelling, and more idling. Knots of men stood at all the corners, slightly underfed, but kept going by the tea-and-two-slices which the Londoner swallows every two hours. One seemed to breathe a less feverish air than in Paris. It was the land of the tea urn and the Labour Exchange, as Paris is the land of the *bistro* and the sweatshop.

It was interesting to watch the crowds ... Here and there were street meetings. In Whitechapel somebody called The Singing Evangel undertook to save you from hell for the charge of sixpence. In the East India Dock Road the Salvation Army were holding a service. They were singing 'Anybody here like sneaking Judas?' to the tune of 'What's to be done with a drunken sailor?' On Tower Hill two Mormons were trying to address a meeting. Round their platform struggled a mob of men, shouting and interrupting. Someone was denouncing them for polygamists. A lame, bearded man, evidently an atheist, had heard the word God and was heckling angrily. There was a confused uproar of voices.

'My dear friends, if you would only let us finish what we were saying – ! – That's right, give 'em a say. Don't get on the argue! – No, no, you answer me. Can you *show* me God? You *show* 'im me, the I'll believe in 'im. – Oh, shut up, don't keep interrupting of 'em! – Interrupt yourself! – Well, there's a lot to be said for polygamy. Take the – women out of industry, anyway. – My dear friends, if you would just – No, no, don't you slip out of it. 'Ave you *seen* God? 'Ave you *touched* 'im? 'Ave you shook 'ands with 'im? – Oh, don't get on the argue, for Christ's sake don't get on the *argue*!' etc. etc. I listened for twenty minutes, anxious to learn something about Mormonism, but the meeting never got beyond shouts. It is the general fate of street meetings.

In Middlesex Street, among the crowds at the market, a draggled, down-at-heel woman was hauling a brat of five by the arm. She brandished a tin trumpet in its face. The brat was squalling.

'Enjoy yourself!' yelled the mother. 'What yer think I brought yer out 'ere for an' bought y' a trumpet an' all? D'ya want to go across my knee? You little bastard, you *shall* enjoy yerself!**" "**

GEORGE ORWELL,
DOWN AND OUT IN PARIS AND LONDON, 1933

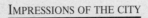

IMPRESSIONS OF THE CITY

LONDON'S BRIDGES

Many of Dickens' novels were originally published in weekly or monthly instalments in magazines and periodicals, and they proved immensely popular with the public. "The Old Curiosity Shop" first appeared in a new weekly called "Master Humphrey's Clock", which was launched in 1840 and written wholly by Dickens.

" Then, the crowds for ever passing and repassing on the bridges (on those which are free of toll at least), where many stop on fine evenings looking listlessly down upon the water, with some vague idea that by-and-by it runs between green banks which grow wider and wider until at last it joins the broad vast sea – where some halt to rest from heavy loads, and think, as they look over the parapet, that to smoke and lounge away one's life, and lie sleeping in the sun upon a hot tarpaulin, in a dull, slow, sluggish barge, must be happiness alloyed – and where some, and a very different class, pause with heavier loads than they, remembering to have heard or read in some old time that drowning was not a hard death, but of all means of suicide the easiest and best.**" "**

CHARLES DICKENS,
THE OLD CURIOSITY SHOP, 1840–1

POETS AND PHILOSOPHERS

One of the last great German Romantics, Heinrich Heine (1797–1856) won recognition and acclaim with the publication in 1827 of a collection of poems "The Book of Songs". At this time he also published two volumes of "Travel Sketches", and a further two volumes were completed between 1826 and 1831.
*   In them, drawing on his travels in Italy, Great Britain and other countries, Heine gave rein to his imagination, sometimes developing his political theories, which were liberal and which resulted in the banning of his works in several German states.*

" I have seen the most astonishing thing that the world has to show: I have seen it and I marvel at it still....I see it now, this forest of bricks bisected by a river and filled with a teeming horde of people who cherish a thousand different passions, rent by love, hunger and hate.... I mean London.
Send a philosopher to London by all means, but for the love of God don't send a poet! Take a philosopher there and set him down at the corner of Cheapside, and he will learn more than ever there was in all the books at the last Leipzig Book Fair put together; and while this tide of humanity goes babbling round him there will rise a sea of thoughts before him too, the eternal spirit which hovers overhead will touch him with its breath and the darkest secrets of humanity will be revealed in an instant, quite clearly shall he see and hear the vital pulse of the world...for if London is the world's right hand, strong and vigorous, this highway with the Stock Exchange at one end and Downing Street at the other must be its artery.
Never send a poet to London! The serious business of putting a price on everything leaves nothing untainted; there is a dreadful uniformity as of a clockwork motor, even pleasure wears a gloomy face. The very pressure of the place stifles the

imagination and destroys the heart; and if by chance you were to send a German poet, a dreamer who stands and stares at anything from a ragged beggar-woman to a gleaming goldsmith's shop, then he'd be trampled underfoot! Jostled and buffeted on all sides, swept off his feet with a friendly curse. Curse those confounded crowds! 🙶🙶

HEINRICH HEINE,
TRAVEL SKETCHES, 1826–31

NOSTALGIA

Charlie Chaplin (1889–1979), the film actor and director, harbored a secret nostalgia for the London of his childhood, which he revealed in his autobiography of 1964.

🙶This was the London of my childhood, of my moods and awakenings: memories of Lambeth in the spring: of trivial incidents and things: of riding with mother on top of a horse-bus trying to touch lilac trees – of the many coloured bus-tickets, orange, blue, pink and green, that bestrewed the pavement where the trams and buses stopped ... of melancholy Sundays and pale-faced parents and children escorting toy windmills and coloured balloons over Westminster Bridge: and the maternal penny steamers that softly lowered their funnels as they glided under it. From such trivia I believe my soul was born. 🙶🙶

CHARLIE CHAPLIN,
MY AUTOBIOGRAPHY, 1964

A LAND OF PRIVACIES

Paul Theroux has written about several countries around the world in works of fiction and non-fiction. His view of London, as an American, is one shared by many visitors to the city.

🙶It had been a mistake to walk from my hotel to this reception. My hotel was in Chelsea, near the Embankment; the party was at Horton's, Briarcliff Lodge, in Kensington. London is not a city. It is more like a country, and living in it is like living in Holland or Belgium. Its completeness makes it deceptive – there are sidewalks from one frontier to the other – and its hugeness makes it possible for everyone to invent his own city. My London is not your London, though everyone's Washington, DC, is pretty much the same. It was three miles from my hotel to Horton's, and this was only a small part of the labyrinth. A two-mile walk through

any other city would take you inevitably through a slum. But this was unvarying gentility – wet narrow streets, dark housefronts, block upon block. They spoke of prosperity, but they revealed nothing very definite of their occupants. They were sedate battlements, fortress walls, with blind windows, or drawn curtains. I imagined, behind them, something tumultuous. I had never felt more solitary or anonymous. I was happy. The city had been built to enclose secrets, for the British are like those naked Indians who hide in the Brazilian jungle – not timid, but fantastically private and untrusting. This was a mazy land of privacies – comforting to a secretive person, offering shelter to a fugitive, but posing problems to a diplomat. **"**

PAUL THEROUX,
THE LONDON EMBASSY, 1982

CHRISTMASTIME

Martin Amis has become something of a commentator on late-20th-century manners and morals in his novels. "Money" was the first of his books to achieve best-seller status, but others have followed since.

" It is Christmastime in London.
In London, Christmastime is the time when cabbies' change feels as hot as coins coughed from the bowels of fruit-machines, when office duds try their hands as wits in the pubs and on the long tables of cheap bistros, when in the dead days before New Year people show their presents to the world in buses and tube trains: collars grip the neck like a cold compress, gloves lie on the lap as stiff as pickled octopi, watches and fountain pens flash their signals in the hired light. Christmastime is the time when all girls talk about things being lovely and warm.
The first annual snowfall caused dismay, breakdown, anarchy, as it does every year. All week I've been walking though the London streets and wondering what they look like. They look like something terribly familiar. People are wiggling on their faulty gyroscopes. Whoops! we all go on the hoof-marked brocades. We stare at the pavements to find our footing but we can't tell what the pavements look like. For fifteen minutes the snow was crispy white and squeaky clean. Then no colour at all – no colour, not even grey. What does it look like? With its murky scurf and banked channels of glint and scum, it looks like washing-up, it looks like the London skies. London summer skies: that's what they look like. And so is everything the same?
The second annual snowfall caused dismay, breakdown, anarchy, as it does every year. This second snow stayed white and hard for a lot longer. It was better-quality stuff: it obviously cost more. The snow surprised everyone, as it does every year. It surprised me. But then, snow surprises. Snow is surprising! It is the element of surprise. For a while the world was lunar. It was silent. It was snowjobbed. It was hushed the next morning until at last you heard the apologetic sounds of whispering cars. We all tiptoed out of doors and blinked at the world. Everyone seems to think that everything is all their fault. But we give ourselves credit too sometimes. **"**

MARTIN AMIS,
MONEY, 1984

A Journey Through London

▲ HMS *Belfast* and Tower Bridge.

▲ Christmas lights in Regent Street.　　　▼ The Isle of Dogs and Canary Wharf.

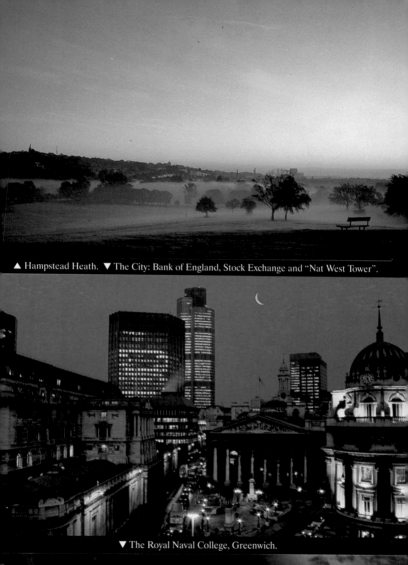

▲ Hampstead Heath. ▼ The City: Bank of England, Stock Exchange and "Nat West Tower".

▼ The Royal Naval College, Greenwich.

▲ Trooping the Colour.

▼ Horse Guards Parade.

▼ A walk in Grovelands Park.

▲ A garden party at Buckingham Palace.

▲ The residential district of Highgate has preserved its village atmosphere.

▲ Syon House.

▼ The gardens at Hampton Court Palace.

THE SIGHTS OF LONDON

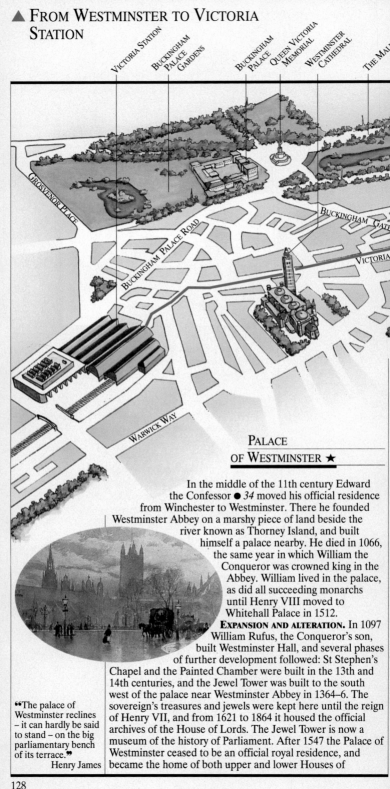

VICTORIA STATION

BUCKINGHAM PALACE GARDENS

BUCKINGHAM PALACE

QUEEN VICTORIA MEMORIAL

WESTMINSTER CATHEDRAL

THE MALL

GROSVENOR PLACE

BUCKINGHAM PALACE ROAD

BUCKINGHAM GATE

VICTORIA

WARWICK WAY

PALACE OF WESTMINSTER ★

In the middle of the 11th century Edward the Confessor ● *34* moved his official residence from Winchester to Westminster. There he founded Westminster Abbey on a marshy piece of land beside the river known as Thorney Island, and built himself a palace nearby. He died in 1066, the same year in which William the Conqueror was crowned king in the Abbey. William lived in the palace, as did all succeeding monarchs until Henry VIII moved to Whitehall Palace in 1512.

EXPANSION AND ALTERATION. In 1097 William Rufus, the Conqueror's son, built Westminster Hall, and several phases of further development followed: St Stephen's Chapel and the Painted Chamber were built in the 13th and 14th centuries, and the Jewel Tower was built to the south west of the palace near Westminster Abbey in 1364–6. The sovereign's treasures and jewels were kept here until the reign of Henry VII, and from 1621 to 1864 it housed the official archives of the House of Lords. The Jewel Tower is now a museum of the history of Parliament. After 1547 the Palace of Westminster ceased to be an official royal residence, and became the home of both upper and lower Houses of

66 The palace of Westminster reclines – it can hardly be said to stand – on the big parliamentary bench of its terrace. 99
Henry James

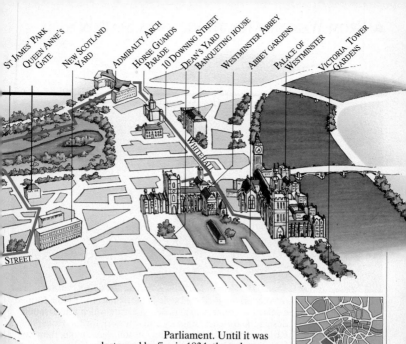

ST JAMES' PARK · QUEEN ANNE'S GATE · NEW SCOTLAND YARD · ADMIRALTY ARCH · HORSE GUARDS PARADE · 10 DOWNING STREET · DEAN'S YARD · BANQUETING HOUSE · WESTMINSTER ABBEY · ABBEY GARDENS · PALACE OF WESTMINSTER · VICTORIA TOWER GARDENS · WHITEHALL · STREET

🏛 One day

Parliament. Until it was destroyed by fire in 1834, the palace towered over a great maze of little streets that were filled with lodging houses, taverns, coffee-houses and shops.

REBUILDING: BARRY AND PUGIN. Out of ninety-seven designs that were submitted for the rebuilding of Parliament, the eventual success of Sir Charles Barry's project was largely due to his collaboration with another architect, Augustus Pugin (1812–52). Pugin was one of the great neo-Gothic stylists of his day, and assisted Barry with his designs from 1836 until his death. The contrasting temperaments of the two men resulted in a design that was both elegant and highly original. Barry provided the building with its classical balance and symmetry, while Pugin supplied the ornamentation and asymmetrical elements, such as the Victoria Tower and the Clock Tower. Pugin was also responsible for much of the interior decoration and furnishings. Albert ▲ *228*, prince consort since 1840, was a keen amateur follower of the arts and was

"Authority still resides in Lords and Commons. They must take decisions, they must govern. Nothing can be done without their approval; patronage is theirs to bestow, and the framing of policy their responsibility. It is not power which Parliament lacks, any more than Louis XVI or Nicholas II lacked power; rather the will to exercise it. Power without resolution is as vain as desire without virility, and evokes as scant respect."

Malcolm Muggeridge
The Thirties

THE FIRE OF 1834
The fire blazed through the night of October 16–17, and several painters hurried to the Palace of Westminster in order to capture the scene. Constable took up a position on Westminster Bridge, while Turner set off in a boat on the Thames with another artist from the Royal Academy, Clarkson Stanfield, and painted several watercolors from there ● *102*. By dawn on the morning of the 17th, nothing was left of the ancient royal palace except for Westminster Hall, the cloisters and the crypt of St Stephen's Chapel.

devoted to the medieval style in particular. In 1841 he formed a selection committee in order to decide which artists should design the frescoes, statuary and ironwork for the Houses of Parliament: Dyce, Maclise and Gibson were among those to be selected. The rebuilding process began in 1839 and was finally completed in 1860, when the roof was put on the Victoria Tower.

WESTMINSTER HALL ★. The hall was built by William Rufus between 1097 and 1099, as an extension of Edward the Confessor's palace. At the time it was probably the largest building of its type in Europe, measuring 240 feet long and about 40 feet high. During the last decade of the 14th century it was altered by Richard II's architects, the walls being raised and a fine porch added. The most significant alteration however was the addition of the magnificent hammer-beam roof, which was 92 feet high in the center. Parliaments were held here, and many famous trials took place, among them those of Anne Boleyn (1536), Guy Fawkes ● *36* (1606) and King Charles I (1649). After the Restoration of Charles II, the head of Oliver Cromwell was displayed on the roof of the hall , and in more recent years the bodies of Gladstone, Edward VII and Winston Churchill have all lain in state here. Westminster Hall is now part of the House of Commons, linked to it by St Stephen's Hall.

PARLIAMENT. The United Kingdom Parliament is composed of two Houses: the House of Lords, which was for many years

the Royal Entrance, the queen puts on her robes and the imperial State Crown in the Robing Room. Accompanied by the Prince of Wales, she is greeted in the House of Lords by the Lord Chamberlain and the Peers in their robes. Once she is seated on the throne, the Members of Parliament are invited by a herald to come to the House of Lords and hear the queen's speech. This outline of government policy for the coming year is always drafted by the prime minister. Only after this ceremony can Parliament get down to business. The

ceremony is preceded by an annual inspection of the palace cellars, a legacy from the Gunpowder Plot of November 5, 1605, when Guy Fawkes and his fellow conspirators attempted to blow up the palace during King James I's speech.

St Margaret's Church

This church in Parliament Square was founded in the 12th century and rebuilt between 1486 and 1523. It is the parish church of the Houses of Parliament, and has innumerable important links with the past. The window was made in honor of Prince Arthur's engagement to Catharine of Aragon, though Arthur died before the wedding, and Catharine married his younger brother, Henry VIII. Also married here were Samuel Pepys ● *40* (1655), John Milton (1656) and Winston Churchill ● *42* (1908). Among historical figures buried in the church are William Caxton (1491), and Sir Walter Raleigh (1618) after his execution in Old Palace Yard.

Westminster Abbey ★

Coronations and burials. With two exceptions (Edward V and Edward VIII), the monarchs of England from William the Conqueror to Elizabeth II have been crowned in Westminster Abbey. It is also the burial place of most of them, from Harold Harefoot (1040) to George II (1760).

Uncertain origins. A church was probably built on this site in the 7th century, followed by a Benedictine abbey between 730 and 740. When Edward the Confessor

Big Ben

The astronomer royal, George Biddell Airy, was appointed to oversee the

accuracy of the new clock in 1846. He specified that the first stroke of each hour should be correct to the nearest second, and that its exactness should be checked by telegraph twice each day at the Royal Observatory, Greenwich.

Central Lobby

This octagonal room (left) in the center of the palace separates the Lords from the Commons. Members of Parliament receive the press here.

Invitation to the coronation
of George IV in
Westminster Abbey.

FRENCH INFLUENCE
Henry III greatly
admired the
cathedrals of Rheims
and Amiens, as well
as the Sainte-
Chapelle in Paris, and
Westminster Abbey
reflects these
influences. The apse
and its radiating
chapels derive from
Amiens, together
with the recessed
portals in the
north
transept.
The tall windows in
the chapels of the
apse derive from
Rheims; and there
are many other
features imported
from France, such as
the flying buttresses,
rose windows and
immensely tall nave.

ascended the throne in 1040, he rebuilt the abbey and added a
Norman church. The church was dedicated on December 28,
1065: a week later the king died and was buried inside it.
When he was canonized in 1139, successive kings gave rich
endowments to the church, keen to have their names linked
with Edward's.

GOTHIC REBUILDING. In 1220 Henry III began to rebuild the
abbey. He started by adding the Lady Chapel (demolished in
the construction of the Henry VII chapel), and the foundation
stone of the new building was laid on July 6, 1245. The old
building was gradually demolished as construction work
continued westward: the east end, choir, transepts and the
first bay of the nave were all complete by the end of
the century. The first master builder to work on
the rebuilding was Henry de Reynes, possibly
brought back by Henry when he visited
Rheims in 1243. There is certainly much
French influence in the abbey's design,
though the style was not simply copied from
Continental models. The ribbed vaulting is a
typically English feature, as are the galleries, the
long nave, wide transepts and the polygonal Chapter House.

ENTER HENRY YEVELE. In 1269, in order to celebrate the
completion of the transepts, the north façade, part of the
cloisters and the Chapter House, the abbey was consecrated
and the remains of Edward the Confessor were moved to the
newly built St Edward's Chapel before the high altar: before
the Dissolution of the monasteries, its upper part was
decorated with gold and jewels, and sick people would spend
the night in the recesses at the base praying for recovery.
Henry III died in 1272 and was also buried in front of the high
altar, having paid for the rebuilding with all his private
fortune. His death brought building work to a halt, to begin
again 104 years later in 1376 under the supervision of master
mason Henry Yevele, who had redesigned Westminster Hall
and built the nave of Canterbury Cathedral. Yevele undertook

**"PROCESSION OF
KNIGHTS OF THE
ORDER OF THE BATH"**
This painting by
Canaletto
(1697–1768) shows
the knights leaving
Westminster Abbey.
The Bath is the
second oldest order
of knighthood in
England, and in 1725
the Henry VII Chapel
became the chapel of
the order. Their
carved stalls divide
the aisles from the
nave, each bearing
their arms engraved
on a copper plaque
with their standards
displayed above.

the construction of the nave, working as far as possible to the former plans of Henry de Reynes, and also built the Jerusalem Chamber in the dean's lodgings, where Henry IV died in 1413 after collapsing while at prayer before the shrine of St Edward. Yevele's devotion to the 13th-century designs gave the abbey a remarkable unity of style, which was in due course respected by his successors. With the exception of the towers on the west front, which were added by Hawksmoor ▲ 311 in the mid-18th century, the abbey was complete by 1532. Apart from looting during the Dissolution of the monasteries ● 36 royal protection has saved this magnificent building from either damage or alteration.

MAUSOLEUM OF THE GREAT AND GOOD. The sheer number of monuments inside it has all but transformed Westminster Abbey into a museum of English sculpture. There are the tombs of no fewer than fifteen monarchs located here, together with a great many other members of the British royal families. They are scattered around the abbey chapels, two of which are of outstanding importance: those of Edward the Confessor and Henry VII. Altogether, Westminster Abbey contains more than five thousand tombs, monuments and memorials. Over the centuries many of the greatest Englishmen and women have been interred here: Isaac Newton, Handel, Charles Darwin, Oliver Cromwell, Cecil Rhodes, Henry Purcell, David Livingstone and literally thousands more.

RESTING PLACES. The tombs and memorials are sometimes grouped together in different parts of the abbey. Part of the north aisle and transept is devoted to statesmen: there are statues here of Benjamin Disraeli (1804–81), his despised rival William Ewart Gladstone (1809–98), Lord Palmerston (1784–1865) and many more. The great radical Charles James Fox (1749–1806) has a statue depicting him dying in the arms of Liberty. In the south transept is the famous Poets' Corner, which was named after the first two poets to be buried here, Geoffrey Chaucer and Edmund Spenser. Many more writers are commemorated than are actually buried here, but John Dryden, Samuel Johnson, Sheridan, Robert Browning and Tennyson are some of those whose remains lie within the abbey. Ben Jonson was buried upright at his own request, so as to take up as little space as possible. Westminster Abbey also has memorials to the two world wars: the Unknown Soldier was interred in the nave in 1920, at the front of which is a memorial plaque to Winston Churchill, with another to the memory of US President Franklin Delano Roosevelt near the west door.

THE NORTH TRANSEPT Its splendid façade overlooks Parliament Square. A large rose window is framed by elegant flying buttresses over a triple entrance.

THE HENRY VII CHAPEL IN 1828 Situated at the east end behind the altar, it contains the tomb of the first Tudor king. This was carved by the Florentine Pietro Torrigiano, who left Italy after he broke Michelangelo's nose in a fight.

WESTMINSTER ABBEY CHORISTERS The abbey has its own choir, composed exclusively of men and boys who sing "with the greatest ease imaginable".

139

EFFIGY OF WILLIAM DE VALENCE (D. 1296)
William was Henry III's French half-brother, and Earl of Pembroke. He fought for Henry at the Battle of Lewes, and went on the last crusade to Palestine with Prince Edward (later Edward I).

The coronation of William IV in Westminster Abbey.

THE NAVE
The dimensions of the nave are exceptional for an English cathedral: 102 feet high and 72 feet wide, including the aisles. It is the highest Gothic nave in England. The central section is separated from the aisles by graceful columns of grey Purbeck marble, which accentuate its height. The interior light comes from the large 15th-century window above the west door.

THE CHAPEL OF EDWARD THE CONFESSOR AND THE CORONATION CHAIR ★. The tomb of the royal saint is in the middle of the chapel. Also here is the Coronation Chair, made around 1300 and used for every coronation since 1308. Beneath it is a block of brown sandstone, the Stone of Scone: the kings of Scotland had been crowned on this piece of rock for as long as anyone can remember, and it was symbolically brought to London by Edward I in 1297 after his conquest of Scotland. Legend also associates the stone with Jacob's pillow at Bethel. In almost seven hundred years the Coronation Chair has only left the abbey three times: once when Cromwell was made Lord Protector in Westminster Hall, and twice for safekeeping during the two world wars. At the east end of the chapel is the oak effigy (once coated with silver) of Henry V (1387–1422). His beloved "Kate", Catharine de Valois (1401–37), whom he married in 1420, is interred above him in the king's chantry chapel. For three hundred years after her death, Catharine's embalmed body lay here in an open coffin.

THE HENRY VII CHAPEL ★. The reign of the first Tudor king, Henry VII (1485–1509), was an important one in the abbey's history. Henry embarked on the construction of a chapel to contain the remains of his murdered uncle Henry VI (1421–71), whom he wished to have canonized. The pope demanded an extortionate fee for this service, so the chapel was dedicated to the Virgin Mary instead. It was finally completed in 1512, three years after Henry's death and in the reign of his son Henry VIII. This enormous chapel at the east end of the abbey is a masterpiece of Tudor building. In the words of the American writer Washington Irving: "Stone seems, by the winning labor of the chisel, to have been robbed

of its weight and density, suspended aloft as if by magic, and the fretted roof achieved with the wonderful minuteness and airy security of a cobweb." There are many royal tombs in the chapel: Elizabeth I (1558–1603) shares one with her sister Mary I (1553–8), not far from their brother, the boy-king Edward VI (1547–53). In the south aisle is the effigy of Mary, Queen of Scots (1542–87); most poignant of all, at the end of the chapel known as "Innocents' Corner" are the bones of the two princes murdered in the Tower in the 15th century.

ROYAL AIR FORCE CHAPEL. This lies at the far end of the Henry VII Chapel, with a window commemorating the Battle of Britain in 1940 and a roll of honor with the names of the 1,497 Allied airmen killed in the battle. Here too is the tomb of Oliver Cromwell. At the Restoration, his body was exhumed and hanged at Tyburn. His head was left on the roof of Westminster Hall for twenty-five years until it fell down.

KINGS AND COMMONERS. Coronations take place in the choir of the abbey and follow a strict procedure laid down in the 14th century. But the abbey has had its share of political life as well. The early House of Commons met in the CHAPTER HOUSE until 1547, to the great annoyance of the monks, who complained about the noise. Access to the Chapter House is through the cloister: it is a beautiful octagonal room with six large windows and 14th-century frescoes including a frieze of animals. Its vaulted roof springs outward from a central column of Purbeck marble. The Chapter House was bombed in World War II and has been carefully restored.

The tiled floor (c. 1250) is the finest of its kind to survive from the 13th century. The ABBEY MUSEUM in the Norman undercroft beneath the Chapter House has wax and wooden effigies of historical figures. Most spectacular are those of Charles II, in his Garter robes, and of Lord Nelson: "It is as if he were standing there," said a contemporary. Nearby is the PYX CHAMBER (c. 1070), originally a Norman chapel, with the oldest altar in the abbey. It was converted in the 13th century to a royal strongroom (note the locks on the double door). Gold and silver coins were brought to be tested against standard pieces, kept in a special box called a pyx. There is a display of church plate.

POETS' CORNER
Geoffrey Chaucer's monument in the south transept was the original landmark that was responsible for the institution of Poets' Corner (he also lived in a house on the site of the Henry VII Chapel). It should be remembered that many of the monuments are merely retrospective and do not mark actual burial places. But among the many notable figures interred here are David Garrick, with a monument representing him making his final bow; Handel, with a fine statue by Roubiliac; Samuel Johnson, with a noble bust of the great Englishman by Nollekens; and John Gay, author of *The Beggar's Opera* and author too of his own epitaph, "Life is a jest, and all things shew it; I thought so once, and now I know it."

TOMB OF QUEEN ELIZABETH I

TOMB OF EDWARD THE CONFESSOR
Only the lower part is original (left). The gilded wooden upper section (1557) replaces a precious shrine decorated with gold and jewels which was vandalized and looted at the time of the Dissolution of the monasteries.

DEAN'S YARD

In this peaceful square is the entrance to one of Britain's most famous public schools, Westminster. Formerly a monastic school attached to the Benedictine abbey, it was refounded by Elizabeth I in 1560, after the Dissolution ● *36*. Famous old boys include Ben Jonson and Christopher Wren.

ASHBURNHAM HOUSE. Built around 1662 for the Ashburnham family (possibly by John Webb, son-in-law of Inigo Jones), the house is now part of Westminster School. The interior has a fine staircase around a square well and lit by a lantern in the roof. It has been called the finest 17th-century domestic interior in London.

AROUND WHITEHALL

Whitehall links Westminster with Trafalgar Square and Charing Cross. It is a wide road, and around it are ministries, government offices and the official residence of the prime minister.

WHITEHALL. York Place, the London residence of the archbishop of York, formerly stood on the site of Whitehall. It was built in 1245, and extensively refurbished in the early 16th century by Cardinal Wolsey. When Wolsey fell into disgrace in 1530, Henry VIII confiscated the Renaissance palace Wolsey had built for himself and chose it for his own London residence, abandoning the old-fashioned Palace of Westminster. He changed its name to Whitehall and embarked on an ambitious building project, purchasing more land to the west of the palace. But in Henry's reign the palace was never more than a disparate collection of buildings, of which none remain today. It was left to the Stuart dynasty to make the greatest changes to the palace. James I

prime minister was created, the house became the premier's official residence. The substantial interior of the house was altered by William Kent, 1732–5, and by Sir John Soane in 1825. The famous Cabinet Room is on the ground floor. Number 11, next door, is the home of the Chancellor of the Exchequer.

HORSE GUARDS AND HORSE GUARDS PARADE
The building on the left, the Horse Guards, was completed in 1758 by John Vardy to the designs of William Kent, who died ten years before. On the Whitehall side this Palladian building forms three sides of a square, while on the other side is Horse Guards Parade (right), reached by the three arches at the back. Only the monarch is allowed to use the central arch.

commissioned Inigo Jones (1573–1652) and Jones' son-in-law John Webb (1611–72) to redesign and enlarge Whitehall, which resulted in plans for a palace of around two thousand rooms, extending for half a mile along the river and reaching back almost as far as Horse Guards Parade. This grandiose scheme was inspired by the Escorial in Spain and the Tuileries Palace in Paris, but it was soon abandoned. Only the Banqueting House was ever completed. After 1685 it was Wren who left his mark on Whitehall, building a Privy Gallery and Catholic chapel for James II. (When William of Orange landed in England in 1688, the king "stole away from Whitehall by the Privy Stairs".) England's new rulers, William and Mary, deserted Whitehall for Kensington Palace, which suited the king's asthma better. Whitehall was damaged by fire in 1691, and when in 1698 it burned to the ground leaving only the Banqueting House, it was not rebuilt.

DOWNING STREET. This narrow street derives its name from the diplomat Sir George Downing (1623–84), who built a cul-de-sac of terraced houses here. Numbers 10, 11 and 12 are the only surviving original buildings. On the south side of the street is the FOREIGN AND COMMONWEALTH OFFICE, while number 10 is known the world over as the prime minister's residence. The street is now blocked off by large security gates, commissioned by Margaret Thatcher.

THE OLD TREASURY. The Treasury Building in Whitehall, below the Horse Guards and on the same side, was built by Sir Charles Barry ▲ *129* in 1844, replacing an earlier one designed by Sir John Soane which had become too small. Barry retained Soane's columns and frieze however.

ADMIRALTY AND ADMIRALTY HOUSE. The last large official building on the west side of Whitehall before Trafalgar Square is the Admiralty. Admiralty House was built between 1786 and 1788 by Samuel Pepys Cockerell as the home of the First Lord of the Admiralty. Access to it is through a

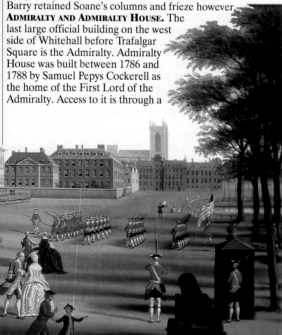

OFFICER OF THE LIFE GUARDS
Reviews and parades have been held on Horse Guards Parade since the 16th century. The ceremony of Trooping

the Colour is held every year on the sovereign's official birthday: it first took place in 1755 and has been a regular event since 1805. The ceremony originates in the practice of parading the colours in front of the troops, so that each regiment would recognize its rallying point on the battlefield ● *50*.

143

CEILING OF THE BANQUETING HOUSE
These huge canvases by Rubens, depicting the *Apotheosis of James I*, so pleased Charles I that he knighted the artist.

ADMIRALTY ARCH
Sir Aston Webb's monumental arch (below right) was built in 1910 as part of the national memorial to Queen Victoria. It is a massive, pompous Edwardian construction, framing a fine view down the Mall to the Victoria Memorial with Buckingham Palace in the background.

CARLTON HOUSE TERRACE
The elegant terraces that overlook the Mall were built between 1827 and 1832 by John Nash on the site of Carlton House, where George IV lived before Buckingham Palace was completed. The short pillars at the base of the façade are an early use of cast iron. Prime ministers Palmerston and Gladstone both had houses here.

wing of the Admiralty. The graceless façade of Thomas Ripley's Admiralty (1722–6) is masked by an elegant stone screen (1759–61), an early work by Robert Adam.

BANQUETING HOUSE ★. Situated on the east side of Whitehall opposite the Horse Guards, this is the only surviving building of Whitehall Palace. In 1581 Elizabeth I approved plans for a reception building here in which to entertain envoys of the Duke of Alençon, her projected fiancé. It was to be a temporary affair made of wood and canvas, but even so it had almost three hundred glass windows. The next banqueting house on the site was built on the orders of James I in 1608, and until its destruction by fire in 1619 it was frequently used as a theater. In the same year, James commissioned the architect Inigo Jones ▲ *272, 326* to replace it.

BANQUETING HALL ★. Jones built a vast double cube, the interior dimensions of the hall itself, on the first floor, being 115 feet long, by 60 feet wide and 55 feet high. There are two stories of seven windows, separated by Ionic half-columns below and Corinthian pillars above. In 1630 Charles I commissioned Rubens to paint the ceiling: installed in 1635, the panels were executed in Brussels, and glorify the union of England and Scotland under the wise rule of Charles' father, James I. The Banqueting House is used for all kinds of state occasions, such as the ritual washing of the commoners' feet by the monarch on Maundy Thursday, and the annual dinner for the Knights of the Garter on St George's Day. In 1649 Charles I was executed on a scaffold set up outside one of its windows, and in 1689 William and Mary consented to become joint sovereigns of Britain in the hall of the Banqueting House. A few years later Wren converted it into a chapel, which it remained until Queen Victoria decided to hand it to the Royal United Services Institute in 1890 to be used as a museum. It was extensively restored in 1963, and the paintings were returned to their correct positions (Rubens' allegorical story begins at the far end of the hall).

THE MALL

Running from Admiralty Arch down to Buckingham Palace, the Mall was formerly a leafy avenue laid out in St James's Park at the Restoration. Its name, like Pall Mall, comes from the game of Pell Mell that was once played here with balls and mallets. The present road was constructed as a processional route beside the old Mall in the first decade of the present century.

WESTMINSTER CATHEDRAL ★

At the far end of Victoria Street from Parliament Square, on the lefthand side in Ashley Place, stands Westminster Cathedral, the headquarters of the Roman Catholic church in

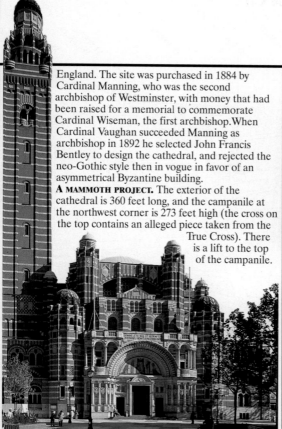

England. The site was purchased in 1884 by Cardinal Manning, who was the second archbishop of Westminster, with money that had been raised for a memorial to commemorate Cardinal Wiseman, the first archbishop. When Cardinal Vaughan succeeded Manning as archbishop in 1892 he selected John Francis Bentley to design the cathedral, and rejected the neo-Gothic style then in vogue in favor of an asymmetrical Byzantine building.

A MAMMOTH PROJECT. The exterior of the cathedral is 360 feet long, and the campanile at the northwest corner is 273 feet high (the cross on the top contains an alleged piece taken from the True Cross). There is a lift to the top of the campanile.

WESTMINSTER CATHEDRAL
In order to avoid unfavorable comparison with the Gothic masterpiece at the other end of Victoria Street, architect John Francis Bentley searched around for a different style. On a trip to Italy in 1894 he explored early Christian buildings, the medieval architecture of Siena and Venice, and visited Constantinople. The final building (left) was constructed in red brick (12½ million bricks were needed) with bands of white Portland stone. The cupola was modeled on that of St Sophia in Constantinople, while the immense campanile was derived from models in Venice and Siena.

The nave is the widest in the whole of England, with seating for twelve hundred people, not counting the side-aisles which can hold several hundred more. The walls, columns and domes are all covered with mosaics made from more than a hundred different varieties of marble. The overall effect is mystical and sumptuous. The dark green marble columns in the nave are made from stone taken from the same quarry that provided the marble for St Sophia in Istanbul. Note the *Stations of the Cross*, which was executed by Eric Gill between 1913 and 1918, and also a 15th-century statue of the Virgin and Child. The decoration is still incomplete, with some rough brick exposed on many of the cupolas.

VICTORIA STATION

This formless building is really two stations joined into one. In the 1860's the London, Brighton and South Coast Railway's terminus at the junction of Victoria Street and Buckingham Palace Road was joined on its east side by the London terminus of the London, Chatham and Dover Railway. The latter handled boat trains to the Continent, and has been the arrival and departure point of more visiting heads of state than any other London terminus. In the First World War troops bound for the trenches in France left from Victoria Station.

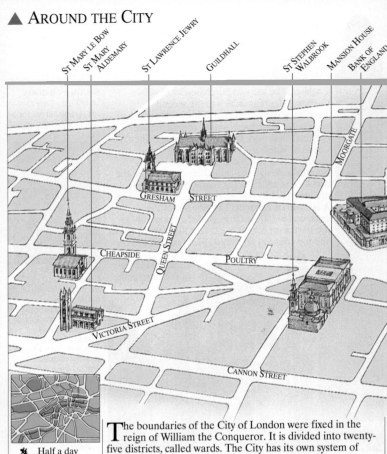

ST MARY LE BOW • ST MARY ALDEMARY • ST LAWRENCE JEWRY • GUILDHALL • ST STEPHEN WALBROOK • MANSION HOUSE • BANK OF ENGLAND

GRESHAM STREET

MOORGATE

CHEAPSIDE

QUEEN STREET

POULTRY

VICTORIA STREET

CANNON STREET

✗ Half a day

THE QUEEN VISITS THE LORD MAYOR Queen Victoria arriving at the Guildhall in November 1837. As head of the world's oldest corporation, the Lord Mayor has privileges within the City and precedence over everyone except the sovereign, with whom he has the right of audience.

The boundaries of the City of London were fixed in the reign of William the Conqueror. It is divided into twenty-five districts, called wards. The City has its own system of government, independent of the crown and Westminster, a privilege that it acquired when the monarchy was weak: in 1191 and again in 1215 King John granted London its commune, or status as a self-governing corporation, with the right to elect its own mayor.

LIVERY COMPANIES. The Livery, or uniformed, Companies, whose name derives from the distinctive uniform which their members wear at banquets and on official occasions, took on the role of governing the City in the 12th century. Although they have now lost the power they wielded in the Middle Ages, Liverymen still have a role to play in City government: each year they elect the Lord Mayor and sheriffs. An order of precedence for the twelve principal guilds was established in 1514: Mercers, Grocers, Drapers, Fishmongers, Goldsmiths, Skinners, Merchant Taylors, Haberdashers, Salters, Ironmongers, Vintners and Clothworkers – an order that is still jealously preserved. The hundredth company, that of Information Technicians, was created in 1992.

ELECTING THE LORD MAYOR. Every year since 1189 or 1192, the approximate date on which the event first took place, a new Lord Mayor is elected at the Guildhall. This is an important event, since within the City the Lord Mayor takes precedence over everyone except the sovereign, and is

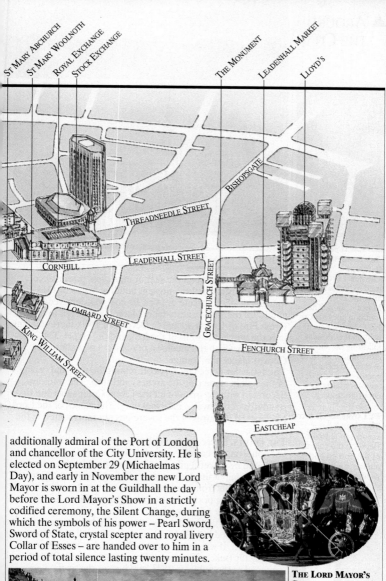

ST MARY ABCHURCH
ST MARY WOOLNOTH
ROYAL EXCHANGE
STOCK EXCHANGE
THE MONUMENT
LEADENHALL MARKET
LLOYD'S

THREADNEEDLE STREET

BISHOPSGATE

CORNHILL

LEADENHALL STREET

GRACECHURCH STREET

LOMBARD STREET

KING WILLIAM STREET

FENCHURCH STREET

EASTCHEAP

additionally admiral of the Port of London and chancellor of the City University. He is elected on September 29 (Michaelmas Day), and early in November the new Lord Mayor is sworn in at the Guildhall the day before the Lord Mayor's Show in a strictly codified ceremony, the Silent Change, during which the symbols of his power – Pearl Sword, Sword of State, crystal scepter and royal livery Collar of Esses – are handed over to him in a period of total silence lasting twenty minutes.

THE LORD MAYOR'S SHOW

A great parade like a carnival escorts the new Lord Mayor on his way to swear allegiance to the sovereign. It accompanies him as far as the Mansion House, his official residence. In the 17th century poets wrote pageants to be performed at the celebrations. The coach has been in use since 1755 and is drawn by six dapple-grays. The panels are by Giovanni Cipriani.

THE GUILDHALL ★

THE LORD MAYOR'S BANQUET
The new Lord Mayor used to host a banquet after the Lord Mayor's Show. The tradition goes back to 1501, though now it is held on the Monday following the show. After dinner, in front of seven hundred guests, the prime minister makes an important speech.

ST LAWRENCE JEWRY
This church has a square stone tower. Between the columns of the portico, niches alternate with windows under a superb frieze showing fruit and flowers, the work of Wren ▲ 171, 174.

The Guildhall has been the seat of municipal power since 1192. Construction of the present building began in 1411 and was practically complete in 1439. Its cost was defrayed by the guilds. Of the 15th-century fabric, largely destroyed in the Great Fire of 1666 ● 40 and in December 1940, there remains only the porch, the walls of the hall, and the crypts. The façade into which the medieval porch is set was altered by George Dance the Younger in 1788.

THE HALL. Sir Giles Gilbert Scott rebuilt the roof and ceiling of the hall in stone (for the arches) and steel. The walls are decorated with the arms of all the Livery Companies and the standards of the twelve principal ones. The names of the Lord Mayors and the arms of the sovereigns are represented in the windows.

THE CRYPTS. There are two crypts beneath the Guildhall: the later one, on the eastern side, with nave and side-aisles separated by graceful pillars of Purbeck marble, dates from the beginning of the 15th century. The one on the western side is probably from the late 13th century, and in spite of the fine vaulting supported by heavy octagonal pillars, is in an altogether more primitive style.

THE LIBRARY. The Guildhall is fortunate to have a magnificent library, founded in 1423 by a bequest in the will of Richard Whittington. It was the first public library, but it was seized in 1549 by the Duke of Somerset. It was restored in 1828 and opened to the public in 1873, and houses the finest collection of artifacts, prints and maps of London, as well as documents relating to the office of Lord Mayor. It also contains one of the most valuable collections of clocks in the world. In 1974 a new library was opened in the west wing.

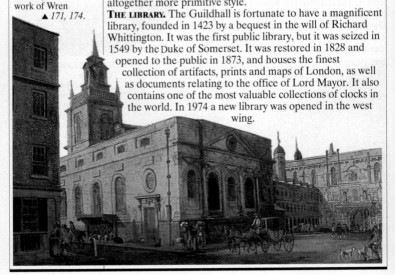

St Lawrence Jewry

St Lawrence Jewry is opposite the Guildhall, within the ancient Jewish quarter from which it gets its name.
THE OFFICIAL CHURCH OF THE CORPORATION OF LONDON. The Lord Mayor and aldermen all have their own pews, and there is a chapel consecrated to the Commonwealth commemorating the part played by the City merchants in the creation of the empire. The original 13th-century church was destroyed in the Great Fire and replaced with a new one to Wren's design between 1670 and 1687. The interior was again destroyed in 1940 and restored by Cecil Brown, who altered it slightly to create more space.

St Mary Woolnoth ★

At the corner of Lombard Street and King William Street is St Mary Woolnoth. The church antedates the Norman Conquest, and was rebuilt by William the Conqueror. Wren

▲ *171, 174* was content to patch up the damage it sustained in the Great Fire; in 1716 the work of reconstruction was given to one of his pupils, Hawksmoor ▲ *311*, who in ten years built the most original church in all the City. The Baroque elegance of the interior is a delight, with four rows of three slender Corinthian pillars forming a square. Among the monuments are those of Edward Lloyd ▲ *153*, founder of the famous insurance company, and John Newton, a former slave trader who repented and preached here.

Mansion House

Mansion House stands at the financial heart of the City. The work of George Dance the Elder, it is a heavy building of Portland stone in Palladian style. Its façade bears a portico of six immense Corinthian columns on a rusticated base. On top is a pediment carved with allegorical figures of London and the Thames. At the end of the 18th century the building was altered by George Dance the Younger, who raised the inside staircase and redecorated the Egyptian Hall (the Lord Mayor's reception room) in Roman style. Barrel vaulting allowed the ceiling to be lowered, and high windows and carved niches were added.

St Stephen Walbrook

The church of St Stephen, built by Wren between 1672 and 1679, seems like a sketch for St Paul's Cathedral ▲ *171*.

INGOTS IN THE BANK OF ENGLAND
The bank continues to hold the country's gold reserves in its strongrooms.

A CITY STREET AT THE TURN OF THE CENTURY
This photograph is an illustration (showing the Mansion House and Cheapside) from the time when the City was still the undisputed financial center of the world.

THE BANK OF ENGLAND
By stages, Soane finally completed the bank's neo-classical building. Behind the large blank wall decorated with Corinthian columns are the Stock Office (1792), the Rotunda (1796) and the Dividend Office (1818–23), showing how light and graceful neo-classical design can be. In the bank's museum is a model showing the originality of Soane's design.

THE CITY

Built on the site of Roman London, the City of London was largely destroyed in World War Two and since the 1950's has presented an ever-changing face to the world. New buildings erected during the 1950's have given way to ultra-

modern blocks of glass and steel which have been put up by property developers cheek by jowl with the few carefully preserved "listed" buildings.

THE BANK OF ENGLAND ★

A national bank enabling the government to raise money as it needed to was conceived by a Scotsman, William Paterson, in order to fund William of Orange's war against Louis XIV of France. It came into existence in 1694. Then, in 1766, Prime Minister Pitt the Elder placed the bank directly under government control. A law passed in 1844 divided the bank into two, separating its note-issuing function from its general banking functions and its responsibility for guarding the country's financial reserves.

"THE OLD LADY OF THREADNEEDLE STREET". What the playwright and politician Sheridan called "The Old Lady of Threadneedle Street" was nationalized in 1946. It is the bankers' bank, overseeing the highly complicated British banking system which was first laid down in the 18th century (with clearing houses that exchange checks and bills, and accepting houses, or merchant banks). It is run by a board of governors who are chosen by the crown, and is the only bank in England with the right to issue notes.

SOANE'S BUILDING. The bank was originally housed in the Mercers' Hall, then in the Grocers' Hall in Poultry, and in 1734 it finally moved to Threadneedle Street. In 1788 Pitt the Younger entrusted the building of new premises to John Soane ▲ *166*, but producing a practicable design proved to be fraught with problems due to the lack of ground space. In addition the fear of riots led to the construction of a solid blank wall on its exterior. The building was greatly enlarged and altered between the wars by Sir Herbert Baker, who retained only a few of Soane's architectural features, such as the outside wall.

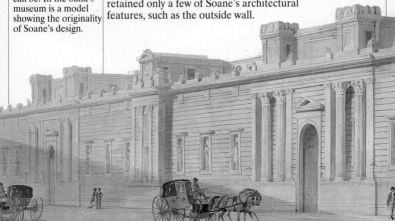

THE ROYAL EXCHANGE

Opposite the Bank of England is the Royal Exchange, the oldest mercantile institution in the City, founded by Sir Thomas Gresham. The Exchange, built on Cornhill by Flemish craftsmen using materials imported from Flanders, opened for business in 1567. Modeled on those at Antwerp and Venice, the Exchange consists of a piazza surrounded by

galleries with dealers' premises above. It was officially opened in 1570 by Queen Elizabeth I, who granted permission for the Exchange to call itself "Royal". The building was destroyed in the Great Fire, replaced by a larger one designed by Jarman which was again destroyed in 1838, and finally rebuilt by Sir William Tite to be officially opened by Queen Victoria in 1844. It is in neo-classical style, and its façade has a portico of eight large Corinthian columns supporting a carved pediment. The figure in the center represents Commerce. It ceased trading in 1939 and since 1983 has been used by the London International Financial Futures Exchange (LIFFE) for the sale of forward transactions. Of Gresham's 1567 original building nothing remains save part of the courtyard paving.
WELLINGTON'S STATUE. In front of the Royal Exchange is an equestrian statue of the Duke of Wellington ▲ 246, cast in bronze from French cannons captured at the Battle of Waterloo. It was unveiled in 1844 in the presence of the Duke, and is the work of Sir Francis Chantrey.

THE STOCK EXCHANGE

The Stock Exchange came into being to supply capital needed by the share-issuing companies and the demands of rapidly developing commerce and industry.

"DIVIDEND DAY"
This picture of 1859 depicts Dividend Day, one of the four annual Quarter Days when stockholders on the London Exchange receive their dividends.

THOMAS GRESHAM
The son of a merchant who became Lord Mayor, Thomas Gresham (1519–79) was the first to lead a double career – in the service of the crown and amassing great wealth as a merchant in his own right. While working as a "king's merchant" on the Exchange in Antwerp, he conceived the idea of building a similar establishment in London for the merchants of Lombard Street. His emblem of a gold grasshopper with a crown still adorns the façade.

THE AGE OF COFFEE HOUSES. Up until the 17th century shares were bought and sold outside the Royal Exchange. But the dealers within were bothered by the noise the brokers made and chased them away. The latter shifted their business to the coffee houses of Change Alley, between Lombard Street and Cornhill. There, at JONATHAN'S COFFEE HOUSE, which opened around 1680, or at GARRAWAY'S, which opened ten years earlier, prospective buyers would go to see how the shares were moving, and stockbrokers dealt with their clients. Then in 1773, when *Jonathan's* ceased to be available, they opened their own premises in Threadneedle Street and called it the Stock Exchange. For sixpence per day, anyone was free to deal there. In 1801 a group of disaffected brokers built a new exchange in Capel Court that housed more than five hundred members, soon including most of those from the former premises. Expansion necessitated a new building in 1888 and again in 1972: there are now around five thousand members of the Stock Exchange.

BROKERS AND JOBBERS. Apart from the admission of women to the floor in 1973, the workings of the Stock Exchange had hardly changed since the 18th century, until October 1986, when the "Big Bang" removed the distinction between *jobbers* and *brokers*. Until then, its members had been of two kinds: jobbers sold stocks, making their profit from the difference between the buying price and the selling price, though they were not allowed to sell stocks directly to clients outside the Exchange.

EXPERIENCING THE CITY LIFE
It is best to explore the City on a weekday during office hours, when the streets are swarming with up to half a million men and women who work there. After 5pm the district is deserted. Gone is the old Victorian look of the place that dominated until the 1950's. The bowler-hatted "city gent", with black waistcoat, striped trousers, white shirt, stiff collar and tightly rolled umbrella is a thing of the past. There is now a substantial proportion of women in the workforce, which was for long a masculine preserve. Customs have also changed: people now call each other by their Christian names in the office, and lunch in a wine bar or delicatessen.

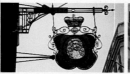

Accordingly, for each deal, prospective buyers needed a broker who, in exchange for a fixed commission, negotiated with the jobber.

THE PRIVATE BANKS. The majority of the large private banks have their headquarters within the City. In 1930 the Midland Bank (founded in Birmingham in 1836) moved to an imposing Portland stone building that had been commissioned from Sir Edwin Lutyens (1869–1944). Its construction was not completed until 1936. You have to stand well back to glimpse the dome on its top, which resembles one that Lutyens had

earlier put on the Viceroy's House in New Delhi. Nearby are the head offices of the NATIONAL WESTMINSTER BANK, a company formed in 1968 from the amalgamation of three other banks. The main building of the so-called "NatWest" is its 600-foot tower between Bishopsgate and Old Broad Street, beside the City of London Club which was founded in 1832 by a group of wealthy bankers. The contrast between the latter's Palladian exterior (built in 1833–4) and the fifty-two-story tower block beside it has with some justification been called "architectural schizophrenia".

LLOYD'S ★

Lloyd's is not an insurance company but a stock exchange for insurance contracts. Two types of people work here: the Lloyd's members (underwriters) have the sole right of selling risk insurance, and the annual subscribers (Lloyd's names) are "invited" to stand surety. Contracts are drawn up between a company or individual and a member, who then distributes both the dividends and risks between a number of subscribers.

FROM AN INN TO LEADENHALL STREET. In the late 1680's, Edward Lloyd opened a tavern in Abchurch Lane at the corner of Lombard Street, where merchants used to buy and sell ships and underwrite their insurance, a growing market in the 18th century. In 1769 a group of underwriters primarily interested in maritime insurance left the tavern to open the *New Lloyd's Coffee House* in Pope's Head Alley, where ships were bought and sold "by candle" (in a candle auction the last bid before a small candle expires secures the property). The coffee house soon became too small and in 1771 Lloyd's moved to the Royal Exchange, where it stayed until 1928. From there it transferred to Leadenhall Street.

LLOYD'S: A CATHEDRAL OF GLASS AND METAL
The new building which opened in 1986 is a testament to the company's modern approach to business. Designed by Richard Rogers, co-designer of the famous Pompidou Center in Paris, it is a glass and metal rectangle with six satellite towers, built round a central atrium culminating in a vast arched roof 190 feet high. In 1991 Lloyd's had 26,500 members. In its museum can be seen the Underwriting Room and the *Lutine*, a bell which is still rung to announce either bad or good news according to whether it is struck once or twice.

SITE OF
LLOYDS
COFFEE HOUSE
1691–1785
THE CITY OF LONDON

"LLOYD'S COFFEE HOUSE"
The origins of Lloyd's are now a legend, and have grown over the years since Edward Lloyd first opened his coffee house for business in the late 17th century.

THE CITY'S OWN MARKET
The present Leadenhall Market was built in 1881 by Sir Horace Jones.

The metal arches painted maroon and cream, the glass panels and the central cupola all contribute to its charm. High-quality produce from here goes to supply the banquets of the Livery Companies ▲ 146. Now the market's cafés, wine bars and sandwich bars do flourishing business at lunchtime.

LEADENHALL STREET

The corn and hay markets were here in the Middle Ages. Leadenhall Market is on the north side of the street, an odd place in the heart of the City. The City acquired the land at the end of the 13th century, and later the right to open a market here, which has continued to the present day.

ST ANDREW UNDERSHAFT. The church's unusual name (literally "under the pole") dates from the 15th century, when each year a maypole was erected beside it, a custom which was prohibited in 1517. This Gothic church, which has undergone much alteration, contains the tomb of John Stow (1525–1605). A Cornhill tailor turned publisher, he was an avid collector of manuscripts and was the first real chronicler and historian of London. On his death his widow placed a terracotta bust of her husband holding a quill pen in St Andrew's: in 1905 the guild of Merchant Taylors replaced it. Each year a ceremony takes place in the presence of the Lord Mayor, when a new goose-feather pen is put in place and the old one presented, together with a copy of *Stow's Survey of London* (first published in 1598), to the schoolchild who has written the best essay on London. Hans Holbein the Younger may also be buried here.

THE LEADENHALL MARKET TRADESMEN
After the Great Fire, Leadenhall Street became a general market selling meat, game, fish, fruit, vegetables and flowers.

CHEAPSIDE AND CORNHILL

In the Middle Ages Cheapside was one of the most important streets in London. Its many fine buildings were completely destroyed in the Great Fire ▲ 40.
CHEAPSIDE MARKET. London's principal market used to be here, a place of ceaseless activity, always with plenty to see, whether a funeral, state procession or even a public execution. The Cheapside pillory was

notorious. Different sections of the market specialized in different types of produce, and have given their names to the streets that cross it. Bread Street, joining Cheapside to Queenhithe Dock, was where the bakers were, Milk Street was the dairy produce market, ironmongers once worked in Ironmonger Lane, and Goldsmith Street was home to scores of goldsmiths.

THE STREET OF PUBLISHERS. The grain market was on Cornhill, the highest point of the City. It also boasted a notorious prison and pillory. It was on Cornhill too that Thomas Guy (philanthropist and founder of Guy's Hospital) had his bookshop and printed Bibles. From 1816 to 1868 the firm of Smith and Elder were at number 32, publishers of Thackeray, Mrs Gaskell and the Brontë sisters, and Leslie Stephen (Thackeray's son-in-law and father of Virginia Woolf ▲ *114*) was a frequent visitor. Now banking and insurance are the businesses of Cornhill. At the corner of Lime Street, East India House once stood, home of the East India Company (1600–1862). Until the Indian Mutiny of 1857 the Company enjoyed the monopoly of Indian trade and acted as the government's agent there.

CORNHILL CHURCHES. Two churches on the south side of Cornhill are worth visiting: St Michael's, the tower of which survived the Great Fire, was rebuilt by Hawksmoor 1715–22 in neo-Gothic style; and St Peter-upon-Cornhill, where Mendelssohn played the organ in 1840 and 1842.

THE GREAT HIGHROAD OF CHEAPSIDE
Rebuilt in 1720 after the Great Fire, the new Cheapside was said to be "a beautiful wide street, bordered with tall houses".

LOMBARD STREET

After the expulsion of the Jews in 1290, the Lombards, who had already settled in this street in the previous century, took over the business of banking.

THE BANKERS' STREET. Nearly all the large British banks are based in Lombard Street, and foreign banks have their main London agencies there. Some have their roots way back in the past: Barclay's, for example, developed from a goldsmith's business set up in Lombard Street around 1694. Between 1736 and 1896 the firm of Barclay took over numerous other

ALEXANDER POPE (1688–1744)
The great poet lived in Lombard Street as a child. This was where his father worked as a linen-draper.

FENCHURCH STREET

BILLINGSGATE MARKET
This has been in existence since the 13th century, and in 1699 a royal charter granted it the monopoly of selling fish. Before World War Two 400 tons of fish used to change hands at Billingsgate every day.

A MEMORIAL TO THE GREAT FIRE
This column of Portland stone has 331 steps leading up to a balcony, with good views over the Thames and the London skyline.

banks, some of which had formerly been goldsmiths themselves. Barclay's presented to the City the fountain of Poseidon in George Yard, the work of Sir Charles Wheeler.
CHARLES DICKENS' FIRST ROMANCE. In 1829 the seventeen-year-old Dickens fell in love in Lombard Street. He was living at number 2, near the bank of Smith, Fayne & Smith, and the object of his affections was Maria Beadnell, the daughter of an employee there.

FENCHURCH STREET

This is a continuation of Lombard Street. Its name may come from the old hay market (from the French word *foin*) in Gracechurch Street.
FOUNTAIN HOUSE. The fountain that stands at the corner of the street was erected 1954–7. It is a copy of the one at Lever House in New York.
LLOYD'S REGISTER OF SHIPPING.
This is at number 71, an Art Nouveau building decorated with columns, turrets and friezes. This is where all documentation concerning merchant shipping is registered and classified. Differences had arisen over the standards of classification, and at the end of the 18th century this led a group of shipowners to set up their own organization. Since 1834 the ties between the insurance company and Lloyd's Register have strengthened.
PLANTATION HOUSE. The Rubber Exchange and the London Commodity Exchange are housed in this building constructed between 1934 and 1937 on a large quadrilateral set among narrow lanes. In nearby Mincing Lane is the neo-Georgian Clothworkers' Hall that was opened in 1958.

AROUND THE MONUMENT

THE MONUMENT. Christopher Wren and Robert Hooke submitted several designs for a memorial to the Great

Fire ● *40* before building this tall Doric column, 202 feet high, which is the precise distance from the base of the monument to the place where the fire started in Pudding Lane. Opened in 1677, it was erected when Parliament had decided to commemorate the Great Fire in suitable fashion. On the monument's pedestal are four panels which describe the extent of the disaster and also tell the story of the rebuilding of London. If the dry weather and a strong wind were thought to be the prime causes of the fire, other explanations were offered in the 1670's, when there was powerful anti-Catholic feeling: agents of the pope were blamed, as was the baker in whose shop it began. The Latin inscription on the north side of the pedestal was rounded off in 1681 with a few words denouncing the fanatical Catholics. When James II ascended the throne these words were removed, only to be restored when William of Orange became king. They were finally taken off in 1830 when the Catholics were at last given their civil rights.

BILLINGSGATE MARKET. "Each morning the hall in Billingsgate takes in its scaly harvest . . . there are always salmon for Belgravia and herrings for Whitechapel", commented the 19th-century French writer Jules Vallès. Billingsgate, once the biggest fish market in London, was famous for its smell, its noise and its foul-mouthed fishwives. After centuries of activity, the market finally closed in 1982. A new fish market has since opened at West India Dock on the Isle of Dogs, keeping at least the name of Billingsgate.

AROUND CANNON STREET

In the Middle Ages Cannon Street was the district where candlemakers lived: the street's name is a corruption of its earlier name of Candlewick Street. Most of its interesting buildings were destroyed in the Blitz, such as the fine 18th-century Cordwainers' Hall, which stood on the site of St Paul's Garden. In the wall of the Bank of China is the London Stone, probably a Roman milestone, which stood on the other side of the road in the wall of St Swithin's church, until that beautiful Wren building was destroyed in 1941.

ST MARY ABCHURCH ★. This church, begun in 1681, is the most graceful of all Wren churches and the one that has best withstood the ravages of time. Square in plan, it is flanked by a red-brick and stone tower topped with a perforated lantern and an elegant lead spire. The square nave, without side-aisles, is underneath a cupola pierced with oval windows that sits on eight arches. The cupola was painted by William Snow. The church also has a reredos, the only one that can be attributed with confidence to Grinling Gibbons ▲ *173*.

ST MARY ALDERMARY. Near Queen Victoria Street is the oldest church consecrated to the Virgin, rebuilt in 1681–2. Here Wren appears to have experimented with the Gothic Perpendicular style ● *70* almost to the point of parody, using fan vaulting with surprising additions.

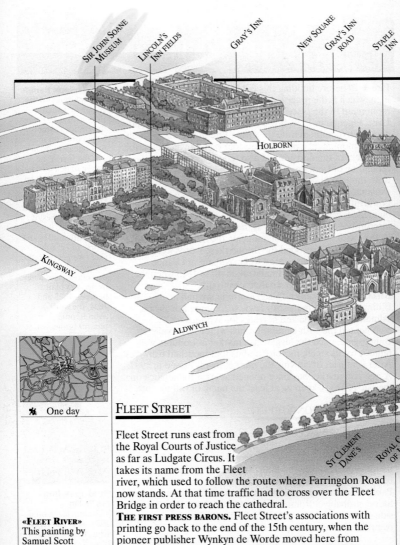

SIR JOHN SOANE MUSEUM   LINCOLN'S INN FIELDS   GRAY'S INN   NEW SQUARE   GRAY'S INN ROAD   STAPLE INN

HOLBORN

KINGSWAY

ALDWYCH

ST CLEMENT DANE'S   ROYAL C OF J

🚶 One day

FLEET STREET

Fleet Street runs east from the Royal Courts of Justice as far as Ludgate Circus. It takes its name from the Fleet river, which used to follow the route where Farringdon Road now stands. At that time traffic had to cross over the Fleet Bridge in order to reach the cathedral.

THE FIRST PRESS BARONS. Fleet Street's associations with printing go back to the end of the 15th century, when the pioneer publisher Wynkyn de Worde moved here from Westminster. Between 1500 and his death in 1535, from his premises *At the Sign of the Sun*, he printed and published hundreds of books, many on legal and religious subjects (the Inns of Court and Blackfriars Monastery were both nearby). Other printers also working in the area included Richard Pynson, printer to the king after 1508, whose office was at the corner of Fleet Street and Chancery Lane. In 1530 Sir Thomas More's nephew William Rastell began printing and selling books from premises in St Bride's churchyard, bringing out an edition of his uncle's works in 1557. It was clear that the publishing

«FLEET RIVER»
This painting by Samuel Scott (1702?–72) shows the mouth of the Fleet River as seen from the Thames. On the left is the spire of Wren's St Bride's Church ● 171, ▲ 174.

158

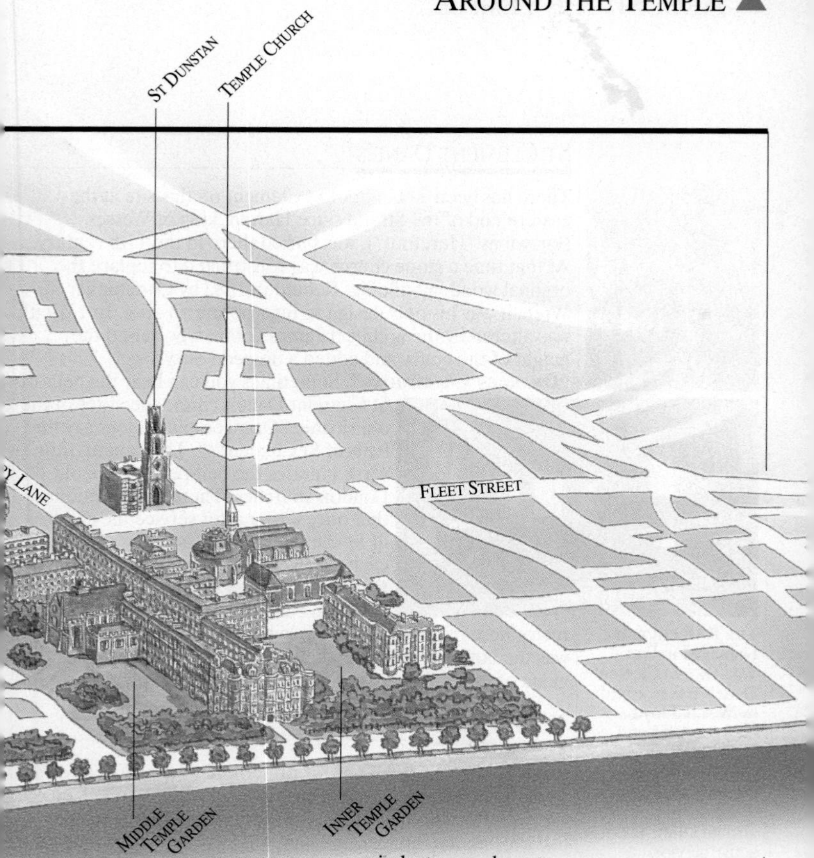

ST DUNSTAN
TEMPLE CHURCH

FLEET STREET

...Y LANE

MIDDLE TEMPLE GARDEN

INNER TEMPLE GARDEN

industry was here to stay. A key date in the history of Fleet Street was the year 1702 when the first newspaper, the *Daily Courant*, appeared. Thereafter the street became home to hundreds of newspapers, and its name is still synonymous with British national journalism. This state of affairs only came to an end in the 1980's, when the British press was going through a period of deep crisis caused by the changeover to the new technology, which necessitated relocating to gain more space. *The Times* led the way, to Docklands, and within a few years Fleet Street was stripped of its soul. The traditional pubs lost their best customers, the journalists. But the great Fleet Street pubs are still worth seeing, most of all YE OLDE CHESHIRE CHEESE, once the haunt of Dickens and, tradition has it, of Samuel Johnson. Look out too for the façade and lobby of the *Daily Express* building, a futuristic construction built in 1931–2.

"The man must have a rare recipe for melancholy, who can be dull in Fleet Street."

Charles Lamb

159

ST CLEMENT DANE'S

There has been a church of St Clement on this site at the eastern end of the Strand since Harold, king of Wessex (known as "Harefoot"), was buried there in the 11th century. At that time a stone church was constructed to replace the original wooden building. Rebuilt in 1682 by Christopher Wren, it was his only design to incorporate an apse. In 1719 it was altered by the architect James Gibbs, who raised the height of the belfry and added a domed vestry.

"ORANGES AND LEMONS". Sometimes you can hear the bells of St Clement Dane's chime the notes of the old rhyme: "Oranges and lemons say the bells of St Clement's". This tuneful little verse imitates the bell-peals of the old London churches. There is a tradition that once a year after service the children of St Clement Dane's primary school each receive an orange and a lemon.

RUGBY AND THE RECTOR. Another tradition claims that William Webb Ellis, rector here in the 19th century, while a pupil at Rugby School was the boy who picked up and ran with the ball during a game of football and so originated the game of rugby.

THE RAF CHURCH
Damaged in World War Two, St Clement Dane's was restored by W.A.S. Lloyd between 1955 and 1958 thanks to contributions from the Royal Air Force. A war memorial lists airmen killed on active service. Together with the insignia of the various units and squadrons and other memorabilia, it serves as a reminder that the church is now dedicated to the RAF.

TEMPLE BAR

From 1191 to 1319 the City of London ▲ *170*, enclosed within walls, asserted its independence from the neighboring City of Westminster, the seat of royal power. Temple Bar, situated just outside the old fortifications, has been one of the boundaries between the two cities since 1222. Originally it was just a chain between two posts barring the entrance to Fleet Street; in 1351 a great gate with a jailhouse in its upper part was built. This was replaced at the start of the 1670's with a design by Wren. In 1877–8 traffic flow necessitated its demolition, and in 1880 the present memorial was erected in its place.

FELON'S GATE. Until 1772 the heads of executed criminals were exhibited at Temple Bar, near a pillory where, among others, Daniel Defoe, the author of *Robinson Crusoe*, passed a nasty few minutes in 1703.

TEMPLE BAR TODAY
Horace Jones' monument of 1880 is surmounted by a dragon, the symbol of the City of London.

AROUND THE TEMPLE

A little to the west, between Fleet Street and the River Thames, is the Temple, a haven of tranquillity. The Templars, established in London in the first half of the 12th century, were granted this piece of land on the bank of the river. There they built a church, consecrated in 1185, and then a monastery. Several monarchs, among them John Lackland, have since stayed there. After the Dissolution of the monasteries between 1536 and 1539, the Temple became crown property, and in 1609 James I granted the land in perpetuity to the members of the MIDDLE and INNER TEMPLES. After the Second World War it was rebuilt to a design by Sir Edward Maufe partly in neo-Georgian style.

THE INNS OF COURT. Lawyers and law schools have been concentrated in the area of Temple Bar since the Middle Ages. At first, lawyers who came to London for the sessions of the Royal Courts of Justice used to put up in local taverns, the Inns. The schools, also called Inns, were founded around the 13th century when the need arose to teach the subject, which was not then a university discipline. Studies took seven or eight years, and faculty members, lawyers, probationers and students were all fed and lodged there, minimizing contact with the outside world. Of the ten inns that existed in the 14th century, only four remain: LINCOLN'S INN (1422), the MIDDLE and INNER TEMPLES (1501 and 1505), and GRAY'S INN (1569). Each of these Inns has its own hall (where students are obliged to eat a certain number of dinners to qualify for call to the Bar), its own church, library, cloister and gardens, all going to make up a little world apart.

TEMPLE CHURCH ★ ● 67

The Temple Church, all that remains from the age of the Templars, is rare among English churches in having a circular plan modeled on the Church of the Holy Sepulcher in Jerusalem. It was built in the transitional period between the Norman and Gothic styles, with elements of each side by side.

● 67

PAPER BUILDINGS OF THE INNER TEMPLE
In the southern part of the Inner Temple, these were designed in the 19th century by the Smirkes, father and son.

SAMUEL JOHNSON
17 Gough Square, a late 17th-century house, was Dr Johnson's home from 1746 to 1759. Here he compiled his *Dictionary of the English Language*, containing definitions of more than 40,000 words and with 114,000 quotations. The house is now a museum, where a first edition of the dictionary can be seen.

THE TEMPLE CHURCH ROTUNDA
The Temple Church rotunda is supported by columns of Purbeck marble and houses the stone tombs of nine Templars, dating from the 12th and 13th centuries. There are figures lying with their feet crossed, carved from Purbeck marble on top of these: (above) the effigy of William Marshal, first earl of Pembroke and brother of King John Lackland, who died in 1219.

161

TEMPLE CHURCH
Temple Church has been altered many times. Above left is the exterior as it was after 19th-century alteration; above right shows the roof structure after damage sustained during World War Two.

Between 1220 and 1240 the church was completed with a Gothic choir, with nave and side-aisles of the same height. The building has been altered many times, notably at the end of the 17th century by Wren ▲ *171*, who designed the reredos carved by William Emmett in 1682. Removed in 1840 by Sydney Smirke, it was returned to its place in the post-war restoration.

MIDDLE TEMPLE ★

MIDDLE TEMPLE GATEWAY. The brick entrance, built in 1684 by Roger North, lawyer and bencher (senior member) of the Inn, has four Ionic pilasters and a pediment fronting on to Middle Temple Lane.

MIDDLE TEMPLE HALL. The Tudor-style Middle Temple Hall (1562–73) is the main building of the Middle Temple, just above FOUNTAIN COURT. Its ornate carved-oak roof in Perpendicular style ● *68* is the finest extant. At the end of the room is an Elizabethan rood screen with a gallery above supported by caryatids.

TWO TABLES. The resplendent "benchers'" table, presented by Queen Elizabeth I and made from Windsor Forest oak trees, is a prominent exhibit in the Middle Temple. Nearby is a smaller table known as the Cupboard, on which newly qualified lawyers sign their names when they become members of the Inn. Legend has it the Cupboard is made of hatch-covers from the ship in which Sir Francis Drake sailed round the world, the GOLDEN HIND: Drake was a member of

ROYAL COURTS OF JUSTICE
These are usually known as the law courts. The task of designing the new buildings was given to George Edmund Street (1824–81). Work was begun on the new courtrooms in 1874, and they were duly opened in 1882 by Queen Victoria. They represent what is probably the most extreme example of the neo-Gothic style that was so dear to the Victorians, at the start of its decline.

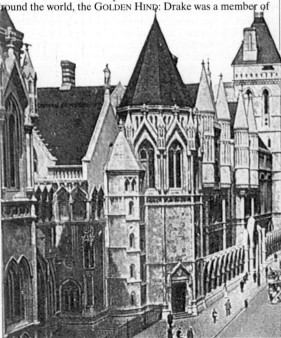

the Inn. For a long time the hall was used as a theater: it was here in 1601 that Queen Elizabeth I attended the first performance of *Twelfth Night*.

THE LIBRARY. Rebuilt in neo-Georgian style in 1956 the library possesses, in addition to a fine pair of globes made by Molyneux in 1600, an important collection of works on American law.

THE WARS OF THE ROSES. Middle Temple Gardens, to the south of Fountain Court, was the birthplace of the Wars of the Roses, a civil war that ravaged England from 1455 to 1485 and inspired two of Shakespeare's tragedies, *Henry IV* and *Richard III*. It is here, in *Henry IV*, that Somerset picks a red rose, the symbol of the House of Lancaster, and Warwick picks a white one, the symbol of the House of York.

A legal bookshop in New Square.

INNER TEMPLE ★

As there are few historic buildings remaining in the Inner Temple, which was badly damaged in the Blitz, go down KING'S BENCH WALK with its view over the Thames and Inner Temple Gardens. Numbers 4 and 5 were built in 1677–8 to designs by Christopher Wren. Number 7 dates from 1685, number 8 (1782) was the home of novelist George Moore, and adventure-story writer Rider Haggard lived at number 13.

THE TUDOR INNER TEMPLE GATEWAY. Opening on to Fleet Street, it dates from 1610, and in spite of reconstruction at the beginning of the 19th century, remains one of the best-preserved buildings of the period in London.

THE LAW COURTS ● 81

The law courts are the Royal Courts of Justice. They used to be housed in Westminster Hall, until they were moved in the second half of the 19th century to be close to the Inns of Court. The brick façade skirts Bell Yard as far as the

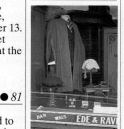

WIGS AND GOWNS
Judges and lawyers wear these wigs in court. Barristers wear black gowns too, made of silk if they are Queen's Counsel (senior barristers). High Court judges wear scarlet robes.

THE LAW COURTS
Looking up Fleet Street from St Clement Dane's. Middle Temple and Inner Temple are behind the houses on the righthand side of the picture.

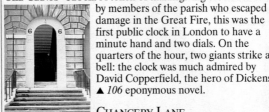

LINCOLN'S INN
Its name comes from the Earls of Lincoln, owners of the land whose arms – a lion rampant gules – are on both buildings.

STAPLE INN AND LINCOLN'S INN
Staple Inn (top) and Lincoln's Inn (above) were established in the 14th century. Since 1884 the former has been the Institute of Actuaries, and the latter is an important barristers' college.

corner of Carey Street, where it ends in a graceful tower of brick checkerwork. The long façade on the Strand is of Portland stone in mock-medieval style. The four dominant features are the clock tower, the entrances to the courts and the hall, and the metal grilles, showing the interest that the neo-Gothic architect G.E. Street had in wrought-ironwork.
THE HALL. The interior is immense, 238 feet long and 80 feet high, with a ribbed, vaulted ceiling. A warren of corridors and staircases leads from it to the hundreds of offices that are all part of the thirty-five courts of the Supreme Court of Justice.

ST DUNSTAN-IN-THE-WEST

Leaving Johnson's Court in the direction of Fleet Street, you pass in front of this octagonal church, built between 1829 and 1833, where Catholic, Anglican and Orthodox services are held. It is an early example of the 19th-century Gothic Revival ● 80, replacing an earlier 12th-century church demolished in the widening of Fleet Street ▲ 158.
THE GIANTS' CLOCK. A token of thanksgiving erected in 1671 by members of the parish who escaped damage in the Great Fire, this was the first public clock in London to have a minute hand and two dials. On the quarters of the hour, two giants strike a bell: the clock was much admired by David Copperfield, the hero of Dickens' ▲ 106 eponymous novel.

CHANCERY LANE

Chancery Lane is on the right as you leave the church. Its name dates back to 1377, after Edward III had bestowed the CONVERTS' HOUSE (a refuge for Jews who had renounced their faith and their money) on the Lord Chancellor. This was demolished in 1896, and on its site stands the PUBLIC RECORD OFFICE, the British national archives. The museum contains a wealth of rare documents such as the 1129 *Pipe Roll*, medieval records, state papers before 1782, legal archives, volumes of the *Domesday Book* (a land census ordered by William the Conqueror), a copy of the *Magna Carta* dated 1225, Shakespeare's will, and many more treasures.

LINCOLN'S INN ★

Undamaged in the Second World War, Lincoln's Inn is the only one of the four Inns of Court to have preserved its original character. The huge entrance in Chancery Lane, with its arch and square towers, dates from 1518. It opens on to OLD BUILDINGS, dating from the Tudor period and built of brick except for the chapel. It forms an irregular square.

FAMOUS ALUMNI. Cromwell studied here, and among its other famous members the Inn boasts Sir Thomas More (1478–1535), who in his role as bencher contributed toward the construction of the Chancery Lane entrance; John Donne, chaplain to the Inn, the writer on jurisprudence Jeremy Bentham, and the founder of Pennsylvania, William Penn.

THE OLD HALL ★. On the west side and built between 1485 and 1492, the hall contains a large Hogarth painting *Paul before Felix* (1748). The arch-braced roof, carved wooden screen, panelling and bay windows are impressive. Dickens set the suit of Jarndyce v. Jarndyce from *Bleak House* in Old Hall.

THE CHAPEL. The stone façade is in Gothic style and was built between 1619 and 1623. The foundation stone was laid by John Donne; another poet, Ben Jonson, took part in the building armed with trowel in one hand and book in the other. The chapel, with a barrel-vaulted roof and mullioned windows in Perpendicular style, has a low gallery used by students as a meeting place. Eighty Members of Parliament held a meeting there in 1659 with the intention of restoring the monarchy. It was renovated by Wren ▲ *171, 174* in 1685, by Wyatt in 1791, and in 1882 by Salter. In December there is a sung service here with lessons read by the senior judges.

LINCOLN'S INN FIELDS ★. This contains some magnificent architecture from the 17th to 19th centuries. In the 1930's the south and west sides were built to William Newton's designs.

LINDSEY HOUSE. Long thought to be the work of Inigo Jones, this house is a fine example from the Stuart period of the search for a national style of architecture, inspired by Palladio. It owes its sense of lightness to the use of brick, now covered in stucco, and tapering pilasters bearing fine Ionic capitals. The purity of design is apparent by comparison with the weighty appearance of the adjacent house, number 57–8, built around 1730 by Henry Joynes in Portland stone, and decorated with pilasters and an architrave.

LINCOLN'S INN FIELDS
In the Middle Ages there were two fields here, used by Londoners (particularly the inhabitants of Lincoln's Inn) for walks and recreation. Their owners, St John's and St Giles' Hospitals, rented them out for grazing. From the time of Queen Elizabeth I public executions were carried out here.

"A Lincoln's Inn beggar was a proverb. The whole fraternity knew the arms and liveries of every charitably disposed grandee in the neighbourhood, and as soon as his lordship's coach and six appeared, came hopping and crawling in crowds to persecute him.**"**
Lord Macaulay,
History of England

A barrister in Lincoln's Inn Fields.

▲ THE SIR JOHN SOANE MUSEUM

In 1790 the architect Sir John Soane (1753–1837) began to collect all manner of objects, and he spent thirty-two years building a house in Lincoln's Inn Fields to contain them. This three-story house (actually three houses converted into one) is of a complicated design and full of surprises. Preserved just as it was when Soane died, this is one of the most remarkable museums in London.

Illustration of the Corinthian order, used in Soane's Royal Academy lectures in 1819.

LIBRARY OF THE SIR JOHN SOANE MUSEUM
Soane collected an astonishing number of books and manuscripts, including the entire library of Robert Adam. He also amassed a fine collection of drawings and engravings.

SIR JOHN SOANE
Under the influence of the Romantic age, this stonemason's son collected classical and Renaissance carvings and casts, fragments of Roman architecture, funeral monuments, bronzes, vases and much more besides.

This space, with a glass dome above, creates a well of light in the middle of the house.

SECTIONAL VIEW OF THE DOME IN THE SIR JOHN SOANE MUSEUM
Soane's friend George Bailey did this drawing showing the collection of classical casts arranged on three floors. The museum has remained much as it was when Bailey made this illustration in 1810.

"IMAGINARY VIEW OF PUBLIC AND PRIVATE DESIGNED BY SIR JOHN SOANE." Soane's colleague J.M. Gandy drew this odd landscape of buildings designed by Soane between 1789 and 1815.

THE GARDENS OF GRAY'S INN
The gardens were a fashionable meeting place in the 17th century. Samuel Pepys liked to walk there, as did Charles

Lamb, who thought them "the most beautiful gardens of the Inns of Court", and the young Charles Dickens, who at the age of fourteen was apprentice clerk to a lawyer's office there.

THE ROYAL COLLEGE OF SURGEONS. The Royal College of Surgeons is on the south side of the square. The surgeons left the Barber-surgeons in 1745 and founded their own separate institution which became a royal college in 1800. The Lincoln's Inn Fields premises, opened in 1797, were designed by George Dance Jr (1741–1825), and were superseded in 1835 by Barry's ▲ *129* building which integrated Dance's huge Ionic portico and which was again enlarged in 1888. In the college is the HUNTERIAN MUSEUM, named after the famous 18th-century Scottish surgeon. Hunter was a forerunner of Charles Darwin and, fascinated by the concept of surgical transplantation, he amassed an enormous collection of anatomical specimens for comparative study. This was acquired by the government in 1799 and gradually expanded until the Second World War, when the collection was greatly diminished in the air raids.

NEW SQUARE ★. Built at the end of the 17th century around a central lawn, New Square is just to the west of Lincoln's Inn Fields, and consists of terraced four-story houses. An archway from New Square leads to Carey Street. On the north side are STONE BUILDINGS, built in Palladian style between 1774 and 1780 by Robert Taylor. These are in sharp contrast to Philip Hardwick's brick-built neo-Tudor buildings of 1843–5: the New Hall, the Treasury and the Library. The latter, established in 1497, has seventy thousand volumes and forms an important collection of legal works. In the New Hall is a large mural by G.F. Watts, *Justice* (1859), in a style that mixes Pre-Raphaelite and Romantic elements.

GRAY'S INN

To the north of Lincoln's Inn is the last of the Inns of Court, Gray's Inn. During the 14th century the Inn became a hotel for lawyers and took the name of Sir Reginald de Grey, the Chief Justice of Chester, whose London residence it had formerly been. In 1594 Shakespeare (whose patron, the earl of Southampton, was a member of the Inn) gave the first performance in the hall of *The Comedy of Errors*. The interior of the hall, destroyed during World War Two and rebuilt by Sir Edward Maufe, has retained some parts dating from the 17th, 18th and the early 19th centuries. An old rood screen carved from the wood of a Spanish galleon survived the damage and is now on view. The gardens are the only ones of the four Inns of Court that are open to the public. They were a notorious dueling ground in the 17th century.

THE PHILOSOPHER'S GARDEN
The gardens are the most beautiful part of Gray's Inn. They were laid out in 1606 by Sir Francis Bacon (1561–1626), who wrote a famous essay about them. The great philosopher was first a student (1576), then a bencher (1586) and finally treasurer of Gray's Inn in 1608. It is said that he planted the catalpa tree behind number 4 Raymond Buildings.

HISTORICAL JOURNEY

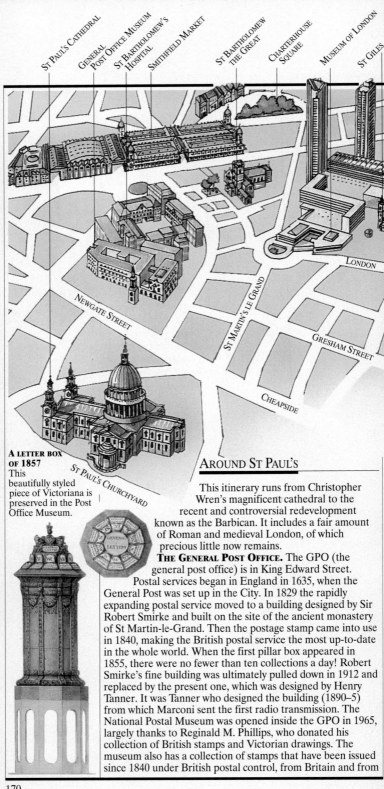

ST PAUL'S CATHEDRAL   GENERAL POST OFFICE MUSEUM   ST BARTHOLOMEW'S HOSPITAL   SMITHFIELD MARKET   ST BARTHOLOMEW THE GREAT   CHARTERHOUSE SQUARE   MUSEUM OF LONDON   ST GILES

NEWGATE STREET

ST MARTIN'S LE GRAND

LONDON

GRESHAM STREET

CHEAPSIDE

ST PAUL'S CHURCHYARD

A LETTER BOX OF 1857
This beautifully styled piece of Victoriana is preserved in the Post Office Museum.

AROUND ST PAUL'S

This itinerary runs from Christopher Wren's magnificent cathedral to the recent and controversial redevelopment known as the Barbican. It includes a fair amount of Roman and medieval London, of which precious little now remains.

THE GENERAL POST OFFICE. The GPO (the general post office) is in King Edward Street. Postal services began in England in 1635, when the General Post was set up in the City. In 1829 the rapidly expanding postal service moved to a building designed by Sir Robert Smirke and built on the site of the ancient monastery of St Martin-le-Grand. Then the postage stamp came into use in 1840, making the British postal service the most up-to-date in the whole world. When the first pillar box appeared in 1855, there were no fewer than ten collections a day! Robert Smirke's fine building was ultimately pulled down in 1912 and replaced by the present one, which was designed by Henry Tanner. It was Tanner who designed the building (1890–5) from which Marconi sent the first radio transmission. The National Postal Museum was opened inside the GPO in 1965, largely thanks to Reginald M. Phillips, who donated his collection of British stamps and Victorian drawings. The museum also has a collection of stamps that have been issued since 1840 under British postal control, from Britain and from

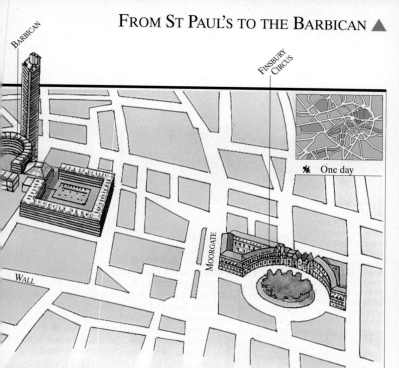

BARBICAN

FINSBURY CIRCUS

MOORGATE

WALL

✺ One day

other countries. With the addition of several series of stamps from members of the universal postal union, the museum has developed into one of the best philatelic collections in the world. There is also a fascinating collection of objects connected with the postal service, such as stamp-boxes, rubber stamps and letterboxes. In the courtyard of the General Post Office, near to St Bartholomew's Hospital, is a part of the medieval London Wall and a section of Roman wall too.

St Paul's Cathedral

History. The cathedral is built on top of one of the hills in the City, where in Roman times ● *34* there was once a temple in honor of Diana. The first cathedral to be built on the site, in 604, was destroyed by fire in 1087. Rebuilt between the 11th and 13th centuries, the new Norman and Gothic structure was said to be the biggest medieval church in the whole of Europe, and it boasted the tallest spire ever built. The spire burned down in 1561. The old cathedral was at the center of a complex of religious buildings: there was the chapter house, the bishop's palace and the free-standing Jesus Bell Tower, for example. After the English Reformation, the cathedral was abandoned for a while and became a market-place, to be restored by Inigo Jones around 1634 by order of King

The Penny Black
This is the pride of the postal museum, the world's first adhesive stamp.

Sir Christopher Wren (1632–1723)
The genius of English Baroque architecture was responsible for rebuilding London after the Great Fire of 1666 ● *40*, a commission which included St Paul's Cathedral.

Charles I. This work was unfortunately interrupted by the outbreak of the English Civil War ● *35*.

Wren's projects. Soon after the Restoration of 1660, Christopher Wren was given the job of restoring St Paul's Cathedral, which he planned to do by encasing the Gothic structure in a classical shell and then replacing the spire with a dome. His plan was finally approved on August 27, 1666, just one week before the Great Fire ● *40* razed it to the ground. So a new cathedral had to be built. Wren was appointed as director of works by the king in 1669, and the architect submitted several different designs: his first and favorite one, which Charles II also liked, featured a Greek cross plan with a dome. But the high-ranking clergy rejected it as being too untraditional. His "Great Model" of 1673 sought to overcome the clerical resistance by the addition of a portico and a vestibule topped with a dome. That too was rejected, so in 1675 Wren came up with the "Warrant Design", which had the "Norman English" Latin cross shape with a long nave and transepts, and a long choir with narrow ambulatories ending in an apse.

LONDON
IT'S QUICKER BY RAIL
FULL INFORMATION FROM ANY L·N·E·R OFFICE OR AGENCY

The dome of St Paul's. The building is crowned with a massive dome which is 107 feet in diameter and whose top is 365 feet above the ground. The dome is supported on eight pillars. Its weight was a problem that Wren eventually solved by building a stone cone between an inner and an outer dome to take the weight of the lantern. The view over London from the Golden Gallery above the dome is quite superb.

The exterior. Apart from the lead-covered dome of the cathedral, on to which all the main lines of the building seem to converge, the cathedral's exterior has three other important features: the great tambour of the dome, which is surrounded by a colonnade with alternate niches and loggias; a screen wall which serves as a buttress concealing the supporting arches and enhances the majestic overall effect (an impression that is further heightened by the semicircular colonnaded porticoes of the north and south transepts); and finally the west front, which was a predominantly Baroque inspiration. It features two graceful towers that frame a double portico with columns surmounted by a carved pediment.

The dome of St Paul's
When his model, with dome, was rejected as too revolutionary, it is said that Wren burst into tears.

THE INTERIOR. The
cathedral's impressive interior is
lacking in warmth and fails to inspire the
same wonder as the exterior. Between 1690 and 1720
Wren employed many different artists to decorate it. There
was Sir James Thornhill ▲ *326*, who painted the cupola with
frescoes illustrating the life of St Paul, and nearly fell to his
death in the process. Grinling Gibbons ▲ *157* carved the
magnificent choir-stalls, the bishop's throne and the organ
case; the French artist Jean Tijou executed the wrought-iron
grilles of the choir and the balustrade leading up to the
library. The best view of the interior (certainly of the
Thornhill frescoes) is probably from the Whispering Gallery.
TOMBS. The cathedral interior was all but free of tombs until
1790. Since then, like Westminster Abbey, it has become a
sort of Pantheon. Great men buried here include Lord
Nelson, the duke of Wellington and, fittingly, Wren himself.

**VIEW OF ST PAUL'S
FROM THE RIVER**
Among the great men
buried in St Paul's is
Lord Nelson, whose
sarcophagus of black
Italian marble was
meant for Cardinal
Wolsey. Henry VIII
took it from him.

**THE MORNING
CHAPEL**

**THIRTY-FIVE YEARS
TO BUILD**
The length of this job
gave rise to a popular
saying: "As slow as the
builders of St Paul's!"

173

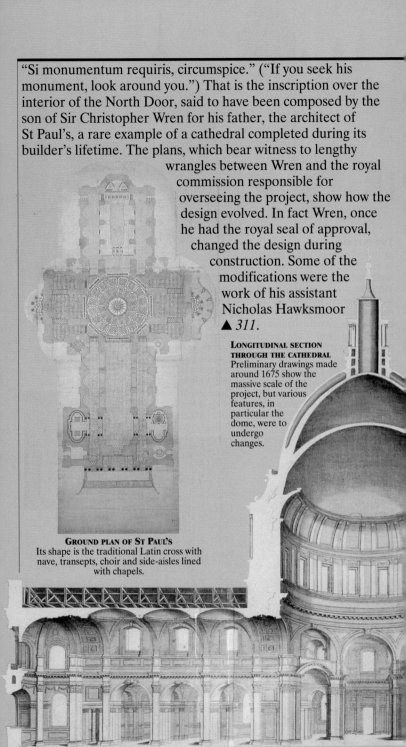

"Si monumentum requiris, circumspice." ("If you seek his monument, look around you.") That is the inscription over the interior of the North Door, said to have been composed by the son of Sir Christopher Wren for his father, the architect of St Paul's, a rare example of a cathedral completed during its builder's lifetime. The plans, which bear witness to lengthy wrangles between Wren and the royal commission responsible for overseeing the project, show how the design evolved. In fact Wren, once he had the royal seal of approval, changed the design during construction. Some of the modifications were the work of his assistant Nicholas Hawksmoor ▲ *311*.

LONGITUDINAL SECTION THROUGH THE CATHEDRAL
Preliminary drawings made around 1675 show the massive scale of the project, but various features, in particular the dome, were to undergo changes.

GROUND PLAN OF ST PAUL'S
Its shape is the traditional Latin cross with nave, transepts, choir and side-aisles lined with chapels.

DESIGNS FOR THE DOME AND THE PERISTYLE
This drawing of 1675 is headed "definitive plan" but this was not to be the case: Wren had not yet conceived the intermediary stone cone or the drum-shaped peristyle.

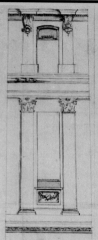

STUDY FOR THE WEST FRONT
In Baroque style, the design has an elegant two-storied portico. At this stage the plan still lacked the two turrets which balance the mass of the dome.

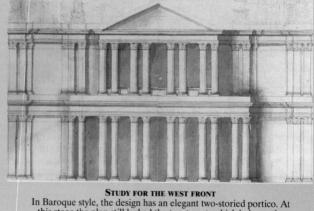

THE PORCH OF ST BARTHOLOMEW THE GREAT
This was rebuilt in 1893 by Sir Aston Webb. The original portal still exists in the gatehouse to the west.

STATE OCCASIONS AT ST PAUL'S CATHEDRAL. A great many state funerals have been held here over the centuries, including those of Lord Nelson (1805), the duke of Wellington (1852) and Winston Churchill (1965). Queen Victoria celebrated her Golden Jubilee here in 1887, and in 1981 Prince Charles broke with recent tradition and chose to marry Lady Diana Spencer in St Paul's Cathedral.

SMITHFIELD

This was a suburb to the north of London that has gradually been absorbed into the city. Smithfield gets its name from "smooth field", since it was originally a vast stretch of grassland at the edge of London.

ST BARTHOLOMEW'S HOSPITAL ★. This is London's oldest hospital. Together with a priory, it was founded in 1123 by Henry I's jester, Thomas Rahere, and then refounded in the 16th century by Henry VIII following the Dissolution of the monasteries before being again rebuilt between 1730 and 1759 by James Gibbs. Nothing now remains of the hospital's original buildings. Above the entrance is a statue of Henry VIII by Francis Bird, a sculptor who also worked for Christopher Wren ▲ 171. William Harvey, who discovered the principle of the circulation of the blood, was chief physician here 1609–33. One of the most illustrious governors of the hospital, during the 18th century, was the painter William Hogarth ▲ 210, who donated two pictures, *The Pool at Bethesda* and *The Good Samaritan* (1735–6), both of which are now to be seen hanging on the main staircase.

ST BARTHOLOMEW-THE-LESS. This church was originally built around 1184 as the hospital chapel. When the hospital was refounded in 1547, it became a parish church. Damaged during the Second World War, it was restored in the 1950's. Many famous surgeons and physicians of the hospital are buried here. The square tower with turret is of 15th-century origin.

ST BARTHOLOMEW-THE-GREAT. The priory, which was founded in 1123 by Rahere, was bought in 1544 by Sir Richard Rich, and then remained in his family until 1862. If the church escaped damage during the Great Fire, down the centuries it suffered in a number of different ways: for instance, the Lady Chapel became a house and then a printer's office, the cloisters became stables, and the north transept was turned into a blacksmith's forge. By the middle of the 19th century the church was no more than a ruin. Its restoration began in 1858; only a part of the nave now remains, although the Norman choir is still most impressive. The tracery of the high windows is from the 14th century, together with the eastern end of the choir and the Lady Chapel. The cloisters are 15th-century in origin, the tower was built in 1628, and the present porch in 1893. The church has undergone many changes over the centuries.

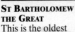

ST BARTHOLOMEW THE GREAT
This is the oldest church in London, and it is a rare example of Norman architecture in the capital. Other examples include St John's, Clerkenwell, the Tower Chapel and the Temple Church.

SMITHFIELD MARKET. Crowds used to flock to this square located just beyond the City walls in the Middle Ages in order to watch the public executions (Smithfield was one of the main places of execution both for Scottish rebels and for Protestant martyrs), to see some jousting, or to attend the popular Cloth Fair, which lasted for three days and was held every year during August. There has been a cattle market in Smithfield since late Saxon times (the 11th century). By the 16th century the area around the market had developed into a considerable community, with its gates at the end of St John Street. The nuisances that an urban cattle market brings with it forced its closure in 1855, and it was then moved to Islington. But the meat market remained, in the new halls which were built to house it.

THE LONDON CENTRAL MEAT MARKET. The four market halls

LONDON CENTRAL MEAT MARKET
As soon as it opened in 1868, the market was an immediate success. It still sells more than a thousand tons of meat per day. Behind the stone and red-brick walls are huge glass-roofed halls.

OTHER SIDE UP | WAY OUT
ANGEL
SMITHFIELD CLUB SHOW
DECEMBER 10ᵀᴴ – 14ᵀᴴ

● *84* were the work of Sir Horace Jones. The future of Smithfield is now under threat from property developers, just like Covent Garden ▲ *272*, Billingsgate ▲ *157* and Spitalfields ▲ *312* before it.

CHARTERHOUSE SQUARE ★. Within this peaceful, paved and gas-lit square is the old monastery of the CHARTERHOUSE, which was founded in the 14th century in order to house monks of the Carthusian order. Subsequently it became first a school and later a retirement home. Thomas More ▲ *197, 320* lived here from 1499 to 1503, and Thomas Cromwell stayed here in 1535. The buildings are not open to the public, although the gardens may be visited by going through the gate.

THE "FAT BOY". This chubby little figure in gilded wood stands at the corner of Giltspur Street and Cock Lane, on the site of an old tavern, marking the site where the Great Fire ended.

"THE OLD SMITHFIELD MARKET"
This painting by Thomas Sydney Cooper shows the cattle market in the 19th century.

THE OLD WALL
Remains of a
3rd-century brick
Roman rampart,
incorporating pieces
of medieval stone.

THE GOD MITHRAS
This 4th-century head
discovered in 1954 in
the Temple of
Mithras, provides
evidence of a
flourishing Mithraic
cult in Londinium.

THE MUSEUM OF LONDON

This enterprise opened on its
present Barbican site in 1976.
It is extremely popular with
Londoners as well as with
tourists, and is an
amalgamation of the old
London and Guildhall
Museums.

HISTORY. The Guildhall
Museum was founded in
1826 to display the
remains of Roman and
medieval London
discovered in the City
and surrounding areas or donated. The London Museum was
founded by Viscounts Harcourt and Esher in order to give
London an equivalent of the Musée Carnavalet in Paris, and
it was intended to house all that could be found concerning
the capital's history. It opened in 1912 in Kensington Palace,
and then moved to Lancaster House. Archeologist Sir
Mortimer Wheeler suggested a fusion of the two in 1927, but
the plan was forgotten until after the Second World War, the
City and the government having other, more important
priorities. The decision was finally made in 1965, and the
Museum of London was born. Adequate space was
eventually found for it in 1971, and a modern building
was constructed in the Barbican. Now it contains a
number of superb and informative collections
relating to the economic and social history of the
capital. Whole buildings, houses and shops have been
reconstructed here. The main entrance by the
rotunda leads to the upper level. This is where to
begin exploring the ten rooms tracing the history of
London.

THE THAMES IN PREHISTORY. This room leads the
visitor through prehistoric and protohistoric London,
from its earliest recorded origins to 42 AD. There is
paleolithic and neolithic silex, pottery which was found
at Heathrow, and some bronze weapons.

ROMAN LONDON. This is the history of Londinium
● *34* from 43 to 410 AD. One of the remains from
this period is the Temple of Mithras, which was
unearthed in 1954 in Walbrook and moved to Temple
Court, 11 Queen Victoria Street.

MEDIEVAL LONDON. This room covers a thousand years
of history from 410 to 1484. Among the treasures from this
period are some 11th-century Norman battleaxes, objects
such as the carved-wood
panel (left) from a chest
dated 1400 and illustrated
with scenes from the
Canterbury Tales, and a
heavy 6th-century gold
brooch of Saxon origin
(above right), found in an
Anglo-Saxon necropolis at
Mitcham, Surrey.

TUDOR LONDON. This room shows the astonishing growth of the City, and the daily life of Londoners between 1485 (the year of Henry VII's accession) and 1603 (when Queen Elizabeth died and the first Stuart king, James I, ascended the throne). The room is filled with arms, jewelry and costumes of the period, and there are watches and clocks made by Flemish craftsmen living in the City.

EARLY STUART LONDON. The early Stuart period (1603–66), including the Commonwealth, is covered in this room. There are models of a Shakespearean theater and London Bridge, and a death mask of Oliver Cromwell, as well as a diorama of the Great Fire complete with sound effects.

This 13th- or 14th-century vase is of Venetian origin.

THE LATER STUARTS. The history of the period 1667–1714 is illustrated in this room, which ends with the accession of George I. There is a fine example of a Londoner's costume of the time, a fascinating sectional model of the new St Paul's Cathedral ▲ *171*, and a gaming table for backgammon and chess.

GEORGIAN LONDON. The terrific expansion that went on in this period (1714–1800) is well covered here; there is also the reconstruction of a prison interior, a pillory, and arms.

PLATE
Dated 1602, this earthenware tin-glazed plate is probably the work of a Flemish potter working in Aldgate. It bears an inscription celebrating Elizabeth I.

NINETEENTH-CENTURY LONDON. In this room, covering the period 1801–80, there some excellent models, such as one of a barge dated 1807, one of the Crystal Palace (constructed in 1851 for the Great Exhibition), and a fire truck of 1862.

IMPERIAL LONDON. This room displays the late Victorian and the Edwardian eras from 1881 to 1910, with reconstructions of a street and a public house.

TWENTIETH-CENTURY LONDON. There are objects here from the period between the wars that will be familiar to many older visitors, such as a 1928 elevator from the big department store *Selfridges*, an air raid shelter and even a broadcasting studio.

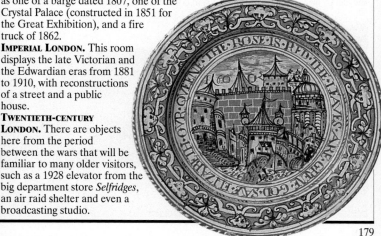

Around the Barbican

In the 1960's to the north of St Paul's there grew up a high-rise district of blocks and terraces. It is an enormous development of both commercial and residential properties and with its own arts center, a confusing network of modern buildings in the middle of which are still Gothic and neo-classical churches and other remains of historic London. The name Barbican comes from one of these remains, a section of the Roman and medieval wall.

BARBICAN
This maze of tower blocks, courtyards, stairways, tunnels and passages was built on land flattened in the Blitz ● *42*.

REBUILDING. Though St Paul's Cathedral survived the Blitz ● *42* relatively unscathed, a third of the City was destroyed. The worst-hit area was around the Barbican. Post-war

problems delayed the bulk of reconstruction work until 1955. It was decided to rebuild in a contemporary style and to make a clean break with the past, constructing new houses and flats, office blocks, recreation and cultural centers. The work was entrusted to three architects who shared the design and planning of the scheme: Chamberlain, Powell and Bon.

A CONTROVERSIAL DEVELOPMENT. Work started in 1962 and went on for the next twenty years, to be finally completed on March 3, 1982. Derelict for many years, the Barbican now houses almost two-thirds of the City's population. With the traffic re-routed underground, it has the appearance of an area entirely dedicated to pedestrians. For the latter, there is a network of terraces, passageways, squares and fountains that are designed to link the various disparate features of the development. Critics say that the development is difficult to get to and easy to get lost in, a dreary concrete world that lacks the human touch appropriate for its cultural institutions. These include the GUILDHALL SCHOOL OF MUSIC AND DRAMA and the CITY OF LONDON SCHOOL FOR GIRLS.

"FINSBURY CIRCUS"
This 19th-century painting by an unknown artist shows the northern side, with the now demolished London Institution where there were lectures "by eminent scientific and literary men".

THE BARBICAN CENTRE FOR THE ARTS AND CONFERENCES. Officially opened in March 1982, this is one of the most important socio-cultural complexes in the whole of Europe. There are ten floors in all, some of them underground, and its two-thousand-seat concert hall is home to the London

Symphony Orchestra. Its theater (with
fifteen hundred seats) houses the ROYAL
SHAKESPEARE COMPANY, and there is also the
smaller PIT THEATRE, a library, an art gallery,
three cinemas, conference halls and
auditoria, as well as restaurants and
cafeterias.

ST GILES-WITHOUT-CRIPPLEGATE. The church
gets its name from one of the five Roman
gates to the City: Cripplegate, Aldgate,
Bishopsgate, Newgate and Ludgate. The
present building dates from the mid-16th century, and
the tower is from a century later. It is one of the few
churches to have escaped the Great Fire of 1666, although it
was rather less fortunate during the Blitz. In the choir of the
church are the tombs of the explorer and navigator Martin
Frobisher (c. 1535–94) and of the poet John Milton
(1608–74). Oliver Cromwell (1599–1658) was married here in
1620.

THE WALL. Several remains of the old wall encircling the City
are still visible in the street named London Wall, particularly
in the garden of St Alfege and at West Gate. The
wall is a mixture of Roman foundations,
medieval sections with gray stone supports
from the 14th century, and some 15th-
century sections built with red brick.

ALL HALLOWS CHURCH. Built between
1765 and 1767 in London Wall by
George Dance the Younger ▲*149*, this
church is constructed in neo-classical style.
The altar painting is by the architect's
brother, Nathaniel Dance. A section of the
original Roman fortifications is still visible in
the church garden.

FINSBURY CIRCUS. This fine circular "square" is on the east
side of Moorgate. Unfortunately none of George Dance
the Younger's early 19th-century houses remain; but there
are some imposing buildings, such as LUTYENS HOUSE
(1924–7, by Sir Edwin Lutyens), surrounding an
attractive garden.

**"ST BOTOLPH'S,
ALDERSGATE"**
This Victorian
painting shows the
sub-tropical plants in
the churchyard, which
in 1880 became a
most unusual garden,
Postman's Park. It is
in Noble Street, on
the other side of the
Barbican.

WESLEY'S CHAPEL
The "Methodists'
Cathedral" was
consecrated in 1778
by the evangelist and
missionary John
Wesley (1703–91).

▲ THE TOWER OF LONDON AND TOWER BRIDGE

FENCHURCH STREET STATION   CORN EXCHANGE   TOWER PIER   TRINITY SQUARE   TOWER OF LONDON   ROYAL MINT

Two hours

BYWARD STREET

TOWER HILL

LOWER THAMES STREET

By the year 200 London had become one of the wealthiest cities in the Roman empire, surrounded by walls (traces of which are still to be seen in Trinity Square and inside the Tower). But in spite of its fortifications London was still taken by William the Conqueror in 1066. Ten years later he built the White Tower. His successors each added various features, Edward I adding the outer curtain wall and moat in the late 13th century. The White Tower was so called not from the Caen limestone and Kentish ragstone of which it was built, but because in 1240 Henry III had the entire building whitewashed. In the 17th century the Norman windows were enlarged by Christopher Wren ● *70*, ▲ *171*. The White Tower now houses a magnificent collection of arms and armor, the HERALDS' MUSEUM, and ST JOHN'S CHAPEL (the oldest church in London and a masterpiece of early Norman architecture).

THE WHITE TOWER
The keep known as the White Tower is the oldest part of the Tower of London. Its only staircase spiraled clockwise to make it easier for defenders to fight with their swords in their right hands.

ROYAL PALACE AND ROYAL PRISON ★. The Tower first became a royal residence when Henry III (1216–72) built a palace to the south of the White Tower. It was partially rebuilt in the reign of Henry VIII, and in 1540 the half-timbered houses on Tower Green, including the QUEEN'S HOUSE, were constructed. The palace was redecorated for the coronation of Henry VIII's second wife Anne Boleyn, but the Tower ceased to be a royal residence and became a prison for enemies of the crown. Many famous men and women were imprisoned and sometimes executed here on Tower Green, such as the seventeen-year-old Lady Jane Grey, Anne Boleyn and Catharine Howard (second and fifth wives of Henry

182

VIII). Execution on Tower Green instead of in public on Tower Hill was a privilege reserved for high-ranking prisoners, who also had the right to be buried in the 13th-century chapel of ST PETER AD VINCULA; this was destroyed by fire in 1512 and rebuilt three years later. Sir Thomas More ▲ *197* and John Fisher, bishop of Rochester, were also beheaded on Tower Green, the latter so weak he had to be carried to the block. They were executed for refusing to take the Oath of Supremacy (1534), which put the Church of England under the control of the sovereign.

In 1413 Sir John Oldcastle (Shakespeare's Falstaff) was confined in the Tower to await execution, but he escaped the following year only to be recaptured and hanged. Shakespeare dramatized another incident which took place in 1483, when the boy-king Edward V and his brother were reputedly murdered in the Garden Tower (afterwards known as the Bloody Tower). The skeletons of two children were found in 1674 under the stairs leading to St John's Chapel, and when the remains were exhumed in 1933 they were thought to be those of "the Little Princes". Other famous prisoners include Sir Walter Raleigh (who spent twelve years there), the Earl of Essex (beheaded on Tower Green), Guy Fawkes and his fellow conspirators, who were tortured in the basement of the White Tower, and the Duke of Monmouth after the failure of his rebellion in 1685. Two famous prisoners in the 20th century include Sir Roger Casement (hanged at Pentonville) and Hitler's deputy Rudolf Hess, after his mysterious flight to Scotland in 1941.

THE RAVENS. Legend has it that the kingdom will fall if the ravens leave the Tower. The origin of this superstition is not known but may derive from Charles II, who wanted to get rid of the birds but was advised against it.

YEOMAN WARDER OF THE TOWER Commonly known as Beefeaters. They are ex-servicemen, and wear blue Tudor costume (red on state occasions).

183

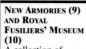

NEW ARMORIES (9) AND ROYAL FUSILIERS' MUSEUM (10)
A collection of weapons is on display in this maritime warehouse of 1680. The Fusiliers' Museum traces the history of the regiment from its formation in 1685 to the present.

MIDDLE TOWER (1, 13th century), with access to BYWARD TOWER (2, with 14th-century wall paintings) beside the Main Gate. From here Water Lane leads to the BELL TOWER (3), once the prison of the future Queen Elizabeth I, Sir Thomas More and Monmouth, where curfew is rung every evening. Beyond this on the right is ST THOMAS' TOWER (4, 13th century) with an oratory dedicated to St Thomas à Becket.

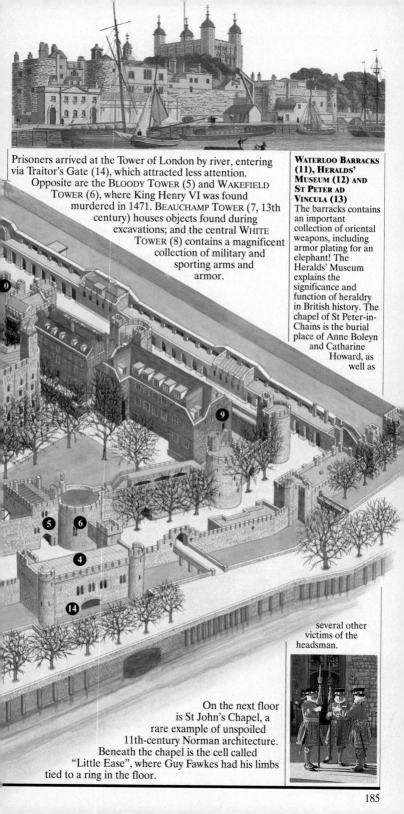

Prisoners arrived at the Tower of London by river, entering via Traitor's Gate (14), which attracted less attention.

Opposite are the BLOODY TOWER (5) and WAKEFIELD TOWER (6), where King Henry VI was found murdered in 1471. BEAUCHAMP TOWER (7, 13th century) houses objects found during excavations; and the central WHITE TOWER (8) contains a magnificent collection of military and sporting arms and armor.

WATERLOO BARRACKS (11), HERALDS' MUSEUM (12) AND ST PETER AD VINCULA (13)
The barracks contains an important collection of oriental weapons, including armor plating for an elephant! The Heralds' Museum explains the significance and function of heraldry in British history. The chapel of St Peter-in-Chains is the burial place of Anne Boleyn and Catharine Howard, as well as several other victims of the headsman.

On the next floor is St John's Chapel, a rare example of unspoiled 11th-century Norman architecture. Beneath the chapel is the cell called "Little Ease", where Guy Fawkes had his limbs tied to a ring in the floor.

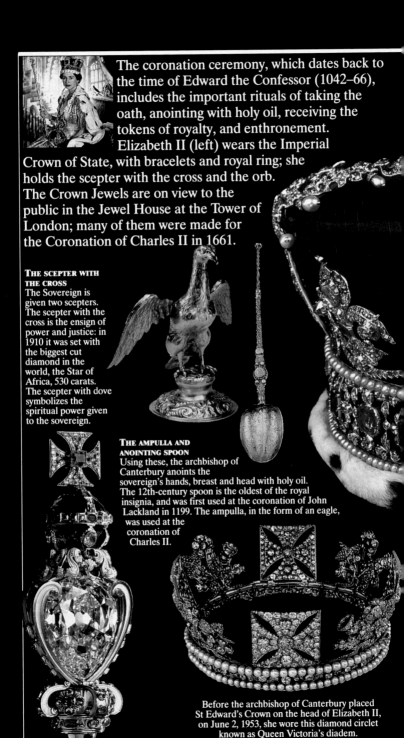

The coronation ceremony, which dates back to the time of Edward the Confessor (1042–66), includes the important rituals of taking the oath, anointing with holy oil, receiving the tokens of royalty, and enthronement. Elizabeth II (left) wears the Imperial Crown of State, with bracelets and royal ring; she holds the scepter with the cross and the orb. The Crown Jewels are on view to the public in the Jewel House at the Tower of London; many of them were made for the Coronation of Charles II in 1661.

THE SCEPTER WITH THE CROSS
The Sovereign is given two scepters. The scepter with the cross is the ensign of power and justice: in 1910 it was set with the biggest cut diamond in the world, the Star of Africa, 530 carats. The scepter with dove symbolizes the spiritual power given to the sovereign.

THE AMPULLA AND ANOINTING SPOON
Using these, the archbishop of Canterbury anoints the sovereign's hands, breast and head with holy oil. The 12th-century spoon is the oldest of the royal insignia, and was first used at the coronation of John Lackland in 1199. The ampulla, in the form of an eagle, was used at the coronation of Charles II.

Before the archbishop of Canterbury placed St Edward's Crown on the head of Elizabeth II, on June 2, 1953, she wore this diamond circlet known as Queen Victoria's diadem.

THE IMPERIAL CROWN OF INDIA (1911) AND THE STATE CROWN OF QUEEN ELIZABETH THE QUEEN MOTHER (1937)

The first crown (1) is set with more than six thousand precious stones from India: it was only worn once, when George V was crowned Emperor of India in Delhi. The second (2), made of platinum, contains the famous Koh-i-Noor diamond (Mountain of Light).

1

2

3

4

THE IMPERIAL STATE CROWN

This crown (above) was made for the coronation of Queen Victoria in 1838. Set with more than 2,800 diamonds, it also contains the Black Prince's ruby, worn by Henry V at the Battle of Agincourt. Elizabeth II wore this for her coronation procession.

THE CORONATION RING AND THE QUEEN'S RING

After the crowning ceremony, the archbishop places the Coronation Ring on the third finger of the monarch's right hand. These rings were made for the coronation of William IV and Queen Adelaide in 1831.

SAINT EDWARD'S CROWN AND QUEEN MARY'S CROWN

St Edward's Crown (3) weighs almost 5lbs. It was made for the coronation of Charles II in 1662: most of the Crown Jewels had been scrapped during the Commonwealth. This crown is only used for the crowning ceremony. Queen Mary's Crown (4) was worn by Mary at the coronation of George V.

▲ THE TOWER OF LONDON AND TOWER BRIDGE

The Prince of Wales unveiled this commemorative plaque on Monday June 21, 1886.

Formerly there was a menagerie within the Tower of London: in 1235 the Holy Roman Emperor presented Henry III with three leopards, as an allusion to the leopards which figured on the Plantagenet coat of arms, and it was this gift that began the royal menagerie. Next, in 1252 a polar bear arrived as a gift from the king of Norway; it was kept on a long chain which allowed it sufficient freedom to catch fish in the River Thames. Louis IX of France gave Henry an elephant; over the years a number of other animals were added, and the menagerie became a popular attraction. But by 1822 the royal collection had dwindled to just a grizzly bear, a single elephant and a few assorted birds. So a new royal keeper, Alfred Copps, was appointed and he enlarged it to include fifty-nine species. In 1835, when a lion attacked some soldiers in the Tower, the animals were all transferred to the Zoological Gardens in Regent's Park ▲ 257.

TOWER BRIDGE ★

Tower Bridge has long symbolized the city of London to people from all over the world. It was the gateway to the capital for ships coming upriver to dock in the port, and it is the first bridge over the Thames coming upriver from the east. Its design and its brilliant engineering encapsulate the heart and soul of Victorian London. Today the bridge continues its threefold function, permitting the efficient movement of road vehicles, river vessels and pedestrians.

CONSTRUCTION. The construction of a new bridge across the Thames was necessitated by the density of traffic that was traveling over the river in the 1880s, particularly over London Bridge. As its site roughly corresponded with the City limits, the City's own architect, Sir Horace Jones, was commissioned to build it. His design was inspired by the lift bridges over the canals in Holland. His daring plan was to have a relatively low through bridge,

"STEEL SKELETONS CLOTHED WITH STONE", WAS HOW ARCHITECT SIR HORACE JONES DESCRIBED HIS TOWERS AT EITHER END OF THE BRIDGE.

only 30 feet above the water, with a double lift giving ships access to Upper Pool, the basin between Tower Bridge and London Bridge. Two other men of vision must also share the credit for this immense project: engineer John Wolfe-Barry (the son of the famous architect Sir Charles Barry), and architect G.D. Stevenson, who modified the plans after Jones died in 1887.

THE ARCHITECTURE. Parliament and the City both specified a neo-Gothic design for the bridge (at the request of Queen Victoria and the War Office), with towers that would conceal the hydraulic lifting machinery as well as blend in well with the nearby Tower of London. An additional factor was that the neo-Gothic style was at its height at this time. The influence of Scottish castle architecture is due to Stevenson, who was a Scot himself, and this is apparent in the decoration of the towers as well as in the use of steel for the superstructure of the bridge. The stone cladding over a metal framework offered the best resistance to the stresses that were imposed by the two lifting bascules. The foundation stone of the river's "Gateway to the City" was laid by the Prince of Wales in 1886. Its length is approximately 800 feet between the two towers, and though today Londoners think of Tower Bridge with considerable affection, it was the subject of some harsh criticism at its opening in 1894.

SHIPS UNDER THE BRIDGE. At any hour of the day or night, a ship with a superstructure or fixed mast that is more than 33 feet in height can signal to Tower Bridge from the level of Cherry Garden Pier that it requires to pass through. There is a similar procedure in operation for vessels that are going downriver.

THE LAST BRIDGE OVER THE THAMES
Tower Bridge was specifically designed to facilitate the passage of river traffic.

DETAIL OF THE PARAPET
The metal parts of the bridge, painted red, white and blue, are decorated with royal insignia.

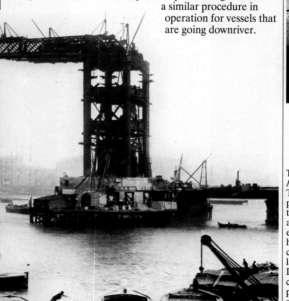

TOWER BRIDGE IN APRIL 1892
The bridge is a perfect example of the Victorian blend of architecture and engineering, historical detail combined with the latest technology. During its construction many people spoke out against covering a metal framework with stone.

189

Many architectural plans for the bridge were put forward before the design of Sir Horace Jones was accepted. In 1879 Sir Joseph Bazalgette submitted a design for a single-arch bridge, which was rejected because of insufficient headroom. The final form of the towers was settled on after Jones' death and simplified long after the bridge was completed, at the end of the Second World War.

EVOLUTION OF A DESIGN
The plans on the left are part of a project that was never realized. Those on the right represent the final project: front view and section (far right).

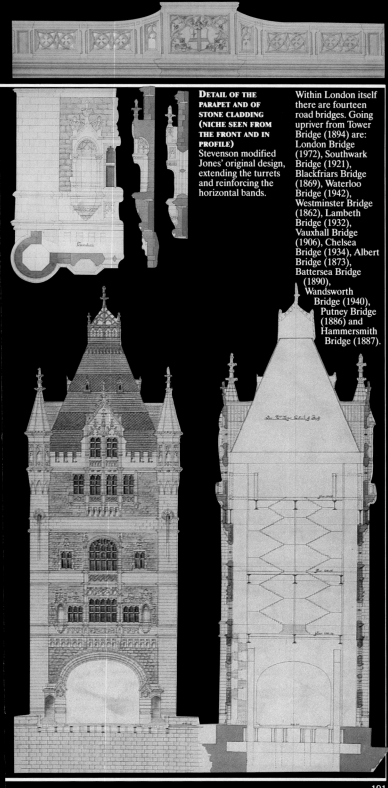

DETAIL OF THE PARAPET AND OF STONE CLADDING (NICHE SEEN FROM THE FRONT AND IN PROFILE)
Stevenson modified Jones' original design, extending the turrets and reinforcing the horizontal bands.

Within London itself there are fourteen road bridges. Going upriver from Tower Bridge (1894) are: London Bridge (1972), Southwark Bridge (1921), Blackfriars Bridge (1869), Waterloo Bridge (1942), Westminster Bridge (1862), Lambeth Bridge (1932), Vauxhall Bridge (1906), Chelsea Bridge (1934), Albert Bridge (1873), Battersea Bridge (1890), Wandsworth Bridge (1940), Putney Bridge (1886) and Hammersmith Bridge (1887).

191

THE FOOTBRIDGE
Each tower has a lift to take pedestrians up to the walkway, necessary in the days when the bridge was opened very frequently. It was closed in 1911 because of the large number of suicides. But it was glassed in and reopened in 1982, and now offers superb views over the river.

"At every mooring chain and rope, at every stationary boat or barge that split the current into a broad arrow-head, at the offsets of the piers from Southwark Bridge, at the paddles of the river steamboats as they beat the filthy water, at the floating logs of timber lashed together lying off certain wharves, his shining eyes darted a hungry look.**"**
Charles Dickens,
Our Mutual Friend

Note that the ships are not required to wait: rather, the road traffic must give way to the traffic on the river. A tugboat is always waiting at the ready at the northeast corner in order to assist the passage of sailing boats through the bridge.

THE BRIDGE AT WORK. At one time there were eighty men at work on Tower Bridge. When it has to be opened, the look-out on duty warns the policeman in charge of the traffic on the bridge, which is then closed by the use of traffic lights. Careful synchronization between the river and road traffic is necessary at this point in order to prevent an accident: there are many stories of incidents that have happened here. There was the driver of a London bus who went through the red light and was caught on the opening bascules. The bus jumped a gap of several feet to land safely on the other side. When they reach the bridge, ships have to wait only one and a half minutes before they can pass through. The original hydraulic lifting machinery was made by the Newcastle firm of Armstrong-Mitchell Ltd, and never once failed to work. River traffic diminished in 1970 when the wharves in Upper Pool closed down. Scarcely any more large vessels came far enough upriver to use the bridge, whose running costs were extremely

high. There was talk of abandoning the lifting facility, or at least switching to new machinery that would be less costly to maintain. Tower Bridge was used almost exclusively by road traffic and as its once-revolutionary Victorian machinery became aged and impractical, it was in danger of becoming just another monument. But in 1976 the hydraulic system was replaced by electric motors, so that the bridge, although seldom called into use by passing ships, remains in working order.

TOWER BRIDGE MUSEUM AND "HMS BELFAST". A museum opened in the old power house on the south side in 1982. It traces the history of the bridge. Stevenson's original drawings are on display, and the original hydraulic lifting machinery is demonstrated. The old walkway high above the road has also been reopened. *HMS Belfast* (11,500 tons), which was opened as a museum in 1971, is moored nearby. It is the largest cruiser ever to have been built by the Royal Navy: it saw service in World War Two on the Arctic convoys.

VILLAGES
AND MUSEUMS

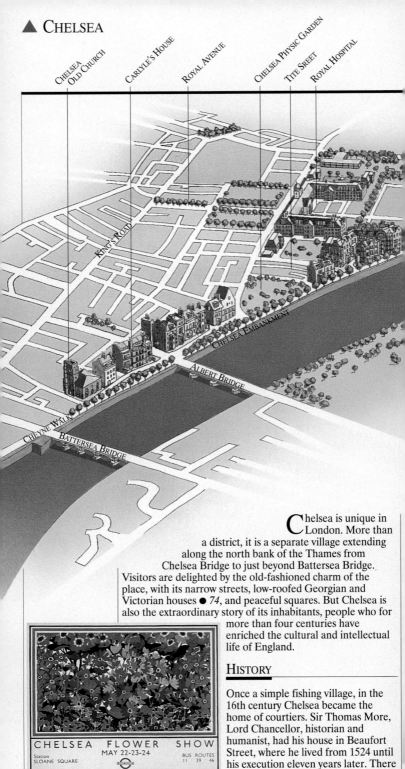

CHELSEA OLD CHURCH

CARLYLE'S HOUSE

ROYAL AVENUE

CHELSEA PHYSIC GARDEN

TITE SREET

ROYAL HOSPITAL

KING'S ROAD

CHELSEA EMBANKMENT

ALBERT BRIDGE

CHEYNE WALK

BATTERSEA BRIDGE

Chelsea is unique in London. More than a district, it is a separate village extending along the north bank of the Thames from Chelsea Bridge to just beyond Battersea Bridge. Visitors are delighted by the old-fashioned charm of the place, with its narrow streets, low-roofed Georgian and Victorian houses ● *74*, and peaceful squares. But Chelsea is also the extraordinary story of its inhabitants, people who for more than four centuries have enriched the cultural and intellectual life of England.

CHELSEA FLOWER SHOW
MAY 22-23-24
Station
SLOANE SQUARE
BUS ROUTES
11 · 39 · 46

HISTORY

Once a simple fishing village, in the 16th century Chelsea became the home of courtiers. Sir Thomas More, Lord Chancellor, historian and humanist, had his house in Beaufort Street, where he lived from 1524 until his execution eleven years later. There he received such friends as Erasmus

One day

CHELSEA FLOWER SHOW
The Flower Show is a feature of the London social season. Below, the cover of a piano piece written to celebrate the famous event attended by high society from the Royal Family downwards.

(1469–1536) and the German painter Hans Holbein (1497–1543), who was to have a marked influence on English portrait artists after him. In 1537 King Henry VIII

● *36* built the NEW MANOR HOUSE beside the Thames, which in the 17th century came into the possession of the Cheyne family and was bought in 1712 by the celebrated physician Sir Hans Sloane ▲ *301,* who kept his famous Cabinet of Curiosities there.

THE HOME FOR OLD SOLDIERS. Over the years Chelsea changed a great deal and it was definitively put on the map in the 17th century with the construction of the Royal Hospital. Retired soldiers, or "Pensioners", of the Hospital probably boasted about the fresh air and the peace they found there, far from the smoke and fog of the city, and from 1742 all London started coming to Chelsea to take the air. Their favorite spot was RANELAGH GARDENS, to the east of the Royal Hospital, where there were regular concerts, balls, grand dinners and firework displays.

BOHEMIA. Artists, writers and intellectuals of all kinds started to move to Chelsea at the beginning of the 19th century, seduced by the peace and quiet they found there. The poet Shelley and the landscape painter Turner ● *102,* ▲ *215, 216* were among the first. Word spread, and its popularity increased. Later in the century Chelsea could number among its inhabitants the painters Dante Gabriel Rossetti ▲ *218,*

195

▲ CHELSEA

Holman Hunt and James Abbott McNeill Whistler ● *104*; and the writers George Eliot, Henry James and Oscar Wilde ● *111*. It was not long before Chelsea acquired a reputation as a cultural Bohemia, and then followed famous men from the worlds of science and beyond, such as the historian Thomas Carlyle and that extraordinary architectural genius of bridges and tunnels, Sir Marc Brunel (father of the great Isambard Kingdom Brunel).

IN MEMORY
Some houses in London have blue ceramic plaques recording the name and dates of a famous personality who lived there.

SIR CAROL REED FILM DIRECTOR LIVED HERE 1948 - 1978

THE TEMPLE OF FASHION. Chelsea became fashionable again during the 1950's. First of all the new generation of dramatists, the so-called "Angry Young Men", had their plays staged at the Royal Court Theatre. These were playwrights such as John Osborne and Arnold Wesker, who were reacting against what they called the "Establishment". Then, during the 1960's, Chelsea became the musical Mecca for rock music devotees, with the Rolling Stones leading the field, and for fashion too, with the young Mary Quant well up front. The media personalities and rock stars took over from the dreamy intellectuals who had gone before them, but Chelsea remains the lively little village it has always been, with its pretty cottages and landscapes, never getting bogged down in the past. Right through the 20th century it has continued to be a home for all manner of creative personalities, from the thriller writer Agatha Christie, philosopher Bertrand Russell and writer-director Peter Ustinov, to such unlikely figures as millionaire Paul Getty and the ex-prime minister Margaret Thatcher.

A HOST OF CELEBRITIES
Among the famous people who settled in Chelsea are (below, left to right): Whistler (1834–1903), an American painter celebrated for his riverscapes; George Eliot (1819–80), author of *Middlemarch* and *Silas Marner*; Oscar Wilde (1854–1900), dramatist and wit; and Algernon Charles Swinburne (1837–1909), English poet and critic.

EXPLORING CHELSEA

Invaded as it has been for the last thirty years by trendy boutiques catering primarily for fashion-conscious youngsters, the commercial parts of Chelsea at least have changed, yet somehow without relinquishing all links with the past. A walk around will reveal an attractive jumble of fashion shops, traditional pubs (some with their own little theaters attached), delightful statues, good restaurants, antique shops and historic gardens.

RED BRICK AND WHITE STUCCO
Detail of a typical 19th-century Chelsea house.

SLOANE SQUARE. This extremely busy square, with the Royal Court Theatre on the east side opposite the famous *Peter Jones* department store, marks the boundary between northern Chelsea and the start of Belgravia. It is named after Sir Hans Sloane ▲ *301*, the 18th-century physician and benefactor of Chelsea.

THE KING'S ROAD. This road was laid out during the 17th century at the orders of Charles II as a link between the Palace of Whitehall ▲ *142* and Hampton Court ▲ *352*. It was a private road until 1830, and a special pass was needed to use it. Today it must be the busiest road in Chelsea, and it is crowded with shops, pubs and restaurants and a colorful mass of people thronging the pavements. It is Chelsea's High Street, and the meeting place of London's "gilded youth". Once there were Hippies, then came the Punks: the latest trends are sure to be on show here. This is particularly true on Saturdays, when well-off young people drive up and down the road, perhaps showing off their expensive Jaguars and Morgan cars, or maybe sitting astride a noisy Harley Davidson motorbike. The King's Road also has plenty of antique shops, the best-known of them being the *Antiquarius Center* at number 131–141; an arcade of antique shops at number 181; and the Chelsea Antique Market at numbers 245–53.

THE OLD TOWN HALL. This building was constructed between 1885 and 1907 in the English Baroque style. Every year there is an important antique fair held here that attracts a large number of visitors from all over the world.

NUMBER 152 KING'S ROAD. Only the façade remains of THE PHEASANTRY with its portico supporting a quadriga. This was once a magnificent private house, built in 1881 for the artist Amédée Joubert.

ARGYLL HOUSE. Opposite the new Chelsea College of Art is a group of listed 18th-century buildings. Argyll House is at number 211, built in 1723 by the Venetian Giacomo Leoni. Dr Thomas Augustine Arne (1710–78), composer of *Rule, Britannia*, and the writer-director Peter Ustinov have both lived here.

THE ROYAL AVENUE. This elegant space, bordered with lime trees and lined with rows of fine houses, is all that remains of an ambitious urban development that was initiated by William III, who wanted to build an avenue from the Thames up to Kensington Palace. The Royal Avenue bisects the grassy lawns of Burton's Court and finishes up outside the central building of the Royal Hospital.

THE ROYAL HOSPITAL ★

The hospital was built in 1682 by King Charles II as a retirement home for old soldiers of his lately reconstituted army. Sir Stephen Fox, the army's paymaster general, was entrusted with the job of raising the money. The diarist and courtier John Evelyn roughed out the plans for the hospital, whose design and construction was the work of Sir Christopher Wren ● *70*, ▲ *171, 353*. It was only completed in

STENDHAL IN CHELSEA
"I loved London for its beautiful walks along the Thames to Little Chelsea. The tiny cottages wreathed in roses brought tears to my eyes," said the French novelist Stendhal, author of *Scarlet and Black*.

SIR THOMAS MORE
This statue of England's great Lord Chancellor was erected in 1970 opposite Chelsea Old Church in Cheyne Walk.

A HAVEN OF TRANQUILLITY
In this painting by Peter Tillemans (1684–1734) the buildings of the Royal Hospital, set among lawns and the Ranelagh Gardens (right), rise above the Thames to show the classical severity of their architecture – which prompted the historian Thomas Carlyle to call it: "Quiet and dignified and the work of a gentleman".

A HARMONIOUS EFFECT
This canvas by Edward Haytley dates from 1746 and captures the building's elegant proportions. Its geometric simplicity is enhanced by the bright red brickwork contrasted with white stone. Before the construction of Chelsea Embankment, the hospital gardens ran right down to the Thames.

A CELEBRATION
On special occasions during the summer, and when they go out, the Chelsea Pensioners wear a tricorn hat, trimmed with gold braid, and a scarlet coat bearing their medals.

1692 in the reign of William III, though 476 Pensioners were admitted in 1689. The number of inmates has changed little in the time since then. Between 1765 and 1782 Robert Adam ● 76, ▲ 256, 263 made some alterations. Between 1819 and 1822 some additional buildings in a severe neo-classical style were erected to the east and west. They were designed by Sir John Soane ▲ 150. The Royal Hospital was seriously damaged by enemy action during World War Two and has been largely rebuilt since then.

A TOUR OF THE ROYAL HOSPITAL. The Royal Hospital is constructed of red brick and white Portland stone and it consists of a central building with a lantern turret. The two long wings that house the Pensioners form courtyards on either side, with additional wings on each side of them. In the middle of the central courtyard is a statue of Charles II, depicted as a Roman emperor, by Grinling Gibbons ▲ 157, 173. The main portico, with its Doric columns, divides the chapel from the Great Hall. The chapel was consecrated in 1692. Its fine woodwork was carved by William Emmett and Renatus Harris, while the apsidal vaulting was decorated 1710–15 with a fresco by the Venetian artist Sebastiano Ricci. Both Pensioners and visitors come to worship in this chapel every Sunday. On the other side of the portico, the Great Hall was used as a refectory until the end of the 18th century; in 1852 it was used for the lying-in-state of the duke of Wellington ▲ 246, and many thousands of Londoners came here to pay their last respects to the great soldier. Replicas of the flags that were captured from the French during the revolutionary and Napoleonic wars hang from the refectory walls. On the front wall is an allegorical fresco by the Italian Antonio Verrio (1639–1707), which was begun around 1667. It, too, represents Charles II. On the eastern side of the buildings, in an annex near the Royal Hospital's cemetery, is a small museum which traces the history of the institution. Here there is a fascinating collection of medals and decorations that belonged to the Pensioners.

THE CHELSEA PENSIONERS. The old soldiers are easily recognizable by their distinctive uniform, which has not changed since the end of the 18th century. During the

summer they wear red to go out, and also on festival days. Summer here begins on May 29, which is known as Oak Apple Day, the birthday of King Charles II. Pensioners must be at least sixty-five years old; and they receive an allowance "for beer and tobacco", pocket money, and are fed and lodged at the expense of the state. In exchange they are bound to attend military church services and parades. Custom dictates that in the refectory these old soldiers from the ranks are served before officers. It is a common sight to see Chelsea Pensioners walking down the King's Road or in one of the local pubs.

CHELSEA FLOWER SHOW. The Royal Hospital Gardens slope down toward the bank of the river, and each May the Chelsea Flower Show is held here, opened by the queen in person. It is organized by the Royal Horticultural Society, whose members provide the exhibits. The show is also a competition and lasts for four days; the winner's picture appears in *The Times* the following day. The show attracts thousands of visitors, some from as far away as the United States.

are predominantly veterans of World War Two. Only some parts of the hospital are open to the public: the chapel, a small museum, the Great Hall (above), and also the huge gardens (below).

RANELAGH GARDENS. Redesigned around 1860, Ranelagh Gardens are now on the east side of the Royal Hospital Gardens. They are on the site of what was once the estate of Lord Ranelagh, paymaster general to the Forces until his death in 1712. For more than half a century, from 1742 to 1804, the gardens were a fashionable walking and recreation place for Londoners.

NATIONAL ARMY MUSEUM. This museum was opened in 1971, in modern buildings to the west of the hospital in Royal Hospital Road. It displays the history of the British Army and its regiments from 1485 until the outbreak of World War One.

AROUND CHEYNE WALK

Leaving King's Road and the Royal Hospital, the visitor also leaves Old Chelsea, toward less opulent but perhaps even more attractive sights. There is a subtle charm to be found in the maze of little residential streets such as Oakley Street, Old Church Street and Upper Cheyne Row; and in the elegant Georgian ● 74 town houses of Cheyne Walk, facing the river. Ceramic blue plaques ■ 373 on some façades give the name and dates, together with a few other details, of various famous men and women who have lived in Chelsea; they are a satisfying stimulus to the imagination.

WINTER UNIFORM
The heavy, dark blue outfit worn in winter keeps the Pensioners warm, but is duller than the summer one.

199

THE PHYSIC GARDEN
The illustrations above show the garden as it was in the 19th century.

A CERAMIC PLAQUE
This type of ornament (right) is often seen on houses in Chelsea.

SLOANE'S TOMB
In the graveyard of All Saints, Chelsea (known as Chelsea Old Church), is a great urn marking the grave of Sir Hans Sloane (1660–1753), the Chelsea physician, botanist and collector. His museum and library helped to found the British Museum.

CHELSEA PHYSIC GARDEN ★. With the exception of the one at Oxford, this is the oldest botanical garden in England. It was founded in 1673 by the Apothecaries' Company, which wanted a collection of medicinal plants for educational and scientific study. The land it occupies was originally the gift of Sir Hans Sloane. One of the greatest horticulturalists of the day, Philip Miller, was put in charge of it and he made the Physic Garden the envy of his contemporaries. The first cedar trees in England were planted here in 1683, and here also were raised cotton plants from the South Seas which went to found an industry in the colony of Georgia in 1732. Behind the Physic Garden's wrought-iron railings, there is still a horticultural and botanic study center of the highest quality. There are many trees that are more than a hundred years old and more than seven thousand varieties of herbs, fruits and vegetables. The garden is open to the public during the summer, and visitors can enjoy the benefit of an expert and dedicated staff, as well as a number of books and leaflets available from the information bureau. From the entrance gate, an avenue leads to the imposing statue of Sir Hans Sloane. This is a copy of the one that was carved by Rysbrack in 1737. From this point, there is a magnificent view over the whole of the rest of the garden.

CHEYNE WALK ★. Facing the river bank is Cheyne Walk, an extremely pleasant and shady street that is lined with a row of fine Georgian ● *74* brick houses. The most beautiful of these buildings are gathered at the beginning of the street, and perhaps the most remarkable of them all is CROSBY HALL, a much earlier house, which was built between 1466 and 1475 by the wool merchant Sir John Crosby. This street has been much involved with painting and poetry: the Pre-Raphaelite Brotherhood was founded here, since this was where several of its members also lived.

FAMOUS RESIDENTS. Mary Ann Evans, who, writing under the pseudonym of George Eliot, was a famous novelist of the realist school, died in 1880 at 4 Cheyne Walk. At number 16 lived Dante Gabriel Rossetti. He was an eminent poet and painter, the son of an Italian immigrant teacher and the leader of the Pre-Raphaelite movement. He lived here from 1862 until his death. The poet Algernon Charles Swinburne (1837–1909), novelist George Meredith (1828–1909) and the critic John Ruskin (1810–1900) were among the frequent visitors to his house (which was built in 1717). The American novelist Henry James (who became a British citizen in 1915) died at 21 CARLYLE MANSIONS in Cheyne Walk. During the 1920's, the historian Arnold Toynbee (1889–1975), author of a controversial ten-volume *History of the World*, and the poet T.S. Eliot (1888–1965) also lived here for a while.

LINDSEY HOUSE. At 95–100 Cheyne Walk is Lindsey House, which was built around 1674 by the earl of Lindsey. In the late 18th century it was divided into a number of separate dwellings: the American painter James Abbott McNeill Whistler (1834–1903) ● *104* lived at number 96. He believed in "art for art's sake" and disliked the quasi-literary approach of the members of the Pre-Raphaelite movement. The paintings he made of Battersea Bridge, together with his portraits of his mother and of Thomas Carlyle, are probably among his most famous works. J.M.W. Turner (1775–1851) ● *102* spent the last ten years of his reclusive life at 118–19 Cheyne Walk, living under the name of Booth. Turner was one of the greatest English landscape painters, and he derived much of the inspiration for his work from the River Thames. He was a precursor of Impressionism. Within the Tate Gallery, the Charles Clore Gallery is entirely devoted to Turner's work ▲ *207*.

THE PRE-RAPHAELITES ▲ *218*. The originators of the Pre-Raphaelite Brotherhood were three Royal Academicians: William Holman Hunt (1827–1910), John Everett Millais (1829–96) and Dante Gabriel Rossetti. Reacting against the academic painting of the period, they affirmed the social and religious duties of art. They were the forerunners of Symbolism, and of naturalism too, for their work is characterized by a precise and minute attention to detail.

18TH-CENTURY ELEGANCE
Many of the houses in Cheyne Walk date from this period, and are first-rate examples of the Georgian style.

CARLYLE SQUARE
Its yellow brick houses ornamented with stucco are typical of the period 1830–40. Charles Dickens found the style ugly, and in his novel *Nicholas Nickleby* (1839) he spoke out against the design of prosperous Belgrave Square houses as well as what he called "the barbaric chaos of Chelsea".

The movement only survived into the 1870's, but its influence on 20th-century Symbolism remained important.

CHELSEA OLD CHURCH. This is Chelsea's old village church. Although it is partly medieval, most of the church was built during the 17th century, and it was again heavily restored following the bombing of 1941. The SIR THOMAS MORE CHAPEL, which was rebuilt by the man himself in 1528, now contains a monument to him. After More's execution, however, his head was buried at Canterbury. Popular legend has it that Henry VIII married his third wife Jane Seymour here in 1536.

CHELSEA AND SIR THOMAS MORE. Before the King's Road ran through Chelsea, its main road was Old Church Street, which was lined with little cottages. Sir Thomas More was Henry VIII's Lord Chancellor ▲ *197, 320*, and also the author of the fantasy *Utopia* and some other philosophical writings. But after Henry's divorce and the consequent rejection of the Catholic church, More felt himself unable to recognize the sovereign as the head of the newly formed Anglican church, and he was accordingly beheaded in the Tower of London. He was beatified in 1886 and then made a saint in 1935. The Irishman Jonathan Swift (1667–1745), author of *Gulliver's Travels*, lived for a time in Old Church Street. The many friends who came to visit him there included John Gay (1688–1732), William Congreve (1670–1729) and Alexander Pope (1688–1744).

CHEYNE ROW ★. The Scottish historian Thomas Carlyle (1795–1881) lived at 24 Cheyne Row for almost fifty years, from 1834 until his death ▲ *112.* His writings, among the most famous of which were the *History of the French Revolution* and a six-volume *Life of Frederick the Great*, were tremendously influential. Carlyle loved the sense of history and the bohemian disorder that he found in Chelsea. His house has now become the Carlyle Museum.

PAULTON'S SQUARE
This attractive Georgian square was built in the 1830's. It faces onto the King's Road near the area known as World's End.

CHEYNE WALK
One of the most attractive streets in London, it has the Thames on the south side and fine 18th-century houses on the north.

RIVERSIDE PUBS
The pubs around Cheyne Walk have carefully preserved their traditional atmosphere. The *King's Arms* at number 114 is still a village inn, likewise the *King's Head and Eight Bells* at number 50.

TITE STREET. The Irish writer Oscar Wilde ● *111* (1854–1900) settled at 3 Tite Street in 1880 and a few years later he moved into a different house in the same street, at number 34. Born in Dublin, Wilde was friends with James Abbott McNeill Whistler ● *104*, the art critic John Ruskin (1842–1900), the French poet Stéphane Mallarmé (1842–98), Sarah Bernhardt (1844–1923) and Mark Twain (1835–1910). Wilde made himself the darling of society thanks to his brilliant wit and his dandified elegance. It was at number 34 that he wrote his only novel, *The Picture of Dorian Gray*, the homosexual implications of which were to cause a scandal when the work appeared in 1890. Four years later its creator caused an even bigger scandal when he was arrested in the Cadogan Hotel, Sloane Street, and charged with having homosexual relations with Lord Alfred Douglas, son of the Marquis of Queensberry. Wilde was found guilty and sentenced to two years' hard labor, which he served at Reading jail; after his release he became an impoverished alcoholic exile in France, where he died. The American painter John Singer Sargent (1856–1925) lived at number 31 from 1885 until his death. In his work he was much influenced by two of his friends, Monet and Whistler. His painting fell into disfavor after his death but he is now recognized as a great portrait artist of the Edwardian era. Finally, two Art Nouveau houses designed by architect E.W. Godwin are well worth a look: number 44, built in 1878 for Wilde's friend the painter Frank Miles; and number 46, built a couple of years later and consisting of four artists' studios one on top of the other.

CHELSEA EMBANKMENT ★. The Embankment was completed in 1874 and runs parallel to Cheyne Walk. It is lined with houseboats and barges that continue to attract the attention of tourists.

Cheyne Walk now overlooks scores of houseboats and converted barges.

THOMAS CARLYLE A statue of the great historian is in the gardens at Cheyne Walk.

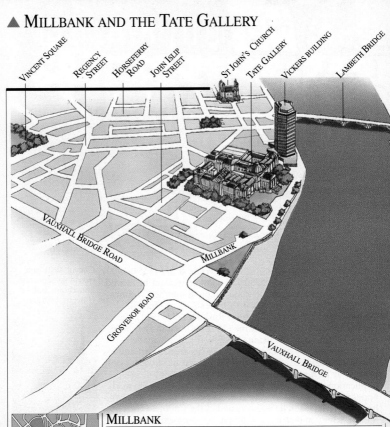

VINCENT SQUARE

REGENCY STREET

HORSEFERRY ROAD

JOHN ISLIP STREET

ST JOHN'S CHURCH

TATE GALLERY

VICKERS BUILDING

LAMBETH BRIDGE

VAUXHALL BRIDGE ROAD

MILLBANK

GROSVENOR ROAD

VAUXHALL BRIDGE

🚶 Half a day

MILLBANK

Until the early 18th century Millbank was an ordinary road that crossed fields full of crops and water meadows linking Westminster and Chelsea. Its name derives from the mill of Westminster Abbey, which stood at the end of what is now Great College Street; this was pulled down by Sir Robert Grosvenor in 1736 so that he could build himself a manor house.

MILLBANK PENITENTIARY. In 1809 the seat of the Grosvenor family was demolished to make way for the Millbank Penitentiary, which was to be London's biggest prison in the 19th century. Liberal thinker Jeremy Bentham's ideas for prison reform were the motivating force behind its construction. He thought the prison should be circular, with the warders in the middle. Prisoners should learn to enjoy work through sharing in the profits of the goods they made

THE PRISON WALLS
Inside the walls was a maze of corridors 3 miles long. It is said there was one warder who had to mark his way with a piece of chalk even after working there for seven years.

(boots and mailbags). In 1794 Bentham persuaded the government to finance the building of a model prison, putting up some of the money for the project himself. The penitentiary was completed in 1821, a star-shaped building with six arms extending over 7 acres of marshland on the bank of the river. Bentham's reforming ideas were never adopted, and in 1843 the penitentiary became an ordinary prison, to be closed in 1890 and demolished soon after. The Tate Gallery was built on the site.

PIMLICO

The district of Pimlico is bounded to the east by Vauxhall Bridge Road, to the west by Chelsea Bridge Road and by Ebury Street in the north.

THE ORIGINS OF THE NAME.
Where the district of Pimlico's name actually comes from remains obscure. Some say it was the name of a drink for which the recipe is lost, others associate it with the Pamlicos, a tribe of North American Indians who exported timber to London during the 17th century. It may alternatively have been the name of a bird that used

to make its home in these parts, or it may have referred to a 16th-century publican called Ben Pimlico. The earliest traces of occupation in the area date from 1626. These were the NEAT HOUSES, some cottages that were built on land belonging to Westminster Abbey. The land where Pimlico now stands was composed mainly of vegetable gardens, willow coppices and untenanted ground that in 1830 belonged to the Grosvenor family. They leased it to Thomas Cubitt (1777–1855), who pursued his policy of developing the area as he had already done successfully in both Bloomsbury and Belgravia.

THOMAS CUBITT. He started his career as a carpenter, before advancing to become a contractor of public works whose influence on urban development in London was probably as profound as that of Christopher Wren ▲ *171–4* and John Nash ▲ *257* before him. He built houses on the Russell lands in Bloomsbury, and then became a property developer in Belgravia. Pimlico always lacked the fashionable cachet of Belgravia: it was respectable, but never really smart. Yet if this district lacks the real elegance of some of Cubitt's other developments, there are still some exceptionally fine terraces of stuccoed houses to be seen here, which he built near the beginning of the 19th century.

ECCLESTON SQUARE. Begun by Thomas Cubitt in 1835, this square is named after one of the duke of Westminster's country properties. Winston Churchill lived at number 33 from 1908 to 1911. The same house was later to become the headquarters of the Workers' Party during the General Strike of 1926.

EBURY STREET. This road crosses some of the most attractive residential streets to be found just south of Belgravia. The

"Vauxhall Gardens, the Grand Walk about 1751"
Canaletto ● 97 painted Vauxhall Gardens, which bordered the opposite bank of the Thames, when they were known as New Spring Gardens. They were opened in 1660: Samuel Pepys ● 40 liked walking here.

eight-year-old composer Amadeus Mozart wrote his first symphony at number 180. Across the road is a fine example of tenement dwellings, which were built in 1871, the Coleshill Flats.

Pimlico Road. This is the area's main shopping street, and there are indeed some first-class antique shops. The small Victorian Gothic church of St Barnabas was built between 1847 and 1850 by Thomas Cundy. St Saviour's is in George Square, a rectangle between Grosvenor Place and Lupus Street. It was built in 1864 to a design submitted by Thomas Cundy the Younger.

Churchill Gardens. This prize-winning housing development for 6,500 people was built by Westminster Council between 1952 and 1960. The architects responsible were A.J.P. Powell and J.H. Moya.

Sir Henry Tate.

The Tate Gallery ★

The Gallery of Modern British Art has become one of the most famous museums in the world under the name of the Tate Gallery. It was opened on Millbank facing the Thames in 1897, in response to a growing demand for a single gallery to represent British painting and sculpture. Up to this time existing major collections, such

A NEO-BAROQUE BUILDING
Sydney Smith designed the museum in a neo-Baroque style: the imposing façade consists of a portico with Corinthian pillars approached by a staircase from the embankment.

as the Chantrey bequest, the Sheepshanks collection, the Vernon collection, and the Turner bequest, were kept in the Victoria and Albert Museum or the National Gallery.

SIR HENRY TATE. The museum is named after a businessman, sugar merchant and art collector, Sir Henry Tate. He gave his private collection of British art to the nation (sixty canvases and three sculptures), and this became the nucleus of the museum's collection. Tate also funded the construction of a building in which to exhibit it.

EARLY DEVELOPMENTS. Another benefactor of the museum, Lord Duveen, financed the building of the wing housing the paintings that Turner bequeathed to the nation, and which up until then had hung in the National Gallery. In 1926 a first extension was built to exhibit the foreign collections, and the museum was enlarged for a third time in 1937, financed by Lord Duveen's son. A fourth extension was started in 1971.

THE CLORE GALLERY. This was designed to hold the enormous collection of Turner's works: three hundred oil paintings and more than nineteen thousand drawings and watercolors which are the pride of the Tate Gallery.

The Tate Gallery is based around three separate collections, the quality of which has won the museum an enormous worldwide reputation. Housed here is the largest collection of English painting from the 16th century to the present day (Historic British); there is also the largest collection of 20th-century painting since the Impressionists (Modern Collection); and last of all an important collection of recent works of art (Contemporary Collection). If the first collection is relatively stable, the other two are regularly increased by new acquisitions.

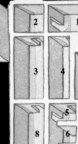

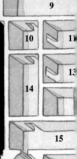

"POMPEII"
Hans Hofmann (1880–1966). This German painter who lived in the USA from 1931 founded a school of art in New York in 1933. Until 1940 his work remained figurative in the Expressionist tradition. Then he developed an abstract style, represented by this canvas of 1959.

Each year, on January 1, the names of the rooms as well as their contents are changed. Below is the layout as it stood in 1993.

1. Tudor and Stuart painting
2. A Decade of Growth: London and the Arts in the 1740's
3. The Group Portrait in the Later 18th Century
4. Robert Vernon's

Gift: British Art for the Nation 1847
5. Robert Vernon's Gift: British Art for the Nation 1847
6. Robert Vernon's Gift: British Art for the Nation 1847
7. William Blake and Landscape
8. Constable and Early 19th-Century Landscape Painting
9. The Pre-Raphaelites and Symbolists

"SELF-PORTRAIT" (1797)
Joseph Mallord William Turner.

"FAA IHEIHE"
The Tahitian title of this work has been translated as "Pastoral Symphony"; it was painted by Gauguin (1848–1...) during his last sta... Tahiti. It portrays... vision of Paradise... hymn to the harm... existing between... and nature, and v... painted after a pe... of profound crea... pessimism. It is o... the landmarks in... collection of mod... European and American art from... Impressionism to... new avant-garde... the 1970's which... Tate Gallery bega... assemble between... 1910 and 1920.

TURNER AND THE CLORE GALLERY
Since 1987 the Tate Gallery's east wing has housed the prestigious Turner collection. It was designed by James Stirling.

"THE FORGE"
Joseph Wright (1734–97), known as "Wright of Derby", started out as a painter of the Industrial Revolution in the Midlands. In a uniquely recognizable style influenced by Caravaggio, Wright combined realism with sentiment, and made much use of the effects of light.

"THE ARTIST AND HIS DOG"
This self-portrait of 1745 by William Hogarth (1697–1764) is resting on works of Shakespeare, Swift and Milton: from now on, painting took its place beside literature as a noble art form. X-ray examination reveals that Hogarth originally painted himself dressed like a gentleman.

IN MY BEST ROOM IS A CHOICE COLLECTION OF THE WORKS OF
HOGARTH, AN ENGLISH PAINTER OF SOME HUMOR."

CHARLES LAMB

"CAPTAIN THOMAS LEE"

Captain Lee, officer of the County of Essex, took part in the conquest of Ireland. Estimating that he lacked the means to continue the war, he returned to England in 1594 to plead his cause before Queen Elizabeth I, and had his portrait painted by Marcus Gheeraerts the Younger (c. 1561–1636). Lee is richly dressed, but has bare feet like a poor soldier. He is standing in an Irish landscape under an oak tree, symbol of courage. He was executed at Tyburn for his part in the conspiracy of 1601.

"THE SALTONSTALL FAMILY"

This painting by David des Granges (1611–75) is a fine example of 17th-century family portraiture. At first glance it seems to be simple enough: a husband congratulating his wife who has just borne him a third child. In fact, as was often the case during the Elizabethan era, the living and the dead are painted together. Saltonstall is depicted here with his two wives: his deceased first wife holds out her hand toward her two children. His second wife is holding her new baby.

"THREE DAUGHTERS OF SIR WILLIAM MONTGOMERY AS GRACES ADORNING A STATUE OF HYMEN"

Joshua Reynolds (1723–92), first president of the Royal Academy, elevated relatively unimportant genres of painting, especially the portrait, by introducing elements of Grand Genre. His painting of the three sisters (1773) bears witness to his efforts. At the request of the gentleman who commissioned the painting, Reynolds incorporated symbolic features derived from classical antiquity and the Old Masters. The sisters are seen raising the god of marriage in poses used by Poussin and Rubens. To the right of Elisabeth is Anne, dressed in white and already married; on the left is Barbara, who married the following year.

"THE HARVESTERS"

The self-taught painter George Stubbs (1724–1806) became during his lifetime the most famous animal painter in England, working for the aristocracy and adapting the grand style to his pictures of animals. Above all, he was famous for painting horses; but he also produced some delightful scenes of English country life. In an age when peasants were held to have a merely decorative value in paintings, Stubbs shows them in a more sympathetic light, making them real personalities. This painting (1785) is nevertheless composed in a severely classical style. A girl is in the center, while a horseman on the right balances a couple binding corn. Men bent at their work link the two groups.

"GIOVANNA BACCELLI"

Thomas Gainsborough (1727–88) is unusual in that he never left England, having arrived in London fairly late in life, in 1774. It was there that the duke of Dorset, who was also the ambassador to Paris, commissioned Gainsborough to paint a portrait of his mistress Giovanna Baccelli, the prima ballerina at the Haymarket Theatre. She had started her career at the Opéra in Paris, and is depicted executing a dance step. Here the artist's technical mastery and his feeling for line result in a composition where exceptional grace and lightness combines with fresh colors to produce a portrait of great subtlety and beauty. The picture was exhibited at the Royal Academy in 1782.

"BEATRICE ADDRESSING DANTE FROM THE CAR" William Blake (1757–1827) believed himself entrusted with the mission of preserving the Divine Vision in a troubled age. This watercolor, painted between 1824 and 1827, is from a series of a hundred illustrations to Dante's *Divine Comedy*. It represents a scene from the *Purgatorio*, describing Dante's first sight of Beatrice.

"THE BLIND FIDDLER" David Wilkie (1785–1841) was a Scottish artist who enjoyed an immense success in England during the early 19th century. Early in his career he painted scenes of rustic life that were derived from Dutch and Flemish models. His influence later extended all over Europe.

"THE OPENING OF WATERLOO BRIDGE". In this scene depicting the opening of the bridge on June 18, 1817, the English painter John Constable (1776–1837) makes a direct reference to one of Canaletto's paintings as a symbol of England's superiority over other nations.

THE BRIDGE OF SIGHS, THE DUCAL PALACE AND THE CUSTOM-HOUSE, CANALETTI PAINTING". When Joseph Mallord William Turner (1775–1851) visited Venice for a second time in 1832, he became obsessed with painting the city. This bold, sunlit canvas was in homage to Canaletto, the great Venetian painter; and there is also an underlying desire on Turner's part to make himself part of the great artistic tradition

"THE DOGANO, SAN GIORGIO, CITELLA, SEEN FROM THE STEPS OF THE EUROPA" Painted in 1842 after his third visit to Venice, this returns to Turner's more subdued range of colors, a testament to his emotions at the collapse of the great republic.

"PETWORTH, SUNSET IN THE PARK". Turner had a studio at Petworth, the country seat of his friend and patron Lord Egremont. This watercolor dates from around 1830, and is one of more than a hundred that he painted there.

"SNOWSTORM –
STEAMBOAT OFF A
HARBOR'S MOUTH
MAKING SIGNALS IN
SHALLOW WATER AND
GOING BY THE LEAD.
THE AUTHOR WAS IN

THIS STORM ON THE
NIGHT THE ARIEL
LEFT HARWICH."
Snowstorms and
storms at sea are
recurrent themes in
Turner's work. This

picture, where the
tempest's power is
centered on the frail
mast at the heart of a
whirling mass of
paint, was exhibited
in 1842, after the

artist had spent four
hours lashed to the
mast of a boat
crossing from
Harwich in such a
storm that he did not
expect to survive.

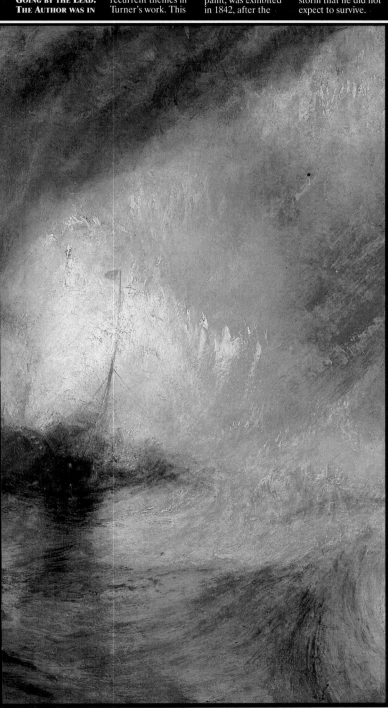

"BEATE BEATRICE"
Dante Gabriel Rossetti (1828–82) was, together with Hunt and Millais, a founder of the Pre-Raphaelite Brotherhood. Their principal aim was to paint only serious subjects, and to portray them with the utmost realism. The title of this work, painted in 1863, refers to the death of Dante's beloved Beatrice. Rather than paint a corpse, Rossetti chose to treat his subject symbolically, undergoing a spiritual transfiguration. The painting is in homage to the artist's wife, Elizabeth Siddal, who died from a drug overdose in February 1862, and he used her face for the figure of Beatrice.

"THE AWAKENING CONSCIENCE"
The young mistress of a wealthy man remembers the innocent days of her childhood and turns toward the light from the garden, reflected in a mirror. Holman Hunt (1827–1910) uses the effects of light and the room's decoration to reflect the state of mind of the young woman.

"THE GOLDEN STAIRS"
Edward Burne-Jo (1833–98) belong to the late Pre-Raphaelite period. He was influenced by Rossetti and then by the Italian Old Masters. The sinu curved lines in th painting of 1880 a characteristic features of the artist's later work

"OPHELIA"
The inspiration for this picture by John Everett Millais (1829–96) comes from th death of Ophelia described in Act IV of *Hamlet*. The background was painted between July and October 1851 during a visit to the village of Ewell in Surrey. Back in London that winter, the artist used Rossetti's wife Elizabeth Siddal as model, as did many other Pre-Raphaelit The detailed vegetation in the picture includes plants and wild flowers with particular symbolic significance: the poppy, for example, is a symbol of death

"MR AND MRS CLARK AND PERCY"
David Hockney (b. 1937) studied at the Royal College of Art from 1959, and then exhibited at the Whitechapel Art Gallery. His early work reflects the influence of Francis Bacon and of Jean Dubuffet. After a period of abstract painting Hockney evolved a naturalistic approach from 1965. The subjects in this picture, painted between 1970 and 1971, are the famous dress designers of the period Ossie Clark and Celia Birtwell.

"WHAAM!"
The American master of Pop Art Roy Lichtenstein (b. 1923) painted many pictures in the early 1960's that were inspired by strip cartoons. This one, dating from 1963, exemplifies his use of bright colors and exaggerated shapes that tend toward abstraction.

"LIGHT RED OVER BLACK"
An American painter of Russian origin, Mark Rothko (1903–70) was initially influenced by the Surrealists. In the 1950's he evolved an original style of his own, using rectangular bands of color. Up to the middle of the decade his palette was mainly bright, but it gradually darkened, dominated by black or dark red on a brown background (left, a work of 1957).

"Three Studies for Figures at the Base of a Crucifixion" Francis Bacon (1909–92) exhibited these three studies in 1945 after a period of eight years of silence. They show the influence of Picasso's work in the 1920's; the figures have become the Eumenides, the Furies who pursue Orestes in the *Oresteia* of Aeschylus. The zoomorphic shapes have shrieking human mouths, an obsessive image in Bacon's work.

"Weeping Woman" On April 26, 1937, during the Spanish Civil War, German aeroplanes bombed Guernica. Pablo Picasso (1881–1973) began his famous painting *Guernica*, in which a weeping woman carries a dead child in her arms, two days later. Picasso took up the theme again in June 1937, making three sketches and painting four canvases, of which this is the last of the series. His model was the photographer Dora Maar, who was also his mistress.

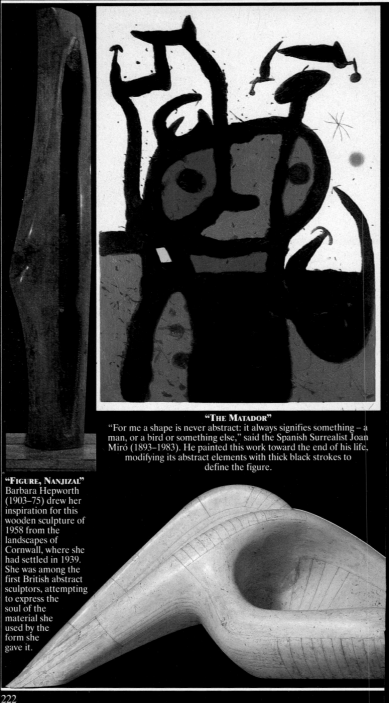

"THE MATADOR"
"For me a shape is never abstract: it always signifies something – a man, or a bird or something else," said the Spanish Surrealist Joan Miró (1893–1983). He painted this work toward the end of his life, modifying its abstract elements with thick black strokes to define the figure.

"FIGURE, NANJIZAL"
Barbara Hepworth (1903–75) drew her inspiration for this wooden sculpture of 1958 from the landscapes of Cornwall, where she had settled in 1939. She was among the first British abstract sculptors, attempting to express the soul of the material she used by the form she gave it.

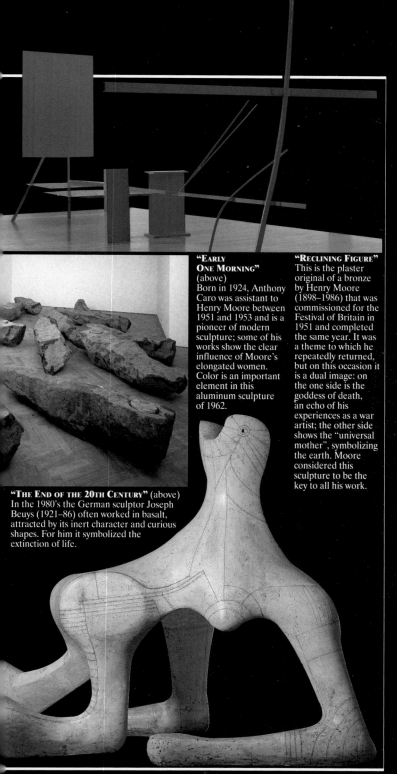

"EARLY ONE MORNING" (above)
Born in 1924, Anthony Caro was assistant to Henry Moore between 1951 and 1953 and is a pioneer of modern sculpture; some of his works show the clear influence of Moore's elongated women. Color is an important element in this aluminum sculpture of 1962.

"RECLINING FIGURE"
This is the plaster original of a bronze by Henry Moore (1898–1986) that was commissioned for the Festival of Britain in 1951 and completed the same year. It was a theme to which he repeatedly returned, but on this occasion it is a dual image: on the one side is the goddess of death, an echo of his experiences as a war artist; the other side shows the "universal mother", symbolizing the earth. Moore considered this sculpture to be the key to all his work.

"THE END OF THE 20TH CENTURY" (above)
In the 1980's the German sculptor Joseph Beuys (1921–86) often worked in basalt, attracted by its inert character and curious shapes. For him it symbolized the extinction of life.

223

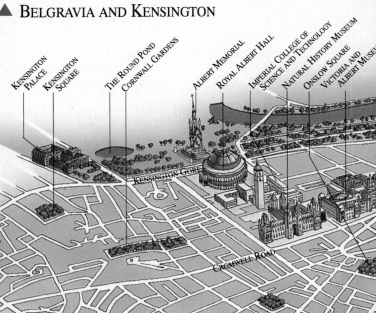

KENSINGTON PALACE   KENSINGTON SQUARE   THE ROUND POND   CORNWALL GARDENS   ALBERT MEMORIAL   ROYAL ALBERT HALL   IMPERIAL COLLEGE OF SCIENCE AND TECHNOLOGY   NATURAL HISTORY MUSEUM   ONSLOW SQUARE   VICTORIA AND ALBERT MUSEUM

KENSINGTON GORE

CROMWELL ROAD

FULHAM ROAD

✶   One day

THE VICTORIAN TERRACE
Painted stucco below yellow London brick is typical of Belgravia's Victorian terraces and also of those in Islington. Islington terraces often have arched front windows with stucco surrounds.

BELGRAVIA

The fashionable district of
Belgravia was once a stretch of
land known as "Five Fields". It was a
notorious haunt of robbers right up to
the time that development started, with the
first houses being built in Grosvenor Place in
1747. When George III acquired Buckingham House
(now Buckingham Palace) in 1762, the area's future was
assured, although large-scale development only began in the
1820's when Lord Grosvenor engaged the builder and town
planner Thomas Cubitt (1777–1855) to help him increase
the value of his property. Cubitt, who had excavated St
Katharine's Dock ▲ *334* near the Tower of London, used
the earth and rubble from the excavations to raise the level
of the marshy land of Belgravia. Then he laid out squares
and terraces lined with large elegant houses. The finest of
all is BELGRAVE SQUARE, the work of

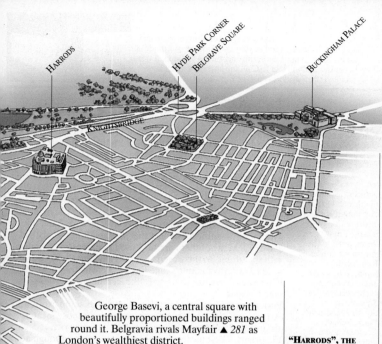

George Basevi, a central square with
beautifully proportioned buildings ranged
round it. Belgravia rivals Mayfair ▲ *281* as
London's wealthiest district.

KNIGHTSBRIDGE

"HARRODS". This enormous store in the
Brompton Road is not exactly in
Belgravia, but in the
neighboring district of
Knightsbridge. In 1849
Henry Charles Harrod
opened a small grocer's shop
in Knightsbridge. The family
business did so well that most of the
present building was constructed
between 1894 and 1903. The store was
completed in 1939. The russet-colored
frontage looks at its best as night falls,
when its outlines are
illuminated by
thousands of light-bulbs.

**"HARRODS", THE
MEAT HALL**
Shoppers at *Harrods*
find it interesting for
two reasons. Firstly,
its interior
decoration, which
alone makes it worth
a visit. The food halls
are magnificent (the
meat hall has ceramic
tiles in Art Nouveau
style decorated with
hunting scenes, the
work of W.J. Neatby).
The second reason is
the store's amazing
variety of stock,
which is all of the
highest quality.

KENSINGTON

Until the 17th century Kensington was
a village located on the outskirts of
London. Then King William III bought
Nottingham House, Kensington, in 1689
and commissioned Christopher Wren
● *70,* ▲ *171, 250, 353* to turn it into a
royal residence, to be known as
Kensington Palace ▲ *250.* Nottingham
House and Holland House between
them transformed Kensington into a
much sought-after residential district.

KENSINGTON SQUARES. Kensington Square was the first of the
district's distinctive squares to be built (Thomas Young,
1681). It was originally named King's Square in honor of
James II, and until 1840 it remained entirely surrounded by

KENSINGTON AND QUEEN VICTORIA

When Queen Victoria died in 1901, Kensington was made a royal borough in her honor, the only one in London. Later this was extended to include Chelsea, and the district is now called the Royal Borough of Kensington and Chelsea.

KENSINGTON HOUSES
Queen Victoria was born in Kensington Palace and spent the first eighteen years of her life living there, until she ascended the throne in 1837. Her long reign was also a period of intense urban development. The enormous houses of Kensington were replaced by squares and crescents ● *76* such as Edwardes Square, Trevor Square, Montpelier Place, Pelham Crescent and many more.

fields. The population of London had doubled by the first half of the 19th century, and Kensington expanded along with it. ONSLOW GARDENS and ONSLOW SQUARE are both in typical early Victorian style. They were built around 1846 by Charles James Freake. Their name comes from the then owner of the land, the earl of Onslow. The elegant houses in Onslow Square are covered in white stucco. Hereford Square is also a typically Victorian design, a peaceful little place that was built in 1847 by Edward Blore. The residential district of Kensington extends behind either side of the busy Kensington High Street. Kensington Palace Gardens (1843) is a long private road bordering Kensington Gardens ▲ *247* and lined with many magnificent houses that were built between 1844 and 1870. Many of them are now used as embassies. Parallel with this street, to the west, is Kensington Church Street, which was once a country lane linking Kensington to Notting Hill Gate. There are some fine 18th-century properties to be seen along it.

FINE FAMILIES AND FINE ART. Kensington has some exotic and extravagant 19th-century houses, particularly those located around Holland Park, which were built by newly rich Victorians. Their owners bought many pictures – though not usually with much discernment. The artist Frederick Leighton (1830–96) was so successful that he made a fortune and built himself a studio-house at 12 Holland Park Road, called LEIGHTON HOUSE. This palatial dwelling includes an Arab Hall (1879) that gives a good idea of the 19th-century taste for exotica. Like the rest of the house, the hall was the work of George Aitchison, and it is an ingenious blend of all kinds of decorative elements, but pays little heed to their artistic quality. The other rooms are hung with a number of pictures by Lord Leighton and his friends. Nearby, at 29 Melbury Road, is TOWER HOUSE. This is a strange medieval-style house that was constructed by the architect William Burges between 1876 and 1881.

SOUTH KENSINGTON

In Queen's Gate (formerly Albert's Road) the houses were built in an Italianate style in the latter part of the 19th century. Some of these have been converted into flats or hotels, and though many more have since disappeared, the street retains a genteel late Victorian air.

To the south of Kensington Village is the residential district of South Kensington, an area that is notable for some interesting mews streets. These were formerly alleys consisting of stables and coach houses which were located behind the streets. These alleyways have now become delightful cobbled lanes, and the stables have been converted into some charming town cottages. The Great Exhibition of 1851 set in motion the building of museums and colleges in this district, projects that were initiated by Prince Albert: the ALBERT MEMORIAL and the ROYAL ALBERT HALL were both built in his memory. Taking a walk down Cromwell Road, with its imposing porticoed houses, or down into "South Ken", the visitor can hardly fail to notice the French flavor of the area. This is hardly surprising since located here are the French Lycée, the French Institute, the French Consulate and the cultural department of the French Embassy. Around these institutions have sprung up several French bakers, patisseries, butchers and bookshops to cater for the substantial expatriate population living here.

Around the beginning of the 20th century the middle classes began to reject the showy opulence of their houses in favor of comfort. Interior décor quietened down, and they evolved the neo-Georgian style in imitation of the old Georgian. And as fewer families had servants, gradually the houses were broken up into flats. It became a familiar sight to see a front

door with fifteen bells on it, where formerly there had been only one.

❝Before reaching Knightsbridge, Mr Verloc took a turn to the left out of the busy main thoroughfare, uproarious with the traffic of swaying omnibuses ... and ... marched now along a street which could with every propriety be described as private. ... The only reminder of mortality was a doctor's brougham arrested in august solitude close to the curbstone. The polished knockers of the doors gleamed as far as the eye could reach, the clean windows shone with a dark opaque lustre. And all was still.❞

Joseph Conrad,
The Secret Agent

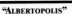

"ALBERTOPOLIS"
This aerial view shows
the Royal
Geographical Society,
Albert Hall Mansions,
the Royal Albert Hall
and, in the
foreground, the
Albert Memorial.

MUSEUM LAND

The southern part of Kensington, between
Chelsea and Kensington Gardens, might be
seen as a separate center of learning devoted to
the study or appreciation of science and the arts.
In this one relatively small area is a concentrated
group of museums, colleges and learned societies
that is quite unique in London. The area is
sometimes known as "Albertopolis", a symbol of the
19th-century middle-class reverence for learning and
a general thirst for knowledge. And no-one was
more active in this movement for self-improvement
than Prince Albert, the husband of Queen
Victoria.

THE HIGH POINT OF THE VICTORIAN ERA. The first
Great Exhibition ▲ *38* in London was held in 1851.
It was considered a huge success, the apogee of
Victoria's reign, and attracted some six million
visitors. The vast Crystal Palace, built in Hyde Park
by Joseph Paxton to house the exhibition, drew the
attention of the government and of Prince Albert to
the need for a cultural center in the west of London,
an area which was then expanding rapidly. From 1856
onwards, museums and teaching institutions for
science and the arts began to spring up in an area
north of the Cromwell Road, the thoroughfare opened
up in 1855 in imitation of Louis-Napoleon's new Paris
boulevards.

PRINCE ALBERT. For long confined to the role of a royal
figurehead, the German prince Albert (left) devoted
himself to the education of his and Victoria's nine
children. This then developed into an obsession with
educating the British nation, scientifically and

culturally. He was determined that the people should have specialized schools, colleges and museums. His friend Sir Henry Cole shared this view and and helped him to organize the new South Kensington developments. A collection of artifacts purchased during the Great Exhibition was put on display at MARLBOROUGH HOUSE, and this was such a huge success that the two of them decided to add to it and build a museum especially to house it. From 1852 to 1856 a museum of arts and sciences was moved from one temporary location to another, but it was only in 1859 that the home for the collection was finally built, providing the germ of what would subsequently become the Victoria and Albert Museum. Oddly enough, Prince Albert's premature death in 1861 had the effect of hastening the realization of this enormous project.

THE MUSEUMS. Two monuments were erected to the memory of the prince consort: the Albert Memorial (1863–72) and the Royal Albert Hall (1867–71). Less ostentatious, though of incalculable value, were the museums, colleges and institutes that opened, creating a form of living encyclopedia of science and art. This has never stopped growing: from 1873 up to the present such institutions as the NATURAL HISTORY MUSEUM, the ROYAL GEOGRAPHICAL SOCIETY, the ROYAL COLLEGE OF ORGANISTS, the ROYAL COLLEGE OF MUSIC, the GEOLOGICAL MUSEUM and the SCIENCE MUSEUM have opened here. Most recently, the IMPERIAL COLLEGE OF SCIENCE AND TECHNOLOGY and the ROYAL COLLEGE OF ART have rounded off this extraordinary area of learning. The museums are astonishing.

THE VICTORIA AND ALBERT MUSEUM ★

The masterpiece of Museum land. It opened in 1852 as the Museum of Manufactures, to become the South Kensington Museum in 1859; and finally in 1899 the Victoria and Albert Museum.

FIFTY YEARS OF CONSTRUCTION. This extraordinary building is the result of no fewer than six quite unrelated architectural designs, successively assembled by Francis Fowke, and after his death in 1866 by Henry Young Darracott Scott and Aston Webb ▲ 243. The result is something of a muddle, with decoration only on certain parts of the edifice. In a rather haphazard way it is centered round a rectangular courtyard, the QUADRANGLE, inspired by the Italian Renaissance. The oldest wing is the one lying to the east of the Quadrangle, built between 1856 and 1858 to house the collection of English painting donated by a rich Yorkshire industrialist, John Sheepshanks; its façade is rather later, dating from 1901. The west wing was designed by Geoffrey Sykes and his assistants in 1864, and set the style that was used for the rest of the museum (and for many other buildings in Museum land as well), i.e. brick with terracotta and mosaic decoration. The north building was constructed (1856–9) as the museum's main entrance. Between 1877 and 1884 the Quadrangle was closed to the south by a wing holding the National Art Library. Last of all, the main façade was added by Aston Webb between 1899 and 1909. The decoration on the great bronze doors is a reminder that the "V & A" is devoted to science as well as the arts.

"CHRIST'S CHARGE TO PETER"
For this design, Raphael (1483–1520) drew on the Gospel according to St John. Peter is depicted receiving the keys, on his knees before Christ. The cartoon underlines the primacy of St Peter, and by extension affirms the supremacy of the pope.

"FLATFORD MILL"
Together with Turner, John Constable (1776–1837) is one of the greatest English landscape painters. The artist's "light and shade of nature" is everywhere in the painting, which also shows his fascination with painting the sky.

AN ELIZABETHAN MEDALLION
This miniature of a courtier was painted by Nicholas Hilliard (c. 1547–1619).

A MUSEUM OF FINE ARTS AND THE APPLIED ARTS. The museum is an extraordinary assembly of collections taken from all over the world. There are no fewer than 145 rooms: to see them all would represent a walk of more than 5 miles! Three rooms in particular encapsulate Victorian taste: the "Green Dining Room" decorated by William Morris; the Gamble Room or central dining room, which is covered in ceramic tiles; and the Grill Room, decorated by Edward Poynter. Finally the visitor should make a point of seeing the ceramic staircase, completed in 1871 by students to the designs of F.W. Moody.

THE MUSEUM'S COLLECTIONS

THE RAPHAEL CARTOONS ★. These are the most important large-scale works of Renaissance art in the whole of England. In 1623 the future Charles I, then in Genoa, bought seven of ten cartoons by Raphael (the remaining three have never been found), depicting scenes from the lives of St Peter and St Paul. They were designs for tapestries originally commissioned by Pope Leo X to decorate the Sistine Chapel on special feast days. From Rome the cartoons went to Brussels, where they were cut into strips and copied in the workshops employed to fulfil the commission. When Charles bought them, he sent them to one of the great English tapestry-makers at Mortlake that had recently been founded by Charles' father, James I. Centuries later the reassembled cartoons were loaned by Queen Victoria to the V & A. Since tapestries are woven from the back, the cartoons are really mirror images of the intended effect and so should be read from right to left. They are shown in chronological order, beginning with *The Miraculous Draft of Fishes*. The same room has a tapestry woven at Mortlake to this design.

THE INDIAN COLLECTIONS ★. The presence of these artifacts in the V & A is the result of the demolition in 1956 of the Indian Museum that was situated on the other side of Exhibition Road. From the end of the 18th century India became the object of serious study by a number of British

> "It was worthwhile to come here, if only to see Raphael's cartoon in pencil of . . . Julius II. It has all the immense power of . . . the oil painting, and . . . verifies Mr Power's assertion, that colour is not needful to expression."
>
> Sophia Hawthorne

"St Paul Preaching at Athens"
This cartoon was executed for the *Acts of the Apostles*; Raphael shows St Paul preaching the Word of God.

"The River Goddess Yamuna"
The V & A has Indian sculptures dating from 2000 BC up to the 19th century AD, depicting such figures as gods of the earth and nature, and scenes from the life of Buddha. Below: a Hindu sculpture from central India, c. 900 AD.

scholars. In 1801 the East India Company opened a private museum in London in order to display antiquities, curios and historical souvenirs that were sent home by the company's employees working out there. When the company was dissolved in 1858, following the Indian Mutiny, the sub-continent came directly under the control of the crown, and the collection was then moved to the India Office. Public interest in Indian art and civilization, which had already been aroused by the Great Exhibition of 1851, now grew even more rapidly. The South Kensington Museum received the main body of the India Office collection in 1880, and it was greatly expanded during the second half of the 19th century with pieces that were brought back by British manufacturers to copy and sell over here, undercutting the Indian market. An exploration of the collections on display gives the visitor an excellent overview of religious, ceremonial and domestic life in India, and demonstrates what can be learned from the study of other civilizations.

The English collections ★. The V & A is the only museum to offer the visitor a survey of five centuries of British art. There are two different categories in which to trace the history of British art over this period: decorative arts and painting. Two decorative artists who each embody important movements are well represented here: Robert Adam ▲ *256*, who was one of the initiators of neo-classicism, and William Morris, who originated the Arts and Crafts movement. Both these men wanted to create a style that was modern (one in the late 18th century, and one in the late 19th century) and at

"Prince on Horseback"
Gouache on paper; Moghul art, c. 1720.

"The Tippoo Tiger"
Made in 1790 for the sultan Tippoo Sahib, this tiger devouring an Englishman has a mechanism that emits groans and roars. The sultan had recently been defeated by the English at the siege of Seringapatam.

The V & A has costume collections too. Above is an evening gown made by the Callot sisters around 1922.

THE SCULPTURE GALLERY
This displays European sculpture from the 15th to the 19th centuries.

THE CAST ROOM
This houses casts of sculptures and bas-reliefs. Opposite: a cast of the Roman emperor Trajan's column.

the same time to reinvent a historical style, both were bold experimenters, using new industrial techniques and at the same time placing great importance on traditional methods. The V & A was partially conceived as a museum of industrial and artisanal design, which included the responsibility for inspiring contemporary British artists and decorators, as well as educating the common man: a look round the exhibition galleries will make this intention quite apparent. Last of all, English painters are very well represented thanks to numerous legacies and donations made between 1857 and 1908. Works donated by the textile magnate John Sheepshanks include two remarkable collections: there are a total of 233 oil paintings by such masters as Mulready, Landseer, Etty, Turner, Gainsborough and Reynolds; and there is also Sheepshanks' huge collection of watercolors, to which have been added some Pre-Raphaelite paintings and early 20th-century pictures. The most important collection of paintings by Constable is also on display in the V & A: no fewer than 95 canvases and 297 drawings and watercolors were the gifts of his daughter Isabel, of Sheepshanks and of Henry Vaughan. The latter left *The Hay Wain* and *The Jumping Horse* to the museum. Constable is now regarded as the leader of the English landscape school.

THE MINIATURES ★. The V & A has the most important collection of English miniatures, allowing the visitor to follow the development of an art form that began with Hans Holbein the Younger and Nicholas Hilliard, and continued up to the early Victorian age.

THE JONES COLLECTION ★. The Jones Collection has works in several different departments. John Jones (1799–1882) was actually a military tailor who bequeathed to the museum a collection that he started around 1850, when he retired from business. This was predominantly composed of works of French decorative art from the time of Louis XIV to Louis XVI. Jones was one of those collectors who was shrewd enough to take advantage of the sale and dispersal of the

contents of châteaux and other noble houses after the French Revolution, and he acquired some first-class pieces in this way. All of this material bears witness to the taste and the bargaining skill of a quite exceptional Victorian collector. Jones managed to acquire a collection of 18th-century French furniture, with works signed by André-Charles Boulle (1642–1732) and Martin Carlin, as well as some English pieces, such as this cabinet designed by Crosse and built in the workshops of Wright & Mansfield in London for the Paris Exhibition of

1867 (below right). The latter pieces bear witness to the limits of Jones' knowledge, for he bought them as 18th-century work when in fact they were from the 19th century. He also had a fine porcelain collection, chiefly of Sèvres but also with a few rare specimens of Vincennes and Chelsea. His collection of miniatures was a particularly important bequest, both for its quantity (more than 160 pieces, including an interesting selection by the 17th-century artist Jean Petitot) and its diversity: the earliest examples are Renaissance. Jones also collected French sculpture of the 18th century, such as Houdon's bust of *Voltaire*, a *Cupid and Psyche* by Clodion, and *Perronet* by Pigalle; as well as contemporary English sculpture such as John Gibson's *Grazzia Puella Capuensis*. Last of all, paintings, watercolors and drawings are all well represented in this collection: there are French works (Boucher, Lancret, Pater, de Troy) hanging side by side with paintings by Guardi and Jones' English contemporaries (Turner, Mulready, Etty, Frith and Landseer), painters whose charms were also working their magic on Sheepshanks at the time. The appeal of the Jones rooms has been enhanced by the restoration of certain pieces, such as the boudoir of Mme de Serilly, a music desk and table decorated with Sèvres porcelain that once belonged to Marie-Antoinette, and the Italian Oval Salon.

THE WORLD OF SCIENCE

THE NATURAL HISTORY MUSEUM ★ ● 82. In 1860 it was decided to move the natural history department of the British Museum to a base in South Kensington. Most of its contents had been collected by the physician Sir Hans Sloane (1660–1753) ▲ *200, 301,*

THE DINOSAUR GALLERY ★

The Natural History Museum was built with exceptional symmetry. The huge central hall displays dinosaur skeletons. It resembles the nave of a vast cathedral, vaulted in glass and metal and decorated with terracotta panels.

POST-WAR RESTORATION

Several of the museum's galleries were destroyed by enemy action in World War Two. They were rebuilt in the late 1950's and early 1960's; a new wing housing laboratories was added on the Exhibition Road side between 1971 and 1975.

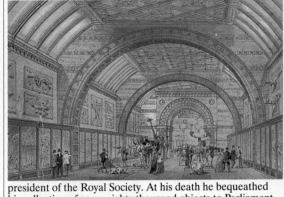

president of the Royal Society. At his death he bequeathed his collection of some eighty thousand objects to Parliament in exchange for a suitable pension for his daughters. From then until the middle of the 19th century, the collection was repeatedly enlarged by numerous donations, and in particular by those of Captain Cook. In 1866 the commission to design a new museum was awarded to Alfred Waterhouse. Construction began six years later, and the first departments were duly opened in 1881. The interior layout was the work of the museum's first director, the zoologist Richard Owen. It was decided to divide the layout of the museum into five sections: Paleontology, Zoology, Entomology, Botany and Mineralogy. The west and east halls were devoted to birds, fossils and geology. In 1990 the east gallery was rearranged in order to accommodate a new Ecology section. The Natural History Museum now operates as both a museum and a research center, and it is endowed with a magnificent library.

THE SCIENCE MUSEUM. The collections assembled since 1852, greatly enlarged by those of Woodcroft (who donated the

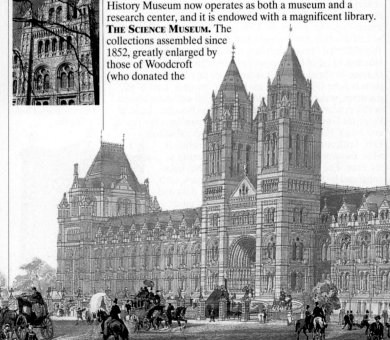

"Puffing Billy", one of the first steam locomotives, built in 1813) and Maudsley (who presented a great number of machine tools and marine engines), were installed in the present building, begun in 1913 by Allison and finally completed in 1977. The five floors are laid out along an instructive route displaying instruments and models (some of them working), to give a general survey of discoveries and inventions that assured Britain's industrial and scientific pre-eminence from the late 18th century onwards. Here too are the great inventions of the 20th century from all over the world, with displays of their use and applications.

THE GEOLOGICAL MUSEUM. This museum goes back to 1835, when it was housed in Craig's Court, Whitehall. It has been in its present home only since 1933. It connects to the Science Museum by means of a covered passageway. Originally it was devoted to British minerals and geology. Mining and oil prospecting in the North Sea are thoroughly explained. The museum has about one million mineral specimens, including fossils and precious stones.

THE IMPERIAL COLLEGE OF SCIENCE AND TECHNOLOGY. The present Imperial College dates back to 1953, when it decided to double its intake of students. Until then it was three separate institutions, including the Royal College of Chemistry (founded in 1845 by Prince Albert). The changes in 1953 involved demolishing old buildings such as the Imperial Institute: only the central tower, a Victorian mock-Renaissance building, was left. Imperial College has several engineering departments, and is one of the most famous colleges in the world.

THE ROYAL ALBERT HALL ★ ● *83*

The idea of building a cultural center and concert hall on the site of Gore House was first mooted in 1853, but it was not until just after Prince

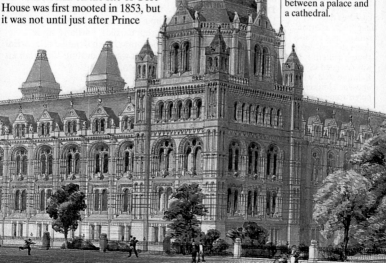

THE AUDITORIUM
The Albert Hall can seat eight thousand people. It is not in fact circular but oval, topped with a glass and iron cupola 135 feet high.

THE ALBERT MEMORIAL
It took twelve years, from 1861 to 1872, to complete this extraordinary monument from which a 14-foot statue of Albert contemplates the hall that was named after him. The design of George Gilbert Scott was the personal choice of Queen Victoria.

BROMPTON ORATORY
This picture by Herbert Gribble (1847–94) perfectly captures the impressive character, with all its excessive decoration, of the church's interior. It was designed in Baroque style, with unusual additions of polychrome marble.

Albert's death that the plan finally came to life. Prince Albert's friend, Sir Henry Cole, who initiated the project, also came up with the idea of selling 999-year leases on the seats to help finance the construction. The architect Henry Darracott Scott was responsible for the final building, which has rather unkindly been likened to the lid of a Wedgwood soup tureen. Queen Victoria laid the building's foundation stone in 1867, and the hall was opened on March 29, 1871, in the presence of the Prince of Wales. The exterior is predominantly of red brick, and the façade is relieved by a terracotta frieze which illustrates the theme of the Triumph of Arts and Letters. Just about every one of the world's great conductors has performed here at some point in his or her career, but the hall's popularity soared to even greater heights after 1941. Until then, the famous London "Proms" (the Henry Wood Promenade Concerts, begun in 1895), an annual summer season of music that combines popular symphony concerts with a broad range of other less fashionable works, were held in Queen's Hall. This was bombed by the Germans in 1941, and the Proms were then transferred to the Royal Albert Hall, where they have continued to take place during an eight-week season starting in July each year.

THE ROYAL GEOGRAPHICAL SOCIETY.
Founded in 1830, the society moved to LOWTHER LODGE in 1913. This is a large house built between 1873 and 1875 by Norman Shaw. It organized and financed a number of major expeditions, such as those of Livingstone to Africa and of Captain Scott to the South Pole. The society's library contains 130,000 books, to which the 7,500 members have ready access.

THE ALBERT MEMORIAL. This giant neo-Gothic monument is 175 feet high. It is built from a dazzling variety of materials (among them different colored marbles, Portland stone, mosaic and bronze) and is decorated with detailed allegorical figures. It illustrates the gulf that was separating Victorian art from the industrial achievements of the age.

BROMPTON ORATORY ★

When he converted to Roman Catholicism in 1845, Cardinal John Henry Newman (1801–90) introduced to Britain a branch of the brotherhood of St Philip Neri (founded in Rome in the 16th century). They settled at Brompton in 1847. The Baroque church was built between 1878 and 1884 to the designs of Herbert Gribble. Inside, visitors are often surprised at the size of the enormous nave. Round the sides of the building is a series of chapels. The life-sized statues of the twelve Apostles are the work of Guido Mazzuoli (1644–1725), and were purchased at Siena in 1895. In 1896 a monument to Cardinal Newman was erected in front of the Oratory.

London's Parks

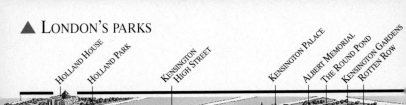

HOLLAND HOUSE · HOLLAND PARK · KENSINGTON HIGH STREET · KENSINGTON PALACE · ALBERT MEMORIAL · THE ROUND POND · KENSINGTON GARDENS · ROTTEN ROW

THE PARK IN SUMMER
The green and white striped deck chairs are ideal for dozing in the sunshine. A small fee is charged for use.

❝It is a park of intimacy. . . . There are few hours of the day when a thousand smutty children are not sprawling over it, and the unemployed lie thick on the grass and cover the benches with a brotherhood of greasy corduroys.❞
Henry James,
English Hours

"ST JAMES'S"
Watercolor by Benjamin Read (c. 1838).

Seen from the air, London appears as a spacious town dotted with sizeable patches of green (parks, football pitches, cricket grounds and thousands of private gardens) set around a long and meandering river. The Englishman's love for his garden prompted Emerson to remark in his *English Traits*: "England is a garden. Under the sooty sky, the fields, combed and rolled, appear to have been created with a brush instead of a plough". Whitehall, home of the Horse Guards and just to the east of St James's Park, is an ideal starting point from which to explore the great parks of London: St James's Park, Green Park, Hyde Park, Kensington Gardens and Holland Park.

ST JAMES'S PARK

This, the oldest of the royal parks, is also the smallest, and the most ornamental. The Mall cuts it off from the district called St James's.
RECLAIMING MARSHLAND. In 1536 Henry VIII decided he wanted a park on the boggy lands between the palaces of St James and Whitehall, so he had the marsh drained and stocked the land with deer, for decorative purposes rather than for hunting. Dotted with trees and with leafy avenues (of which the Mall is the only one to admit traffic), it was opened to the public in 1662 during the reign of Charles II, who asked

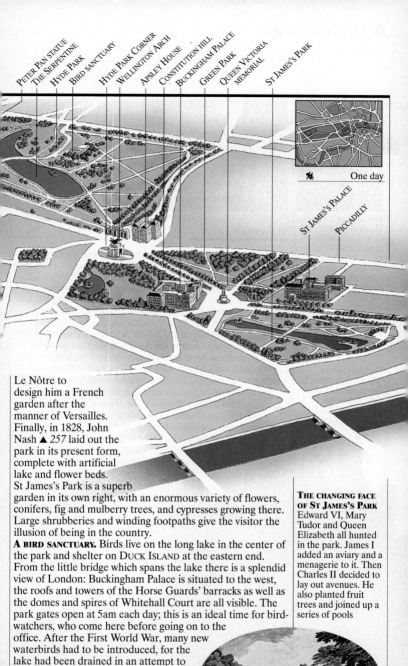

PETER PAN STATUE
THE SERPENTINE
HYDE PARK
BIRD SANCTUARY
HYDE PARK CORNER
WELLINGTON ARCH
APSLEY HOUSE
CONSTITUTION HILL
BUCKINGHAM PALACE
GREEN PARK
QUEEN VICTORIA MEMORIAL
ST JAMES'S PARK

ST JAMES'S PALACE
PICCADILLY

🏛 One day

Le Nôtre to design him a French garden after the manner of Versailles. Finally, in 1828, John Nash ▲ 257 laid out the park in its present form, complete with artificial lake and flower beds.

St James's Park is a superb garden in its own right, with an enormous variety of flowers, conifers, fig and mulberry trees, and cypresses growing there. Large shrubberies and winding footpaths give the visitor the illusion of being in the country.

A BIRD SANCTUARY. Birds live on the long lake in the center of the park and shelter on DUCK ISLAND at the eastern end. From the little bridge which spans the lake there is a splendid view of London: Buckingham Palace is situated to the west, the roofs and towers of the Horse Guards' barracks as well as the domes and spires of Whitehall Court are all visible. The park gates open at 5am each day; this is an ideal time for birdwatchers, who come here before going on to the office. After the First World War, many new waterbirds had to be introduced, for the lake had been drained in an attempt to stop the gleam of the water acting as a landmark for Zeppelins, guiding them to nearby Buckingham Palace. Pink flamingoes, pelicans, swans (the property of the queen), gulls, geese and ducks – thirty different species of bird now perch round the edge of the lake. BIRDCAGE WALK, which borders the park to the south, is named after the aviary that James I had installed near this tree-lined avenue. During the summer, in fine weather, there is live music in the bandstands, usually played

THE CHANGING FACE OF ST JAMES'S PARK Edward VI, Mary Tudor and Queen Elizabeth all hunted in the park. James I added an aviary and a menagerie to it. Then Charles II decided to lay out avenues. He also planted fruit trees and joined up a series of pools to form a canal. He left the romantic Rosamond's Pool (above) intact.

239

by military brass bands. It is extremely pleasant to visit the park in the calm of the evening: after dark, the lake is floodlit and the air becomes full of the scents of trees and flowers, while the lights of the city twinkle brightly in the background.

THE QUEEN'S CHAPEL
This was built for Queen Henrietta Maria, King Charles I's Catholic wife. It was the first church in England to be built in classical style.

THE KITCHENS
Above right: a 19th-century impression.

THE GATEHOUSE
The main entrance to the palace, in Tudor style, is reached from Pall Mall or St James's Street.

ST JAMES'S PALACE

AN ANCIENT ROYAL PALACE. Construction of this Tudor building, situated on the site of an old lazar-house, began in 1532 on the orders of Henry VIII. The Palace of Whitehall ▲ *142* was destroyed in a fire, and after 1698 St James's Palace became a permanent royal residence. The English court is still known as "The Court of St James". Queen Victoria preferred to live in Buckingham Palace when she acceded to the throne in 1837. Now St James's Palace houses the Yeomen of the Guard (the royal bodyguards), and also the Gentlemen at Arms ● *50* (the sovereign's personal guard), the Lord Chamberlain and other court officials.

A MIXTURE OF STYLES. The incongruous medley of buildings that makes up St James's Palace is the result of several centuries of alterations. Of the original building there is still the guardhouse left, constructed in brick with crenellated walls and octagonal towers. Another old part of the palace is the GATEHOUSE, the main entrance to the palace and a fine fortified Tudor building, which opens into COLOUR COURT, one of the palace's total of four courtyards. The three others are: AMBASSADOR'S COURT, FRIARY COURT and ENGINE COURT. Located off the latter is the Chapel Royal, which was built by Henry VIII and then altered at the beginning of the 19th century. Friary Court,

rebuilt after a fire in 1809, is a fine example of the neo-Tudor style. The accession to the throne of a new monarch is always proclaimed from a balcony overlooking this courtyard.

THE GUARDHOUSE. This old building is easily identified from Pall Mall thanks to its distinctive octagonal towers. It contains the THRONE ROOM (the carved mantelpiece of which is signed by Grinling Gibbons), the TAPESTRY ROOM and also the ARMS ROOM, designed by William Morris (1867).

THE CHAPEL ROYAL. The Chapel Royal, where the queen's choristers sing, is between Colour Court and Ambassador's Court. George IV, George V and Queen Victoria were all married here.

THE QUEEN'S CHAPEL AND CLARENCE HOUSE. The Queen's Chapel was built using Portland stone between 1632 and 1635 by Inigo Jones ▲ *69, 325*, and was attached to the palace before Marlborough Road was driven through. Inside there are some fine English Baroque features, among them a sculpture by Grinling Gibbons. To the west of the chapel is Clarence House, which was completed by John Nash in 1827. It is now the home of the Queen Mother.

THE HORSE GUARDS' BARRACKS. This was built in the mid-18th century in Palladian style, which lends it a rather palatial appearance. Its U-shaped design was the work of William Kent just before his death in 1748, and it was completed by John Vardy; it is a curious mixture of arches, pediments and eaves. The painter William Hogarth thought little of it and called it lifeless. The "U" encloses a courtyard on the Whitehall side, while on the side of St James's Park are three arches giving access to the piece of land known as HORSE GUARDS PARADE. The building has an imposing clock-tower that times the changes of the guard every hour between 10am and 4pm. There are two guardsmen posted in front on Horse Guards Parade, and two mounted troopers of the Household Cavalry on the Whitehall side. The latter are quite unruffled by the crowds of tourists constantly clicking cameras. The barracks houses the forty mounted sentries of the Royal Guard ● *50* responsible for protecting the royal residences of London. There are two regiments of Horse Guards: the Life Guards (scarlet coat, white-plumed helmet, and horse with black or white saddlecloth), and the Blues and Royals (blue coat, red-plumed helmet and horse with black saddlecloth).

HORSE GUARDS PARADE
From the entrance to the barracks an arched passageway leads to a large patch of ground where the ceremony of the Changing of the Guard takes place during the summer; in winter it is held in the inner courtyard. This square, known as Horse Guards Parade, is flanked by statues of Generals Wolseley and Roberts and there are two cannons.

BUCKINGHAM PALACE SEEN FROM ST JAMES'S PARK
The palace is on the site of Buckingham House, which was built on the edge of London at the start of the 18th century for John Sheffield, first Duke of Buckingham and Mulgrave. This in turn replaced thousands of mulberry trees that were planted here by James I to promote the silk industry.

241

THE PICTURE GALLERY, BUCKINGHAM PALACE
The present appearance of the Picture Gallery owes much to Queen Mary, wife of George V. She changed the lighting, reduced the number of paintings on display and replaced the great crimson carpet with smaller rugs.

THE GREEN DRAWING ROOM, BUCKINGHAM PALACE
This gets its name from the color of the silk chair-coverings and brocade wall-panels. Guests at royal receptions first have to cross the Green Drawing Room, past the door leading to the Picture Gallery.

THE MUSIC ROOM, BUCKINGHAM PALACE
The Music Room has hardly changed since the days of Queen Victoria. It contains a fine harpsichord; though the room is only used at royal baptisms and for receiving official visitors.

BUCKINGHAM PALACE

In 1762 King George III, who was not over-fond of the neighboring St James's Palace, bought Buckingham House, which became the home of Queen Charlotte in 1775.

JOHN NASH REBUILDS IT. Soon after his accession to the throne, in 1820, George IV (who had been regent since 1811) decided to commission John Nash ▲ 257 to transform the house into a royal palace. But the cost of the works far exceeded the money that was made available by the government, and on the king's death in 1830 the palace, which included the shell of Buckingham House, remained incomplete. Nash was dismissed and replaced by Edward Blore. Building started once again in 1837, when Victoria ascended the throne: Blore replaced Nash's dome with an attic, and in 1847 he enclosed the courtyard with an Italianate east wing. He also removed Marble Arch from outside the palace and moved it to the top of Park Lane. In 1913 Aston Webb added the present façade constructed of Portland stone. The ground floor and the two upper floors of the palace have more than six hundred rooms, which are linked by several miles of corridors. The finest parts of the palace are those designed by Nash.

THE GREAT HALL. The GRAND STAIRCASE rises up from here to the next floor and the state apartments. It is decorated in white marble with bas-reliefs. The stairwell was designed by Nash, and is topped with a dome. The richly gilded walnut balustrades are blended with one of the finest examples of Regency wrought-ironwork. The north wing of the quadrangle, housing the queen's apartments, overlooks Constitution Hill. The state apartments, also by Nash, are in the south and west wings on either side of the Picture Gallery.

THE PICTURE GALLERY. This was completed in 1914 and hung with many paintings from the royal collection, started in the reign of Henry VIII, who put Holbein the Younger in charge of it. Charles I purchased works by Titian and Raphael, George III added Canalettos and Gainsboroughs, and George IV bought pictures by Van Dyck, Rembrandt and Vermeer. Queen Victoria further enriched the collection with paintings by Constable, Turner, Hogarth and Reynolds.

THE STATE DINING ROOM. This is used for official balls, diplomatic receptions and royal weddings. The original interior was designed by John Nash, but Edward Blore changed it and added the three

BUCKINGHAM PALACE IN THE 19TH CENTURY
The watercolour painted by John Nash in 1846 (top) shows Marble Arch in its original position at the entrance to the courtyard of Buckingham Palace.

MUSIC AT THE PALACE
This is the invitation that guests received to a soirée held on Friday June 13, 1890.

THE KING IS ILL
When Edward VII was confined to his bed in 1902, an anxious crowd gathered outside Buckingham Palace.

"SUMMER DAY IN HYDE PARK"
This picture by John Ritchie, a genre painter who exhibited at the
Royal Academy from 1858 to 1875, looks north from the Serpentine
toward Marble Arch.

"Walked up to Hyde Park. . . . The South Middlesex Volunteers were to be inspected by Lord de Grey on the site of the old Crystal Palace, one of the dearest and most sacred spots in this neighbourhood to me.**"**

A.J. Munby,
Diaries

GREEN PARK
To the east of the park, between Piccadilly and the Mall, is Queen's Walk. Notable among the buildings on the east side of Green Park is the Palladian Spencer House, designed by John Vardy and James Stuart and built for the 1st Earl Spencer in 1756–66. Spencer House's splendid terrace and garden overlook the park. It has a number of state rooms that can be hired for private functions.

BANDSTAND IN GREEN PARK
Around 1900 bands, protected from the weather by bandstands, were a great favorite with the public.

cupolas. The walnut dining table can seat sixty people. On the other side of the Picture Gallery, next to the Green Drawing Room (which was formerly used by Queen Charlotte), is the Throne Room. On this wing and overlooking the Mall is the famous balcony, which was first used in 1854 by Queen Victoria. The royal family ● *48* still come out on to the balcony on important occasions.

THE QUEEN'S GALLERY. Opened in 1962, the Queen's Gallery is on the site of the chapel that was built by John Nash and then destroyed by enemy action in 1940. Pictures from the royal collection are on show here.

THE ROYAL MEWS. Until the National Gallery was built, the Royal Mews used to be near Charing Cross. Nash's 1826 buildings are virtually a small village inside Buckingham Palace. The name Mews comes from buildings that used to house falcons in moult. The Master of the Queen's Horse is the head of the Royal Mews, a title which goes back to 1391. His house is located at the entrance to the buildings. In former days the Royal Mews used to hold only the state coaches (the Gold State Coach of 1762, used for coronations, and the Irish State Coach of 1851, which is used for the opening of Parliament), the State

Landau, used for state visits, other carriages, and also the royal horses.

THE PALACE GARDENS. Buckingham Palace has a park of some 45 acres, with fine gardens laid out in the 19th century by W.T. Aiton: the lake on the west side of the park is named after him. In February 1841 Prince Albert misjudged the thickness of the ice when skating here and was rewarded with an involuntary bath!

GREEN PARK

To get to this attractive park well furnished with cast-iron benches, all the visitor has to do is cross the Mall. There are great stretches of lawn to walk on, and in season there is the heady scent of the lime trees. The avenue called Broad Walk is covered with grass and lined with plane trees. Picnics are popular here in fine weather: people who work around Piccadilly, as well as schoolchildren, take advantage of the shade under the trees.

HYDE PARK

The largest of the royal parks starts at the west end of Piccadilly. Hyde Park and its adjoining neighbor Kensington Gardens

"FLY TO BRITAIN WITH BOAC"
The British Overseas Airways Corporation was an ancestor of British Airways. This publicity postcard shows Constitution Arch (1846) or Wellington Arch, at Hyde Park Corner.

245

ROTTEN ROW
Of all the London parks, Hyde Park is probably the least formal.

have between them a total of 615 acres of parkland in the heart of London. It is like an immense lung. Hyde Park was first opened to the public in the 17th century by Charles I, and at once it became extremely popular. People loved walking along its country paths, though duels were frequently fought in the more secluded corners. The gibbet at Tyburn in the northeast corner of the park attracted huge crowds in search of sensation. Fashionable beaux and ladies used to walk along here wearing masks, a practice which led to so many unseemly excesses that it was ultimately forbidden by royal edict in 1695. George II added the Serpentine in 1730 and then the famous Rotten Row seven years later.

THE DUKE OF WELLINGTON (1769–1852)
He is best known for his defeat of Napoleon on June 18, 1815, at Waterloo. He was a High Tory of the old school, and he played a leading role on the domestic and international political stage for many years. He was prime minister from 1828 to 1830.

THE SERPENTINE. This artificial lake was constructed for Queen Caroline, who adored the countryside. The damming of the river Westbourne began in 1730. When this was finished two boats were moored here for the express use of the royal family. A great fair was held in Hyde Park in 1814, which included a reconstruction of the Battle of Trafalgar on the Serpentine. The lake is also associated with the death of Shelley's first wife Harriet Westbrook: pregnant by the husband who had left her, she drowned herself here. Today boats can be hired and there is public bathing. There is also an old tradition of bathers who come here for a dip on Christmas Day, come wind or snow, and even if the ice has to be broken. The Serpentine Gallery is an old tearoom built in 1908 by Sir Henry Tanner. Today it is used for exhibitions of contemporary art organized by the Arts Council.

HYDE PARK CORNER
On the left of the photograph are the three arches linked by columns known as the Hyde Park Screen, designed by Decimus Burton in 1825 as the southeast gate to the park. Beyond it is Apsley House, formerly Wellington's home and now open to the public.

SPEAKERS' CORNER. At the northeast corner of Hyde Park, near Marble Arch ▲ 252, is Speakers' Corner. In 1855 at least 150,000 people gathered here to demonstrate against Lord Robert Grosvenor's Sunday Trading Bill, authorizing shops to open on Sundays. Mobs like this were illegal, but when police appeared to arrest the ringleader they were too late. Then, in 1872, after many demonstrations of similar

RIDING IN ROTTEN ROW
High society went riding here in the 19th century.
In Rotten Row fashionable people drove up and
down in carriages to look at each other and to
make sure of being seen themselves.

proportions, the right to hold meetings here
was finally granted, and the area became
known as Speakers' Corner.
Everyone has the right to
stand up here and to say
whatever he or she thinks,
provided that it is not
obscene, blasphemous
or slanderous.

APSLEY HOUSE. This was
originally a house built of
red brick by the Adam
brothers between 1771 and
1778 for Henry Bathurst, the Lord
Chancellor of England (Baron Apsley and second earl of
Bathurst). It later became the London home of the duke of
Wellington, with the impressive address of Number One,
London. In 1829 Wellington commissioned Benjamin and
Philip Wyatt to put a Bath stone cladding on the walls, and to
add the Corinthian portico and build the Waterloo Gallery.
Each year on June 18 a great banquet is held at Apsley House
to celebrate the famous victory at the Battle of Waterloo. The
tradition is still upheld using the silver Portuguese dinner
service that is on display in the Waterloo Gallery. Apsley
House is now also the magnificent WELLINGTON MUSEUM,
with pictures by Goya, Murillo, Velásquez, Rubens and many
others.

ROTTEN ROW. The name comes from the French *route du roi*
(King's Way), which was gradually corrupted into its present
form. It links Kensington Palace to St James's, and was the
first road in England to have street lighting. It was William III
who ordered three hundred lanterns to be hung from the
trees that lined it as a precaution against the footpads who
made it a dangerous place at night. In 1687 a malefactor was
hanged for killing a lady who had
swallowed her wedding ring to prevent its
theft. But it remained a haunt of cut-
throats: in 1749 Horace Walpole, on his
way home from Holland House, was
attacked by two men who held him up
with a blunderbuss, relieving him of his
watch and eight guineas. Today there are
plenty of horsemen and children on
ponies from the riding school at the

Serpentine exercising here. This is also the road that the
Horse Guards ● *50* use every morning. Some
Londoners know this road as "The Mile".

KENSINGTON GARDENS

Sir Christopher Wren replanned the
private gardens of Kensington Palace
before the joint monarchs William and
Mary took it over as their London
residence. Queen Anne, who disliked the
formal Dutch gardens, had most of them
dug over. During the 1720's Henry Wise
and Charles Bridgeman embarked on a
new layout.

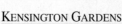

**"THE CRINOLINE
EQUESTRIAN"**
"No one can fail to
admire the elegant
simplicity of my
dress!", ran the
caption to this mid-
19th-century
lithograph.

THE CRYSTAL PALACE
Joseph Paxton
designed the building,
a metal framework
with panes of glass,
that housed the Great
Exhibition of 1851.
In 1854 the Crystal
Palace was taken
down and
reassembled at
Sydenham. Once
much larger and
divided into separate
galleries, the Crystal
Palace now became
an entertainment
center with plays,
concerts, exhibitions
and even circuses
staged inside it.
Statues and fountains
ornamented the
surrounding park,
where firework
displays were regular
features. Eventually
there were football
matches here. The
palace was destroyed
by fire in 1936.

"AUTUMN IN KENSINGTON GARDENS"
A painting by the landscape artist James Wallace (1872–1911). Queen Mary, wife of William III, took a great interest in the arrangement of the park and summoned the royal gardeners Henry Wise and George London to create Dutch gardens: beds bordered with low box hedges and yew bushes. George II opened Kensington Gardens to the public (by which he meant the genteel public), and its main avenue Broad Walk soon became as fashionable a place to be seen in as the Mall ▲ *144*.

THE SUNKEN GARDEN
Kensington Gardens is much more formal than Hyde Park, and it is crossed by tree-lined avenues. The Sunken Garden was created out of an old gravel pit.

Kensington Palace

THE MONUMENTS IN THE GARDENS. It was probably William Kent who in 1726–7 built the small temple at the southeast end of the gardens, which later became part of Temple Lodge. King William IV first opened the park to the public, and a Flower Walk was planted here in 1843. The ALBERT MEMORIAL was unveiled in 1863, and then enlarged in 1872. A granite obelisk was erected here in 1864 commemorating the discovery of the source of the Nile by John Hanning Speke, followed by the statues of Queen Victoria in 1893 and then of William III in 1907. The statue *Physical Energy* by G.F. Watts dates from 1904, while the *Elfin Oak* by Ivor Innes is a treetrunk carved with woodland creatures. It is close to the children's playground on the north side of the park, near Black Lion

Gate. The bronze does and fawns decorating the Queen's Gate are the work of P. Rouillard (1919).

The Peter Pan statue. This is one of London children's favorite statues, and has been so ever since it was first put here in 1912. George Frampton's bronze depicts the boy who was first created by J.M. Barrie in *The Little White Bird*, a story set in Kensington Gardens. The character was immortalized in the eponymous play which still regularly thrills young audiences in London and elsewhere. Nina Boucicault, who created the role of Peter, sat for the sculptor. He is depicted here playing the pipes, while fairies, mice and rabbits frolic round his feet.

The Round Pond. In the middle of the park is a small lake that also attracts London children (especially on Sundays), who sail their model boats here. There are even some old sailors too, dressed in navy blue and a white cap, who come to launch some exquisitely fashioned models.

The Sunken Garden. This garden, which was laid out in 1909, is on the east side of the park. Rows of flowers are planted on the three terraces to form a rectangle round a

The Queen's Chamber in Kensington Palace One of the magnificent interior designs created by Sir Christopher Wren around 1690, and altered in the 1720's.

249

KENSINGTON GARDENS
Seen from across the Round Pond.

❝We walked out to Kensington and strolled through the delightful Gardens. It is a glorious thing for the King to keep such walks so near the Metropolis, open to all his subjects. We were very calm and happy. Our conversation was most agreeable.❞
James Boswell, *Diary for May 21, 1763*

"MY LADY'S GARDEN"
This picture by John Young Hunter, painted in 1899, shows the walled Dutch Garden in Holland Park very clearly in the background. It was laid out by Buonaiuti in 1812, and consisted of flower beds in geometric shapes edged with low box hedges. It is still there today. One feature is not in the picture: the niche in the northeast wall known as ROGERS' SEAT, above which is an inscription by Lord Holland in tribute to his friend the banker and Romantic poet Samuel Rogers.

pool, and with a delightful walk under a vault of lime trees. Leaving the park on the left by the northwest gate, the road then leads west into Notting Hill, a lively and extremely cosmopolitan quarter. It then proceeds down to Holland Park. On the lefthand side is the beautiful Campden Hill Square, which was built on a slope, making it a magical sight, particularly at Christmas time, when all the occupants put lighted candles in the bow windows of these early Victorian houses.

KENSINGTON PALACE. This manor house was first built for Sir George Coppin, before being bought by the earl of Nottingham, who duly called it Nottingham House. Following the 1689 revolution, it became the home of the young royal couple William III and Mary, since the king suffered from asthma which was greatly exacerbated when he lived beside the Thames. In addition, the setting of Kensington delighted him, for he loved the countryside. He commissioned Sir Christopher Wren ● *70*, ▲ *171, 349* to enlarge and transform the house into a palace, and employed Nicholas Hawksmoor ▲ *311* to supervise construction. Wren added a new façade and royal apartments to the building. He also designed a magnificent wrought-iron staircase (executed by Jean Tijou) and built new stables. Queen Anne added the Orangery in 1704, probably to plans drawn up by Hawksmoor that were then modified by Vanbrugh. Under George I, three of the state rooms were rebuilt in Palladian style. George II and Queen Caroline moved here in 1727. After his death in 1760, his grandson, who was now King George III, decided to live instead at Buckingham House. Kensington Palace, as it was now called, was therefore abandoned for a time, before some of the royal children took apartments here. At the beginning of the 19th century James Wyatt made some extensive alterations to the palace in neo-classical style. Princess Victoria was born here in 1819, and it was here too that news came to her in 1837 that she was now queen. Today Princess Margaret has apartments in the palace, which is also the traditional home of the Prince of Wales. Still open to the

public, the palace contains a fine collection of costumes that were worn at court after 1750. The state apartments are decorated with paneling and Old Master paintings dating from the 17th and 18th centuries. In the queen's apartments there are mirrors with carved and gilded frames by the famous Grinling Gibbons ▲ *157, 173, 276*, and also William Kent's cupola room, while in the king's apartments the Privy Council chamber was created by the same architect.

HOLLAND PARK

Surrounded by imposing Victorian houses, Holland Park is a most delightful retreat from the busy world outside its walls, with squirrels, peacocks, Australian emus and many other rather less exotic birds. It was once part of the land belonging to Holland House, which was built in 1607 and almost entirely destroyed by enemy action in 1941 during the Second World War. There are three gardens laid out around it, namely the ROSE GARDEN, the DUTCH GARDEN and the IRIS GARDEN. The flowers are a mixture of the exotic and indigenous, among them catalpas, bamboos, yuccas, lime trees, holly, oaks, poplars and ash trees ● *24*. There are also several statues, including a monument to Lord Holland (1872) by Watts and Boehm, *The Boy and the Bear Cubs* (1902) by John MacAllan Swan, and also a work by Eric Gill. The small conical 18th-century stone construction was once an ice house. There are refreshments for sale at the café, which makes a perfect spot in which to get away from the crowded city. Last of all there is the magnificent Orangery, built together with the stables in 1638–40, where there are bronze copies of statues. Art exhibitions and concerts are also held here.

RELAXING IN HOLLAND PARK
In common with the other London parks, Holland Park is an ideal place to relax in, whatever the season. To the south the park slopes gently down, giving visitors a fine view over the roofs of the town.

HOLLAND HOUSE. Only parts remain of the original building, which was called Cope Castle and built for Sir Walter Cope, who was Chancellor of the Exchequer under James I. All that remains are the east wing, some arcades in the courtyard, and a gateway that is attributed to Nicholas Stone and Inigo Jones. The property was for a long time in the family of Charles James Fox, who became a Member of Parliament at just nineteen years of age and then leader of the Whig party. In the first part of the 19th century Lady Holland had a salon here, attended by such famous names as Sheridan, Sir Walter Scott, Lord Byron, Wordsworth and Dickens, and all the great Whig politicians who opposed the war with France. After the 1941 bombing Holland House was abandoned until 1952, when the London County Council took control of it.

HOLLAND HOUSE, THEN AND NOW
The engraving below shows the original Holland House, while in the oval picture (above left) is the house as it appears today. In summer there are plays, ballets and operas given in front of the façade. This open-air terrace is called the Court Theatre.

251

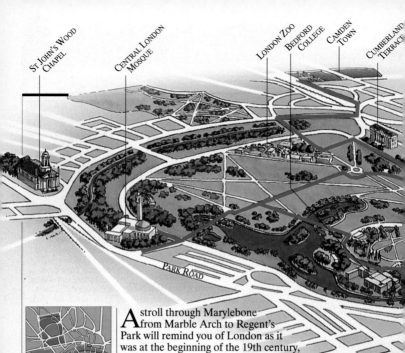

※ One day

A stroll through Marylebone from Marble Arch to Regent's Park will remind you of London as it was at the beginning of the 19th century, a residential quarter with squares and gardens, the streets lined with opulent houses.

AROUND MARYLEBONE

MARBLE ARCH. At the top of Park Lane, which runs up the eastern side of Hyde Park, is Marble Arch roundabout. The triumphal arch which stands there is of white Italian marble. It was executed in 1828 by Decimus Burton (1800–81). Originally intended as a ceremonial gate for Buckingham Palace ▲ *242*, Marble Arch was moved to its present position in 1851 as its wrought-iron gates proved too narrow to let the state coach through. At the beginning of the present century it became apparent that Marble Arch was insufficient to meet the needs of the new motor traffic, so it was placed on an island around which the traffic now flows.

MARBLE ARCH
Just a few steps from Marble Arch, a stone triangle set into the road marks the site of Tyburn, where, for six centuries, criminals and martyrs from the Tower of London were publicly executed.

MARYLEBONE. The district extends from both sides of Marylebone Lane and Marylebone High Street. In the middle of the 18th century many important building projects were initiated in the village of Marylebone, which rapidly became incorporated into London with the construction of new streets, squares and grand town houses. These improvements were partly the work of Robert Adam (1728–92) assisted by his three brothers ▲ *268*. Adam brought a freedom of movement into architecture, reacting against the suffocating restraints of the noble Palladian style, in a great variety of private houses which can still be seen.

HARLEY STREET. Laid out in 1820, Harley Street has been the preserve of the medical profession since the middle of the 19th century. Eighteenth-century houses jostle with Victorian and Edwardian dwellings. In buildings that date from 1765 at

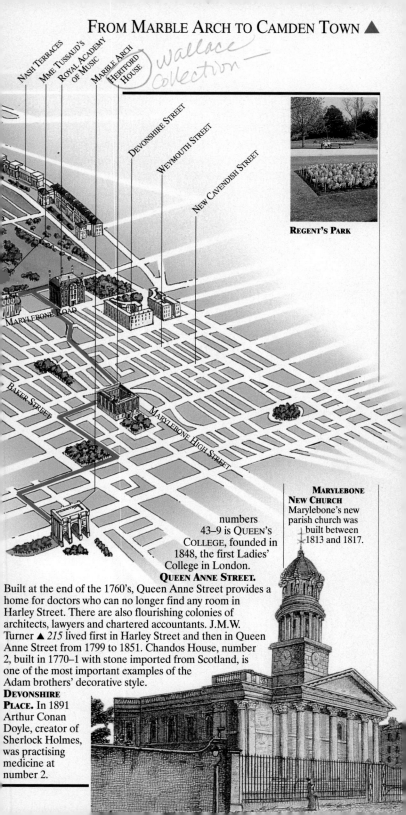

NASH TERRACES

MME TUSSAUD'S

ROYAL ACADEMY OF MUSIC

MARBLE ARCH

HERTFORD HOUSE

Wallace Collection

DEVONSHIRE STREET

WEYMOUTH STREET

NEW CAVENDISH STREET

REGENT'S PARK

MARYLEBONE ROAD

BAKER STREET

MARYLEBONE HIGH STREET

numbers 43–9 is QUEEN'S COLLEGE, founded in 1848, the first Ladies' College in London.

QUEEN ANNE STREET. Built at the end of the 1760's, Queen Anne Street provides a home for doctors who can no longer find any room in Harley Street. There are also flourishing colonies of architects, lawyers and chartered accountants. J.M.W. Turner ▲ *215* lived first in Harley Street and then in Queen Anne Street from 1799 to 1851. Chandos House, number 2, built in 1770–1 with stone imported from Scotland, is one of the most important examples of the Adam brothers' decorative style.

DEVONSHIRE PLACE. In 1891 Arthur Conan Doyle, creator of Sherlock Holmes, was practising medicine at number 2.

MARYLEBONE NEW CHURCH
Marylebone's new parish church was built between 1813 and 1817.

Hertford House in Manchester Square houses the famous Wallace Collection. Assembled by the four first Marquises of Hertford and the illegitimate son of the last Marquis, Sir Richard Wallace (1818–90), the collection was bequeathed to the nation on the death of Sir Richard's widow, and opened in 1900. There is a magnificent collection of French art (Fragonard, Boucher, Watteau), as well as Italian painting (Guardi), Spanish (Velásquez, Murillo) and Flemish, not forgetting the work of English artists and 19th-century French painting as well. The gallery, which also houses collections of furniture and all manner of other objects, was refitted between 1976 and 1981.

"VENUS ARISING FROM THE WAVES" This majolica (glazed Italian ceramic ware) tablet was executed in 1553 by Francesco Xanto Avelli.

"THE LAUGHING CAVALIER" This familiar portrait was painted in 1624 by the Dutchman Frans Hals (c.1585–1666). The brushwork was a great influence on 19th-century painters, notably Manet.

CLOCK WITH ASTRONOMICAL DIAL This clock in gilded, patinated bronze, the work of Michel Stollerwerck (c.1746–75), is just one example from a substantial collection of clocks.

"MADAME DE POMPADOUR"
This painting of Louis XV's mistress by Francois Boucher (1703–70) is part of a collection of French art that was assembled by the Marquis of Hertford during the Revolution.

MILANESE GORGETS (c.1610)
These pieces of armor protected the soldier's neck and throat. It is part of a collection of armor purchased from the Count of Nieuwekerke.

PORTLAND PLACE. The Adam brothers began work on one of London's grandest development schemes in 1773. Ten of the original houses are still standing.

MARYLEBONE HIGH STREET AND THAYER STREET. The main road and the very heart of old Marylebone, it still retains something of a village atmosphere, and is lined with shops.

TOWN SQUARES. PORTMAN SQUARE was laid out between 1764 and 1784 on land belonging to the Portman family. At number 30 is HOME HOUSE, Robert Adam's finest town house and witness to his genius for combining different elements in one harmonious whole. MANCHESTER SQUARE contains the Wallace Collection; and though it is in no sense a square, this is the place to mention STRATFORD PLACE (just off Oxford Street), an elegant little impasse dating from 1774.

BAKER STREET. Baker Street's most celebrated tenant lived at number 221B. This was Sherlock Holmes, whose museum is in the *Sherlock Holmes* pub in Northumberland Avenue, south of Trafalgar Square. The upper part of the street is one of the best preserved sections in the area.

MARYLEBONE ROAD

MARYLEBONE NEW CHURCH. From 1813 to 1817 on land donated by the duke of Portland, Thomas Hardwick built a new parish church, the third, with a heavy Corinthian portico and a domed tower supported by caryatids.

THE ROYAL ACADEMY OF MUSIC. The present red-brick

English Baroque building was constructed in 1910–11. When the Academy first opened in 1823, an early pupil was Charles Dickens' sister Fanny.

"MADAME TUSSAUD'S". In 1802 Marie Tussaud (1761–1850) arrived in London from France with thirty-five wax figures and death masks of famous revolutionaries who had fallen victim to the guillotine. By 1884 the museum boasted four hundred figures. Today, among many other features, it contains a Hall of Fame, Chamber of Horrors, gruesome relics of the old London prisons and many historical tableaux. It is one of the most popular tourist attractions in London, attracting millions of visitors every year.

THE LONDON PLANETARIUM. This opened in 1958. With optical lenses supplied by

the Zeiss laboratories, the sky is projected on to a great copper dish. On certain evenings the space is used as a Laserium, and sometimes concerts are held here.

REGENT'S PARK ★

● 24

For the French historian Hippolyte Taine, who came to London in 1864, Regent's Park appeared "a solitary place with no noise of traffic; London is forgotten and you are quite alone". The newest of London's parks is the most splendid and varied too. This giant green space of more than 500 acres was formerly a hunting ground of King Henry VIII. In 1811 the Prince Regent (the future George IV) gave his favorite architect John Nash the job of developing the land. The plan called for no fewer than 56 villas, a summer residence for the Regent, and a Pantheon dedicated to England's greatness, while the park was to be ringed with gracious terraces of houses. Nash dreamed of creating a new, idealized garden city landscape. The project never came to completion thanks to lack of funds and customers, but over the years the park became a delightful and original environment. Nash began work on the park in 1812, and worked on it with his assistant Decimus Burton until 1827 ▲ 278. But Regent's Park was not opened to the public until 1838.

VISITING THE PARK. Except for the northern area, occupied by the zoo, and the lawns in the center, most of the park is given over to sports, such as cricket ● 56. There are long, tree-lined avenues for walks, clearings planted with willows to relax in, plenty of cooling lakes and countless beds planted with all kinds of flowers. To see the park and the Nash terraces it is best to set out from the semicircular PARK CRESCENT, with its magnificent Ionic colonnade. If the west side of the park is centered around the BOATING LAKE, the middle or INNER CIRCLE is the most beautiful part. It contains QUEEN MARY'S GARDEN and rose gardens (as fine as any in England), and the Open-Air Theater, where each summer there are performances of *A Midsummer Night's Dream* against a natural setting of trees and woods.

ST JOHN'S LODGE. On the southwest side of Regent's Park stands this 18th-century villa (above, inset) with a wing that was added in the 20th century, surrounded by a delightful garden which remains largely undiscovered, in spite of being open to the public.

> "The Crescents and gardens alike had a faint Regency character, partly, perhaps, because they faced remote light blue distances, such as one sees in watercolors of the period."
>
> Edith Sitwell,
> *I Live under a Black Sun*

CUMBERLAND TERRACE
The most grandiose of the Nash terraces in Regent's Park looks like a palace.

257

THE NASH TERRACES ★ ● *76.* These are the fruits of Nash's town-planning project. They are made up of gracious town houses in Regency style, each terrace forming a substantial palace with long stuccoed façade. Among the most remarkable terraces on the west side are YORK TERRACE and CORNWALL TERRACE (which was the first one to be built, in 1820–1), and Sussex Place, decorated with Corinthian columns and domed towers. Perhaps the two most imposing terraces on the eastern side are CHESTER TERRACE, 325 yards long and decorated with Corinthian columns, and CUMBERLAND TERRACE, Nash's most accomplished work, built in 1825. This has the grandest façade of all of them, with an arrangement of Ionic columns surmounted by a pediment carved by G.H. Bubb and topped by three statues. After World War Two, these delapidated terraces were tempting investments for property developers, and have since been converted to luxury apartments.

THE REGENT'S PARK MOSQUE
On the west side of Regent's Park, the mosque is next to Winfield House, the residence of the American ambassador.

ST KATHARINE'S HOSPITAL. The northeast entrance to the park, by Gloucester Gate, faces the old hospital of St Katharine. The neo-Gothic complex of buildings includes the old church of St Katharine, which is now the Danish church in London, and houses built in 1826 by Ambrose Poynter. St Katharine's, a charitable foundation, was moved here from its original site near the Tower when the land was taken over for the construction of St Katharine's Dock ▲ *334.*

THE CENTRAL LONDON MOSQUE. London's new central mosque is beside Hanover Gate on the west of the park. With its minaret and copper dome, it is an impressive building built between 1972 and 1978 by Frederick Gibberd, a testament to the importance of the Islamic religion in London.

LONDON ZOO

ZOO LIFE
Each new birth in London Zoo is announced on a noticeboard at the main gate.

Today the zoo covers 37 acres in the northern part of Regent's Park. Sir Stamford Raffles founded the Zoological Society in London in 1826, and in 1828 its members opened a zoological garden to plans laid out by Decimus Burton. It was immediately popular, and two years later the collection of animals from the Tower was added. Within the next few years came giraffes, lions, snakes and apes, and the famous African elephant, Jumbo.

THE CANAL
Regent's Canal runs along beside the zoo in lush green surroundings before turning off toward the East End.

A MODERN ZOO. London Zoo was a real pioneer when it opened the MAPPIN TERRACES in 1913. For the first time in the world, people could watch animals in something approaching their natural habitat. The remarkable penguin enclosure, opened in 1934, was followed 1962–5 by the elephant and rhinoceros houses. A more general reorganization of the zoo took place during the 1960's to plans laid down by Sir Hugh Casson. Lord Snowdon, at that time the husband of Princess Margaret, designed the giant aviary in 1967 with the intention of giving the birds at least a modicum of freedom. Finally, in 1976, the NEW LION TERRACES allowed the great beasts to shelter or take advantage of an open-air green space as they wished. London

FOR THE ZOO, BOOK TO REGENT'S PARK OR CAMDEN TOWN

Zoo also has an Institute of Comparative Physiology, an animal hospital, and a Twilight House (the Charles Clore Pavilion), home of nocturnal mammals. The zoo has thousands of animals, representing 1,162 species. A library with more than 100,000 volumes allows visitors to discover or improve their knowledge of the habits of the zoo's inmates.

CHILDREN'S ZOO AND FARM. This is situated on the southern side of the zoo. It is a place where children can play with tame animals.

CAMDEN LOCK
Artists, sellers of bric-à-brac and secondhand clothes have been coming to set up shop here at weekends for the last twenty-five years, on the old quays beside the locks of the Regent's Canal.

AROUND CAMDEN LOCK

Regent's Park is bounded on the north by the Regent's Canal, with its picturesque locks which create an attractive backdrop to the craft and antique stalls of Camden Lock.

PRIMROSE HILL ★. This dominates the Thames valley beyond the canal: being 203 feet high, it offers some splendid views over London. Covered with grass and set with groups of chestnut and plane trees, Primrose Hill was once a favorite place for duelists.

REGENT'S CANAL ▲ *18* . The prettiest parts of the canal are just beside the zoo and near Macclesfield Bridge. The Regent's Canal was opened in 1820, linking the Thames to Paddington and thence, via the Grand Union Canal, to Birmingham and beyond. In contrast to its earlier days, the canal is now used relatively little. Walkers and anglers enjoy the towpath today, and the old horse-drawn barges have been replaced by pleasure craft.

CAMDEN LOCK. This is now an antique market beside the Regent's Canal. It is situated in former commercial premises (warehouses or stables) that were used by the canal and the nearby railway. Camden Town is an old-fashioned working-class district. When the French poets Verlaine and Rimbaud stayed there in 1873 (aged twenty-nine and eighteen, respectively), they attempted to earn some money by placing an advertisement in the *Daily Telegraph* newspaper offering to give French conversation lessons.

STIFF COMPETITION
Camden Lock now rivals the famous Portobello Road flea market and the antique shops of Camden Passage in popularity.

▲ From Hampstead to Highgate

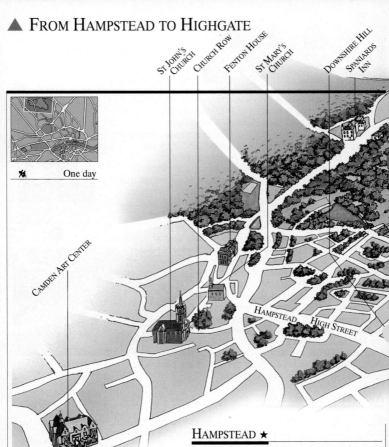

St John's Church · Church Row · Fenton House · St Mary's Church · Downshire Hill · Spaniards Inn

Camden Art Center

Hampstead High Street

🏃 One day

Hampstead ★

HAMPSTEAD FROM PARLIAMENT HILL FIELDS, WITH THE BATHING POND
This ancient bathing place, a mixture of Georgian and Victorian styles perched on the side of a hill, has attracted many famous people to its waters: Keats, Shelley, Lord Byron, Kipling, D.H. Lawrence, H.G. Wells, and Sigmund Freud.

Hampstead is the perfect place for a fascinating stroll. Its streets are lined with houses like country cottages, with neat front gardens. The area is enormous fun to explore on holiday, rain or shine. The High Street is packed with interesting shops: some are open on Sunday too. Hampstead was once woodland, but a lot of it was cut down to rebuild the City after the Great Fire ● *40*. Well-to-do Londoners built their country houses here in the 18th century near the heath, which was well known for its fresh air and spring water. The water used to be sold in the taverns: it was bottled in Flask Walk. There used to be a thermal spring in Well Walk; and in the same street once lived John Keats and the landscape painter Constable ▲ *214*. (Formerly he lived for a while at 2 Lower Terrace.) Many media personalities still live here today. To see more of the history and architecture of Hampstead, go to Church Row and marvel at its magnificent Georgian houses, just before you reach St John Street.

Hampstead from Parliament Hill.

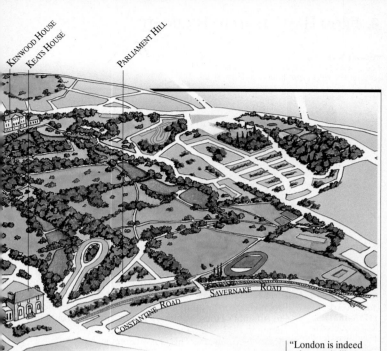

SAVERNAKE ROAD

CONSTANTINE ROAD

HAMPSTEAD CHURCHES. ST JOHN'S CHURCH
● 72 was built 1744–7 out of brick, and then enlarged
in the 19th century. Its crenellated belfry gives it a medieval
air. The painter John Constable is among those buried in the
churchyard. Along Holly Walk is ST MARY'S, a Roman
Catholic church founded by a Frenchman, Abbé Morel. Its
white walls form an attractive contrast with the brown brick of
Hampstead houses. There are some interesting 20th-century
mosaics to be seen inside its two chapels. Skirting the
National Institute of Medical Research (built in 1880), you
come to Mount Vernon. On Holly Bush Hill is a timber-built
house which was constructed in 1797 for George Romney, a
portrait artist whose work was very popular with the nobility
of that time.

KEATS' HOUSE, KEATS GROVE. From 1818 to 1820 John Keats
(1795–1821) lived in Wentworth Place (as it
was then called), in a double-fronted house
built for his friends Charles Armitage Brown
and Charles Wentworth Dilke. Keats first
came to Hampstead in 1816 to meet the
journalist and poet Leigh Hunt, who lived in
the Vale of Health, and it was through his
connections that Keats came to know Shelley,
William Hazlitt, Wordsworth and Charles
Lamb. In 1817 he moved to Well Walk with
his brothers George and Tom; then, when he
was left by himself (George had emigrated to
America and Tom had died from a chest
infection), he accepted his friend Brown's
invitation and went to live in the lefthand part
of this house. Dilke rented his half to a Mrs
Brawne, whose daughter Fanny was later to
become Keats' fiancée. Keats' House, like so
many others in the suburbs, boasts a luxuriant
garden. Inside the house can be seen
autograph manuscripts and personal effects

"London is indeed
a thousand villages;
remove them and
all that is left is a
vast hulk peppered
with spectacular
buildings . . . ."
Ian Nairn

261

"ADMIRAL'S HOUSE"
This landscape was painted by Constable in 1820 and captures the village atmosphere of Hampstead.

JOHN KEATS (1795–1821)
The poet lived in Hampstead for three years. His *Ode to a Nightingale*, the longest of his odes, was written on a May evening in the garden at Wentworth Place.

HOME, SWEET HOME
The name Hampstead derives from *"homestead"*. It is said that long ago a Saxon cut down part of the forest here and built himself a farm.

that belonged to the poet. Not far away, and still in Keats Grove, is the courtyard of an old brewery surrounded by 17th-century buildings, Old Brewery Mews.

FENTON HOUSE ● *74.* Built in 1693, the house is named after the merchant who bought it in 1793. Inside there is a collection of early keyboard instruments, including a magnificent harpsichord that Handel used to play. There is also a fine collection of porcelain that once belonged to Lady Binning, who bequeathed the house to the National Trust in 1952 along with some pictures by Constable and Breughel the Elder. **HAMPSTEAD GROVE** and **ADMIRAL'S WALK** are lined with some early 18th-century houses and cottages. The novelist John Galsworthy (author of *The Forsyte Saga*) lived next door to Admiral's House at **GROVE LODGE** from 1918 until his death in 1933.

HAMPSTEAD HEATH. This grassy common, covering 420 acres, includes Parliament Hill Fields and Kenwood, and separates Hampstead from Highgate. Until the 13th century its only inhabitants were wolves; it was not until late in the 17th century that the medicinal qualities of its spring waters were discovered, when the place suddenly became extremely popular. Today Londoners use this beautiful spot with its open spaces, lakes and wooded groves for picnics and walks. Music lovers will be pleased to learn that at Concert Pond there are frequent open-air concerts held in the summer. The view over London from Parliament Hill Fields is

most impressive. There are also several famous pubs in the area. The 18th-century Kit-Kat Club used to meet in *Upper Flask Inn* in Flask Walk. This was basically a club of Whig politicians ▲ *251,* but it had some illustrious members including the writers Alexander Pope ▲ *155,* Richard Steele and Joseph Addison, the painter Sir Godfrey Kneller and many others. Keats and Shelley drank here too. The club took its name from the pastrycook Christopher Katt, in whose house the first meetings were held. On top of the heath, near Whitestone Pond, is **JACK STRAW'S CASTLE,** a historic pub frequented by Charles Dickens ● *110,* ▲ *299.* You can make your way to Kenwood House along Spaniards Road and stop at the *Spaniards Inn,* which is four hundred years old and was the Spanish ambassador's residence during the reign of James II. In 1780 the landlord got the Gordon Rioters drunk

here, and attempted to stop them burning Kenwood House. The inn was also a meeting place for writers such as Keats, Shelley, Byron and Dickens.

KENWOOD HOUSE ★. In 1754 the chief justice of the King's Bench, Lord Mansfield, bought the estate of Kenwood. (He was not at all popular with the general public, which is why his house was attacked during the Gordon Riots.) It is a brick house, and parts of the original can still be seen today. It was already fifty years old when Mansfield purchased it. He commissioned Robert Adam to transform the place: the resulting parts added by the young architect on the south façade overlooking Hampstead Heath are imaginative and beautifully proportioned. The finest room in the house is undoubtedly the LIBRARY. After Mansfield's death in 1793, his nephew added the two wings on either side of the north façade, where the main entrance is, with a portico by Adam. Lord Iveagh (grandson of the founder of the brewing dynasty, Arthur Guinness) purchased Kenwood in 1925 and filled it with his collection of paintings (including notable works by Rembrandt, Vermeer, Gainsborough and Stubbs). He presented the house and all its contents to the nation before his death in 1927.

HIGHGATE

Highgate High Street crosses Highgate Hill and was built in 1386 on the order of the bishop of London, for the route round the hill was proving difficult in winter. Travelers used to pay a toll at the top of the hill in front of a large gateway, after which both hill and street are named. At the foot of the hill, the Whittington Stone commemorates the spot where Richard Whittington, while he was a poor apprentice turning his back on London, is supposed to have heard the bells of St Mary-le-Bow (Bow Bells) calling him to return and become Lord Mayor. He was to be Lord Mayor four times, and at his death in 1423 he left his fortune to finance the building of the Guildhall ▲ *148*.

ADAM AT KENWOOD
The south façade of Kenwood House (above) is decorated with ornate pilasters in classical style.

At each end of the library (above) is an apse guarded by two Corinthian pillars. Robert Adam was particularly proud of the curved ceiling.

THE PARK AT KENWOOD
In the 18th century there was a decorative "English" garden here. Today, open-air symphony concerts are given regularly at Kenwood in what is a beautiful rustic setting.

THE KINGDOM OF SHADES
Many famous people lie buried in this romantic Victorian cemetery: Karl Marx,

Christina Rossetti, Michael Faraday, George Eliot and Ralph Richardson are just a few of them.

THE FREUD MUSEUM
Fleeing from the Nazi invasion of Vienna in 1938, Sigmund Freud, the father of psychoanalysis, took refuge at 20 Maresfield Gardens in Highgate, and died there the following year. His daughter Anna lived there until her death in 1982.

CROMWELL HOUSE
This magnificent dwelling, built of brick in 1637–8, is on the east side of the summit of Highgate Hill.

LAUDERDALE HOUSE. Highgate grew up around a group of grand country houses that had been built by the nobility in an attempt to escape from the ever-increasing noise and bustle of London. The place has managed to retain its village atmosphere ever since. An example is Lauderdale House, a 16th-century dwelling that was remodeled in the middle of the following century by the duke of Lauderdale. In 1871 it was bought by the philanthropist Sir Sidney Waterlow, who let it to St Bartholomew's Hospital as a rest home. In 1889 he gave the house and gardens to the London County Council. The house is now used for exhibitions and concerts. There is also a museum and restaurant.

HIGHGATE SCHOOL. This famous school is situated on North Road. In 1565 Queen Elizabeth I authorized Sir Roger Cholmley to open a school that would offer the best education to children of good families, and also serve the needy of the village. In 1571 the school had just forty pupils; in 1993 the school numbered 930 boys. Its French-style neo-Gothic buildings date from 1865 to 1868. POND SQUARE, in the middle of the village, owes its name to a pool (filled in in 1864) formed by the repeated removal of gravel from the spot to mend the roads. The poet Samuel Taylor Coleridge and the violinist Yehudi Menuhin lived at numbers 3 and 2 THE GROVE, a road that is well known for its elegant houses. In South Grove there is a fine group of 18th-century houses. At the foot of Swain's Lane is HOLLY VILLAGE ★, a group of eccentrically designed cottages that were built in 1865 by Henry Darbishire. Among the more modern buildings should be mentioned Highpoint 1 and 2, which were built on North Hill in 1938 by Lubetkin and Tecton. Filled with admiration, Le Corbusier called them "a vertical garden city".

HIGHGATE CEMETERY ★. ST MICHAEL'S CHURCH, a neo-Gothic building, was constructed by the architect Lewis Vulliamy in 1830 on the site of the old home of Sir William Ashurst, who was Lord Mayor of London in 1694. Soon afterwards the rest of the land was bought by Stephen Geary, who then founded the London Cemetery Company and laid out the cemetery. As soon as it was opened in 1839 it proved to be an incredible success. Everyone wanted to be buried there, and since then visitors have flocked to explore the place. In fact, so great was Geary's success that in 1857 he had to create an extension in Swain's Lane. On the west side are Egyptian Avenue and the catacombs, housing the remains of rich families, which have lost nothing of their magnificence.

THE WEST END

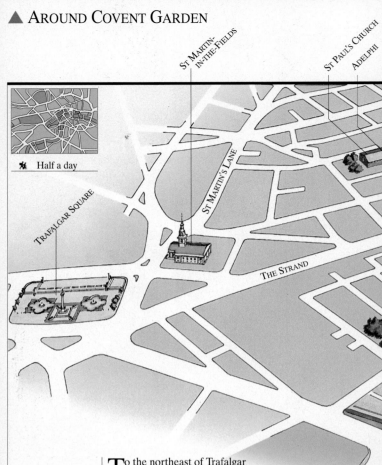

ST MARTIN-IN-THE-FIELDS

ST PAUL'S CHURCH

ADELPHI

ST MARTIN'S LANE

TRAFALGAR SQUARE

THE STRAND

⚔ Half a day

To the northeast of Trafalgar Square, just a few steps from the City, is the very heart of London. The route leads from the Strand to Covent Garden, past theaters and along the river. It is a district packed with history, but unfortunately heavily redeveloped in the 20th century.

THE STRAND

This broad main road runs between Fleet Street and Charing Cross Station, linking the City of London to the City of Westminster. It is one of the busiest streets in the whole of the capital, packed with traffic and with many thousands of commuters hurrying to and from the station. Already by the middle of the 19th century, when Charlotte Brontë came to London to see her publishers, she found that crossing the road here was a hazardous affair.

HISTORY. The street started out as a track running east above the riverbank, hence its name. During the 16th century courtiers wanting to live near the royal palace of Whitehall

ST MARY-LE-STRAND
Like its neighbor, St Clement Dane's, this church has the distinction of sitting in the middle of the Strand, which widens here to form a sort of square.

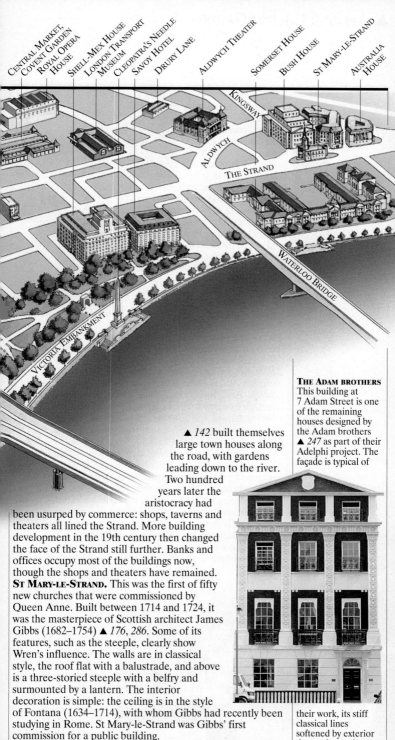

CENTRAL MARKET, COVENT GARDEN · ROYAL OPERA HOUSE · SHELL-MEX HOUSE · LONDON TRANSPORT MUSEUM · CLEOPATRA'S NEEDLE · SAVOY HOTEL · DRURY LANE · ALDWYCH THEATER · SOMERSET HOUSE · BUSH HOUSE · ST MARY-LE-STRAND · AUSTRALIA HOUSE

KINGSWAY · ALDWYCH · THE STRAND · WATERLOO BRIDGE · VICTORIA EMBANKMENT

THE ADAM BROTHERS
This building at 7 Adam Street is one of the remaining houses designed by the Adam brothers ▲ *247* as part of their Adelphi project. The façade is typical of

▲ *142* built themselves large town houses along the road, with gardens leading down to the river. Two hundred years later the aristocracy had been usurped by commerce: shops, taverns and theaters all lined the Strand. More building development in the 19th century then changed the face of the Strand still further. Banks and offices occupy most of the buildings now, though the shops and theaters have remained.

ST MARY-LE-STRAND. This was the first of fifty new churches that were commissioned by Queen Anne. Built between 1714 and 1724, it was the masterpiece of Scottish architect James Gibbs (1682–1754) ▲ *176, 286*. Some of its features, such as the steeple, clearly show Wren's influence. The walls are in classical style, the roof flat with a balustrade, and above is a three-storied steeple with a belfry and surmounted by a lantern. The interior decoration is simple: the ceiling is in the style of Fontana (1634–1714), with whom Gibbs had recently been studying in Rome. St Mary-le-Strand was Gibbs' first commission for a public building.

THE ADELPHI. In Adam Street and John Adam Street are the remains of one of the most ambitious urban redevelopments in London, and indeed in all of Europe as far as neo-classical

their work, its stiff classical lines softened by exterior decoration and delightful ironwork.

267

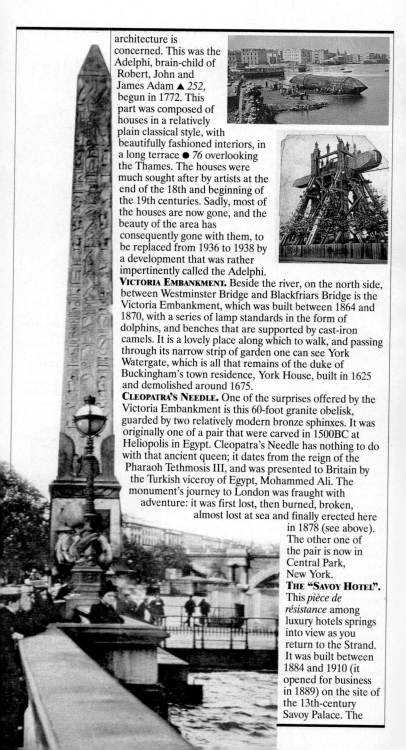

architecture is concerned. This was the Adelphi, brain-child of Robert, John and James Adam ▲ *252*, begun in 1772. This part was composed of houses in a relatively plain classical style, with beautifully fashioned interiors, in a long terrace ● *76* overlooking the Thames. The houses were much sought after by artists at the end of the 18th and beginning of the 19th centuries. Sadly, most of the houses are now gone, and the beauty of the area has consequently gone with them, to be replaced from 1936 to 1938 by a development that was rather impertinently called the Adelphi.

VICTORIA EMBANKMENT. Beside the river, on the north side, between Westminster Bridge and Blackfriars Bridge is the Victoria Embankment, which was built between 1864 and 1870, with a series of lamp standards in the form of dolphins, and benches that are supported by cast-iron camels. It is a lovely place along which to walk, and passing through its narrow strip of garden one can see York Watergate, which is all that remains of the duke of Buckingham's town residence, York House, built in 1625 and demolished around 1675.

CLEOPATRA'S NEEDLE. One of the surprises offered by the Victoria Embankment is this 60-foot granite obelisk, guarded by two relatively modern bronze sphinxes. It was originally one of a pair that were carved in 1500BC at Heliopolis in Egypt. Cleopatra's Needle has nothing to do with that ancient queen; it dates from the reign of the Pharaoh Tethmosis III, and was presented to Britain by the Turkish viceroy of Egypt, Mohammed Ali. The monument's journey to London was fraught with adventure: it was first lost, then burned, broken, almost lost at sea and finally erected here in 1878 (see above). The other one of the pair is now in Central Park, New York.

THE "SAVOY HOTEL". This *pièce de résistance* among luxury hotels springs into view as you return to the Strand. It was built between 1884 and 1910 (it opened for business in 1889) on the site of the 13th-century Savoy Palace. The

present hotel also includes the Savoy Theatre, which was built in 1881 for performing the comic operas of Gilbert and Sullivan. One of the hotel's most famous guests was Claude Monet, who painted his finest views of London from the balcony of his room ● *96*.

SHELL-MEX HOUSE. Built in 1931, this giant building has a proportionally large clock on its façade, from which it is much easier to tell the time if looking from across the river. Formerly it was the *Hotel Cecil*, then the largest in Europe with eight hundred bedrooms, before becoming the headquarters of the Shell-Mex company. The Austrian painter Oskar Kokoschka was given permission to paint from its flat roof.

CHARING CROSS STATION. "The full tide of human existence is at Charing Cross", said Samuel Johnson (1709–84), long before the great railway terminus serving southeast England was built here. The building incorporates the *Charing Cross Hotel*, and was opened in 1864. In the forecourt is Queen Eleanor's Cross, which was erected in 1865 by Edward Middleton Barry, and is a copy of one of the twelve crosses put up by King Edward I to commemorate his wife Eleanor of Castile, who died in 1290.

COUTTS BANK. The old building of this famous bank located opposite the station was redeveloped in the 1970's, with a spacious modern atrium but retaining the elegant Nash ▲ *257* façade. Coutts and Co. are the queen's bankers.

SOMERSET HOUSE. It is a good idea to view Somerset House from Waterloo Bridge before exploring the inside. This immense Georgian residence is the sole remaining example of the great houses that once lined the Strand. It was built on the site of a Renaissance palace, which was in turn constructed around 1547 by Lord Protector Somerset, regent in the reign of Henry VIII's son, the boy-king Edward VI. The original building was altered by Inigo Jones ▲ *328* and John Webb in the 17th century, then gradually fell into disuse and was finally demolished in 1775 on the orders of George III. The present Somerset House was built between 1776 and 1786 by the Scottish architect Sir William Chambers (1723–96) ▲ *280, 348* to house government offices, as well as the Admiralty, the Royal Academy, the Royal Society and the Society of Antiquaries. Two additional wings were added in the 19th century: the west wing in 1856, designed by Sir James Pennethorne; and the east wing (1835), designed by Robert Smirke and intended for King's College. Somerset House contains part of the National Archives, and since 1990 the Courtauld Institute of Fine Art. In the center of the courtyard, surrounded by four wings with bases of Portland stone, is a bronze statue of King George III holding a rudder. This was executed in 1778 by John Bacon.

KING'S COLLEGE. The east wing of Somerset House is occupied by King's College (founded in 1828 by the duke of Wellington), part of the University of London since 1908.

SOMERSET HOUSE
This great neo-classical building on the banks of the Thames once extended right down to the water's edge.

SHELL-MEX BUILDING AND SAVOY HOTEL
These buildings dominate the skyline above Victoria Embankment.

SOMERSET HOUSE
This illustration shows the ornate porch of the great palace.

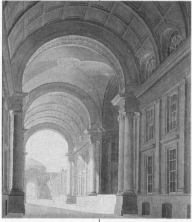

"A BAR AT THE FOLIES-BERGÈRE"
Manet's most famous painting is to be seen here in the Courtauld Institute Galleries.

"A QUACK ADDRESSING A CROWD AT A FAIR"
Rembrandt (1606–69) was one of the greatest line artists of his time, as this ink and wash sketch shows.

"ADAM AND EVE"
A marvelous biblical painting by Lucas Cranach the Elder (1472–1553).

THE COURTAULD INSTITUTE GALLERIES ★

Having been relegated for more than half a century to some cramped premises in Woburn Place, the collections of the Courtauld Institute were finally moved in 1990 to Somerset House. The pictures are now to be seen hanging in some elegant rooms that were once occupied by the Royal Academy and by other learned societies, namely the eleven rooms on the upper floor of the east wing, in which the main collections of canvases, painted panels, gold and Venetian glass as well as Italian ceramics are displayed. The Courtauld Institute's worldwide reputation rests chiefly on its collection of French Impressionist and Post-Impressionist paintings, though it does possess many fine Old Masters and some more recent works.

SAMUEL COURTAULD. The heart of the institute's collection is composed of the series of paintings belonging to Samuel Courtauld (1876–1947), who was descended from a French Huguenot family that fled to London in 1685, when the Edict of Nantes was revoked. Courtauld was the head of a huge company manufacturing synthetic fibers, and he consequently made a fortune in the textile industry. He was a passionate devotee of late 19th-century painting, and assembled a magnificent collection of pictures, which he presented to London University in 1932.

THE ITALIAN AND FLEMISH SCHOOLS. The collections of Lord Lee, of Mark Gambier-Parry and the Prince's Gate collection of Count Antoine Seilern are principally of Flemish and Italian Old Masters from the Renaissance period to the 17th century. Do not miss an Italian triptych and a polyptych from the 14th

century, a Botticelli *Trinity with John the Baptist and Mary Magdalene* (15th century) and a painting by Breughel the Elder (16th century). There are some fine 18th-century portraits too, notably by the English masters Romney and Gainsborough ▲ *213*. Count Seilern bequeathed to the institute a total of thirty-two paintings by Rubens from the 16th and 17th centuries. These are displayed in the first rooms and include three sketches for a *Descent from the Cross* from Antwerp Cathedral, a painting depicting the *Placing of Christ's Body in the Tomb*, and six sketches for the Jesuit church in Antwerp. There are also some fine canvases by Rubens' pupil Van Dyck.

A WEALTH OF FRENCH IMPRESSIONISTS. The pictures which Samuel Courtauld acquired include just about all of the leading names of French Impressionism: there are works by Manet (*A Bar at the Folies-Bergère*), and by Monet (*Autumn at Argenteuil*), by Renoir (*La Loge*), Pissarro (*Lordship Lane Station*), two of Gauguin's Tahiti pictures and two Van Goghs, including his self-portrait with his ear cut off. There are also some fine pictures by Sisley, Boudin, Degas, Berthe Morisot and many more. One of the rooms is devoted exclusively to the French Post-Impressionists, such as Seurat (*Jeune Femme se poudrant*), Utrillo (*A Street in Sannois*), Cézanne (*Mont Sainte-Victoire*), Toulouse-Lautrec (*Jeanne Avril*) and a *Nude* by Modigliani.

CONTEMPORARY ART. As well as the above-mentioned material, the Courtauld Institute collections have received bequests and donations of more recent works, particularly from the English artist and critic Roger Fry (1866–1934), including works by Bonnard, Browse, Derain, Hunter and Fry himself, gouaches by Rouault, African sculptures and a number of pieces from the Omega Workshops that Fry founded in 1913.

"THE CONVERSION OF ST PAUL"
This painting by Peter Paul Rubens (1577–1640) is typical of the Flemish master's colorful style. He was the greatest master of the Baroque style in northern Europe.

"MONT SAINTE-VICTOIRE"
This picture of a mountain near Aix-en-Provence was painted by Paul Cézanne (1839–1906) around 1886–8, when he had married and finally settled in his native Provence.

"COVENT GARDEN IN THE 18TH CENTURY"
This picture by Balthazar Nebot, painted around 1735–7, shows the piazza's arcades and St Paul's Church, both designed by Inigo Jones ▲ 328.

"Turning from the Temple gate . . . I got a late Hackney chariot and drove to the Hummums in Covent Garden. In those times a bed was always to be got there at any hour of the night. . . ."
Charles Dickens, *Great Expectations*

"COVENT GARDEN IN THE 19TH CENTURY"
This watercolor by John Wykeham Archer gives a good idea of the busy market in the 19th century. In his play *Pygmalion* (1913) the hero Professor Higgins first meets the cockney flower girl Eliza Doolittle under the portico of St Paul's, Covent Garden. *Pygmalion* later became familiar to millions when transformed into the musical *My Fair Lady*.

COVENT GARDEN ★

The market and the theater were the two dominant features of Covent Garden for almost three hundred years. The area's restoration in 1980 then gave it another lease of life.

A MONASTERY GARDEN. Covent Garden was originally the vegetable garden of the monks of Westminster Abbey ▲ 137, then with the suppression of the monasteries in the reign of Henry VIII ● 36 it came into the possession of the Russell family, earls of Bedford. In 1631 the fourth earl decided to construct a piazza on the spot and he entrusted the project to the royal architect Inigo Jones ▲ 328. Jones incorporated features from the Place des Vosges in Paris and also the piazza at Livorno into his designs, which were built between 1631 and 1635 on a rectangular space backing on to the Russells' property ▲ 298, Bedford House. Because of the considerable cost, the square was lined with arcades on only two sides; the south side was bordered by the gardens of Bedford House, and the west by St Paul's Church. With its terraces of matching houses and elegant right-angled streets, Covent Garden was London's first "square". It was predominantly a residential district inhabited by courtiers, but in 1661 it was partially restored to its old purpose when the Russells decided to start a fruit, flower and vegetable market there. This was such a success that it was soon the principal market of its kind in England. In an attempt to keep

this colorful but chaotic market under control, in 1829 and 1833 architect Charles Fowler built the market halls ● 85. These were three long, parallel buildings in the center of the piazza. They were divided into stalls with iron colonnades and with a glass roof. Nothing remains of Jones' original piazza, though the arcades on the north side of the square give some idea of how it must once have looked.

THE MUSES GO TO MARKET. The opening of the Theatre Royal, Drury Lane, in 1663, and then of Covent Garden Theatre in 1732, transformed the area and brought in crowds of theatergoers. But it was in the 19th century that the district found its greatest theatrical vocation, with the construction of forty new theaters in an area that was already famous for its liveliness and fun.

COVENT GARDEN MARKET IN 1950
The market continued working in the halls built by the duke of Bedford in 1829 right up to the 1970's, and was a familiar part of the London scene.

A SUCCESSFUL FACELIFT. The market retained its cheerful and somewhat scruffy appearance until 1974. When it finally moved to Nine Elms on the other side of the river, the character of the quarter was quickly lost, and plans were made to redevelop the site as offices. Thanks to the determination of the people who lived there, such as artists and architects, the authorities were eventually persuaded to restore Covent Garden. The work was successfully completed in 1980, with a central pedestrian area and NEAL STREET, a lively collection of small shops, contributing to a new lease of life for the old market.

THE FLOWER MARKET. Opposite the main halls, the Jubilee Market (1904) is still in business, with a flea market operating on Mondays. The old Flower Market beside it, which was built in 1891, houses a fascinating theater museum, and there is also the LONDON TRANSPORT MUSEUM to be visited, where horse-drawn ancestors of the famous red London buses are on show. A substantial collection of buses, trams, models, paintings, posters, tickets and other ephemera all help to tell the story of the history of public transport in the capital city.

ST PAUL'S CHURCH. There is a legend attached to the building of this church. It is said that the earl of Bedford thought the building of a church to be essential to the whole success of his development scheme, but he was wary of the expense. In 1613 he accordingly asked Inigo Jones to build something simple, "like a barn". Jones promised his employer "the handsomest barn in England". The result is a simple, Palladian building with a gently sloping roof and a

COVENT GARDEN MARKET TODAY
When the market moved away to new premises south of the Thames, its elegant old buildings were saved from demolition and subsequently restored. Since 1980 they have been home to a range of craft and antique stalls, restaurants, fashion boutiques and a host of other ventures.

pillared porch, in front of a blind façade looking on to the piazza. St Paul's was badly burned in 1795, and then faithfully restored by Thomas Hardwick.

THEATERLAND ● 54

There are a number of major theaters in the neighborhood of the Strand, such as the Savoy Theatre, the Vaudeville Theatre, the Fortune Theatre, the Adelphi, the Strand and the Aldwych. With the addition of the two big ones in Covent Garden, the Theatre Royal, Drury Lane, and the Royal Opera House, the area has long supplied the very lifeblood of the London stage.

THE DRURY LANE THEATRE. The present theater in Drury Lane is the work of Benjamin Dean Wyatt (1755–1850), and it was actually the fourth theater to be built on the site. It was opened in 1812. The second theater had been designed by Wren ▲ *171* in 1672–4, but this was demolished in 1791. Here the actor Edmund Kean (1789–1833) performed many of his great Shakespearean roles, such as Shylock, Iago and Richard III. The auditorium, which was rebuilt in 1922, is the largest in all of London with a seating capacity for three thousand people.

THE ROYAL OPERA HOUSE. This building first opened its doors in 1732 as the Covent Garden Theatre. The present building, which was constructed between 1856 and 1858 by Edward Barry, was the third theater to be built on the site. The previous ones were both destroyed by fire. Its façade is decorated with a Corinthian portico shielding reliefs and a frieze from the previous building by John Flaxman (1755–1826). The auditorium's acoustics are famous throughout the opera world, and there is seating capacity for more than two thousand people. A new west wing was added in 1982. The foundation of the Royal Opera Company in 1946 and of the Royal Ballet ten years later helped to enhance the theater's reputation as one of the finest opera houses in the world.

"This is a fascinating street for anyone wishing to study the ladies doing their

shopping, as the shops and other establishments are close together, and the

displays in the shop windows are such that the emotions proper to the gentler sex

are forever in danger of being undermined." Henry Mayhew, *The Shops and*

Companies of London and the Trade and Manufactures of Great Britain, 1865.

MARBLE ARCH · APSLEY HOUSE · WELLINGTON ARCH · GROSVENOR SQUARE · GROSVENOR CHAPEL · BERKELEY SQUARE

OXFORD STREET

PARK LANE

CURZON STREET

PICCADILLY

🏃 Half a day

ST JAMES'S, PICCADILLY
The church, constructed of brick and Portland stone, was built in 1674 by Wren ▲ 172 and restored after World War Two by Sir Albert Richardson. It has a gallery and a vaulted ceiling ornamented with plaster molding. The organ was made for the Chapel Royal in Whitehall; its case is decorated with gilded figures, the work of Grinling Gibbons ▲ 157, 173, 198, who also decorated the marble fonts and the limewood reredos.

AROUND ST JAMES'S

The exclusive district of St James's is at the very center of fashionable London. Peaceful and opulent, it is an area of gracious town houses and gentlemen's clubs, bounded on the north side by Piccadilly, by the Haymarket in the east, with St James's Park on its southern boundary and Green Park to the west side. Its links with royalty go back as far as the 17th century, but today many of its fine, original houses are gone, replaced by commercial developments of the 19th and 20th centuries.

A ROYAL DISTRICT. Ever since Charles II moved into St James's Palace ▲ 240 the surrounding district has acquired

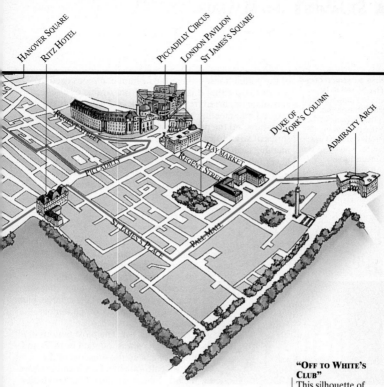

HANOVER SQUARE
RITZ HOTEL
PICCADILLY CIRCUS
LONDON PAVILION
ST JAMES'S SQUARE
DUKE OF YORK'S COLUMN
ADMIRALTY ARCH
REGENT STREET
HAY MARKET
PICCADILLY
REGENT STREET
ST JAMES'S PLACE
PALL MALL

a touch of royal glamor. Henry Jermyn, Earl of St Albans was the first to develop the area: he took advantage of the king's residence nearby to build houses on land that was granted him by Charles II. Then he sold the elegant town houses that line St James's Square to a number of wealthy noblemen who wanted to be as near to the court as possible. The district took off again during the 18th century, with government ministries and foreign embassies settling in St James's. Numerous coffee-houses and shops also opened up, notably in St James's Street, to cater for the needs of such a high-class clientèle. In spite of the young Queen Victoria's decision to move to Buckingham Palace in 1837, St James's continued to be the home of high society.

THE AGE OF ELEGANCE. Dandyism was born in England at the start of the 19th century. Dandies were young men of high birth who expressed their contempt for political democracy and social equality by their exquisite dress, affected speech, exaggerated manners and refined taste. The dramatist Richard Brinsley Sheridan (1751–1816) and the Romantic poet Lord Byron (1788–1824) were among the founding fathers of the fashion, whose unchallenged leader was George Brummell (1778–1840), known as "Beau". Brummell's friendship with the Prince Regent, the future George IV, opened the doors of society for him, and he soon became the arbiter of good taste and the king of fashion. He even chose the clothes that his manservant wore, and would spend hours tying his cravat. A break with the prince obliged Beau Brummell to take refuge from his creditors in France, where he died in Caen, destitute, dirty and mad.

CLUBLAND. The gentlemen's clubs of St James's are some of the pillars of the English establishment. They are descendants

"OFF TO WHITE'S CLUB"
This silhouette of 1819 by Richard Dighton shows William Archer strolling to his club, recalling the observation by a French visitor to London that "a dandy should have a victorious, carefree and insolent air, and take immense pains with his toilette . . ."

NINE HUNDRED CLUBS
There used to be around nine hundred clubs in London. Billiards (below: the billiard room in Brooks's Club) was a typical activity, as was conversation.

The Marquis of Hertford in 1818.

of the coffee-houses where the fashion-conscious used to gather to sip either this new drink from Arabia or else chocolate imported from the Americas. These gradually evolved into meeting-places for discussions about politics, literature and the pressing topics of the day. The clubs have a series of strict rules and restricted membership policies, but members can relax, meet each other (on condition that they never talk "shop"), drink, dine and stay overnight. All rules are carefully observed by the club members, who are still almost exclusively men.

PALL MALL

On turning into Cockspur Street or Pall Mall East, one can see at the end the featureless façades of Pall Mall, which takes its name from an old game, somewhat resembling croquet, that was once played there. Now these large, plain buildings house many of the famous gentlemen's clubs.

THE ATHENAEUM. The most famous of all London clubs was founded in 1823, and it has long been the preserve of the British cultural élite. Past members have included the naturalists Thomas Huxley (1825–95) and Charles Darwin (1809–82), and the writers Charles Dickens (1812–70) ● *110–11, 118,* Joseph Conrad (1857–1924) ● *112*, and Rudyard Kipling (1865–1936). The club has also been popular with many politicians and bishops. Membership of the Athenaeum, which carries great kudos in certain circles, is by application, followed by a ballot where members vote with white or black balls. If a member expresses his objection by the use of a black ball, the candidate is said to be "blackballed" or turned down. Bertrand Russell ▲ *308* had to wait forty years after being blackballed before he was finally admitted to membership of the club. Naturally enough the building is in quasi-Grecian style, built in 1828–30 by Decimus Burton ▲ *257*. It is a most spectacular affair, with a majestic hall dominated by a statue of Apollo, reading room, dining room, games room and a magnificent library where the walls are lined with precious books. Members' private apartments are situated on the upper floors. Certain rules must be observed. For example, it is forbidden to discuss business or to take any paper out of your pocket in the dining room: a lady dining there once with her husband was called to order by the club steward when she took a sample of wallpaper out of her bag.

THE TRAVELLERS' CLUB. This club was founded in 1819 for travelers to meet, exchange experiences and possibly tell a few tall tales. It is at 106 Pall Mall in a clubhouse

designed by Charles Barry ▲ *131* in 1829–32. To be eligible for membership, a candidate must have traveled at least a thousand miles from London. Many diplomats are members.

THE REFORM CLUB. The "Italian palazzo" at numbers 104–5 is the home of the Reform Club, traditionally the preserve of wealthy radicals. It was built in 1837 by Charles Barry.

THE ROYAL AUTOMOBILE CLUB. The present building at 80 Pall Mall was built 1908–11 by the architects of the *Ritz Hotel* ▲ *280*, and now has fifteen thousand members up and down the country. The clubhouse incorporates a much older building, Schomberg House (1698), where the artist Gainsborough ▲ *213* lived from 1774 to 1778.

THE OXFORD AND CAMBRIDGE CLUB. This was founded by Lord Palmerston in 1830. The building, at 71 Pall Mall, was the work of the Smirke brothers, who were also the architects of the British Museum ▲ *300*. Membership is open to those who have studied at one or other of the two universities.

ST JAMES'S STREET

Pall Mall leads to St James's Street, which is one of the most elegant and aristocratic in London. An atmosphere of luxury and quiet refinement rules here, among the old businesses for which the street is world-famous.

THE CLUBS. Boodle's (number 28) together with Brooks's and White's (number 37) are some of the oldest clubs in the street. The Carlton Club, in a building dating from 1827, is another Tory institution, founded in 1832 by the duke of Wellington.

"BERRY BROTHERS AND RUDD". This family business founded in the 17th century is at 3 St James's Street. It is renowned for its excellent clarets and whisky. The large scales inside have been used to weigh famous patrons since 1765, the results being recorded in nine leather-bound volumes.

"LOCK'S". The famous hatter's shop has been at 6 St James's Street since 1759. High society still comes to *Lock's* for top hats and bowlers. Before Lord Nelson ▲ *284* left for his final victory at Trafalgar, he came here and ordered a hat specially fitted with an eyeshade.

"LOBB'S" BESPOKE BOOTMAKERS. "The world's finest bootmaker" is at 9 St James's Street. He makes boots and

shoes for the royal feet, and among his many other famous customers have been Winston Churchill, Katharine Hepburn and Frank Sinatra.

BYRON HOUSE. This was built in 1960 on the site of Lord Byron's house where, as he said, he awoke one beautiful morning in 1812 after the publication of his poem *Childe Harold's Pilgrimage* to find himself famous.

JERMYN STREET

The world-famous parfumier *Floris* (above) is here. Founded in 1730, the shop is noted for its pots-pourri, its stephanotis scent and its rose geranium bath salts. Famous clients have included Queen Victoria, the duke of Windsor, Oscar Wilde, Queen Elizabeth II and Prince Charles. Other notable establishments on Jermyn Street are the famous cheese shop *Paxton & Whitfield*, the cigar merchant *Davidoff* and the goldsmith's *Grima*. There are also several fine shirtmakers.

PICCADILLY

This broad avenue was laid out in the 18th century. It runs from Hyde Park Corner to Piccadilly Circus, separating the district of St James's from Mayfair. Today it is lined with first-class hotels, expensive shops, majestic old town houses and other splendid dwellings converted into clubs.

THE "RITZ HOTEL". This is the biggest hotel in London. Built of Norwegian granite on a steel frame by Mewes and Davis at the corner of Green Park, it opened in 1906.

BURLINGTON ARCADE. There are forty-one small shops in this Regency arcade of 1819, selling luxury goods such as jewelry and cashmere.

THE ROYAL ACADEMY OF ARTS. Burlington House has been home to the Royal Academy for more than a century. The building was altered and enlarged between 1867 and 1874 by Banks and Barry, and again more recently by Norman Foster. It retains its Palladian interior. The academy was founded in 1768 to teach fine arts, and holds an exhibition every summer. Each elected academician is obliged to donate one of his or her works. The list of donors includes Gainsborough ▲ *213*, Benjamin West, Sir William Chambers ▲ *269, 348*, Turner ▲ *215–217* and Constable ▲ *214*. Acquisitions have also enriched the permanent collection, which boasts a lovely marble tondo by Michelangelo: *Madonna and Child with the Infant St John.*

"FORTNUM & MASON'S". This superb grocery store restocks the royal larders. Its orange marmalade is much in demand, likewise its pickles and tea.

"HATCHARD'S" BOOKSHOP. John Hatchard opened here in 1797, and his shop soon began to resemble a club, especially attracting residents of the Albany nearby, such as Lord Byron.

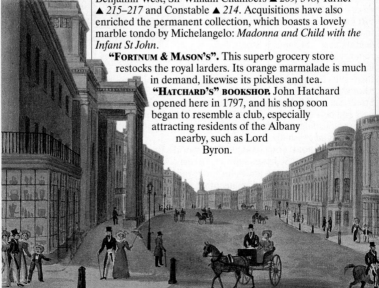

"TO BE ENGLISH IS TO BELONG TO THE MOST
EXCLUSIVE CLUB IN THE WORLD."

OGDEN NASH

Other famous customers have included Wellington, Gladstone and Oscar Wilde.

MAYFAIR

The little district of Mayfair, on the edge of Hyde Park, is bounded by Oxford Street, Regent Street and Piccadilly. The name comes from the "May Fairs", local livestock and grain markets that from 1688 were held in the first week of May. The area was first developed in the 18th century by the Grosvenor family, the dukes of Westminster, then grand houses and numerous squares were added. Mayfair is the wealthiest and most expensive part of London. It divides fairly neatly into two: the area around Bond Street with its prosperous businesses, and west toward Hyde Park, which is the elegant residential quarter. Many celebrated people have lived here, such as Lord Byron, the historian Macaulay and prime minister Gladstone; and more recently the novelist Graham Greene, and former Conservative premier Edward Heath.

CURZON STREET. This street still has some 18th-century houses such as Crew House (number 15), built in 1730 for Edward Shepherd. The shop of *Geo. F. Trumper* (number 9), perfumer and hairdresser, is well worth a look. His shaving creams in such scents as rose, violet, almond and sandalwood, as well as his goats' milk soap and other items, are a delight.

SHEPHERD MARKET. This little area was designed by architect Edward Shepherd around 1735 on the site of the former May Fair. Shepherd's shops and houses were altered in 1860, but it still remains a charming little maze of old-fashioned shops selling food (such as *Bendick's Chocolate Shop*) and antiques. There are interesting restaurants too.

BERKELEY SQUARE. This was laid out 1737–47 to designs by William Kent (1685–1748), the protégé of Lord Burlington. Queen Elizabeth II was born at 17 Bruton Street in Berkeley Square House on the east side of the square.

GROSVENOR SQUARE. This was built between 1720 and 1725 at the end of Upper Brook Street. In 1785 John Adams, future president of the USA, moved to number 9 when he was ambassador here. Ever since, the area has been known as "Little America".

BROOK STREET. Along Brook Street towards Hanover Square is the Savile Club with its French 18th-century-style interior. The composer George Frederick Handel (1685–1759) spent the last thirty years of his life at number 25. Just before Bond Street is the famous *Claridge's Hotel*,

THE ROYAL ACADEMY
Sir Joshua Reynolds was the first president of England's oldest society devoted to the fine arts.

BURLINGTON ARCADE
This private thoroughfare is supervised by "beadles" in coats and bowler hats. By day they watch over the behavior of passers-by (singing is not allowed); and at night they close the gates ● *84.*

NAMES DOWN THE AGES
The noble families who developed Mayfair in the 18th century, with its beautiful houses and elegant squares, have their memorials in many street names. They include Thomas Bond, Lord Dover, Sir Nathaniel Curzon, Hugh Audley, Lord Chesterfield, Lady Berkeley of Stratton and the Grosvenor family.

THE "CAFÉ ROYAL"
This famous restaurant is on the curve of the Regent Street Quadrant. It opened in 1865 and was the haunt of notable writers and artists, such as Oscar Wilde (1854–1900), and the artists Aubrey Beardsley (1872–98), James Abbott McNeill Whistler (1834–1903) ● *104* and Augustus John (1878–1961).

"LIBERTY'S"
This enormous store, renowned for its cottons and silks, is at the corner of Regent Street and Great Marlborough Street ● *89*. The building dates from 1924–5. Behind it is another section in mock-Tudor style, giving on to Great Marlborough Street.

which since 1860 has enjoyed the reputation of being London's best hotel.

SAVILE ROW. The great tradition of British tailoring is centered here: there is *Henry Poole* (tailor to Emperor Napoleon III), *H. Huntsman & Sons*, *J. Dege & Sons*, *Gieves & Hawkes*, and many more.

THE MUSEUM OF MANKIND. This building at 6 Burlington Gardens was built in 1866–7 in the Renaissance style, and was part of the University of London until 1972, when it was transformed to house the ethnographic collections of the British Museum. Here are magnificent primitive works of art (pre-Colombian pieces, African sculpture), artifacts (fabrics and pottery) and objects brought back from the Pacific in the 18th century by Captain Cook.

BOND STREET

This is the main street in Mayfair. It runs down to Piccadilly under the name of Old Bond Street, and in the other direction up to Oxford Street as New Bond Street. Lord Nelson ▲ *274* once lived here with his mistress Lady Hamilton; Beau Brummell and Lord Byron are among other famous residents of Bond Steet.

SUPPLIERS TO THE COURT. Bond Street is also the home of luxury shops such as *Beal & Inman* and *Herbie Frogg* for clothes, *Church & Co.* for shoes, and *Asprey's*, which sells leather goods and jewelry as well as antiques. Above certain shops gleams the sign *By Appointment to Her Majesty*; these

are suppliers to the court, a guarantee of high
quality and the best workmanship.

REGENT STREET

Regent Street runs from the Athenaeum in Pall
Mall up to the north of Oxford Circus, and was
built to designs by John Nash ▲ *257* between 1813
and 1823. This majestic road, lined with gracious
stucco-faced houses linked the Prince Regent's
home of Carlton House in St James's Park to
Regent's Park in the north. The street was entirely
rebuilt between 1898 and 1928, and along it are
large luxury shops such as *Liberty's*, *Aquascutum*,
and *Hamley's* ◆ *386*, one of the biggest and most
celebrated toyshops in the world.

"LIBERTY'S". *Liberty's* was founded in 1875 by Arthur Liberty,
whose fabrics were all the rage in the days of Art Nouveau
● *89*. Today the printed fabrics have become classics of the
English style and some can be reordered in exactly the same
design from year to year. But this is a department store too,
selling men's and ladies' fashions and household goods.

THE QUADRANT. This is the name of the impressive curve
made by Regent Street as it sweeps down toward Piccadilly
Circus. In the façades, rebuilt at the beginning of the century,
no trace remains of Nash's original work.

PICCADILLY CIRCUS. This road junction has come to represent
the heart of London for millions of tourists. But it is in fact
only a busy intersection. At night it is brightly illuminated by
giant neon signs, the first of which was erected in 1890. The
little statue in the middle does not in fact depict Eros, as is
generally thought, but the Angel of Christian Charity. It was
put up in 1893 in memory of the Victorian philanthropist
Lord Shaftesbury.

**REGENT CIRCUS AND
OXFORD STREET**
Oxford Circus was
originally called
Regent Circus. It was
built in the 19th
century at the
junction of
Regent Street and
Oxford Street.

**"OLD REGENT
STREET"**
This painting by
J. Kynnersley Kirby
shows the busy
clothing stores
around the Quadrant,
before the street was
rebuilt.

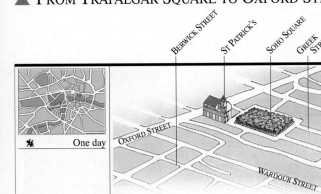

BERWICK STREET
ST PATRICK'S
SOHO SQUARE
GREEK STREET
FRITH STREET
DEAN STREET

OXFORD STREET

WARDOUR STREET

🚶 One day

TRAFALGAR SQUARE

CHRISTMAS CAROLS IN TRAFALGAR SQUARE
The Christmas tree is decorated with lights, and around it the singing is led by a number of different choirs who collect money for charity.

CHRISTMAS IN TRAFALGAR SQUARE
An enormous Christmas tree has been erected here every year since 1947. This gift from the people of Norway is in recognition of the refuge that Britain gave to the Norwegian royal family during World War Two.

In 1820 it was the architect John Nash's idea to lay out a square at the top of Whitehall on the site of the former Royal Mews. The only existing constructions to antedate Trafalgar Square in this area are the church of St Martin-in-the-Fields, and the equestrian statue of Charles I, which was made by Le Sueur in 1633 and then erected on its present site around 1767. The construction of this famous square began in 1829: the sloping land was leveled and then paved in 1840 by Sir Charles Barry, who also added the north terrace below the National Gallery. There are statues of George IV and Generals Havelock and Napier at three corners of the square. The fountains by Sir Edwin Lutyens were added in 1939.

NELSON'S COLUMN. A statue of Lord Nelson over 17 feet tall dominates the square. It was erected in 1843 on a granite column that is 172 feet high, the base of which is ornamented with four bronze lions (1867) by the artist Sir Edwin Landseer. The pedestal of the monument has a number of bas-reliefs, cast from French cannons, which depict the great admiral's naval victories at Cape St Vincent, the Battle of the Nile, Copenhagen, and Trafalgar. It was during the latter, on October 21, 1805, that Nelson was killed.

MEETINGS IN TRAFALGAR SQUARE. The square has been a traditional place for public meetings ever since the time of the Chartists in 1848. Many political marches end here with rallies, at which speakers usually address the crowds from the base of the column. Every year at Christmas there is a huge illuminated fir tree, the gift of the Norwegian people in memory of the Second World War. The tradition is for huge crowds of Londoners to flock here on New Year's Eve in order to hear Big Ben chime midnight and then to wish each other a Happy New Year. The gatherings can get extremely noisy and

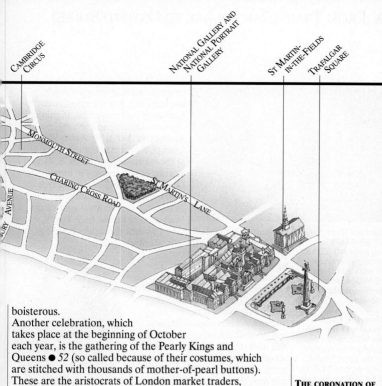

MONMOUTH STREET

CHARING CROSS ROAD

ST MARTIN'S LANE

...BURY AVENUE

boisterous.

Another celebration, which takes place at the beginning of October each year, is the gathering of the Pearly Kings and Queens ● *52* (so called because of their costumes, which are stitched with thousands of mother-of-pearl buttons). These are the aristocrats of London market traders, whose original function was to protect the costermongers' interests and to preserve good relations with the police; their work now is devoted to fund-raising for various charities.

SOUTH AFRICA HOUSE. Sir Herbert Baker (1862–1946) designed this seven-story building in 1935 on the site of the former *Morley's Hotel* (1831). There is a striking sculpture of a springbok at the entrance; the building's portico echoes the design of the portico of the adjacent church of St Martin-in-the-Fields.

CANADA HOUSE. Sir Robert Smirke's original building (1824–7), situated on the west side of the square, was intended for the Royal College of Physicians. Smirke's

THE CORONATION OF QUEEN VICTORIA
Victoria (b. May 24, 1819) became queen on June 20, 1837. Her coronation the following year, and the jubilees in 1887 and 1897, were scenes of great celebration. Her reign (she died in 1901) was also the high point in Britain's status as a world power.

EDWARD BAILY (1788–1867)
An unsigned picture showing the sculptor at work on his statue of Nelson, which surmounts the column.

HORATIO, LORD NELSON (1758–1805)
Sir William Beechey painted this portrait of the great English hero around 1800. In it he omitted to show Nelson's blind right eye, lost at the siege of Calvi in 1794.

❝May the Great God, whom I worship, grant to my Country and for the benefit of Europe in general a great and glorious victory; and may no misconduct in anyone tarnish it; and may humanity after Victory be the predominant feature of the British Fleet. For myself, individually, I commit my life to Him who made me, and may His blessing light upon my endeavours for serving my Country faithfully. To Him I resign myself and the just cause which is entrusted to me to defend. Amen. Amen. Amen.**❞**
Extract from *Nelson's Diary* on the eve of the Battle of Trafalgar

original exterior has been much altered since, but the magnificent interior is well preserved, in particular the fine staircase and library.

ADMIRALTY ARCH. Sir Aston Webb's triumphal arch was completed in 1911 at the southwest corner of Trafalgar Square. It was erected in memory of Queen Victoria. The central arch is only opened on a few state occasions, as it stands on the royal route from Buckingham Palace to St Paul's Cathedral. Named after the adjacent Admiralty buildings, it stands on the site of the 17th-century Spring Gardens.

ST MARTIN-IN-THE-FIELDS. The unusual design of this church, built between 1722 and 1726 by James Gibbs ▲ *176, 267*, is a curious mixture of styles. It rather resembles a rectangular Roman temple, with a Corinthian portico and high steeple. Many famous people are buried here, such as the actress Nell Gwyn, Charles II's mistress; the artists William Hogarth and Sir Joshua Reynolds, the cabinet-maker Thomas Chippendale and the highwayman Jack Sheppard. By tradition it is also the royal parish church: Charles II was one of the many royal babies to be christened here.

THE PIGEONS. Although Trafalgar Square would lose some of its character without the pigeons, they constitute a serious nuisance. Many schemes for reducing their numbers have been tried out, but so far all in vain.

NATIONAL GALLERY ★

In 1824 the government purchased thirty-eight paintings from the estate of the wealthy merchant John Julius Angerstein, including works by Titian, Raphael, Rembrandt and Rubens, for £57,000. They were first exhibited in Angerstein's Pall Mall house, until the construction of a new gallery was entrusted to William Wilkins, who built it on the north side of Trafalgar Square between 1832 and 1838. It is a long and repetitive low structure in classical style which has been much enlarged, with mock-Grecian colonnades, and a dome separating the two wings. One wing formerly housed the Royal Academy before its removal to Burlington House in 1869 ▲ *280*. Since it was opened in 1838, the original shallow design has greatly increased in depth, the latest addition being the Sainsbury wing on the west side, built by Robert Venturi in 1975. A regular grant for the acquisition of pictures was voted by Parliament in 1855. The interior is much more successfully designed and holds one of the greatest collections of paintings in the world. Its marvels were more than enough to depress the frustrated young artist Branwell Brontë (1817–48), brother of Charlotte and Emily: "When after several days of desultory wandering through the streets . . . he eventually visited the National Gallery and saw the work of the great masters after which he had yearned all his life, his reaction was one of despair. He saw their perfection and realized his own incapacity, in the same horrible moment of truth."

TRAFALGAR SQUARE THEN AND NOW
The north side of the square is occupied by the recently extended façade of the National Gallery. Below, to the right of the picture, is the tower of St Martin-in-the-Fields. The photograph above shows Nelson's Column, St Martin-in-the-Fields, South Africa House and the National Gallery.

The National Gallery is one of the most important art galleries in the world. Altogether there are more than two thousand works here, including the finest collection of Italian art to be found outside Italy (particularly Primitive and Renaissance paintings). There is also a superb collection devoted to the work of Dutch and Flemish artists.

"VIRGIN AND CHILD"
Duccio di Buoninsegna (c. 1260–c. 1318) was one of the greatest masters of the Sienese school. His work is among the oldest in the possession of the National Gallery. This piece shows the influence of Byzantine art on the school of Siena, but the depth of color against the gold background shows the evolution toward the Gothic style.

"THE BATTLE OF SAN ROMANO"
Paolo Uccello (c. 1397–1475) painted four versions of this battle for the Medici family. San Romano (1432) was a celebrated victory for the Florentines over their Sienese neighbors: in the foreground the knight without armor represents the Florentine commander Niccolò da Tolentino. Except for the two white horses, the overall color scheme is very dark; but the eye clearly discerns Uccello's experiments in perspective.

"THE DOGE LEONARDO LOREDAN"
Loredan was doge of Venice from 1501 to 1521, and Bellini's magnificent portrait seems to have been painted in the year he took office. The Venetian Giovanni Bellini (c. 1430–1516) was very much influenced by Mantegna, who became his brother-in-law. Mantegna's influence is apparent in the neutral background to the picture, adding to its feeling of austerity.

"THE MADONNA OF THE MEADOW"
"He is very old, but still the best painter there is," Dürer wrote home from Venice. Giovanni Bellini was around seventy-five when he painted this serene and colorful Madonna. Its pose resembles that of a Pietà, of which he executed several that show the influence of his artist father Jacopo.

"THE VIRGIN AND CHILD WITH ST ANNE AND ST JOHN THE BAPTIST"
Leonardo da Vinci (1452–1519) executed this cartoon around 1503 in Florence. It represents an experiment in creating a unified compositional form out of two figures with children. It was one of a series: there is another in the Louvre.

DUAL MATERNITY
Sigmund Freud was fascinated by this cartoon, from which he made a psychological study of the role of the mother in the artist's work. Leonardo was the illegitimate son of a twenty-three-year-old lawyer called Piero da Vinci and a young peasant girl, Caterina. Piero married the daughter of a noble family the year after Leonardo was born, and they adopted the boy, who always retained a great affection for his stepmother. Freud thought that in making the Virgin and her mother St Anne appear the same age, Leonardo was actually reflecting the dual maternity in his own life.

"YOUNG MAN HOLDING A SKULL"
The greatest gift of the Dutch artist Frans Hals (c. 1585–1666) was for portraiture. If his portraits lack the psychological depth of his contemporary Rembrandt, no-one else's come to life more vividly. It is hard to think of another artist who could use oil paint with such virtuosity. This particular portrait is a Vanitas, a popular genre in the 16th and 17th centuries derived from a passage in *Ecclesiastes*: "Vanity of Vanities ...". These images incorporated symbolic features such as hour-glasses with the sand running out, guttering candles and skulls to represent mortality. The model, with thick sensual lips and an irregular nose, also appears in other portraits by Hals.

"THE AMBASSADORS"

Hans Holbein the Younger (c. 1497–1543) was born in Augsburg, Germany, but settled in England in 1532. The next year he painted *The Ambassadors*, which probably helped his appointment as court painter by Henry VIII in 1536. This double portrait depicts Jean de Dinteville, French ambassador from February to November 1533, on the left; and Georges de Selve, bishop of Lavaur, who arrived to visit Dinteville at 10.30am on April 11, indicated by the globe and clock. The shape in the foreground is a distorted skull, which assumes correct proportions when viewed from a certain angle. Other Vanitas symbols include the broken lute string and the brooch in the ambassador's hat.

"THE MARRIAGE OF THE ARNOLFINI"

The Flemish artist Jan van Eyck (c. 1385–1441) painted the Bruges-based Italian merchant Giovanni Arnolfini and his wife Giovanna Cenami in their home. The picture is charged with symbols such as the single candle in the candelabra representing the unity of marriage.

SELF-PORTRAIT OF THE ARTIST, AGED THIRTY-FOUR

Throughout his life, Rembrandt (1606–1669) observed the effects of age and care upon his own face. This canvas, although apparently destined for a patron, does not seem to have been commissioned, and would rather seem to be a studio version of a type of artists' self-portrait painted for public appreciation.

"THE ROKEBY VENUS"
Diego Velásquez (1599–1660) probably painted this picture of the Toilet of Venus in Italy. It is his only existing nude, and a rare example of a female nude in Spanish painting, with rich, warm colors inspired by Titian. Before the National Gallery acquired it, the picture was in Rokeby Park, Yorkshire, hence its name.

"LES GRANDES BAIGNEUSES II" (1900–5)
Toward the end of his life Paul Cézanne (1839–1906) painted many nude figures

"AVENUE AT MIDDELHARNIS"
Meindert Hobbema (1638–1709) was last in the line of great Dutch landscape painters. This, his most famous work, is dated 1689; and though the artist was never very successful during his lifetime, his work became highly prized in England in the 18th and 19th centuries: Hobbema was to prove a great influence on the English landscape painters.

"THE MARRIAGE CONTRACT"
The first in a series of six paintings *Marriage à la Mode* by William Hogarth (1697–1764), executed between 1743 and 1745. It is a comment on decadent society, with the artist satirizing marriages founded on money and snobbery. An impoverished nobleman is arranging the marriage of his son to the daughter of a wealthy merchant. Engravings of *Marriage à la Mode* were very popular.

in a landscape, though his reluctance to use nude models caused problems. This picture is a key work in art history, pointing the way to Cubism.

"BATHERS AT ASNIÈRES"
Georges Seurat (1859–91) was concerned with the static quality o his pictures rather than the flickering play of light favored by the Impressionists. This is an early example of Pointillism, where the colors are mixed in the viewer's eye rather than on the artist's palette, supposedly giving a cleaner and brighter effect.

Left to right: Samuel Cooper's portrait of Oliver Cromwell; George IV by Sir Thomas Lawrence; William Blake by Thomas Phillips.

The first directors had a free hand to make what purchases they wished and made important acquisitions, particularly of Italian Renaissance and Flemish and Dutch masters. Today the National Gallery has a well-balanced collection of more than two thousand pictures, representing five hundred years of painting from the Italian Primitives to the French Impressionists.

The National Portrait Gallery ★

Since 1896 this gallery has been in a specially constructed building behind the National Gallery on its east side. It is a history of England in pictures, with more than nine thousand portraits (paintings, etchings, drawings, photographs and sculptures) of kings, statesmen, musicians, writers and artists from the time of Henry VIII to the present day. It was founded in 1856, to represent "a Gallery of the Portraits of the most Eminent Persons in British History". Precedence was given to statesmen, men of letters, artists and musicians. The result is a unique, wonderful panorama of British history rather than an art gallery, and though the overall quality may be uneven, the gallery houses great treasures such as Holbein's portrait of Henry VIII, a self-portrait by George Stubbs, and the "Chandos" portrait of William Shakespeare.

Sir Edwin Landseer (1802–73)
John Ballantyne painted this picture around 1865 of Landseer at work on a model of one of the four bronze lions that were placed round the base of Nelson's Column in 1867.

A GUIDED TOUR. The works of art in the National Portrait Gallery are exhibited chronologically, beginning on the top floor, which covers the Tudor period to the Regency. There are some magnificent portraits of Elizabeth I in all her finery, of Shakespeare (the best authenticated likeness), Mary Queen of Scots, Sir Walter Raleigh, Ben Jonson, John Donne and many others.

THE STUART PERIOD. This section of the gallery features a miniature portrait of Oliver Cromwell, which has been signed by Samuel Cooper (1609–72), a portrait of Samuel Pepys depicted wearing an Indian robe by John Hayls, and also a beautiful painting of Louise de Keroualle, the universally loathed duchess of Portsmouth who was a mistress of Charles II. The actress Nell Gwyn was another of the king's beauties, and she is painted here by Sir Peter Lely, together with a lamb.

THE GEORGIAN AGE. Among the most interesting pictures in this fascinating collection are Hudson's portrait of Handel, a self-portrait by William Hogarth, Reynolds' portraits of Johnson and Boswell, and Captain Cook, painted at the Cape of Good Hope in 1776. Two rooms are given over to Kneller's portraits of members of the 18th-century Kit-Kat Club ▲ *262*, including Congreve and Vanbrugh. A more unlikely portrait is the one of Charles Lamb by the writer William Hazlitt. In Room 15 there is an amateurish miniature of Jane Austen by her sister Cassandra, which is the only known likeness of the novelist.

THE ROMANTIC ERA. On display here is a portrait of Robert Burns, painted by his friend Alexander Nasmyth, Sir Walter Scott by Landseer, Byron in Albanian dress (1813) by Phillips, Wordsworth by his friend the eccentric Benjamin Robert Haydon, and Keats by Joseph Severn, who accompanied him on his last journey to Rome.

VICTORIANS AND EDWARDIANS. These portraits occupy the upper floor of the gallery. Look out in particular for the Brontë sisters, painted by their brother Branwell, and for Sargent's portrait of Ellen Terry as Lady Macbeth, as well as the likenesses of Oscar Wilde, Gilbert and Sullivan, Max Beerbohm and many of the Pre-Raphaelite painters. The ground floor is crowded with literally hundreds of famous faces from the 20th century.

Jerry Barrett painted Florence Nightingale (1820–1910) among the soldiers she nursed at Scutari in the Crimean War around 1856 (top of page). Vanessa Bell (above left), a painter herself, sat for this picture by Duncan Grant c. 1918. There are many contemporary portraits of Henry VIII (above center): this one is by an anonymous artist. Sir Peter Lely painted this portrait of Nell Gwyn (c. 1650–87) around 1675. Left, a photograph of the illustrator Aubrey Beardsley (1872–98) taken in 1894 by Frederick Henry Evans.

GEORGE BERNARD SHAW (1856–1950) A watercolor by the Punch cartoonist Bernard Partridge.

CHINESE NEW YEAR IN SOHO
The Chinese community is based around Gerrard Street. Their New Year celebrations are a great attraction, with parades, dragons and firecrackers. There are a great many Chinese restaurants here, and gourmets should look out for the places where the Chinese themselves eat.

LEICESTER SQUARE

Just a few yards down Pall Mall from Trafalgar Square on the righthand side is the Haymarket, where there are situated two famous theaters with beautiful façades: the HAYMARKET THEATRE, and directly opposite, HER MAJESTY'S THEATRE ● 54. On the righthand side of the Haymarket, Panton Street leads directly into Leicester Square, a pedestrianized thoroughfare which is usually crowded. The square is lined with souvenir shops, amusement arcades and the garish fronts of discotheques. On the west side is a booth (generally with a long line of people outside it) selling theater seats for West End productions at reduced prices. Formerly Leicester Square was a garden, developed in the 17th and 18th centuries: Hogarth and Joshua Reynolds had houses here. It has recently been extensively cleaned and renovated. There are several large cinemas in the square, which is at the heart of THEATERLAND ▲ 274, close to St Martin's Lane, Monmouth Street, Shaftesbury Avenue, the Haymarket, Charing Cross Road and the Strand. The shows are of all kinds: musical comedies, classic plays, and whodunnits such as Agatha Christie's *The Mousetrap,* which has been playing without interruption for more than thirty-five years.

SOHO

The busy little district of Soho lies within a clearly defined square bounded by Oxford Street, Charing Cross Road, Coventry Street and Regent Street. It is a fascinating and cosmopolitan part of London, which has become famous for its sleazy strip-tease clubs, high-class foreign restaurants and food shops. By day, the district of

THE OTHER SIDE OF SOHO
Soho has long been associated with prostitution, though the girls are no longer permitted on the streets. Strip clubs and pornographic bookshops abound, although what they sell is mild in comparison to the equivalent in Hamburg, Copenhagen or Amsterdam.

> "IF YOU GET SOHOITIS, . . . YOU WILL STAY THERE ALWAYS
> DAY AND NIGHT AND GET NO WORK DONE EVER.
> YOU HAVE BEEN WARNED."
>
> JULIAN MACLAREN-ROSS

Soho is primarily a business center, especially WARDOUR STREET, which is the heart of Britain's film industry. Parallel to this, and one street to the west, lies Berwick Street, the food market for local restaurateurs and gourmets from all over London. There are a number of lively pubs all around Soho, although they are probably best visited at lunchtime: in the evening, theatergoing crowds are replaced by those in search of erotica, though the restaurants still do good business. CARNABY STREET became a Soho legend thanks to Mary Quant and other dress designers of the "swinging sixties": now it is one of the least interesting and most exploited streets of Soho.

BERWICK STREET
Most of the food shops in Soho are Continental, but Berwick Street Market is pure Cockney.

OXFORD STREET

Stretching for 1½ miles from Marble Arch to Tottenham Court Road, Oxford Street is the longest shopping street in London. None of the shops found here is particularly original, but all the famous British trademarks and chain stores are well represented: *Marks & Spencer*, *Boots*, *The Body Shop*, *Littlewoods* and many, many more. There are also some high-quality department stores as well, such as *Selfridge's* ● *88*, *John Lewis*, and *Debenham's* ● *88*. The visitor really should not miss a visit to the little shops in ST CHRISTOPHER'S PLACE, access to which is via a narrow passage beside number 350 (almost opposite Bond Street Underground Station). *Liberty's* ● *88* ▲ *283* is a store famous for its scarves and fabrics. It is situated on the corner of Great Marlborough Street (from where one can observe the shop's impressive Tudor façade) and Regent Street ▲ *283*.

OXFORD STREET

> "He found a place just off Oxford Street, one of those humble teashops with tall urns or geysers on the counter, a slatternly girl in attendance, a taxi-driver or two sitting at the first table and three Italians sitting at the back. He had a poor tea and it cost him fourpence-halfpenny more than he thought it would. When he went out again, it was drizzling, and miserably cold and damp. The queues for the pictures were enormous. All the cheaper seats were probably filled for the night."
>
> J.B. Priestley, *Angel Pavement*

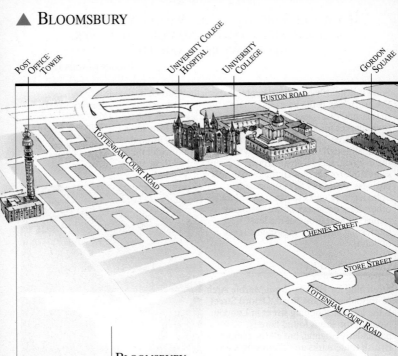

POST OFFICE TOWER

UNIVERSITY COLLEGE HOSPITAL

UNIVERSITY COLLEGE

GORDON SQUARE

EUSTON ROAD

TOTTENHAM COURT ROAD

CHENIES STREET

STORE STREET

TOTTENHAM COURT ROAD

BLOOMSBURY SQUARES
Bloomsbury was a fashionable place to live in the 18th century. Most of its handsome squares were built then, such as Russell Square (below) and Bedford Square (foot of page) ● 76, and in spite of the traffic they retain much of their old-world charm.

BLOOMSBURY

This part of the city is an echo in stone of Georgian and Victorian London. There are quiet streets and squares lined with lovely houses. Naturally enough, the gracious district of Bloomsbury has strong cultural traditions too, since it is set in the shadow of the British Museum. Bloomsbury's attractive streets and squares were first laid out in the late 17th century by the earl of Southampton, but its real expansion came later when celebrities moved in, such as John Constable (1776–1837), Dante Gabriel Rossetti (1828–82), and writers Charles Dickens (1812–70) and George Bernard Shaw (1856–1950). Then, early in the 20th century, the intellectual status of Bloomsbury was boosted again by the novelist Virginia Woolf, who, together with her talented friends, formed what is now known as the Bloomsbury Group.

TAVISTOCK SQUARE. This long, rectangular square has an attractive garden at its center, and was laid out in the early 19th century. The Woolfs, the composer Charles Gounod and Charles Dickens have all lived here; on the north side is a JEWISH MUSEUM with an interesting collection of Jewish historical items.

DICKENS' HOUSE ● 76. From 1837 to 1839, Charles Dickens ● 110–11, 118, lived at 48 Doughty Street, where he wrote *The Pickwick Papers*, *Oliver Twist* and *Nicholas Nickleby*, his first three novels. The house is now a museum containing many souvenirs such as autographs, furniture and first editions of his books. In the basement is a reconstruction of the Dingley Dell kitchen from *The Pickwick Papers*.

RUSSELL SQUARE. This enormous square is at the top of Bedford Place. It was built in 1800, and at the beginning of the 20th

TAVISTOCK SQUARE · BEDFORD SQUARE · CARTWRIGHT GARDENS · SENATE HOUSE · RUSSELL SQUARE · BRITISH MUSEUM · BLOOMSBURY SQUARE

TORRINGTON PLACE · TAVISTOCK PLACE · SOUTHAMPTON ROW · GREAT RUSSELL STREET · BLOOMSBURY WAY · NEW OXFORD STREET

🚶 One day

century many well-to-do businessmen had their houses here. The square is dominated by the heavy Victorian style of the *Hotel Russell* (1898–1900) on the east side.

LONDON UNIVERSITY. The university is made up of many separate colleges and faculties scattered all over London. It began with University College, a lay institution (Oxford and Cambridge were under the jurisdiction of the Church of England) which was founded in 1826 in Gower Street. Since then the university has spread through Bloomsbury, at the cost of many of the district's Georgian houses. Its administrative center, Senate House, is on the west side of Russell Square. Other departments of the university nearby include the School of Oriental and African Studies and the Warburg Institute.

BLOOMSBURY SQUARE. This is the geographical and historical center of Bloomsbury, and one of the oldest of the London squares as well. Nothing remains of the palace that the earl of Southampton built here around 1660 except for the gardens, which are practically intact and make up what was once called Southampton Square. In the 1670's Lady Rachel, the heiress to the Southampton estates, married William, Lord Russell, the earl of Bedford's son, whose family had successfully developed Covent Garden ▲ *272* some years earlier. With the two great London landowning families

CHARLES DICKENS (1812–70)
The house where he lived from 1837 to 1839 is now a museum.

299

UNIVERSITY COLLEGE
The north wing of University College houses the Slade School of Art.

"I passed four hours yesterday with my children in the British Museum. It is now put upon the best possible footing, and exhibited courteously and publickly to all. The visitors when I was there were principally maid-servants."
Sydney Smith,
Letter to Lady Grey,
January 12, 1819

united, Southampton House was renamed Bedford House and Southampton Square became Bloomsbury Square. Elegant Georgian terraces surround the gardens, which were laid out in 1800 by Humphrey Repton. Bloomsbury soon became a fashionable place in which to live, and expanded northwards across fields in the direction of Hampstead ▲ 260.

ST GEORGE'S CHURCH, BLOOMSBURY WAY. This church was completed in 1731 after fifteen years of construction work, to plans by Nicholas Hawksmoor ▲ 311. Its majestic portico is Corinthian, and its remarkable pyramidal steeple derives from Pliny's description of the mausoleum at Halicarnassus; on top of this is a statue of George I dressed as a Roman. It may have been this which led Horace Walpole to call St George's "a masterpiece of absurdity".

BEDFORD SQUARE ● 76. This was the first development on the Bedford estate to the north of Bloomsbury Square. The family still owns the land on which these elegant terraced Georgian houses ● 74 were built around 1775. The statue of the great statesman Charles James Fox (leader of the Whigs at the end of the 18th century) is by Sir Richard Westmacott (1775–1856), and has stood on the north side of the square since 1816. Many of the great and famous have lived in Bedford Square, such as Lord Chancellor Eldon (number 6), the actor Johnston Forbes-Robertson (number 22) and writer of adventure stories Anthony Hope (number 41). Today the square houses several publishers' offices.

THE BRITISH MUSEUM ★

It would take more than a week to see all the British Museum and its collections of treasures (six or seven million objects). Internationally, it is one of the best-known British institutions. Work began on the present building in 1823, to replace Montagu House, Bloomsbury, which had become too small to hold the 120,000-volume library of George III. The architect Robert Smirke ▲ 170 worked on the building from 1823 to 1847, designing it in neo-classical style with an imposing portico of Ionic columns. His brother Sydney Smirke ▲ 162 built the

famous Reading Room (1852–7) on what had been the central courtyard. Between 1884 and 1938 the museum was enlarged by adding the King Edward VII Galleries (1914) to the north, and the West Gallery for Greek sculpture.

THE ORIGINS OF THE MUSEUM. The museum grew around the private collection of Sir Hans Sloane (1660–1753) ▲ *197*, the Chelsea physician and botanist. He had many thousands of specimens of minerals, corals, insects, shells and birds' eggs, as well as some 32,000 antiquities, all housed in his home at 3 Bloomsbury Square. It eventually became too cramped for him to live in, so he bought the house next door. After his death Parliament organized a public lottery to raise funds for purchasing Sloane's collections. To these were added the collection of manuscripts belonging to Robert and Edward Harley, 1st and 2nd earls of Oxford. In 1756 George II presented the Royal Library with 17,000 manuscripts. These were assembled into the British Museum, which first opened its doors in 1759, the doors being those of Montagu House. Not that it was easy to go and see the collections: a detailed written application had to be made, and only ten tickets were initially issued for any one day. The museum continued to expand throughout the 19th century, especially the world-renowned archeological collections. In addition, the British Museum has notable collections of Asiatic, Islamic and European medieval art, and an important department of drawings and engravings. The natural history collections were transferred to the Natural History Museum ▲ *234* in South Kensington in 1870, while the book collections have become the British Library. The museum carries its age and its old-fashioned rules very lightly on the whole, and is expanding all the time. The British Library ▲ *308* is in the process of moving to new premises beside St Pancras Station, expected to be ready by the year 2000, at which time the great round Reading Room will be returned to the museum.

"SEATED MAN", BY MICHELANGELO
A study from the priceless collection of drawings in the British Museum.

THE TEMPLE OF HISTORY
The massive frontage of the British Museum stands imposingly behind tall railings, in an illustration of 1852, at a time when the museum's collections were expanding rapidly.

 ▲ BRITISH MUSEUM

One of the most famous of the British Museum's collections is its Greek Antiquities section, which started with its acquisition of the Elgin Marbles. At the beginning of the 19th century Greece was occupied by the Turks, and the Parthenon in Athens, which had been severely damaged by a Venetian bomb, was left to decay. The British ambassador in Constantinople, Lord Elgin, loved classical architecture and, between 1802 and 1804, with authority granted to him by the sultan of Turkey, he removed various fragments from the Parthenon and shipped them back to London. The total sent was twelve statues, twenty slabs from the building's Ionic frieze and fifteen metopes. The rightful ownership of the Elgin Marbles is still disputed by the Greek government.

"HEAD OF APHRODITE" (GREEK ANTIQUITIES)
This bronze from the 2nd or 1st century BC was found at Sadagh in northeastern Turkey.

"THE NEREID MONUMENT" (GREEK ANTIQUITIES)
This reconstructed façade is from a funeral monument, which dates from around 400 BC. It was found at Xanthos in Lycia, Asia Minor. Statues of Nereids, sea nymphs who accompanied souls to the other world, stood between the Ionic pillars.

"THE HORSE OF SELENE" (GREEK ANTIQUITIES)
This horse's head is from the 4th century BC. It would have been one of four drawing the goddess Selene's chariot, and comes from the Parthenon's east pediment.

302

THE ELGIN MARBLES

Removed from the temple of Athena (Parthenon) on the Acropolis in Athens, the Marbles include twenty sections of the frieze around the building, which depicts a great procession during one of the feasts in honor of the goddess.

An amphora dating from 550–525 BC. On the neck are wrestlers watched by teachers and referees. The main body of the vase shows youths boxing, and carries the painter's signature, Nikosthenes. The black-figure technique was developed in the 7th century BC; red-figure vases became common a century later.

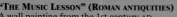

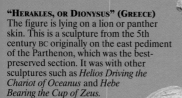

"THE MUSIC LESSON" (ROMAN ANTIQUITIES)
A wall painting from the 1st century AD that was brought back from Herculaneum, Italy.

"HERAKLES, OR DIONYSUS" (GREECE)
The figure is lying on a lion or panther skin. This is a sculpture from the 5th century BC originally on the east pediment of the Parthenon, which was the best-preserved section. It was with other sculptures such as *Helios Driving the Chariot of Oceanus* and *Hebe Bearing the Cup of Zeus*.

THE EGYPTIAN COLLECTION

This is one of the most important in the world outside Egypt, and has the museum's most spectacular exhibits. Initially it was assembled from pieces collected by the French expedition to Egypt, which were lost to the English after the Treaty of Alexandria in 1801. Since 1882 the collection has grown, largely thanks to excavations by the Egypt Exploration Fund.

"THE HUNT IN THE MARSH" (EGYPT)
This scene was discovered in the tomb of the scribe Nebamun (18th Dynasty, c. 1400 BC). It shows Nebamun and his family out hunting birds in a flimsy reed boat.

THE ROSETTA STONE (EGYPT)

This remarkable stone, carved in 196 BC, was found at Rashid (Rosetta) in the Nile Delta in 1799. The text is a decree of Ptolemy V written in Egyptian, in hieroglyphics (the language used by priests), in Demotic (the common language), and in Greek. A comparative study of the writing led the Frenchman Jean-François Champollion (1790–1832) to find the key to the written language of ancient Egypt.

THE "GAYER-ANDERSON" CAT (EGYPT)
This bronze (after 30 BC) dates from the Roman occupation of Egypt. It was offered to the museum by John Gayer-Anderson and Mary Stout. The cat was worshipped in ancient Egypt as the goddess Bastet incarnate.

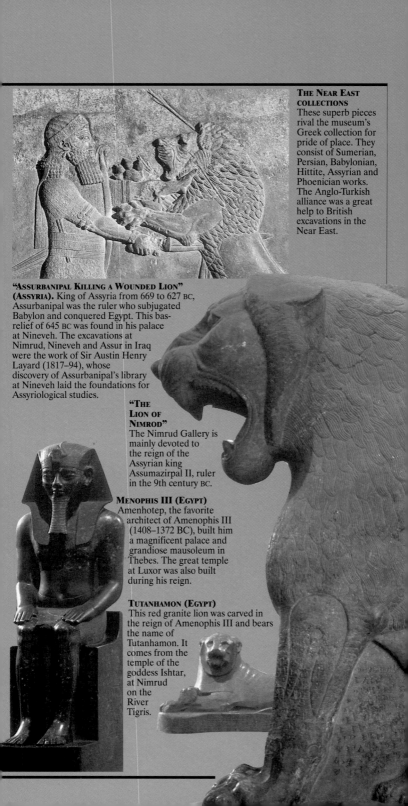

These superb pieces rival the museum's Greek collection for pride of place. They consist of Sumerian, Persian, Babylonian, Hittite, Assyrian and Phoenician works. The Anglo-Turkish alliance was a great help to British excavations in the Near East.

"ASSURBANIPAL KILLING A WOUNDED LION" (ASSYRIA). King of Assyria from 669 to 627 BC, Assurbanipal was the ruler who subjugated Babylon and conquered Egypt. This bas-relief of 645 BC was found in his palace at Nineveh. The excavations at Nimrud, Nineveh and Assur in Iraq were the work of Sir Austin Henry Layard (1817–94), whose discovery of Assurbanipal's library at Nineveh laid the foundations for Assyriological studies.

"THE LION OF NIMROD"
The Nimrud Gallery is mainly devoted to the reign of the Assyrian king Assumazirpal II, ruler in the 9th century BC.

MENOPHIS III (EGYPT)
Amenhotep, the favorite architect of Amenophis III (1408–1372 BC), built him a magnificent palace and grandiose mausoleum in Thebes. The great temple at Luxor was also built during his reign.

TUTANHAMON (EGYPT)
This red granite lion was carved in the reign of Amenophis III and bears the name of Tutanhamon. It comes from the temple of the goddess Ishtar, at Nimrud on the River Tigris.

A VARIETY OF COLLECTIONS
The museum's possessions are by no means limited to classical antiquity or any specialized field: there are all kinds of artifacts from all over the world such as coins, engravings, fans, bookplates and playing-cards.

THE BODHISATTVA TARA (SRI LANKA)
Found near Trincomalee in Sri Lanka (Ceylon), this gilded 12th-century bronze is from the Oriental collections, which include South-East Asia and the Far East.

SAXON CUP (BRITISH ANTIQUITIES)
A 4th-century iridescent glass goblet, discovered in a tomb at a Saxon cemetery in Mucking, Essex.

BRACELET (PERSIA)
This gold bracelet with two griffins' heads is just a small reminder of the splendor that passed with the Persian empire. Together with other finely worked gold ornaments, hairpins, combs and coins, it comes from the Oxus Treasure (c. 500–300 BC), a horde discovered near the River Oxus in central Asia. The Oxus is now called the Amou-Daria, and flows into the Aral Sea.

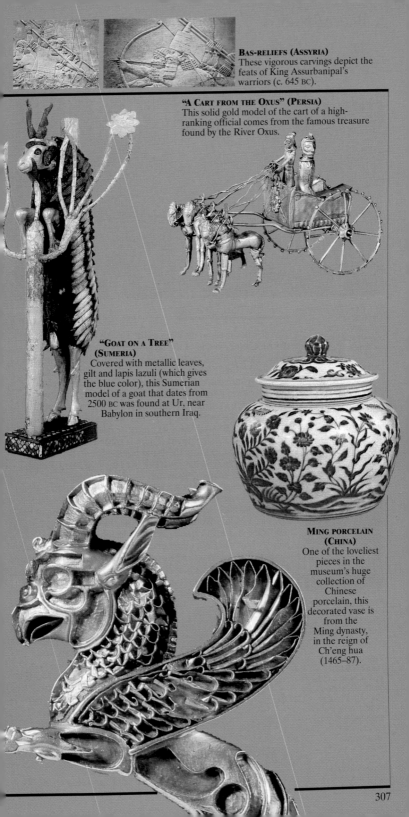

BAS-RELIEFS (ASSYRIA)
These vigorous carvings depict the feats of King Assurbanipal's warriors (c. 645 BC).

"A CART FROM THE OXUS" (PERSIA)
This solid gold model of the cart of a high-ranking official comes from the famous treasure found by the River Oxus.

"GOAT ON A TREE" (SUMERIA)
Covered with metallic leaves, gilt and lapis lazuli (which gives the blue color), this Sumerian model of a goat that dates from 2500 BC was found at Ur, near Babylon in southern Iraq.

MING PORCELAIN (CHINA)
One of the loveliest pieces in the museum's huge collection of Chinese porcelain, this decorated vase is from the Ming dynasty, in the reign of Ch'eng hua (1465–87).

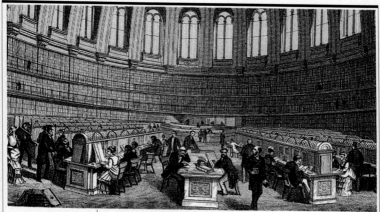

THE BRITISH LIBRARY

Situated in the same building as the British Museum, the
British Library is one of the largest in the world. It contains
more than eighteen million books, some of which are unique,
such as the Lindisfarne Gospels (c. 700, in manuscript); or
extremely rare, such as the Magna Carta of 1215 (England's
first charter of democracy); and first editions of Shakespeare
(1623) and the Gutenberg Bible (1453). Its famous circular
READING ROOM was built by Sydney Smirke in 1857 ▲ *162,
279, 301*, and is notable for its immense dome (140 feet in
diameter and 106 feet high). There is space for 375 readers,
and free access to thirty thousand books around the walls.
Famous people who have worked here include Marx, Lenin,
Sun Yat-Sen, Bernard Shaw and Rudyard Kipling.

THE BLOOMSBURY GROUP. This was the name given to a group
of artists, writers and intellectuals who lived in Bloomsbury
early in the 20th century and used to meet at the house of the
novelist Virginia Woolf. Along with her husband, the
publisher and writer Leonard Woolf, and her sister, the
painter Vanessa Bell, members included artist Duncan Grant,
economist John Maynard Keynes, art critics Quentin Bell and
Roger Fry, the poet T.S. Eliot and the novelist E.M. Forster.
Even if their ideas sometimes clashed with one another, they
were united in their desire to reject the conformity of the age.

Their way of life was as great an
influence on the younger generation
as anything that they wrote. At the
same time there was another
group of intellectuals who
used to meet at the salon
of Lady Ottoline Morrell
near Fitzroy Square,
across Tottenham Court
Road. The Fitzrovians
included novelist Aldous
Huxley, painter and designer
Leon Bakst, the great dancer
Nijinsky and
philosopher
Bertrand Russell ▲ *278.*

AROUND THE EAST END

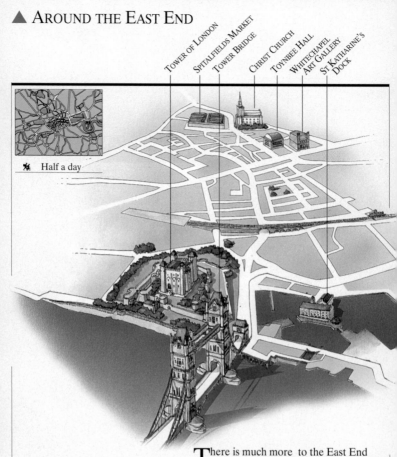

Labels: TOWER OF LONDON, SPITALFIELDS MARKET, TOWER BRIDGE, CHRIST CHURCH, TOYNBEE HALL, WHITECHAPEL ART GALLERY, ST KATHARINE'S DOCK

✄ Half a day

There is much more to the East End than its often repetitive architecture. It is a microcosm of the real London, where the poor have lived for centuries, cheek by jowl with immigrants from the four corners of the world.

HISTORY

Early on, the jumble of roads leading east out of London had no clearly defined districts except for the area comprising Spitalfields, Stepney and Whitechapel. First and foremost the history of the East End belongs to the successive hordes of immigrants who landed here and made their homes.

THE HUGUENOTS. In the 16th century the French Calvinists (Protestants) sought refuge here, and their numbers increased by another forty thousand after the Edict of Nantes was revoked in 1685. The majority of them were skilled craftsmen or weavers, who lost no time in finding profitable work, and gradually moved further west when their fortunes were made.

A HOME FOR THE POVERTY-STRICKEN. Space left by the enterprising Huguenots was taken over in the 18th century by the poor and hungry from all over Britain and Ireland, who abandoned their overcrowded or destitute homes in search of work in the capital. Their plight has

CHRIST CHURCH, SPITALFIELDS
Early in the 18th century a tax was levied on charcoal to build fifty new churches in London. This was one of them, the masterpiece of its architect Nicholas Hawksmoor.

been frankly and sympathetically described by Charles Dickens and others, with its appalling overcrowding, alcoholism, disease and starvation. The poor lived huddled together in street after street of filthy, leaking houses, and so the East End acquired its unenviable reputation.

NINETEENTH-CENTURY IMPROVEMENTS. During the reign of Queen Victoria there were two more floods of immigrants here: the Irish fleeing the potato famine of 1847, and then around 1880 thousands of European Jews escaping pogroms in their homelands. Among the latter were many bakers and garment-makers who quickly found their place in the community. Many attempts were made to improve the quality of life in this wretched part of London throughout the 19th century. William Booth started his famous Salvation Army here in 1878.

IMMIGRANTS FROM THE BRITISH EMPIRE. The 1950's saw an influx of thousands of dispossessed optimists from former British colonies, particularly Pakistanis, Indians, and then families from Bangladesh who opened many clothing businesses. With all this the character of the East End was once again transformed, though it always retained its poverty. There is still the friendly neighborhood spirit that helped this deprived area through its earlier, horrific times, but in recent years affluent City workers have been moving into the area.

> "He went straight off to Stepney, where she lived, as soon as the ship was berthed. He walked all the way, so as to 'ave more time for thinking, but wot with being nearly run over by a cabman with a white 'orse and red whiskers, he got to the 'ouse without 'aving thought of anything."
>
> W.W. Jacobs

> "Certain small fried fish are sold in the area for breakfast, and are said to be known as Spitalfield weavers."
>
> 19th-century guidebook

SPITALFIELDS

CHRIST CHURCH, SPITALFIELDS ★ ● 71. This church on the corner of Commercial Street and Fournier Street was built between 1714 and 1729 by Nicholas Hawksmoor. It owes its existence to Queen Anne (1665–1714), who was trying to put a stop to what she saw as a grave moral decline in England. Of fifty new churches she commissioned, only twelve were ever built (most of them by Hawksmoor), three of them in the East End. As well as Christ Church, there are St Anne's, Limehouse ▲ *336*, and St George-in-the-East ▲ *335*. The portico has an unusual central arch, and the spire is octagonal.

NICHOLAS HAWKSMOOR. Christ Church is probably the masterpiece of its architect Nicholas Hawksmoor (1661–1736) ● *71, 73,* ▲ *139, 149, 174,* after Wren the greatest genius of Baroque English architecture. Hawksmoor became clerk to Christopher Wren ▲ *171–5* at the age of eighteen, and later assisted his master in substantial projects such as the rebuilding of St Paul's Cathedral ▲ *171.* Starting in 1699, Hawksmoor worked on designs for a series of churches commissioned by Queen Anne, in collaboration with Sir John Vanbrugh (1664–1726) and Thomas Archer (1668–1743).

The East End has been making garments since the 16th century. This silk coat was made in 1787. Below is an official document concerning the weaving industry in this part of London.

BENGALI SARIS
Saris like these in a Spitalfields shop are still worn by Bangladeshi women.

FOURNIER STREET AND ELDER STREET ★ ● 75.
Among the French Protestant refugees fleeing the revocation of the Edict of Nantes in Spitalfields in the 17th century were a number of silk-weavers. Several of the houses they built can still be seen on either side of these two streets. The houses in Fournier Street (which was named after one of the Huguenot immigrants) and Elder Street have some fine doorways and large upper windows so as to admit as much light as possible for the weavers working inside. Such a group of houses, built between 1720 and 1750, is extremely rare in London. They have recently been restored.

SPITALFIELDS MARKET. This fruit and vegetable market in Commercial Street was founded under the authority of Charles II in 1682, but it moved from here in the 1980's. The turn-of-the-century buildings that housed it are now occupied by stalls selling organic fruit and vegetables and handicrafts.

COLUMBIA ROAD. This attractive flower market takes place each Sunday morning beside Spitalfields Market. This is the spot in which to hear the broad cockney ● 44 accent, and the rhyming slang that remains a part of life around here. Contrary to those who think that third-world immigration is killing off the old way of life, the old cockney ways continue to flourish – thanks in part to the popularity of a television soap opera *EastEnders,* which is set in a modern, working-class part of east London.

PETTICOAT LANE ★. This unusual open-air market is held every Sunday in Middlesex Street. It resembles the English version of an oriental souk. Its name comes from all the skirts which the tailors and stallholders used to sell, along with other new and used clothes, at the start of the 20th century. Today the street is packed with several hundred stalls, attracting dealers and customers from many different communities: Bangladeshi, Pakistani, Indian and Arab. At 90 Whitechapel High Street the famous kosher restaurant *Bloom's* continues to cater for the long-established Jewish population. Middlesex Street also has an enormous variety of shops and restaurants, many of which are open on Sundays.

BRICK LANE. This old part of town was once famous for brewing and brickmaking. Truman's Brewery is set among a fascinating jumble of shops and garment factories in what is now the Bangladeshi quarter of London; it is the sole survivor of these traditional crafts. Around Brick Lane now are some of the finest Indian restaurants in London. Brick Lane Market sells a wide variety of cakes, fish, oriental spices and household goods, along with the ubiquitous ready-to-

SPITALFIELDS

wear clothes. More surprisingly, there are also many political pamphlets and books on sale here. Behind all the bright colors and the enticing smells of this lively scene is the grim reality of the garment-makers' "sweat shops". In cellars and small back rooms, there are more than thirty thousand Asian immigrants making clothes for European boutiques, working in appalling conditions and for pitifully small wages. Poverty and unrest seem always to have been endemic to this part of London. In 1978 the Brick Lane Riots took place. These were a series of pitched battles between the militant racists of the British National Front party and the immigrant community of Brick Lane. They went on for several days.

A COCKNEY SPECIALTY. In BETHNAL GREEN, a small green area behind Vallance Road, they still sell jellied eels, an old cockney delicacy. These are prepared fresh every morning in huge enamel bowls, and then sold to the whelk-and-cockle stalls or the old-fashioned eel-and-pie shops of the area. Jellied eels are eaten cold, while pie and mash, covered with spoonfuls of green parsley sauce ("liquor"), is a delicious and inexpensive hot meal.

THE HUGUENOT QUARTER
In Fournier Street (above) and Elder Street (below) there are still a number of houses built by Huguenot silk-weavers. These houses have been carefully restored, and are very rare in the capital.

WHITECHAPEL

Right at the heart of the East End, on the fringe of the City, is one of the busiest quarters of London. It gets its name from the white stone walls of St Mary Matfelon, a church that was built in the 13th century and which became the parish church of St Mary Whitechapel around 1338.

THE ROAD TO ESSEX. From Aldgate, Whitechapel High Street was once the departure point for the main road to the fields of Essex. Its former traffic of wagons and ox-carts explains the unusual width of Whitechapel Road and Mile End Road: the houses that line these highways were built at a safe distance from the mud and cow dung in the center. Behind these busy main roads, Whitechapel is actually filled with a fascinating maze of alleyways, courtyards and narrow, winding, sunless streets.

A SINISTER REPUTATION. For centuries Whitechapel has been one of the most dangerous parts of town. During the 19th century it was a refuge for gangs of anarchists and communists, and in 1888 the famous Whitechapel murders made Jack the Ripper a household name all over the world. The poverty of the district also made it an attractive target for Victorian philanthropists,

JACK THE RIPPER. Whitechapel will always be associated with Jack the Ripper. On August 3, 1888, in a thick fog in

SPITALFIELDS MARKET
This sign (below left) indicates one of London's oldest markets, which may soon become a thing of the past if the area is cleared to make way for another shopping mall.

FLOWER MARKET

POVERTY AND SQUALOR
"Oh God, what I saw! People having no water to drink, hundreds of them, but the water of the common sewer which stagnated, full of dead fish, cats and dogs, under their windows. At the same time the cholera was raging, Walsh saw them throwing untold horrors into the ditch, and then dipping out the water and drinking it!"
Charles Kingsley

the heart of the busy East End, a prostitute was murdered and mutilated on a stairway in George Yard. Then, on September 8, the police found the body of another prostitute cut up in the same way. Panic ensued when a London press agency received a cheerful letter from the murderer, who announced his intention of continuing the killings and signed himself "Jack the Ripper". A large-scale hunt by Scotland Yard produced nothing. It certainly failed to stop the murder of two more prostitutes in the streets of Whitechapel on September 30. The last murder attributed to Jack the Ripper was the most horrible of all: on November 9 the body of a pretty young prostitute named Mary Jane Kelly was discovered in Hanbury Street cut up into pieces, and after this the murders abruptly ceased. Eventually the police closed the file on Jack the Ripper, though rumors and speculation still continue as to the possible identity of the killer. But these killings, happening at a time when the social structure of England was fundamentally threatened, revealed to the privileged classes of London the grinding poverty that existed alongside them in the capital. The exposure consequently set in motion several programs of social welfare and reform.

THE MARKETS. From 1708 Whitechapel was one of the three great hay markets of London, along with Smithfield ▲ *177* and Haymarket. The capital's consumption of hay and straw was enormous, thanks to the size of its horse population. Huge trains of wagons loaded with hay arrived in the city every Tuesday, Thursday and Saturday from the farmland of Essex, Suffolk and Hertfordshire. Early in the 20th century the hay was even being brought in by train and lorry. From 7am until lunchtime, Whitechapel

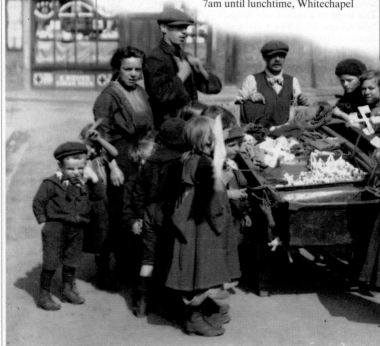

Road and the streets running off it were packed with carts and swarming with people, and over everything hung the sweet, pervading odor of hay. The market finally closed in 1927, removing the last remnant of the countryside from the middle of London. But there are still some traditional markets operating in the area: the WASTE MARKET started in the middle of the 19th century, and further to the north there is MILE END WASTE.

A COSMOPOLITAN DISTRICT. Whitechapel was also famous for its many Jewish butchers and kosher slaughterhouses. They served the large Jewish community that was living here as far back as the 17th century, and an important food market grew up around them. Pakistani and Bangladeshi immigrants are gradually replacing the old Jewish community today, but they still keep up the traditional clothing industry.

REBUILDING THE EAST END. Attempts to improve the living conditions in the area were stepped up after 1888. But in spite of many new developments and the arrival of office blocks, Whitechapel retains its Victorian working-class atmosphere.

WHITECHAPEL BELL FOUNDRY. This famous bell foundry opened at 32–4 Whitechapel Road in 1738, though the foundry had already been in existence since the 15th century. It was established in 1420 in Houndsditch, then moved to Whitechapel in 1583, before transferring to its present site in the grounds of the 17th-century *Artichoke Inn*. The biggest bells in the world were cast here, and many of them

THE "PENNY" Articles about the Whitechapel murders, like those in the *Penny Illustrated Paper*, struck fear into the hearts of the public all over London.

WHODUNNIT? Three suspects for the identity of Jack the Ripper were George Chapman, hanged in 1902 for other offences; Montague John Druitt, the most likely suspect, who committed suicide in 1889; and the duke of Clarence, Queen Victoria's grandson, who had alibis that prove his innocence.

In the old buildings of the Whitechapel Bell Foundry (above right), a set of bells four hundred years old was discovered.

recast following World War Two. Big Ben ▲ *128*, the Liberty Bell (in Philadelphia, Pennsylvania, USA), the bells of Westminster Abbey and countless more were all created here. The foundry buildings and its 18th-century house form one of the most remarkable examples of pre-Industrial Revolution commercial sites in London.

ST DUNSTAN AND ALL SAINTS. The church is in Stepney High Street, south of Mile End Road. It was probably founded by St Dunstan, bishop of London in the 10th century. Its oldest part dates from the 13th century. The exterior was refaced in 1871–2; the church was heavily restored after a fire in 1901, and again after the bombardments of 1944. There is a large nave, and the glass in the windows is modern. The Renatus Harris organ of 1678 was sold to the Drury Lane Theatre.

WHITECHAPEL ART GALLERY
This holds many top quality exhibitions of modern art, as well as Old Master shows.

THE WHITECHAPEL ART GALLERY ★. The gallery was founded at the end of the 19th century by Canon Samuel Barnett, vicar of St Jude's Church, Whitechapel, "to bring the West End to the East End". In 1884 he opened the TOYNBEE HALL as a

university for the common man, which grew into the Workers' Educational Association. This gave him the idea for the gallery, built at the corner of Commercial Street and Whitechapel High Street between 1897 and 1899 with private funds, notably from John Passmore Edwards. Already in the 1890's Barnett had organized several art exhibitions to get the locals used to the idea. It is a splendid Art Nouveau building designed by C.H. Townsend, with a mosaic over the door by Walter Crane. There are frequent exhibitions of modern art here, as well as exhibitions of local interest and an annual show each October.

A BUILDING IN COMMERCIAL ROAD
The front windows are decorated with fine moldings and medallions, all in white stucco.

WHITECHAPEL MARKETS. The WASTE MARKET, opposite the London Hospital, dates from the mid-19th century; fruit, vegetables and jewelry are sold here every day except Sunday. On Saturdays there is an additional market further north at MILE END WASTE; part of the Waste has been made into gardens, where there stands a statue of William Booth, founder of the Salvation Army.

ALDGATE. One of the six gates to the City in Roman times, Aldgate marked the entry point to London from the east. It was rebuilt between 1108 and 1147. The room above the gate was leased to Geoffrey Chaucer 1374–85. Again rebuilt 1606–9, the gate was finally demolished in 1761; the site is now covered by a corner of the street of the same name. In the 17th century this quarter was home to dressmakers and tailors, and it remained a center for this trade until the 20th century. A number of old buildings still stand, among them one of London's oldest inns, the *Hoop & Grapes*, at 47 Aldgate High Street.

MIDDLETON STREET
Among its many shops and stalls is the famous *Tubby Isaacs' Sea Food Kiosk*, where one can try all kinds of fish and seafood.

ALONG THE THAMES

▲ From Lambeth to Southwark

BIG BEN · WESTMINSTER BRIDGE · LAMBETH PALACE · ST THOMAS'S HOSPITAL · HUNGERFORD BRIDGE · COUNTY HALL · JUBILEE GARDENS · WATERLOO BRIDGE · ROYAL FESTIVAL HALL · ARCHBISHOP'S PARK · NATIONAL THEATRE

PALACE ROAD

LAMBETH

LAMBETH ROAD

LAMBETH BRIDGE

🏃 Half a day

"YACHTS OF THE CUMBERLAND FLEET STARTING AT BLACKFRIARS"
A late 18th-century painting. River traffic acquired greater importance after Henry VIII had founded a naval shipyard at Deptford, near the palace of Greenwich.

B etween Lambeth Palace and Southwark Cathedral is a pleasant walk along the south bank of the Thames. This peaceful stretch commands an excellent view of the opposite bank, showing some of the City's historic buildings to their best advantage. The south bank was once all swamp as far as

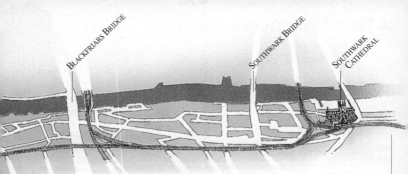

Blackfriars, and was known as Lambeth Marsh: the name Lambeth derives from loam hithe, "mud place". The ancient Celtic name for London, *Llyn Din* ("town on the lake") possibly refers to this area. Until the 18th century this district south of the river remained bogland, with a few fields and causeways. Its most important feature is Lambeth Palace, a rare surviving example of a 13th-century building. Until the 19th century, a ferry plied between Lambeth Palace and the Palace of Westminster on the other side of the river. It was known as Horse Ferry, and was the only boat licensed to carry wagons and horses.

ART AND INDUSTRY. Manufacturing began in north Lambeth around 1670. At the start of the 19th century the Doulton pottery company set up in business: its stoneware with relief decorations of hunting scenes was very popular. In 1720, on the site where County Hall now stands, Richard Holt started a factory that made artificial terracotta for sculptures. When Mrs Coade bought the business, it became the Coade Artificial Stone Manufactory. Coade stone was an exceptionally hard and weatherproof material, and there are still many examples of it on London buildings, but when the company ceased trading in 1840 the formula for Coade stone disappeared as well.

"Lambeth Walk is a long, narrow street and at this hour was so thronged with people that an occasional vehicle with difficulty made slow passage. On the outer edges of the pavement, in front of the busy shops, were rows of booths, stalls, and barrows, whereon meat, vegetables, fish and household requirements of indescribable variety were exposed for sale.**"**

George Gissing,
Thyrza

LAMBETH PALACE ★

Built between 1207 and 1229, the palace has been the residence of the archbishops of Canterbury for seven and a half centuries. The building shows signs of alterations made by many successive occupants.

THE CRYPT AND CHAPEL. The vaulted crypt beneath the chapel is the oldest part of the palace and dates from the beginning of the 13th century. Most of the archbishops were consecrated in the little chapel. In 1633 Archbishop Laud restored it, putting in a new altar, windows, throne and stalls. It had to be rebuilt almost entirely after World War Two.

THE MORTON TOWER. The massive red-brick gateway was built for Archbishop John Morton at the end of the 15th century.

THE GREAT HALL. This was rebuilt in 1663 in Gothic style by Archbishop Juxon. The hammerbeam roof is more than 80 feet high. The residential quarters were rebuilt in 1828 by Edward Blore, and the hall is now the library, founded thanks to a bequest from Archbishop Bancroft in 1610. The library has notable treasures, such as Queen Elizabeth I's prayer book and some fine illuminated manuscripts.

LAMBETH PALACE AND ST MARY'S
A museum devoted to 17th-century landscape painters is in the 14th-century church tower.

SHELL CENTRE AND COUNTY HALL
The immense power of industry is symbolized by the massive outline of the Shell Centre, built between 1953 and 1963. County Hall is easily identifiable from far away, thanks to its roof of Italian tiles. It was built on the site of a former brewery.

THE GUARD ROOM. It was here in 1534 that Thomas Cromwell and the Lords of the Council questioned Sir Thomas More ▲ *177, 197* when he refused to sign the Oath of Supremacy. There is a collection of portraits of archbishops hanging here, including works by Holbein, Van Dyck, Reynolds and Hogarth.

TRIALS AND REVOLUTIONS ● 36. In 1378 the English reformer John Wycliffe, accused of heresy and depravity, was interrogated in the chapel. The palace has been the victim of attack on numerous occasions: in 1381 during the Peasants' Revolt, Wat Tyler's mob ransacked the place. The LOLLARDS' TOWER, actually a water tower built in 1435, is named after Wycliffe's followers who were imprisoned near this spot. From 1646 to 1658, during the Civil War and Cromwell's Commonwealth, Lambeth Palace was a prison. The poet Richard Lovelace was imprisoned here in 1648.

ST THOMAS'S HOSPITAL

Founded at the beginning of the 12th century, St Thomas's Hospital was once part of the Priory of St Mary Overie in Southwark. It was renamed St Thomas the Martyr in memory of Archbishop Thomas à Becket, who was murdered in 1170 and canonized three years later.

IMPERIAL WAR MUSEUM
Situated in Lambeth Road, the museum is devoted to military exploits involving Britain and the Commonwealth since 1914.

During the 13th century it was moved to Borough High Street. At the Dissolution of the monasteries in 1540, Henry VIII, at loggerheads with the church, decided to close the hospital. Edward VI reopened it in 1551 under the new name of St Thomas the Apostle. Its land was purchased by the Charing Cross Railway Company in 1859 in order to build a new station; and so the hospital had to move once more, this time to Lambeth Palace Road. Queen Victoria laid the foundation stone for the new premises on May 13, 1868, and the building was completed in 1871. Its design as a series of blocks was the work of Henry Currey. After World War Two, W. Fowler Howitt and then Yorke, Rosenberg & Mardall were commissioned to rebuild the hospital completely, a project that eventually had to be abandoned. Three of the seven original blocks remain as well as a chapel decorated with scenes in Doulton pottery.

FLORENCE NIGHTINGALE
The nurses at St Thomas's are called "Nightingales".

THE FLORENCE NIGHTINGALE MUSEUM. In 1854, just before leaving for the Crimea, Florence Nightingale initiated numerous changes to the administration of this hospital. Then in 1860 she opened the first training school for nurses. Progress in the science of medicine led to the opening of a medical school here in 1871, and to the opening in 1900 of eleven specialist departments. The hospital also houses a museum that is dedicated to the memory and work of Florence Nightingale.

County Hall

The former city hall of London is an enormous building sitting beside Westminster Bridge and with a magnificent view across the River Thames to another formidable seat of power, the Houses of Parliament. Work on this building's foundations began in 1909, and it finally opened in 1922, although it was not actually completed until 1963. County Hall was designed by Ralph Knott in "Edwardian Renaissance" style ● 88. It is constructed around a series of interior courtyards and is clad in Portland stone (except for the base, which is made of granite, like the quayside wall). In shape, the building is a concave arc with a tower and a rectangular wing on each side. On the lefthand side is a lion that was carved from the famous Coade stone in 1837. It was once the symbol of the old Lion Brewery and is now the emblem of the whole South Bank Centre. The Jubilee Gardens, set beside County Hall, were opened in 1977 to celebrate the Silver Jubilee of Queen Elizabeth II. County Hall has been empty since 1986, when the Greater London Council was abolished by the Conservative government. Several development schemes have since been considered, and the property is now being converted into a luxury hotel.

Southwark

From the Roman occupation up to the middle of the 18th century, Southwark was the only district of London on the south side of the River Thames. Linked to the City by a bridge, Southwark was not entirely under its domination. There were areas called "liberties", pieces of land that had formerly been church property, and which remained self-governing. This independence was ideal for the building of theaters.

A departure point. Southwark was the entrance to London for those travelers coming up from the south, and its many

The sculptures of County Hall
The exterior sculptures just above the first upper floor are the work of Ernest Cole and Alfred Hardiman.

"The Thames at Lambeth"
This painting of 1706 shows the Horse Ferry crossing the Thames. Westminster Bridge was opened downriver in 1750, but the ferry continued to make the crossing until the 19th century.

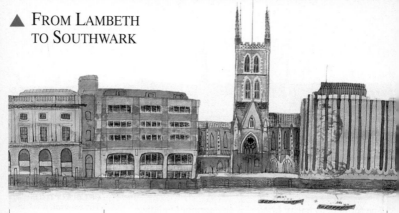

**A DOCK NEAR
SOUTHWARK
CATHEDRAL**
This old three-master
in an unlikely setting
(below) seems to be
waiting for her
captain to return
and take her away
from all this . . .

**THE FIRST
SOUTHWARK BRIDGE**
This was built
between 1814 and
1819 with three cast-
iron arches and a
span of 240 feet. It is
mentioned by
Dickens in *Little
Dorrit*. The present
bridge of five steel
arches was designed
by Sir Ernest George
and built between
1912 and 1921.

inns and taverns had a wide reputation. Among them there
was the *Tabard*, from where Geoffrey Chaucer (c. 1340–1400)
had his twenty-nine pilgrims set out for Canterbury. The
White Hart is mentioned in Shakespeare's play *Henry VI* and
Charles Dickens' novel *The Pickwick Papers*. Of these old
places, only the *George Inn*, which was built in 1677 on the site
of an earlier tavern, remains today.

THEATERS. It was at Southwark (particularly Bankside, which
runs just beside the river) that the first fixed London theaters
were built (with the exception of the Theatre and the Curtain,
which were both in the north of the City). The Rose Theatre
opened in 1586. This was in the shape of a polygon, made of
wood and plaster with a thatched roof over a section of it, and
was destroyed in 1605. Its foundations were recently
excavated. Until 1603 plays by Marlowe, Kyd and
Shakespeare were performed here. Most famous was the
Globe Theatre, and there were two others of less renown, the
Swan and the Hope.

THE GLOBE THEATRE AND SHAKESPEARE GLOBE MUSEUM ★.
As well as acting here, Shakespeare was also a shareholder in
the business. The name of the round wooden building (1598)
comes from its sign, which showed Atlas
bearing the world on his shoulders. At
the start of *Henry V* the Chorus speaks of
"this wooden O". In 1613 a cannon fired
in a performance of *Henry VIII* started a
fire that burned the theater down.
Rebuilt the following year, it was finally
demolished in 1644. The Shakespeare
Globe Museum is in an 18th-century
warehouse close by the site of the old
theater, with illustrations of sets and Shakespearean
characters, as well as models showing the history of
Elizabethan theater. The old tradition of the south bank as
the headquarters of entertainment is preserved today, thanks
to the Royal Festival Hall, the National Theatre, the Museum
of the Moving Image ("Momi"), the National Film Theatre
and the Hayward Gallery. The revival of this quarter began in
1951 at the Festival of Britain, with the construction of the
ROYAL FESTIVAL HALL. Designed by Robert Matthew and
Leslie Martin and altered in 1962 by T.P. Bennett, the
auditorium can seat three thousand people. The year 1968
saw the completion of the QUEEN ELIZABETH HALL, the
PURCELL ROOM, and the HAYWARD GALLERY (where art
exhibitions are held). Attached to the NATIONAL FILM
THEATRE (which moved here in 1958) is the NATIONAL
THEATRE (1977). The MUSEUM OF THE MOVING IMAGE
(cinema museum) is located a little further on.

SOUTHWARK CATHEDRAL ★

In 1106 the Augustinian monks of St Mary Overie built a Norman church on this site. The priory, which burned down in 1212, was then replaced by a Gothic building. After the Reformation it became the parish church of St Saviour, and was finally made a cathedral in 1905. The nave was rebuilt during the 19th century by A.W. Blomfield. Inside is an oak figure of a knight (1275), and an effigy of John Gower, the poet and friend of Chaucer. There is a monument to Shakespeare (1912) by Henry McCarthy in the south aisle; and above are stained-glass windows by Christopher Webb illustrating his plays. Not far from the cathedral is the operating theater of Old St Thomas's Hospital, which has been restored.

SOUTHWARK CATHEDRAL AND PICKFORD'S WHARF
The old and the new sit side by side. It is an incongruous setting for the cathedral, which is the most beautiful medieval building on the South Bank.

WINCHESTER HOUSE
This palace was the residence of the bishops of Winchester from when it was built in 1109 until 1642, when Parliament suppressed the bishopric. It served next as a royalist prison, and then gradually fell into decay. In 1814 a fire exposed its great 14th-century rose window.

SOUTHWARK CATHEDRAL
The founder of Harvard University, John Harvard, was baptized here in 1607. The cathedral also contains the tombs of dramatists Philip Massinger and John Fletcher.

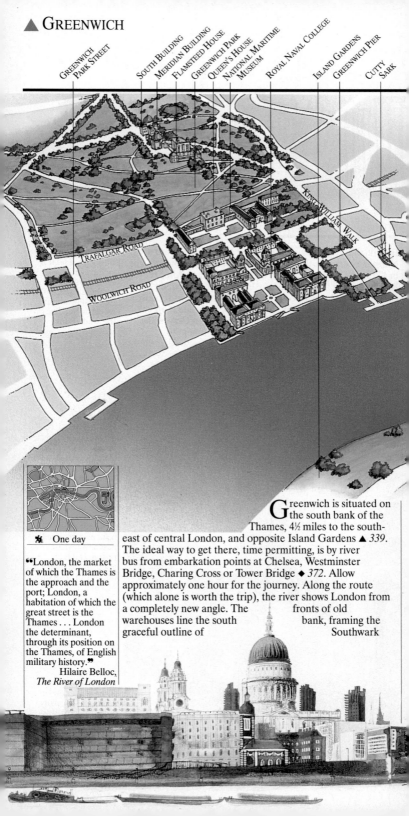

▲ GREENWICH

GREENWICH PARK STREET · SOUTH BUILDING · MERIDIAN BUILDING · FLAMSTEED HOUSE · GREENWICH PARK · QUEEN'S HOUSE · NATIONAL MARITIME MUSEUM · ROYAL NAVAL COLLEGE · ISLAND GARDENS · GREENWICH PIER · CUTTY SARK

KING WILLIAM WALK

TRAFALGAR ROAD

WOOLWICH ROAD

✹ One day

"London, the market of which the Thames is the approach and the port; London, a habitation of which the great street is the Thames . . . London the determinant, through its position on the Thames, of English military history."
Hilaire Belloc,
The River of London

G reenwich is situated on the south bank of the Thames, 4½ miles to the south-east of central London, and opposite Island Gardens ▲ 339. The ideal way to get there, time permitting, is by river bus from embarkation points at Chelsea, Westminster Bridge, Charing Cross or Tower Bridge ◆ 372. Allow approximately one hour for the journey. Along the route (which alone is worth the trip), the river shows London from a completely new angle. The fronts of old warehouses line the south bank, framing the graceful outline of Southwark

Cathedral ▲ 323 while, on the opposite side of the river, the City ▲ 146 appears as a succession of church towers, dominated of course by the dome of St Paul's Cathedral ▲ 171. Then comes the journey through Docklands ▲ 330, and the great loop made by the river around the Isle of Dogs ▲ 336.

"THE FERRY" IN 1784
The Thames was once the main thoroughfare of London, as this illustration shows.

GREENWICH

The name of Greenwich is always associated with the zero Meridian, from which point longitude and world standard time (GMT, or Greenwich Mean Time) are measured. But Greenwich is filled with a great variety of other things to see, and has some magnificent buildings such as the Queen's House and the Royal Naval College.

HISTORY. Greenwich (literally "green village") was a fishing and agricultural settlement where in 1427 the Duke of Gloucester, Henry V's brother, built himself a sumptuous palace he called Bella Court, and later enclosed the 200 acres of Greenwich Park. After the Wars of the Roses the palace became the favorite resort of the Tudor monarchs: Henry VIII, Mary Tudor and Elizabeth I were all born here. Henry loved to go hunting in the park, and kept careful watch over the English fleet moored nearby in the royal dockyards. He enlarged the palace, adding a royal armory, banqueting hall and tiltyard. Three years after his second wife Anne Boleyn gave birth to Elizabeth here, Henry signed Anne's death warrant in Greenwich Palace. His son, the boy-king Edward VI, died here in 1553, and although Mary I disliked the palace, her sister Elizabeth made it her official summer residence on her accession in 1558. It was here that Sir Walter Raleigh is supposed to have laid his cloak over a puddle so that Elizabeth could keep her shoes dry. In 1615 James I commissioned Inigo Jones ▲ 269, 274 to build a house for his wife Anne of Denmark, now known as the Queen's House.

❝ The chief place of resort in the daytime, after the public-houses, is the park, in which the principal amusement is to drag young ladies up the steep hill which leads to the Observatory, and then drag them down again, at the very top of their speed, greatly to the derangement of their curls and bonnet-caps, and much to the edification of lookers-on from below. ❞
Charles Dickens, *Sketches by Boz*

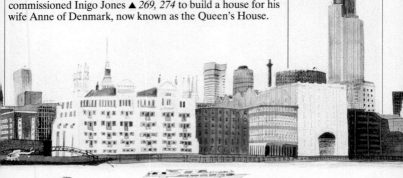

FLAMSTEED HOUSE AND GREENWICH OBSERVATORY
Wren built the observatory and Flamsteed House for the astronomer royal, the Reverend John Flamsteed. The Royal Observatory is now at Herstmonceux, near Battle, Sussex.

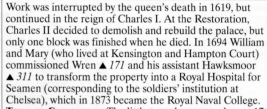

THE QUAYSIDE AT GREENWICH
The charm of the old port of Greenwich and its gracious houses was captured in this painting by John O'Connor (1850–89).

Work was interrupted by the queen's death in 1619, but continued in the reign of Charles I. At the Restoration, Charles II decided to demolish and rebuild the palace, but only one block was finished when he died. In 1694 William and Mary (who lived at Kensington and Hampton Court) commissioned Wren ▲ *171* and his assistant Hawksmoor ▲ *311* to transform the property into a Royal Hospital for Seamen (corresponding to the soldiers' institution at Chelsea), which in 1873 became the Royal Naval College.

TOUR OF GREENWICH. The little town has many elegant 17th- and 18th-century houses. The ancient Croom's Hill is a steep and winding residential road lined with some beautiful houses: one of them, "The Grange", has 12th-century timbers. In the town center are some fine Georgian façades which are decorated with stucco, many good restaurants and historic pubs. The *Trafalgar Tavern* (1837) in Park Row was visited by Thackeray, Dickens and Lord Macaulay, and was famous for its whitebait dinners.

ST ALFEGE. This church in the center of Greenwich derives its name from Alfege, archbishop of Canterbury, taken hostage by the Danes and murdered at Greenwich in 1012 when he refused to allow himself to be ransomed. Henry VIII was baptized in the old church on June 28, 1491: the present building by Hawksmoor was completed in 1714. John James built the west tower in 1730. Inside are paintings by Sir James Thornhill ▲ *173*. The church was restored after being badly damaged in World War Two.

THE "CUTTY SARK". This beautiful ship was, in its day, the fastest clipper in the world. It was launched in 1869 at Dumbarton, Scotland, and then used to bring tea from China and wool from Australia. With all her sail up, the *Cutty Sark* once managed to travel a total of 363 miles in just twenty-four hours. But the opening of the Suez Canal and the arrival of the era of steamships eventually changed her way of life: in 1895 the clipper was sold to the Portuguese, only to be brought back to Greenwich and opened to the public in 1954. Now the ship houses a fascinating museum that tells the story of the clipper trade, including a splendid collection of figureheads. Situated nearby is the 53-foot ketch *Gypsy Moth IV*, like the *Cutty Sark* also in dry dock, in which Sir Francis Chichester sailed single-handed around the world in 1966–7 at the age of sixty-five.

OLD ROYAL OBSERVATORY OR FLAMSTEED HOUSE ★. The Royal Observatory is known all over the world, thanks to the Greenwich Meridian. This was fixed as the standard zero meridian at an international conference held in Washington in 1884, all degrees east and west being measured from this point. The actual zero line is marked in the courtyard paving. King Charles II commissioned Wren to build the observatory in 1675 for his astronomer royal John Flamsteed (1646–1719), together with a house "for the observator's habitation and a little for pompe". The interior is now a museum, the present Royal Observatory having moved to Sussex largely because of the air pollution in London. The Meridian Building houses a fine collection of telescopes. Outside on the roof is a red time ball (1833), which still drops every day at 1pm as a time check for shipping on the river. Flamsteed House contains some elegant 17th-century furniture, and there is a superb panorama of London from the terrace.

ROYAL NAVAL COLLEGE. The former Royal Hospital for Seamen was transformed into a naval university in 1873, and is on the site of the old Greenwich Palace beside the Thames. Between its colonnades and Wren's twin domes can be seen the back of the Queen's House. The north wing was designed as part of a palace for Charles II by John Webb between 1662 and 1669, and served as a model for the rest of the building. Wren ▲ *171*–5 and Hawksmoor ▲ *149, 311* designed most of the new buildings, which include the magnificent PAINTED HALL, with its walls and ceiling, decorated in the Baroque style by Sir James Thornhill ▲ *173*, glorifying William and Mary (and successive monarchs). In 1805 the body of Lord Nelson lay in state in this beautiful room before its interment in St Paul's Cathedral. Opposite the Painted Hall is Wren's CHAPEL, which had to be rebuilt after a fire in 1779 by James "Athenian" Stuart (1713–88). His beautifully proportioned neo-classical design contains an altarpiece, *St Paul after the Shipwreck at Malta*, by the American painter Benjamin West (1728–1820), with statues of Faith, Hope, Charity and Humility by the same artist on display in the vestibule.

"GREENWICH HOSPITAL, SEEN FROM THE THAMES"
The fine buildings of Greenwich are clearly visible in the background of this painting by William Lionel Wylie (1851–1931).

"CUTTY SARK"
Its name comes from a haunting narrative poem by Burns, Tam O'Shanter (1791). Cutty Sark was a witch, a "winsome wench", who chased the drunken Tam through the night and nearly caught him.

CEILING OF THE PAINTED HALL
This domed room was built by Wren as a refectory, and is still used as a dining hall. James Thornhill and his assistants decorated it in rich Baroque style from 1708 to1727, being paid £3 per square yard for the ceiling, but only £1 for the walls.

THE QUEEN'S HOUSE. In 1616 James I commissioned Inigo Jones ▲ *269* to build a summer residence for his wife, Anne of Denmark. On her death three years later James gave the house to the future Charles I, whose wife Queen Henrietta Maria asked Jones in 1629 to complete it. It is a white double pavilion in the shape of an "H", built across the old road that ran from London to Rochester. It was the first Palladian building in England, "sollid, proporsionable to the rulles, masculine and unaffected", according to its architect. The queen was so pleased with the result that she called it her "House of Delights". Inside, the entrance hall is shaped as a perfect cube, with a gallery that is reached by the iron "Tulip Staircase". Also upstairs are the royal apartments: six years' work by the finest craftsmen restored the Queen's House to its original splendor in 1990.

NATIONAL MARITIME MUSEUM. The museum was installed in the Queen's House and the two buildings to either side of it and opened in 1937. For more than a century before that it had been used as a school for sailors' orphans, run by the Royal Naval Asylum. The two wings were completed in 1809 and are linked to the Queen's House by colonnades commissioned in 1807 to commemorate the Battle of Trafalgar. This is now one of the finest maritime museums in the world, illustrating the naval history of Great Britain with documents, paintings, models and other memorabilia. Rooms in the Queen's House are hung with naval paintings (opposite and left) as well as royal portraits and many other pictures. The

West Wing is set on three floors: at the top are the sections devoted to the great maritime explorers and the Royal Navy up to 1700. On the middle floor are the James Cook Gallery and the Nelson Galleries. The most poignant exhibit displayed here is Nelson's uniform worn at Trafalgar, with the bloodstained bullet-hole visible in the left shoulder, through which he sustained the wound that was to kill him on October 21, 1805. The Navigation Room houses a superb collection of globes, charts and instruments. The East Wing of the museum houses a section that is devoted to the history of navigation from the earliest days of sail right through to the steam age. There is also the Arctic Gallery to be seen. It is devoted to the polar expeditions.

GREENWICH PARK. This is the oldest royal park in London, enclosed by the duke of Gloucester in 1433 to be used as a hunting ground. Its long avenues were first laid out for Charles II by Louis XIV's landscape gardener Le Nôtre, who designed the gardens of Versailles. It was first opened to the public during the 18th century, and there are many three-hundred-year-old chestnut trees as well as a bronze sculpture, *Standing Figure and Knife Edge* (1979), by Henry Moore ▲ 223. The view from the top of the hill over London and the Thames is well worth the climb, although the fine symmetry of the Queen's House and Royal Naval College is not matched by the tower of Canary Wharf, the highest in London.

LORD NELSON
Horatio Nelson ▲ 284 (1758–1805) is one of Britain's greatest heroes. He confounded Napoleon's invasion plans, and with the victory of Trafalgar (which cost him his life) assured Britain's maritime supremacy for one hundred years.

THAMES BARGE
On its way down river from London, the barge is seen passing through Greenwich.

▲ THE DOCKLANDS

TOWER BRIDGE · DESIGN MUSEUM · ST KATHARINE'S DOCK · TOBACCO DOCK · ST GEORGE-IN-THE-EAST · WAPPING · ST MARY'S ROTHERHITHE · SALTER ROAD · GREENLAND DOCK · SOUTH DOCK

LOWER ROAD

🏃 One day

"WEST INDIA DOCKS"
This view, looking from east to west across the Isle of Dogs from Blackwall, was painted in 1802 by William Daniell, when the docks were opened. They were finally closed in 1980: the new development of Canary Wharf occupies the whole area now.

The Docklands are on the site of the old docks of the port of London. They are the biggest urban development of the late 20th century to be attempted in all Europe, but today they are running into trouble. The creation of a new town was meant to change the whole image of this old built-up area, covering several square miles, an area that was once a symbol of the commercial and industrial supremacy enjoyed by Britain and her empire. Five hundred years of history vanished with the redevelopment of the ancient port of London, and only a few traces remain of its former history, incorporated into a new Americanized landscape.

THE HISTORY OF THE DOCKS

By the 18th century the old docks and their equipment were proving inadequate to meet the needs of London and the economic expansion brought by the Industrial Revolution. The existing docks included Howland Great Dock at Rotherhithe, created in 1696 and later known as Greenland Dock, and the shipyard at Blackwall, constructed c. 1660, which were primarily used for repairing ships. By the end of the century the situation was quite dramatic: each year, 10,000 coastal vessels and 3,500 ships moored near London at

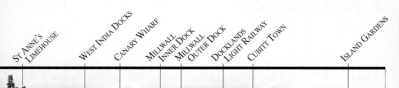

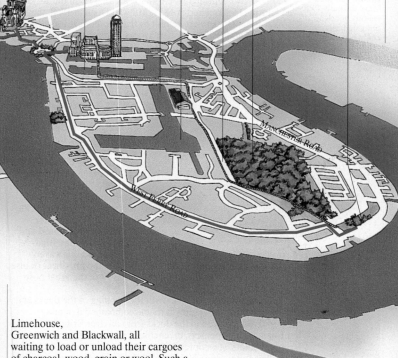

MANCHESTER ROAD

WEST FERRY ROAD

Limehouse,
Greenwich and Blackwall, all
waiting to load or unload their cargoes
of charcoal, wood, grain or wool. Such a
protracted delay inevitably had the effect of raising prices. In
1793 the powerful West India Company threatened to move
elsewhere if new accommodation were not provided.

THE NEW DOCKS. Matters improved quite rapidly after 1799.
West India Docks ● 78, opened in 1802 at Wapping, followed
in 1805 by London Docks. Built by D.A. Alexander and John
Rennie, London Docks had two main basins with room for
more than three hundred ships. In the mid-19th century about

two thousand vessels a year
moored here. Imported goods
from the tropics filled the
warehouses, while in vaulted
cellars beneath the level of the
quays wine and brandy were laid
down to mature. The tobacco
warehouse, which the
government rented out (Queen's
Warehouse), was on one of the
quays. East India Docks opened
in 1806 at Blackwall, followed
in 1812 by Regent's Canal Dock.
The docks' success, the
expansion of British trade, and
the growth of London and of the
empire all contributed to the
area's continuing growth.

Taylor Walker

WATERMAN'S ARMS

A DOCKSIDE PUB
From St Katharine's
in Bermondsey, the
route is marked out
with historic pubs.
The first one, the
Dickens Inn, is in St
Katharine's Dock. In
Wapping there is the
Town of Ramsgate,
where convicts were
locked up awaiting
deportation to
Australia.

St Katharine's Dock opened in 1828, built by Thomas Telford
(1757–1834). During Queen Victoria's long reign the Royal
Victoria Dock opened in 1855, Millwall Dock in 1868, the
West India Docks were rebuilt as the South West India Docks
in 1870, and the Royal Albert Docks were opened in 1880.
The complex was rounded off in 1921 with the completion of
the King George V Dock.

NEW VENTURES. Around the wharves
and warehouses, all kinds of
service industries grew up
during the course of the
19th century. Naval
shipyards provided the
motivating force during
the Napoleonic wars,
then there was the
continued expansion of
trade that flourished
well into the 1860's. All
this was responsible for the
emergence of many other
activities, such as mechanical and
metallurgical industries, and food-
processing factories. A hundred years later all this was in
decline, with businesses having moved to the provinces or else
disappeared altogether, largely as a result of the great post-
war restructuring of London.

A CHANGE IN POPULATION. With the opening of the docks and
the rapid industrial growth that accompanied it, a new
population arrived in the docks from all over Britain.
Engineers, carpenters, mechanics, blacksmiths, coopers,
ropemakers, stevedores, boatmen, lock-keepers, shopkeepers,
skilled and unskilled laborers all flocked here in order to work
at the new docks or in the new businesses that sprang up
around them. A new and heterogeneous community grew up
in the mid-19th century, with the poor in search of work living
side by side with the more prosperous men in search of new
investments. During the 1870's the wealthy and better-off
members of the community began to move out of the district
to make their homes elsewhere. The dockers and laborers
who remained behind developed into a much more closely
knit community with a shared socio-cultural background; and
soon they settled into the domestic round of family life, work,
school and recreation within some clearly defined
geographical boundaries.

A CHANGE OF PACE. One half of all the dockland warehouses
were damaged or destroyed by bombs during the Second
World War, particularly St Katharine's and West India Docks.
They were rebuilt during the 1950's, but the increasing size of
the new ships brought a gradual move downriver toward the
Thames estuary, at the expense of those moorings nearer the
City. Tilbury Docks, some 25 miles away, probably derived the
most benefit from this shift of emphasis.

RECONVERSION. The docks began to close at the end of the
1960's, followed soon after by their redevelopment. This
began in 1969 in St Katharine's Dock, and spread gradually to
both sides of the river. But it was only in 1981, with the
closure of the Royal Docks, that a vast redevelopment
program to convert the entire area was launched by the

THE PORT OF
LONDON

STEAMER CRUISES
visiting the
ROYAL DOCKS
WEDNESDAYS, THURSDAYS AND SATURDAYS
from TOWER PIER 2.30 pm
Near Mark Lane ▆▆▆▆ Station
Return fare 3/6   Children Half Price
Reduced rates for parties. Lunches and teas on board

BOOK IN ADVANCE

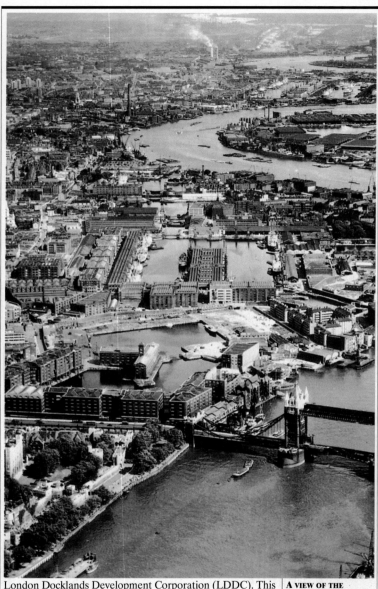

London Docklands Development Corporation (LDDC). This large-scale project first took shape with Canary Wharf on the Isle of Dogs. The tendency to relocate business centers in the east of London involved many significant moves. The great newspapers deserted Fleet Street, mostly in favor of Docklands: *The Times* went to Wapping, the *Financial Times* to Blackwall, the *Daily Telegraph* to Canary Wharf, the *Guardian* to Farringdon, and the *Daily Mail* to Rotherhithe. By the beginning of the 1990's the Docklands population had already risen to 65,000, and almost 70,000 people were

A VIEW OF THE DOCKS IN 1964
The docks begin just past Tower Bridge: to the left are St Katharine's Dock and London Docks in Wapping; to the right, in the bow of the river, are the Surrey Docks.

333

commuting here to work every day. But this enormous expansion was partially checked by the recession that hit Britain in the late 1980's. Many commercial and residential blocks still remain empty, while the Canary Wharf project has run into serious financial difficulty. The projected target of 110,000 residents and 200,000 jobs here by the year 2000 is beginning to seem highly unrealistic.

FROM ST KATHARINE'S TO WAPPING ★

THE ENTRANCE TO THE DOCKS AT WAPPING

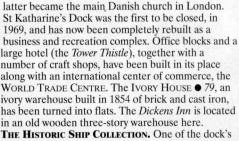

ST KATHARINE'S DOCK ★ ● 78. The preliminary work at St Katharine's in 1826, to make way for the construction of the docks, was spectacular: a whole district with origins that went back to the Middle Ages was razed, and 1,250 houses were demolished. The ancient hospital and church of St Katharine ▲ 258, founded in 1148 near the Tower of London ▲ 182 by Queen Matilda, in memory of her two sons who died at an early age, were just two casualties of this ruthless redevelopment. More than eleven thousand people who lived in the neighborhood of this royal institution, and who lacked the good fortune to be either homeowners or leaseholders, were made homeless because of these demolitions, despite ferocious protests. The authorities justified their actions by saying that the work was necessary in order to clean up an unhealthy part of town. The St Katharine's Foundation was awarded compensation from the St Katharine's Dock Company in the form of land by Regent's Park to build houses, a school and a church. After the First World War the latter became the main Danish church in London. St Katharine's Dock was the first to be closed, in 1969, and has now been completely rebuilt as a business and recreation complex. Office blocks and a large hotel (the *Tower Thistle*), together with a number of craft shops, have been built in its place along with an international center of commerce, the WORLD TRADE CENTRE. The IVORY HOUSE ● 79, an ivory warehouse built in 1854 of brick and cast iron, has been turned into flats. The *Dickens Inn* is located in an old wooden three-story warehouse here.
THE HISTORIC SHIP COLLECTION. One of the dock's basins has been converted into a marina with mooring space for a hundred yachts. Another, the eastern basin, now houses the Historic Ship Collection, which was opened in 1979. The collection of ancient ships on display includes the *Challenge*, a steam tugboat; the *Nore*, a 1931 lightship; and the *Cambria*, a sail-powered trading ship from 1906. The Royal Navy vessel *HMS Discovery* has also been converted into a maritime museum. This was the sail- and steam-powered three-master, built at Dundee, Scotland, which carried the explorer Captain Robert Falcon

Scott on his first expedition to the Antarctic, which took place between 1901 and 1904.

WAPPING. Right beside St Katharine's Dock, the district of Wapping has an unsavory reputation. With its famous gallows and its wretchedly poor people, Wapping could once rival the worst parts of Whitechapel. Bomb damage during World War Two and the closure of many docks and warehouses brought further dereliction and neglect to the area. But with the building of new housing estates, the conversion of old warehouses into flats, and the creation of public gardens on waste land, Wapping is beginning to recover. Its modernization prompted French writer Claude Roy to comment in 1986: "Wapping Old Stairs, where for two hundred years there were thousands of jobless waiting to beg a shilling from passengers as they landed, were rotten when I last saw them. Now they're gone altogether."

TOBACCO DOCK ● 78. The shopping center at Tobacco Dock is intended to be twice as large as the one already thriving in Covent Garden, once work on the *Highway* buildings is complete. Some of the original buildings have been protected and restored, showing the typical design of the old dockside warehouses. A case in point is the SKIN FLOOR in the *Highway* at the corner of Wapping Lane. These buildings are metal-framed, and the 4 acres of space within them has ribbed or cradle vaulting in brick; this is now being converted in order to accommodate shops and cafés.

TOBACCO DOCK
The main docks were linked by Tobacco Dock, which now contains some fine three-masted sailing ships open to the public.

ST GEORGE-IN-THE-EAST. This church, situated to the north of Tobacco Dock in Cannon Street Road, was built between 1714 and 1729 by Nicholas Hawksmoor ▲ *311*, and paid for by a levy on charcoal that was introduced in 1711. It was one of the fifty churches that were voted for by the Tory government and Queen Anne ▲ *311*, who did not want to leave the poverty-stricken parts of London bereft of some spiritual guidance. Although the exterior of the church, with its high tower (160 feet) of Portland stone, has maintained its original appearance, the interior, which was destroyed in 1941, was restored in 1960. There is a modern chapel in the nave.

THE ENTRANCE TO ST KATHARINE'S DOCK

WAPPING HIGH STREET. There is a fine row of 18th-century houses and warehouses to be seen in Wapping High Street, which also houses the Metropolitan Special Constabulary. This is the name of London's river police, a force that was founded in 1798. In Wapping Wall is the *Prospect of Whitby* (left), the oldest of the Thames riverside pubs with roots going back to 1520. It was the haunt of smugglers and thieves, and also of the diarist Samuel Pepys (1633–1703) ● *40* and the artist J.M.W. Turner (1775–1851) ● *102*, ▲ *215–17*.

A HAWKSMOOR CHURCH
St Anne's, Limehouse, completed in 1730, boasts the highest church clock in London.

FROM LIMEHOUSE TO THE ISLE OF DOGS

LIMEHOUSE. In the Commercial Road at Limehouse, where charcoal used to be unloaded during the 18th century, is St Anne's, another church that was designed by Hawksmoor ▲ *311*. Built between 1714 and 1730 in a slum quarter of the town, St Anne's is a typical Protestant English Baroque structure virtually without any curved lines. The church's unusually high tower recalls the Gothic bell-tower in Boston. In Limehouse, *The Grapes* was a pub that Charles Dickens knew particularly well, for it appears in the first chapter of his novel *Our Mutual Friend* (1865).

POPLAR. This is another community that evolved with the opening of the docks and naval shipyards, growing from five hundred inhabitants in 1801 to some fifty thousand in 1881. Skilled craftsmen lived here side by side with the impoverished and jobless. Poplar played a leading role in the development of Socialism under the leadership of men like George Lansbury, who led the Labour Party from 1931 to 1935, when Poplar was the poorest part of London.

ST MATTHIAS. This church was completed in 1654 in Poplar Street and is one of the oldest buildings in Docklands. Originally a private chapel belonging to the East India Company, it was restored and rebuilt in 1776, and again in the middle of the 19th century in "medieval Victorian" style using Kent stone. Since the church was closed in 1977, it has been broken into and badly vandalized. Only the outside can now be seen.

THE ISLE OF DOGS ★. In the 19th century the Isle of Dogs (especially Millwall and Cubitt Town) was a center of naval shipbuilding, first for sail and then for steam. The biggest

QUEENHITHE
Queenhithe is one of the few docks upstream from London Bridge. Only small boats and barges could tie up here.

shipbuilders were all based here. In the mid-1860's Thomas Wright described the Isle of Dogs as the biggest naval shipyard on the whole river: "There are more than a dozen establishments. One of them, the giant Millwall Iron Works, employs around four thousand men and boys". This development is reflected in the population figures for the Isle of Dogs: this area was almost deserted at the beginning of the 19th century; by 1858 there were 5,000 inhabitants, and more than 21,000 from 1901 to 1939. In 1857 the Russell yards launched the *Great Eastern*, designed by Isambard Kingdom Brunel ▲ *332* and five times bigger than any other working steamship in the world.

PRESENT DEVELOPMENTS. Since the middle of the 1980's the Isle of Dogs has again become the focal point of Docklands, and the area is right at the heart of its redevelopment. Forests of cranes no longer unload ships but instead help to build office blocks and luxury apartments on what has become one vast building site. Viewing the site as a whole, it is lacking in architectural unity and overall structure. Although some of the fine old warehouses have been preserved, the neighboring structures – glass and steel towers, and boat-shaped office buildings – are at odds with each other. As for the basins, these have now been turned into a marina. The transformation of the landscape has brought with it a radical change of employment. Any vacancies now are in the worlds of finance, newspaper publishing, or telecommunications, all beyond the reach of unqualified laborers and dockers, whose jobs are long gone. Without the ability to change their careers, and unable to afford homes, the laboring class has given way to the Yuppie class. The latter are the people best equipped to cope with the inflated prices of land speculators, who in turn are in business thanks to the generosity of a government that handed over Docklands to property developers without imposing adequate restrictions on them.

▲ *332*

WEST INDIA DOCK
Two huge warehouses, rebuilt in 1824–5 by George Gwilt & Son, are all that remain from the great age of the docks.

"THE ISLE OF DOGS"
❝The river sweats
Oil and tar
The barges drift
With the turning tide
Red sails
Wide
To leeward, swing on the heavy spar.
The barges wash
Drifting logs
Down Greenwich reach
Past the Isle of Dogs.❞
T. S. Eliot,
    The Waste Land
        (1922)

337

▲ The Docklands

The Thames Tunnel
This was built in 1843 by a French immigrant, the engineer Marc Brunel (1769–1849), and was the first pedestrian underwater tunnel in the world. It is 1,200 feet long.

The Canary Wharf tower
Some Londoners are less than enthusiastic about this development. In 1988 Prince Charles considered the new Docklands a triumph of commercial opportunism over civic values. He thought it had too many mediocre new buildings, as well as a train which would be more suitable for a model village, all of which represented a poor contribution to the reconstruction of the capital.

Billingsgate Market. The famous fish market that used to be in Lower Thames Street in the City is now located on the Isle of Dogs, on the north quay of West India Quay. Billingsgate Market is set inside an enormous modern warehouse, which has been converted into a market hall equipped with huge cold stores.

Canary Wharf. The best way to see the new Docklands developments is to walk the length of Canary Wharf to Heron Quays via West Ferry Road. There you will pass the tallest building in England, designed by the American Cesar Pelli of New Haven, who also designed the World Trade Center in Manhattan. The long pier is on an axis leading to West Ferry Circus. Some time in the relatively near future a huge shopping center, complete with galleries and colonnades, should see the light of day. If the focal point of this future development is the Isle of Dogs, then its crisis point is without doubt the business and financial center of Canary Wharf. This extremely ambitious scheme, which was financed by the Canadian group Olympia & York, was intended to create four million square feet of offices in three towers and open up 55,000 new jobs. Part of the project has been brought to completion, but the recent collapse of Olympia & York has for the moment put a stop to any further work. In contrast to these turbulent business and financial currents, it is agreeable to see that the old dock basins still have pleasure boats and old merchant vessels converted into restaurants.

The Docklands Light Railway. This overhead railway, entirely operated by computer, was built to make the City only a matter of minutes away from Docklands. It serves the whole area, crossing the Isle of Dogs from the south and going almost as far as the Tower of London. But, in spite of all assurances, the space-age train has proved quite inadequate to cope with the number of passengers who use it.

Mudchute Park. It is interesting to visit Mudchute Park before you reach Island Gardens, and to see the farm that was opened in 1977 by Ted Johns. Visitors are usually surprised to find pigs, chickens and ponies, herds of cows, as well as a llama, so close to the urban development. There is also a riding school.

ISLAND GARDENS. This little park set on the south side of the Isle of Dogs has a beautiful view across the river to Greenwich and the Royal Naval Hospital (opposite, bottom right). In order to get there on foot, simply take the Greenwich Footway Tunnel, a pedestrian tunnel that was excavated under the river between 1897 and 1902.

THE SOUTH BANK

To get to the south bank and Rotherhithe from Island Gardens, walk through the tunnel that runs underneath the Thames and then catch a bus, or else go by boat. The south bank has not been spared the great urban alterations of Docklands. This is where London Bridge City was born in the 1980's, set between London Bridge and Tower Bridge.

SURREY DOCKS. These are the only docks on the south bank of the river, and they extend over 300 acres. The first basin opened in 1807. It had a monopoly of trade in Scandinavian timber, and it also dealt in wood pulp and grain. The various old docks on the south bank, faced with the expansion in coastal trade and in the railways, decided to merge in 1864, in imitation of the docks across the river, as the Surrey Commercial Docks Company. They finally closed in 1970. Since 1981 they have undergone radical alterations and have been transformed into a shopping and leisure center.

ROTHERHITHE ★. This was the old port from where the *Mayflower* set sail in 1620. On board were the first 102 colonists, 41 of them Puritans, who founded Plymouth in New England. The Howland Great Dock, ancestor of the future Surrey Docks, opened in 1696 in Rotherhithe for ship repairs and maintenance.

SURREY DOCKS FARM. To cover the distance from Rotherhithe to Bermondsey it is best to take a bus, stopping off first at Surrey Docks Farm, which sells only natural, chemical-free produce. The LAVENDER POND NATURE PARK was established in 1980–1 on the site of St Saviour's Dock.

BERMONDSEY. Two Victorian warehouses, at the boundary of Bermondsey and Southwark in Tooley Street, were built by Sir William Cubitt in 1857. They now

ST MARY'S, ROTHERHITHE
St Mary's (below left) was rebuilt in 1714. Its tower, erected around 1740, is the work of Launcelot Dowbiggin. Nearby, the street running through Shad Thames (below right) leads to the Design Museum ▲ 340.

THE "MAYFLOWER"
This ancient inn (bottom) was named after the ship moored nearby in 1620 that took the Pilgrim Fathers on their voyage to America. The ship's captain, Christopher Jones, is buried in St Mary's Church nearby.

"THE STEELYARD"
This painting of 1811 by George Shepherd depicts the old docks at work.

UNRECOGNIZABLE LONDON
The Czech painter Oskar Kokoschka (1886–1980) disliked the changes to London, which he painted so well. "If the face of London really is changing," he wrote in 1972, "to the point at which it will become unrecognizable, this is not simply the fault of two world wars, but above all it is the fault of speculators and builders. Thanks to them, Londoners will soon be completely ignorant of the organic growth of their city."

TOWER BRIDGE
seen from the docks.

house the shops of Hay's Galleria, under a cradle-vaulted roof of glass and steel which bears some resemblance to the Crystal Palace. To the south, around Bermondsey Square, is BERMONDSEY MARKET, full of fascinating antiques and bric-à-brac. The *Angel*, which was opened in the 15th century by the monks of Bermondsey, is an inn which was once the haunt of robbers and was frequented by the diarist Samuel Pepys (1633–1703), as well as by the navigator Captain James Cook (1728–79).

TOOLEY STREET. The name of the street is a corruption of "St Olave". In the 13th and 14th centuries, rich merchants lived here. Some important clerics also had their London homes here, including the abbots of the Priory of St Augustine in Canterbury. St Olave's Grammar School was also founded here in 1560; one of the school's governors was Robert Harvard. He was the father of the man who subsequently founded the American university of that

name. During the 19th century, between Tooley Street and the river, many groups of warehouses, such as Butler's Wharf, were built. ST OLAVE'S HOUSE, a remarkable Art Deco building, was constructed in 1831 on the site where the old church formerly stood. The young Keats lived in Dean Street, which is just off Tooley Street, while he was studying medicine at St Thomas's Hospital.

SHAD THAMES ● *78*. A huge renovation scheme has taken place in this area. The old warehouses have been completely refurbished and their façades carefully restored, with new buildings integrated. The result is a curious mixture of modern and 19th-century industrial architecture, with apartments, restaurants, shops and art galleries.

THE DESIGN MUSEUM ★. The world's first Design Museum (above) was opened by the entrepreneur Terence Conran in 1989, between Shad Thames and the river. Its permanent collections are arranged in a clear, explanatory fashion, and among them is a collection of furniture ranging from classicism to Post-modernism. Temporary exhibitions are also held here.

THE BRANAM TEA AND COFFEE MUSUEM. This museum has recently opened beside the Design Museum, and traces the history of two important London trades. There is also a collection of objects relating to tea and coffee ● *60*.

OUTSIDE THE CENTER

BUSHY PARK
OSTERLEY HOUSE
OSTERLEY PARK
STRAWBERRY HILL
SYON HOUSE
MARBLE HILL HOUSE
KEW PALACE
HAM HOUSE
RICHMOND PARK
CHISWICK HOUSE

HAMPTON COURT

CHISWICK HOUSE

Lord Burlington's elegant country villa was designed for entertaining rather than for living in, and the ground floor contained the earl's private apartments. At the foot of the monumental staircase are statues by Palladio and Inigo Jones.

PUTNEY

During the English Civil War ● *36*, in 1647, Oliver Cromwell held a council of war in this village southwest of London. It is a pleasant suburb on the south bank of the Thames, with streets of Victorian and Edwardian terraced houses.

PUTNEY BRIDGE. This bridge, which links Putney to Fulham, is also the starting point of the famous Boat Race: every year in March a rowing boat with a team of eight oarsmen from Oxford University (dark blue) races a boat with a team from Cambridge (light blue) over a 4½-mile course from here to Mortlake. The first race was held in June 1829 at Henley. There has only ever been one dead heat, in 1877; in 1912 both boats capsized and the race had to be started again.

FULHAM

A 19th-century commentator described Fulham as "an orchard and kitchen garden on the north bank of the river". It remained largely working-class until the 1970's when it became a fashionable residential area.

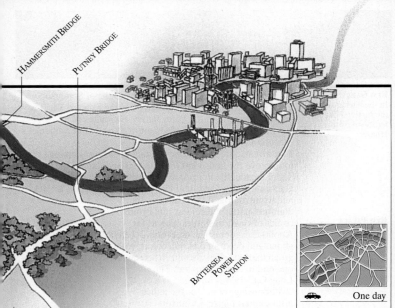

One day

ALL SAINTS CHURCH. The oldest part of this fine church is the 14th-century tower. Inside is a magnificent collection of monuments, most of them 17th-century. In the tower is a painting of 1690 showing a former beadle and sexton with his tankard of ale and churchwarden pipe. In the churchyard are eight tombs of former bishops of London.

BISHOP'S PARK. Once part of the land belonging to Fulham Palace, the residence of the bishops of London from the 7th century until 1973, this riverside park extends from Putney Bridge to Fulham Football Club.

CHISWICK

HOGARTH'S HOUSE. The artist William Hogarth ▲ *210, 292* bought what he called "a little country box by the Thames" in 1749. It became a museum in 1909, and contains a substantial collection of Hogarth prints and 18th-century furniture.

CHISWICK HOUSE. The 3rd earl of Burlington was an amateur architect and keen admirer of Palladio. He built this house between 1725 and 1729, modeled on Palladio's Rotonda (the Villa Capra) at Vicenza. Here he entertained such friends as Handel, Swift and Pope. Much of the interior decoration is the work of William Kent (1685–1748), like Burlington a disciple of Inigo Jones ▲ *274, 326*. On the ground floor is a series of engravings relating to the house. Upstairs are the elegant Blue and Red Velvet Rooms, and the central octagonal Dome Saloon, the ceiling of which forms the cupola which housed the earl's art collection.

SYON HOUSE ★

Situated on the bank of the Thames opposite Kew Gardens, this impressive house stands on the site of a 15th-century monastery. In the 16th century the

THE LONG GALLERY AT SYON HOUSE Robert Adam designed this magnificent room, as well as some of its furniture. Its dimensions are unusual, 136 feet long and only 14 feet wide. It is decorated with landscapes by Zuccarelli.

monastery became the property of the Duke of Somerset, Lord Protector in the reign of the boy-king Edward VI. It is now the property of the Percy family, the dukes of Northumberland, into whose hands it passed after Somerset's execution in 1552.

THE HOUSE. Architect Robert Adam ▲ *268* was commissioned to improve the house in 1761. Though he retained the austere Tudor façade, the interior was redesigned on a grand and elaborate scale. The Great Hall has Doric columns, a black and white marble floor echoed in the diamond-patterned ceiling, and bronze copies of classical statues such as the Apollo Belvedere. The anteroom is heavily gilded and decorated in rich colors, with green marble pillars forming a screen at one end to create a square. The Long Gallery was intended as a "withdrawing room" for the ladies after dinner: pier-glass mirrors disguise the room's narrowness, and the ceiling has a crossline design. The Print Room contains family portraits and two fine 17th-century inlaid cabinets. There are many works of art in the house, principally by Lely, Van Dyck and Gainsborough.

THE PARK. The gardens were laid out in the 18th century by "Capability" Brown. The Great Conservatory was completed in 1827; it contains exotic flowers, in particular orchids, and cacti. The west wing contains an aquarium. Also in the grounds is the London Butterfly House, a tropical conservatory where exotic butterflies are bred. The rose garden contains over four hundred varieties, and there are two mulberry trees planted by Somerset in the 16th century.

ROYAL BOTANIC GARDENS, KEW ★

The world-famous botanical gardens at Kew, which face Syon across the Thames, have their root in a fondness for plants among members of the Hanoverian royal family. Augusta, dowager Princess of Wales, enjoyed "botanizing" and, in 1759, laid out some of her estate at Kew as a small botanic

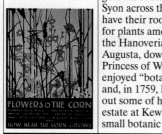

FLOWERS O THE CORN

HOW NEAR THE CORN GROWS

garden. She appointed William Aiton her head gardener, and Sir William Chambers to design some buildings in the grounds, including the lovely Orangery, and the striking ten-story, octagonal Chinese Pagoda. This last was apparently a "surprise" he conceived for her. The dowager princess's son and daughter-in-law, George III and Queen Charlotte, combined the neighboring estate of Richmond with Kew on her death in 1772. They encouraged Sir Joseph Banks, the naturalist, to superintend the botanic garden, and he, in turn, encouraged collectors to search out plants of interest all over the globe. "Capability" Brown directed the landscaping, at George III's request. The king and queen summered at Kew at the White House. Their thirteen children, tutors and governesses were lodged in houses round about, including some on Kew Green. The "Dutch House", or Kew Palace, built in 1631 by a merchant of Dutch extraction, was first an

annex to the White House, then a favored residence of the king and queen when the White House was demolished in 1802. It was a domestic, and deliberately simple, existence, and Kew Palace is "plain as a dainty pikestaff" inside. (The Queen's Garden behind is now planted in 17th-century manner, with tulips, pleached hornbeams, lavender and bergamot.) The princesses kept their pets in a Royal Menagerie, while Queen Charlotte had a cottage orné with thatched roof built, where she often took tea, in the old Richmond grounds. In 1805 Princess Elizabeth designed the decorative scheme of the upper "Picnic Room" in Queen Charlotte's Cottage, where convolvulus and nasturtiums cling to bamboo on a leaf-green background. Framed Hogarth prints ▲ 210 decorate the Print Room below. Queen Victoria kept this cottage and the surrounding acres of woodland till 1897, when she gave it to the public to commemorate her Diamond Jubilee. The woods are a mass of bluebells in late spring. Meanwhile, the Royal Botanic Garden was growing apace, after the state acquired it in 1840. Sir William Hooker was the first appointed director, in 1841, and he established the museums and departments of Economic Botany (1847), the Herbarium and Library (1822). Hooker's son, Joseph, succeeded him as director, and opened the Jodrell Laboratory in 1876. The dowager princess of Wales' botanic garden had occupied 7 acres. The gardens now cover more than 300 acres, and the collection has over thirty thousand different types of plant.

A tour of Kew Gardens. You should begin at Decimus Burton's 1845 wrought-iron main gates, although the lion and unicorn which originally adorned them have been removed to a side gate. Among the trees in the Broad Walk leading into the gardens are some, including a maidenhair tree, which date from the dowager Princess of Wales' botanic garden. First comes Chambers' Orangery, then, on the river side, Kew Palace. The Rhododendron Dell, resplendent with oaks, was dug out by a company of Staffordshire militia in 1773, as part

Queen Charlotte's Summerhouse
Queen Charlotte loved to hold tea parties in this small, thatched cottage, built for her around 1771. It is reminiscent of Marie-Antoinette's "Petit Trianon" at Versailles.

The Chinese Pagoda
The pagoda (above and opposite), which is purely decorative in function, initiated a fashion for Chinese architecture. It may have been partly inspired by the Chanteloup pagoda constructed around the same time for the Duc de Choiseul near Amboise in the Loire

TEMPERATE HOUSE
Decimus Burton's glasshouse is more solidly built and conventional than the more ornamental Palm house.

of "Capability" Brown's landscaping scheme. The grassy paths past the artificial lake and through the Pinetum lead on toward a superb view across the Thames of Isleworth and Syon. Leaving the riverbank, go through the Diamond Jubilee woodland, past the cottage, to the southeast corner of the gardens and the pagoda. (Chambers, who took his inspiration for the folly from an earlier journey to Canton, made fashionable the use of Chinese motifs in garden architecture.) Before losing yourself in the series of glasshouses to come, visit a remarkable one-woman show, the Marianne North Gallery. Miss North, a redoutable Victorian, traveled the world to paint natural vegetation, and then presented 832 of her vivid botanical oil paintings to the gardens, together with a gallery to house them.

THE TEMPERATE HOUSE. Largest of all the glasshouses and the most spectacular, this houses plants from subtropical areas of the world – among them a Chilean wine palm, raised from seed collected in Chile in 1846, which threatens to raise the roof. The Temperate House, the late masterpiece of Decimus Burton, was built in stages between 1860 and 1899, and is planted in geographical sections. The northern wing of the Temperate House contains plants from Asia; the north octagon, from New Zealand and the Pacific Islands; the south octagon contains South African heaths and proteas. The central area is a veritable forest of trees, best seen by ascending the giddy heights to Burton's galleries above. The Temperate House becomes crowded in winter, on account of its delightfully effective heating system. The Australia House next door was built in 1952 of aluminum.

HOLLY WALK. North from the Temperate House lies the decorative Holly Walk, Berberis Dell, and King William's Temple, wherein are inscribed the names of British military victories – oddly, since William IV was known as the

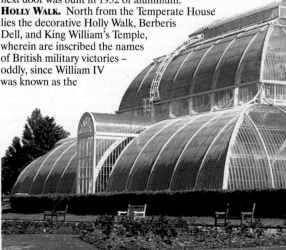

PALM HOUSE
Tropical plants are cultivated here. The atmosphere is kept at a constant 26 degrees centigrade.

"Sailor King". The British Columbia Loggers' Association donated the flagpole – made from a single piece of Douglas fir.

THE PALM HOUSE. This amazed the Victorian public, with its ballooning ironwork and its exotic collection of plants from the tropical world. Rubber plants, banana trees, and a wealth of palms are still cultivated within, as are rare crops like cycads, in danger of extinction in their natural habitat. Decimus Burton and the engineer Richard Turner – who built the Waterlily House next door – collaborated to construct the

house between 1844 and 1848. Condensation and heat conspired at last to endanger its fabric, and it was successfully dismantled and rebuilt between 1984 and 1989. An innovation is the display of tropical marine vegetation in a series of tanks beneath the Palm House.

THE WATERLILY HOUSE. To the north, steamiest of all the glasshouses, this was originally built in 1852 to house the giant Amazonian waterlily, now grown in the Princess of Wales Conservatory. Papyrus and the sacred lotus are grown here now, and curiosities of the cucumber family – the bottle gourd and loofah – climb the inner walls. The Palm House Pond in front of the Palm House boasts a fountain and statue (1826) of *Hercules and Achelous*, which makes an excellent evening perch for fishing herons. Behind the Palm House are the formal rose gardens. The area between the Palm House Pond and the main gate, completing the circular tour, is dense with research and display projects, ancient and innovative. The Princess of Wales Conservatory – the name of which honors also the dowager princess – makes use of the latest glasshouse technology to house plants from varied climes under one roof. The Alpine House (1981) is landscaped within a pyramidal structure. These two glasshouses jostle the Herbaceous Area, where Chambers' Temple of Aeolus (rebuilt by Decimus Burton in 1845) overlooks the Woodland Garden. Close to the Aquatic Garden

CAMPSIS GRANDIFLORA
One of the thirty thousand species of plants at Kew Gardens.

A TROPICAL ENVIRONMENT
The heat and humidity of the Palm House favored the plants it contained, but damaged its structure, which was composed of a cast iron framework and sheets of glass.

347

Entrance to Osterley House.

and Grass Garden are the Order Beds, where students since Sir Joseph Hooker's time have been taught taxonomy, or how to identify, classify and understand plants. (The Herbarium on Kew Green, housing six million preserved specimens and the Jodrell Laboratory are complementary to the Order Beds.) Coming full circle back to the main gate – through the Duke's Garden with Cambridge Cottage, once the Duke of Cambridge's house, and the Kew Gardens Gallery – the Botanic Gardens honor the first of their enthusiastic superintendents with the Sir Joseph Banks Building and Landscape. This exciting, earth-covered, and energy-conserving building houses the Economic Botany Collection and Library. The building has a spectacular exhibition of the interdependence between man and plant life, which it is the work of the scientists and botanists at Kew to promote.

OSTERLEY PARK ★

Delightfully set among serpentine lakes, woodland walks, and arable land, Osterley House is itself an adornment to the landscape. (The noise from the nearby M4 motorway and Heathrow flight path overhead must be ignored.) The original four-turreted house was completed for Sir Thomas Gresham ▲ *151*, founder of the Royal Exchange, in 1575. The 16th-century stable block of soft red Tudor brick still stands. Robert Adam closed the front of Gresham's house in 1761 for another merchant prince, Robert Child of Child's Bank, with one of the finest porticos in England. The architect, Sir William Chambers ▲ *269, 280*, had earlier advised Child on the landscaping which we see today, and erected the Doric Temple of Pan in the grounds. Robert Child died in 1763, but his brother, Francis, retained Adam to continue his remodeling of the 16th-century house, and to instal a great Orangery – burnt down in 1950 – and other buildings in the grounds. The resulting country villa is one of Adam's most pleasing schemes, as ever owing much to classical models and motifs, and employing his favorite master-craftsmen. The design and execution of a door-lock were as important to Adam as those of a ceiling. The State Bed, its dome crowned with silk flowers where once they were cut, is a masterpiece. The hall has a Roman vestibule as its model.

John Linnell carved the bookcases in the library; Pietro Borgnis hand-painted the spidery decorations in the Etruscan Room. In the Long Gallery, fronting the Great Meadow, look out for a marigold, the symbol of Child's Bank, woven into the upholstery of a sofa. Francis Child was disappointed in his daughter, who eloped with Lord Westmorland to Gretna Green, where they were married without parental consent. The estate passed to her eldest daughter, Sarah Sophia, and thus into the Jersey family, when she married the earl. The ninth earl gave the house and furniture to the National Trust, and since then Osterley, with its 18th-century cedars of Lebanon, walks and lakes, has been a favorite weekend resort for Londoners.

TWICKENHAM ★

Just across Richmond Bridge is the town of Twickenham, which has some fine 17th-century houses. The future King Louis Philippe (1830–48) of France (cousin to Louis XVI) took refuge here from Napoleon in the early 19th century, and again after the revolution of 1848, which deposed him.

A HIVE OF CULTURE. The country village of Twickenham on the outskirts of London became fashionable in the 18th century, and several members of the aristocracy built houses here. It also drew writers and painters such as the chronicler Horace Walpole, painters Godfrey Kneller and J.M.W. Turner, and the poet Alexander Pope (1688–1744) ▲ *155, 262*. The latter lived on the bank of the Thames in Pope's Villa from 1719 until his death. It was later demolished. In 1876 Van Gogh lived at 160 Twickenham Road. Today Twickenham is best known as the home of rugby football.

STRAWBERRY HILL. An 18th-century house that is totally different from the classical buildings of the period, Strawberry Hill was created between 1749 and 1766 by the writer Horace Walpole (1717–97), fourth earl of Oxford. He transformed a modest cottage into a miniature Gothic castle. The style is eclectic, reproducing ideas from Gothic buildings all over Europe: the fireplace in the Beauclerc Room is modeled on Edward the Confessor's tomb at Westminster ▲ *137*, and the staircase balustrade is copied from Rouen Cathedral. The house is now a teacher-training college, and has been kept in excellent condition.

MARBLE HILL HOUSE

Built between 1724 and 1729 by Roger Morris to designs by Lord Herbert, Marble Hill House (above) was the home of the future George II's mistress, Henrietta Howard, who later became countess of Suffolk. The three-story Palladian building has been restored after falling into disuse, and there are paintings by Hogarth, Godfrey Kneller and others.

STRAWBERRY HILL
A general view of Horace Walpole's remarkable Gothic creation.

THE GALLERY, STRAWBERRY HILL
Horace Walpole moved here in 1747. He called it "a little plaything of a house, the prettiest bauble you ever did see". Its Gothic gallery has papier-mâché vaulting copied from Henry VII's chapel at Westminster, with niches modeled on a tomb in Canterbury cathedral.

MARBLE HILL HOUSE
Its design was influenced by Inigo Jones.

HAM HOUSE
One of the 17th-century doorways.

HAM HOUSE AND GROUNDS

The re-opening of Ham House on April 2, 1994, after three years' closure, is set to delight all those who know this 17th-century "Sleeping Beauty House", and admire the skillful presentation of its contents by the Victoria and Albert Museum. The fabric, furnishings and decoration of the house have been little altered since the 1670's, when Elizabeth, countess of Dysart and her husband, the duke of Lauderdale, first set their luxurious stamp on the house, built in 1610. They employed the joiner Thomas Carter to create the Grand Staircase. The balustrade is a marvel of carved and pierced panels, featuring trophies of arms. Franz Cleyn, director of the nearby Mortlake tapestry works, was probably employed to supervise the decoration of the North Front apartments. In the holiday atmosphere that followed Charles II's Restoration, the Lauderdales employed the architect William Sanwell to add a South Front, to include state apartments on the upper floor, decorated for the 1680 visit of Charles II's queen, Catherine of Braganza, and sumptuous private apartments for their own use on the ground floor. Elizabeth Lauderdale's son, Lyonel Tollemache, earl of Dysart, was at first hard pressed to make ends meet following her improvements, let alone make alterations. Later generations of Dysarts also chose to leave well alone, with happy results for the late 20th-century visitor. Almost all the paintings, including portraits by Lely and seascapes by Van der Velde, and furniture that is now on view, including adjustable "sleeping chairs" – for the duke's gout – belong to the house. Woolen cut velvet upholstery survives from the 1630's in the Yellow Satin Dressing Room; in the Restoration Library Closet, the blue damask – brownish now – and the embroidered blue velvet frames date from the 1670's. (The library itself, including works that were printed by Caxton and Wynkyn de Worde, was sold in the 1930's.) In the Museum Room, a section of gilded leather hangings ornamented with flowers and cherubs is on show. The National Trust acquired the house and grounds in 1948. In one of the few later alterations to have been made, an avenue which led from the North Front entrance to a landing stage on the Thames was removed. While the V&A administers the house, it is the Trust which restored the Ham House gardens in 1975 to their appearance as created by the Lauderdales, with hornbeam arbors and lavender beds. The summerhouses in the Wilderness which forms a *patte d'oie* before the South Gates replicate those in a 1737 engraving.

STATUE IN THE GARDENS
The 17th-century garden of Ham House is a great rarity. Most formal gardens were destroyed when more natural garden landscapes became fashionable.

MEDALLIONS OF HAM HOUSE
Carved medallions decorate the façade on either side of the entrance.

HAM HOUSE
The house stayed in the family of the Earls of Dysart from 1637 until 1948. It is now in the care of the Victoria and Albert Museum ▲ *229*.

Richmond-upon-Thames ★

Richmond Bridge in 1780, three years after its completion.

The beautiful town of Richmond was the summer residence of the kings of England in Plantagenet times. Henry VII and Elizabeth I both died here. Today Londoners love its elegant buildings, attractive shops and peaceful riverside walks, and its green has been called the finest in England. Historic pubs such as *The Three Pigeons* (1735) at 87 Petersham Street, and *The Roebuck* (1738) at 130 Richmond Hill, enjoy fine views over the Thames valley; and at Richmond visitors should taste

A REFUGE FOR FRENCH ÉMIGRÉS
During the French Revolution and the reign of Napoleon which followed it, a

"*Maids of Honour*", a local specialty and a favorite cake of Henry VIII (the recipe remains a secret). Maids of Honour Row is an attractive terrace of four 18th-century red-brick houses built by the future George II to house his wife's personal attendants.

RICHMOND PARK ■ *24.* East of the town is this magnificent park (right), which was once a royal hunting ground enclosed by Charles I. It covers 2,470 acres, making it the largest park in Greater London. There are several lakes, medieval oak trees, and around six hundred red and fallow deer. From the top of the Henry VIII mound, the magnificent view extends from Windsor Castle to St Paul's Cathedral ▲ *170.*

number of aristocrats managed to escape and find refuge here. The most important were the Duc d'Orléans and his family, which included the future King Louis Philippe.

RICHMOND BRIDGE. James Paine completed the five-arched bridge in 1777 to replace an earlier horse ferry. A toll was payable to cross it until 1859. It is the oldest bridge still standing across the Thames in Greater London, though it was widened in 1937.

WHITE LODGE. A former royal hunting lodge built in 1727 in Richmond Park, the Palladian-style White Lodge has housed the junior department of the Royal Ballet School since 1955. In 1894 the future Edward VIII (later Duke of Windsor) was born here to Queen Mary and George V.

RICHMOND
"We came to Richmond . . . our destination there was a house by the Green: a staid old house, where hoops and powder and patches, embroidered coats, rolled stockings, ruffles and swords, had had their court days many a time."
Charles Dickens,
Great Expectations

RICHMOND HILL. From the top of the hill, the view of the Thames meandering in the valley below has been called the finest in all England. Several painters have been inspired by this superb landscape, among them Joshua Reynolds, who lived at Wick House on Richmond Hill for twenty years until his death in 1792. In the 19th century the view was painted by two of the greatest English landscape artists, Turner ▲ *215–17* and Constable ▲ *214.*

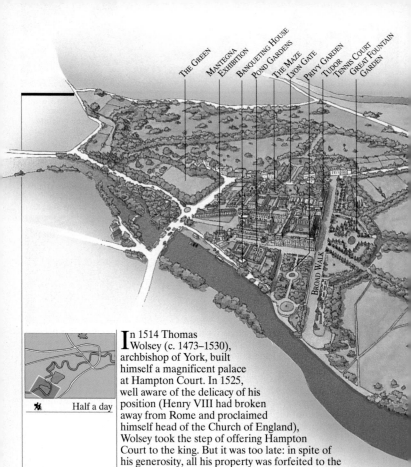

THE GREEN · MANTEGNA EXHIBITION · BANQUETING HOUSE · POND GARDENS · THE MAZE · LYON GATE · PRIVY GARDEN · TUDOR TENNIS COURT · GREAT FOUNTAIN GARDEN

BROAD WALK

★ Half a day

In 1514 Thomas Wolsey (c. 1473–1530), archbishop of York, built himself a magnificent palace at Hampton Court. In 1525, well aware of the delicacy of his position (Henry VIII had broken away from Rome and proclaimed himself head of the Church of England), Wolsey took the step of offering Hampton Court to the king. But it was too late: in spite of his generosity, all his property was forfeited to the crown and he died soon after.

THE HOME OF KINGS
Hampton Court is on the Thames about 14 miles southwest of London. It was a favorite residence of kings and queens from the 16th to the 18th centuries. Queen Victoria preferred Windsor Castle ▲ *356*, and opened Hampton Court to the public in 1838.

THREE PALACES IN ONE. Hampton Court is an English Renaissance building, initially constructed around two courtyards, Base Court and Clock Court. The Round Kitchen Court was added later. The red-brick building of the palace has white crenellation and lead-covered towers, and the interior decoration is magnificent, as witness the ceilings of the offices and apartments that Wolsey commissioned for his own use. Henry VIII decided to enlarge it. Between 1532 and 1535 Wolsey's original hall was rebuilt, the chapel was completed, and a suite of royal apartments was added (of which only the Great Watching Chamber remains). The kitchens too had to be enlarged to accommodate the royal household; and later the king added another room and a tennis court on the west side. In 1689 William of Orange and Queen Mary commissioned Wren ▲ *171–5* to rebuild the palace, which was then decorated by Englishmen James Thornhill, Caius Cibber, Grinling Gibbons ▲ *241, 274* and William Emmett, the Frenchman Louis Laguerre and the

LONG WATER

Neapolitan Antonio Verrio. After the demolition of Henry VIII's state apartments three major projects were built in the Baroque style: Fountain Court, replacing the former Green Court; the Cartoon Gallery, and the Queen's Wing in the east and the north. The king's private apartments were altered, and finally the long

> "Hampton Court is a great garden in the French style, laid out in the reign of William III . . . but the English taste is also apparent in the flower beds full of roses climbing slender trellises and the rows of flowers. Ducks and swans swim in the water and water-lilies open their satiny petals. The old trees are propped up in metal supports; when they die, so as not to lose them completely, great urns are made out of their trunks. Obviously they are loved and respected."
> *Notes sur l'Angleterre*
> Hippolyte Taine

façade on the east side was added.

THE TROPHY GATE. Constructed in the mid-18th century, the Trophy Gate is the main entrance to the palace.

THE GREAT GATEHOUSE. This majestic brick pavilion was built by Wolsey. The two wings leading back were added by Henry VIII in 1536. The mythical beasts beside the entry bridge date from 1950.

BASE COURT. The present palace still reflects Wolsey's original plans. This courtyard, with its crenellated walls, is where the servants' quarters once were.

CLOCK COURT. With the Great Hall on its north side, the courtyard gets its name from the Astronomical Clock that decorates the gateway. The Ionic colonnade on the south side is by Christopher Wren.

FOUNTAIN COURT. Wren drew upon the Château of Versailles for the design of this four-story court, combining Portland stone with pale orange brick. The bull's-eye windows on the façade are covered with monochrome medallions by Laguerre illustrating the Labors of Hercules.

THE ROUND KITCHEN COURT AND THE CHAPEL COURT. The first was built by Wolsey and the second by Wren. Chapel Court was altered in the 18th century.

THE KING'S APARTMENTS. The entrance is on the south side of

THE EAST FAÇADE
This is one of the grandiose alterations made by Sir Christopher Wren. It is broken into two parts by a portico crowned with a pediment carved by Caius Cibber in 1696, and opens on to the gardens.

353

▲ Hampton Court Palace

THE ASTRONOMICAL CLOCK
This is on the façade of ANNE BOLEYN'S GATEWAY which leads into Clock Court, and was made by Nicholas Oursian. It tells the time, day, month, the number of days since the start of the year, the phases of the moon, and even the hours of high tide at London Bridge. Being made before Copernicus and Galileo, it also shows the sun revolving round the earth.

THE TUDOR CHIMNEYS
Hampton Court is topped with lead-domed towers as well as ornamental brick chimneys.

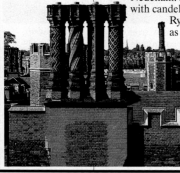

Clock Court, from where the visitor climbs the KING'S STAIRCASE and crosses the guardroom. The ceiling of WILLIAM III'S STATE BEDROOM is the work of Verrio. A corner staircase leads from the King's Study to the Queen's Gallery. Access from the king's apartments to those of the queen is by the COMMUNICATION GALLERY, running the entire length of Fountain Court, where *The Beauties of Windsor* by Sir Peter Lely are exhibited, eleven paintings of ladies of the court of Charles II.

THE CARTOON GALLERY. This is on the south side overlooking Fountain Court. Wren designed it expressly to house the Raphael cartoons (now in the Victoria and Albert Museum), purchased by Charles I in 1632. Access to the QUEEN'S WING, a suite of twenty rooms, partly decorated in the reign of Queen Anne (1702–14), is by the QUEEN'S STATE STAIRCASE, the work of Jean Tijou. The QUEEN'S GALLERY is decorated with a cornice by Grinling Gibbons. To the north is the QUEEN'S BEDCHAMBER with a ceiling by James Thornhill (1715), and the QUEEN'S DRAWING ROOM decorated by Verrio. Its large bay window looks on to GREAT FOUNTAIN GARDEN.

WOLSEY'S CLOSET. The ceilings of this room and also of Wolsey's apartments, which bear his coat of arms, as well as the carved "linen-fold" paneling, are a reminder of the refined and costly decoration the palace enjoyed under its first owner.

THE GREAT WATCHING CHAMBER. The large guardroom is at the entrance to Henry VIII's state apartments, and is all that remains of them. Its cloisonné ceiling is decorated with carved oak pendants and the arms of the Tudor monarchs in papier-mâché. The GREAT HALL was built in the reign of Henry VIII, and has a carved wood ceiling in English style by James Nedeham. Many other features of the hall, decorated with candelabra and acanthus leaves carved by R. Rydge, are in Italian Renaissance style. Just as they would have been in Henry VIII's reign, the walls are hung with tapestries, here illustrating the biblical story of Abraham. The 19th-century stained glass is by Thomas Willement.

THE TUDOR KITCHENS. In 1529 Henry VIII added another room to Wolsey's kitchen with three more fireplaces, as well as an additional one specially for cooking fish. An illuminated model shows the long route followed by those carrying the cooked food, which finally ascended an

THE SOUTH FAÇADE
The façade was decorated with the arms of Wolsey, still to be seen above
Anne Boleyn's Gateway in Clock Court, and with terracotta medallions by the
Florentine Giovanni da Maiano depicting Roman emperors.
These were the first examples of the Italian Renaissance in England.

oak staircase to the HORN ROOM, where it
waited before being served up in the
Great Hall.

THE GARDENS. The gardens owe their
present appearance to work done at the
time of Charles II (r. 1660–85) and then
William III (r. 1689–1702). Charles II had
them landscaped after the French models
of Le Nôtre: the goose-foot pattern and a
canal in front of Wren's façade recall the Palace

of Versailles. William III finished the canal by adding another
semicircular section lined with lime trees specially imported
from Holland. The PRIVY GARDEN is on the south side of the
palace by the river, from which it is separated by twelve 17th-
century wrought-iron grille panels by Jean Tijou. Beside the
Privy Garden a conservatory houses the GREAT VINE, grown
from a single root planted in 1768. The park also contains the
famous maze and, at its northeastern end, an ice-house. The
southern part is now a golf course.

THE BANQUETING HOUSE AND ORANGERY. These were both
built by Sir Christopher Wren. The former, located near the
site of the old Water Gallery (16th century) was decorated by
Antonio Verrio, and in the latter are nine magnificent
canvases painted by Andrea Mantegna in 1492, illustrating
the *Triumph of Caesar*. These were collected originally
by Charles I.

THE GOTHIC HALL
This gallery runs
along the north and
east sides of the
Round Kitchen
Court, and is
supposed to be
haunted by the ghost
of Henry VIII's fifth
wife, Catharine
Howard, beheaded
in 1542.

THE CHAPEL
In 1536 Henry VIII
added a carved
wooden ceiling to
Wolsey's chapel. The
rest of the decoration
including the
furniture is by Wren,
except for the
magnificent reredos
by Grinling Gibbons.

**THE KING'S
STAIRCASE**
This painting by W.H.
Pyne (1819) shows
Verrio's decorations
glorifying William
and Mary, and Tijou's
fine staircase.

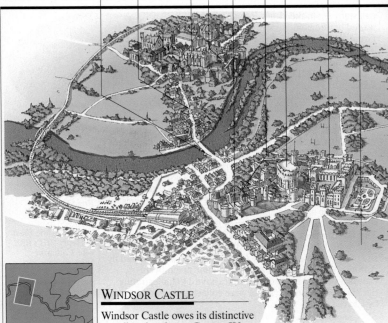

THAMES BRIDGE · ETON HIGH STREET · ETON COLLEGE CHAPEL · ETON COLLEGE · HENRY VIII'S GATEWAY · ST GEORGE'S CHAPEL · ROUND TOWER · STATE APARTMENTS · GREAT PARK

🚕 One day

CHANGING OF THE GUARD
Diverse regiments, including the Grenadier Guards raised by Charles II in exile, guard the castle and Queen Elizabeth II, just as Yeomen of the Guard used to guard Queen Elizabeth I. When the queen is in summer residence, the ceremony takes place in the Quadrangle. In the winter months the soldiers stamp to attention on the parade ground by the Henry VIII Gate.

WINDSOR CASTLE

Windsor Castle owes its distinctive castellated casing to George IV and his architect Jeffrey Wyatville, who homogenized the disparate medieval, Tudor and Stuart precincts in the 1820's. Among other bold flights of fancy, Wyatville added 30 feet in height and battlements to the Round Tower. (The royal standard flies from the tower when the queen is in residence; the Union Jack does so at other times.) The castle and precincts, however, maintain their medieval divisions of Lower Ward, Middle Ward and Upper Ward. William the Conqueror first selected the site for a wooden fortress in 1070; Henry II rebuilt his fortress in stone a century later, and added five rounded towers, including the Curfew Tower in Lower Ward, to the perimeter walls. Edward III, who founded the Order of the Garter, extended the royal apartments in Upper Ward to include St George's Hall (1362–5), where the Knights of the Garter banqueted. Edward IV founded St George's College and built St George's Chapel, which dominates Lower Ward, with Horseshoe Cloisters (1478–81), facing the Great West Door, to accommodate the clergy. The houses are occupied today by members of the staff of St George's Chapel, including the men of the choir. (The boy choristers come from

St George's Choir School, below the castle wall.) Henry VIII provided the castle entrance, or Henry VIII Gate, in 1511. His daughter Queen Mary added to the Military Knights' lodgings in Lower Ward, begun by Edward III. (The military, originally Poor Knights of St George, represent the absent Knights of the Garter in their choir stalls at church services.) Charles II remodeled the royal apartments (1675–83) in Upper Ward magnificently. George III (r. 1760–1820) rescued the castle from a period of neglect thereafter, and began, with James Wyatt, a Gothicizing process, which his son, George IV, and Wyatt's nephew, Jeffrey, pursued to dizzy heights. Windsor Castle is an incomparable treasure house. It houses the bulk of the Royal Collection, which includes the Royal Library, Print Room, Royal Archives, and paintings, furniture, armor, and hangings of inestimable value. Castle and collection were both threatened with devastation in November 1992, when a fire broke out in the queen's private chapel. It spread rapidly through the state apartments, and raged for twenty-four hours. Most moveable treasures were carried to safety. The Gilded Reception Room and St George's Hall, however, were buried under rubble, and the damage is assessed at £8 million.

A TOUR OF THE CASTLE

ST GEORGE'S CHAPEL. The burial place of ten monarchs, and spiritual home of the Order of the Garter. Here the queen and other members of the Order process, in Garter robes from the castle, for an annual June service. Above the stalls in the choir where the Knights of the Order take their places,

357

Shown above from left to right are the King's Audience Chamber, Old Guards' Chamber, the Ball Room and King's Drawing Room, from W.H. Pyne's *Royal Residences* (1819).

GEORGE III
He was known as the "Farmer King" because of his enthusiasm for agriculture. His equerries complained that he would ride 30 miles in a day to inspect a Berkshire neighbor's estate.

NORTH TERRACE, WINDSOR CASTLE

their individual banner, helmet and crest hang all year round. Edward IV founded St George's Chapel in 1475, probably in emulation of Eton College Chapel, that other jewel of Perpendicular Gothic. Henry VII completed the nave, and added the exquisite stone vaulted ceiling. A plate in the floor records the discovery of the tombs of Henry VIII, Jane Seymour and Charles I. Beneath the choir there also lies a vault, containing the coffins of many members of the Hanoverian royal family. Princess Charlotte, heir presumptive, who died in childbirth in 1817, is commemorated in a flowing marble tableau by the Great West Door. Among many other items of interest on show in the chapel is a rare "treacle" Bible, in which the word "balm" is rendered as "treacle".

ALBERT MEMORIAL CHAPEL. Following the death of Prince Albert, her consort, in 1861, Queen Victoria ordered Edward III's disused chapel of St George to be redecorated as a temporary resting-place for his tomb. (It was later moved to the Frogmore Mausoleum.) Sir George Gilbert Scott created the extravagantly decorated interior (1863–73), which now also houses Alfred Gilbert's tomb of the duke of Clarence, who died in 1892. Illustrated marble panels line the walls, the vaulted ceiling is decorated with

Venetian glass mosaic, and the stained glass in the south windows depict ancestors of Prince Albert.

ROUND TOWER. William the Conqueror's wooden Round Tower originally stood on the mound of the Round Tower, which now houses the Royal Archives and Royal Photograph Collection. The mound itself is made of spoil dug in the 1070's from the moat, where there is now a Moated Garden, made in the 1910's by a governor of the castle. Above the Moated Garden may be seen the only two 17th-century windows in the castle to escape Hanoverian Gothicizing.

NORTH TERRACE. This was laid out by Henry VIII on a bluff above the Thames, commanding fine views of the river, Eton Chapel and the Chiltern hills. During the 18th century George III, Queen Charlotte, and their prodigious family used to walk on the castle terraces to provide an example to the nation of marital and domestic harmony. George III later occupied apartments overlooking the North Terrace, when his mind was deranged. His son acted as regent from 1811 until his death in 1820. On the North Terrace is the entrance to the gallery housing Queen Mary's Dolls' House and also to the state apartments.

STATE APARTMENTS. Charles II largely remodeled this area in the 1670's, employing the architect Hugh May, the master wood-carver Grinling Gibbons ▲ 274, 355, and the artist Antonio Verrio, to embellish the apartments. The King's Dining Room, of all the king's suite – otherwise comprising the KING'S DRAWING ROOM, state bedchamber, Dressing Room, and closet – best display the work of Gibbons and Verrio. Charles I's queen consort, Catherine of Braganza, occupied the apartments known as the Queen's Drawing Room, the Ballroom, Audience, Presence and Guard Chambers. (Her state bedroom is now occupied by the Royal Library.) These lie on the southern, sunny side overlooking the Quadrangle, where the Changing of the Guard takes place when the queen is in residence. George IV confirmed the shifted focus of the castle when he linked the private apartments, first occupied by his mother and sisters, and still occupied today by the queen and royal family, by a Grand Corridor, on the eastern and southern side of the Quadrangle. Sir Jeffrey Wyatville also transformed many of

CASTLE VIEWS
The pictures below show a detail of a "Gothicized" window and the approach to the castle through the Henry VIII Gateway (1511). Notice the holes here for pouring boiling oil.

INSIDE THE CASTLE
The wards, towers and terraces accommodate many of the castle's 350-strong community.

The celebrated vista of Eton Chapel and the Chiltern hills from the North Terrace, across "a valley extended every way, and chequered with arable lands and pasture, cloathed up and down with groves, and watered with that gentlest of rivers, the Thames" (Hentzner, 1598).

ST GEORGE'S CHAPEL
The chapel and the buildings associated with this Royal Peculiar – no archbishop or bishop has authority within it – are rich in historical association. Shakespeare's *Merry Wives of Windsor* was first performed in what is now the Chapter Library.

the state apartments during the reigns of George IV and William IV. Among his alterations, he converted King Charles II's Presence Chamber, and part of his Audience Chamber, into the Garter Throne room. Here the queen invests new Knights of the Garter. The WATERLOO CHAMBER adjoining, where the queen lunches with the Knights of the Garter in June, houses portraits, which George IV commissioned Sir Thomas Lawrence to paint, of all the sovereigns, statesmen and soldiers who contributed to the Allied victory over Napoleon in 1815. King Charles II's Baroque chapel, greatly decayed, was demolished to make way for a new St George's Hall, where the Knights of the Garter assemble in June to process down to St George's Chapel for their annual service. This hall is to be restored, following its destruction in the fire of 1992.

THE GRAND STAIRCASE. This was rebuilt by the architect Anthony Salvin for Queen Victoria in 1866–7. (Beneath the statue of George IV by Sir Francis Chantrey is a suit of armor worn by Henry VIII.) Her taste, and that of Prince Albert, are apparent throughout the state apartments, as she lived and entertained here a great deal. The bed hangings in the KING'S STATE BEDCHAMBER, for instance, are of Napoleonic green and violet and embroidered with the arms of Louis Napoleon and the Empress Eugénie, for the latter's state visit in 1855.

QUEEN MARY'S DOLL'S HOUSE. Designed by Sir Edwin Lutyens on a scale of one to twelve and placed here, after exhibition, in a room of his own design in 1925, the display entrances children and adults alike. The palace exterior – in "Wrenaissance" style – is raised aloft by electricity to reveal over forty rooms on four floors, as well as working lifts, flushing lavatories, piped water and Crown Jewels behind a grille. Fifteen hundred companies and individuals contributed to make the Dolls' House a miniature showpiece of early 20th-century manufacturing and artistic standards and ingenuity. The library contains, apart from a pair of Purdey shotguns, a collection of minute prints and drawings by Paul

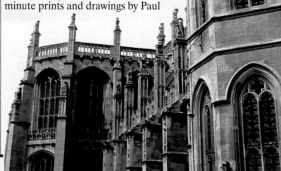

On the walls at Windsor two angels support the royal arms, embossed with the motto of the Order of the Garter.

Nash and Mark Gertler among others, stories by Arthur Conan Doyle and poetry by Siegfried Sassoon. Gertrude Jekyll made the garden – contained, like the garage with its Rolls-Royce Silver Ghost, in a bottom drawer – Broadwood the grand piano, and Singer made the minuscule sewing machine in the linen room.

ETON COLLEGE

Eton College, the public school which has reared so many of England's great and famous men, lies across the river from Windsor, and is best reached by walking across Windsor Bridge – no cars – and sauntering past the ancient and motley buildings which crowd Eton High Street. In this way you are almost certain to bump into some Etonians, as the schoolboys are known, wearing their uniform of coat tails and striped trousers. You may even catch sight of a rarer bird than these penguins. (Their schoolmasters are called "beaks".) Twenty-four members of a select society, founded in the 1820's, called Pop, are entitled to sport fancy waistcoats. The annual Fourth of June celebrations is the time to view Eton from the river, when there are fireworks and processions of boats. Henry VI was only eighteen when he founded Eton College by charter in 1440. The founder, as he is still known, followed closely the model of Winchester College, founded by William de Wykeham in 1382, and poached his first master and scholars from there. As a college of secular priests with a provost and fellows, a charity school and an almshouse, Eton was to be "the first pledge" of Henry's devotion to God. Unfortunately, he was deposed in the wars of the Lancastrians and Yorkists in 1460, when the chapel, a superb example of Perpendicular Gothic, was only half-finished, and the college fortunes languished. Indeed, Henry's Yorkist successor, Edward IV, came near to suppressing Eton College. Today the founder's statue in School Yard stands surrounded by the 15th-century Lower School, cloisters and College Hall, with its octagonal kitchen, and by other buildings added piecemeal in later reigns. Lupton's Tower is of Tudor Gothic. In 1690 Sir Christopher Wren ▲ *171–5*

> "Once admitted, the pupil must choose between rowing and cricket. Studying foreign languages, literature and music . . . are of secondary importance. Swimming, boats, oars, these are the magic formulae. Whoever plays well at football or cricket, plays well at life."
> Paul Morand, *London*

M.R. James, provost of Eton, on Henry VI: "Looking back over fifty years and further, I wonder whether there has ever been any one who has made more boys – more lives – happy than King Henry the Sixth, our Founder, and I hope his ghost, too, crowned with content, sometimes walks among us."

ETON COLLEGE CHAPEL
Stone from Caen, oak from Windsor forest, and bricks from Slough went to build the chapel (below left) which, but for the Wars of the Roses, would have been more than twice the length.

CLOISTERS CHAPEL
The cloister of Eton College (above right) was begun in 1443 and completed in the 18th century. It is still the center of the college.

enclosed the yard to the west with Upper School, later badly damaged in the Second World War. The original seventy King's Scholars of Henry VI's charter are now outnumbered by over a thousand *Oppidani*, or "townsmen" – so called because they live not in the college, but in the dense "town" of buildings which has grown up around it.

WINDSOR GREAT PARK. George II's son, William, duke of Cumberland, created the lake of Virginia Water in the 1750's, when he was an exemplary ranger of the Great Park. He is better known as "Butcher" Cumberland, for his earlier bloody part at Culloden in 1746. The "ruins", or columns, of Lepcis

Magna on the Ascot side of Virginia Water were presented to the Prince Regent in 1816, and were originally destined for the British Museum. A later ranger, Sir Eric Savill, was responsible in the 1930's for creating the garden close by, which bears his name, and also, after the war, the wondrous Valley Gardens, including the Kurume Punchbowl. There are wonderful rhododendrons and azaleas in May. Savill declared that his creations were "not botanic gardens, but should be thought of as private gardens accessible to the public".

THE LONG WALK. Laid out by Charles II, and brought up to the East Terrace of the castle by George IV, this is 3 miles long and connects the castle and Windsor Great Park.

Westmacott's 1831 equestrian statue of George III, known as the Copper Horse, is visible on the horizon. During Ascot week, the queen and her guests process down the Long Walk in carriages en route for the races.

FROGMORE. While Home Park immediately adjoining the castle is private, large stretches of Windsor Great Park are open to the public. Frogmore House and grounds, together with the royal mausolea, which lie between Home and Great Parks, are essential viewing when open for periods in the summer. Frogmore, a sprawling white mansion originally built in 1680 and much adapted since, was for generations of royal ladies an informal retreat from the rigours of castle life. The lake and grounds were landscaped by Uvedale Price's brother Richard. Queen Charlotte, consort to George III, was the first to enjoy Frogmore House. With her six daughters, she gardened, read, walked and painted here each morning. The Green Pavilion is restored to its appearance during her lifetime (she died in 1818). The flower painting in the Mary Moser room which she commissioned remains, and the Cross Gallery was painted by Princess Elizabeth, her most artistic daughter. Queen Victoria offered Frogmore to her mother, the duchess of Kent, in 1841, and twenty years later the duchess was buried in the grounds, in the mausoleum which she had wished to be built in her lifetime. The same Dresden architect, Grüner, designed the royal mausoleum nearby at Queen Victoria's request, following Prince Albert's death in the same year, 1861. The High Italianate interior reflects Prince Albert's reverence for Raphael. The tomb sculpture is somewhat pitiful, in that the figure of Queen Victoria, lying beside Albert, is so youthful. She was, of course, not interred until 1901. Queen Mary, consort to George V, loved Frogmore. In the early 20th century her sons, the future kings Edward VIII and George VI, had their schoolroom here. Queen Mary's Black Museum – a room housing her collection of papier mâché and mother of pearl – has been recreated from photographs in the Royal Photograph Collection.

FROGMORE HOUSE
The duchess of Kent, one of many royal ladies who lived at Frogmore House (above), has a mausoleum in the grounds. Her daughter, Queen Victoria, is entombed nearby with Prince Albert, her consort.

Eton School Library.

"Alas! regardless of their doom
The little victims play!
No sense have they of life to come
Nor care beyond today . . . ."
Thomas Gray,
Ode on a Distant Prospect of Eton College (1742)

363

Dulwich Picture Gallery opened in 1814, six years before the National Gallery ▲ *287*, and was carefully restored after being hit by a bomb in 1944. Among its many rare treasures is a self-portrait of actor Richard Burbage, a friend of Alleyn and Shakespeare.

A GALLERY OF MASTERPIECES
Dulwich Picture Gallery is largely composed of works by Old Masters such as Rembrandt, Rubens, Raphael, Van Dyck, Poussin (right, *The Triumph of David*), Veronese and many others. Many were purchased by Desenfans and Bourgeois from French aristocrats fleeing the French Revolution and the Emperor Napoleon. There is also a fine collection of English pictures by Gainsborough, Hogarth, Reynolds and others.

DULWICH ★

This delightful suburb was once a village that grew up around Dulwich Manor, which originally belonged to Bermondsey Abbey in the Middle Ages and was then demolished in the 19th century.

DULWICH COLLEGE. The school was founded in 1619 by the actor Edward Alleyn in Dulwich Manor. Alleyn had purchased the manor in 1605 for £5,000, which was part of a fortune he had made controlling theatrical licenses and as a partner in a bear-baiting pit. Childless himself, he conceived the idea of a charitable institution for the education of underprivileged boys, and so he spent the next six years transforming the manor into a school. After Alleyn's death the enterprise continued to expand, and eventually moved to its present buildings, which were designed by Charles Barry ▲ *129,* in the mid-19th century. Among the school's old boys are the novelists Raymond Chandler and P.G. Wodehouse. The latter used Dulwich as the setting in several of his books, calling it Valley Fields.

DULWICH PICTURE GALLERY. On his death in 1626 Alleyn bequeathed thirty-nine valuable paintings to Dulwich College, and the school then received a second legacy of 371 pictures in 1811 from the art dealer Noel Desenfans and Sir Francis Bourgeois. Sir John Soane ▲ *166* was then commissioned to build the first public art gallery in the whole of England. Soane's five-roomed gallery is centered around a mausoleum that contains the tombs of Bourgeois and also of Mr and Mrs Desenfans, and it houses many important works of art, such as Gainsborough and Lawrence's portraits of the Linley family, and works by Watteau, Murillo and Rembrandt.

PRACTICAL
INFORMATION

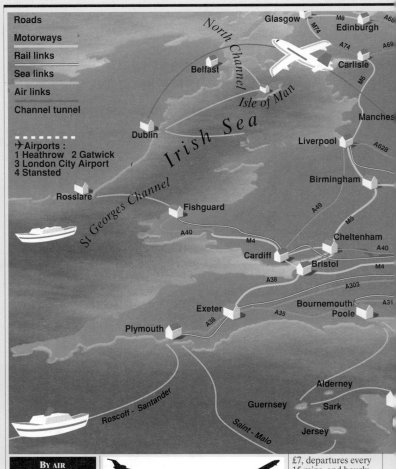

Roads
Motorways
Rail links
Sea links
Air links
Channel tunnel

- - - - - - - -
✈Airports :
1 Heathrow   2 Gatwick
3 London City Airport
4 Stansted

Glasgow — Edinburgh — M8 — A66 — M74 — A74 — A69 — Carlisle — M6

North Channel

Belfast

Isle of Man

Manches

Dublin — Irish Sea — Liverpool — A628

Birmingham

St Georges Channel

Rosslare

Fishguard — A40 — M4 — A49 — M5 — Cheltenham — A40

Cardiff — A38 — Bristol — M4

Exeter — A35 — A303 — Bournemouth/Poole — A31

Plymouth — A38

Alderney

Guernsey — Sark

Roscoff - Santander

Saint - Malo — Jersey

BY AIR

◆ The major British carriers are British Airways (0181-897 4000) and Virgin Atlantic (01293-562000). US airlines offering scheduled flights include American Airlines, Delta, United and US Air. Flight time from New York is about 7 hrs, though Concorde offers a faster service. There are numerous scheduled flights to all major European cities. For advice on discount tickets, phone the ATAB (0171-636 5000).

◆ **AIRPORTS**
Heathrow (15 miles from London), Gatwick (29 miles), Stansted (37 miles) all linked by shuttle service (payment required), and London City Airport (7 miles).
◆ **FROM HEATHROW**
BY UNDERGROUND
Piccadilly Line. Departures every 5 mins. £2.90, journey time about 45 mins.
BY BUS
– National Express or

Greenline bus no. 767. £8, about 1 hr. Arrive at Victoria Coach Station.– Airbus A1 or A2. £5, departures every 20 mins., journey time 1 hr. Stops at Cromwell Road, Hyde Park Corner, Victoria Coach Station.
BY TAXI
£30–£35 to the city center, journey time around 45 mins.
◆ **FROM GATWICK**
BY TRAIN
Gatwick Express.

£7, departures every 15 mins, and hourly through the night. Journey time 30 mins., arrive at Victoria Station.
BY BUS
Flightline 777. £6.30, departures 6.30 am– 8 pm, and every hour 8–11pm, journey time 1 hr 10 mins., arrive Victoria.
BY TAXI
£45–60, about 1½–2hrs journey.
◆ **FROM STANSTED**
BY TRAIN
Stansted Express. £8.50, Bishop's Stortford station, departures every 30 mins., journey time 45 mins., arrive at

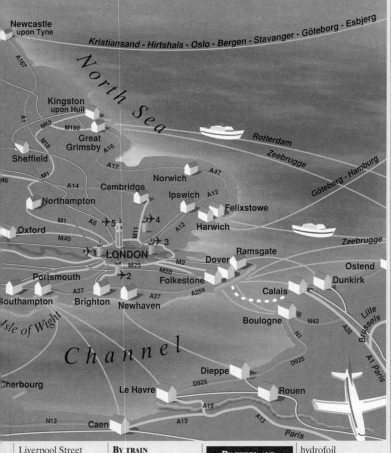

Kristiansand - Hirtshals - Oslo - Bergen - Stavanger - Göteborg - Esbjerg

Newcastle upon Tyne

Kingston upon Hull

Great Grimsby

Sheffield

Norwich

Cambridge

Ipswich

Northampton

Felixstowe

Oxford

Harwich

LONDON

Ramsgate

Dover

Portsmouth

Folkestone

Southampton

Brighton

Newhaven

Calais

Isle of Wight

Boulogne

Lille

Brussels

A1 Paris

Channel

Dieppe

Cherbourg

Le Havre

Rouen

Caen

Paris

Rotterdam

Zeebrugge

Göteborg - Hamburg

Zeebrugge

Ostend

Dunkirk

North Sea

Liverpool Street Station.

BY COACH
National Express or Cambridge Coach Service £6, departures every hour, journey time 1 hr 30 mins., arrive at Victoria Coach Station.

BY TAXI
About £30–40, journey time 1hr 15 mins.

◆ **FROM LONDON CITY AIRPORT**

BY TRAIN
Express train. Journey time 40 mins., arrive at Liverpool Street Station.

BY COACH AND BOAT
£6, coach shuttle from London City Airport to the Riverbus, departures every hour until 4.30pm, journey time 35 mins.

BY BUS
Greenline bus no. 787, arrive at Victoria Coach Station.

BY FERRY AND HOVERCRAFT

All UK ports are linked to the capital by rail. By car the journey takes 1½ to 2 hours. Shorter crossings on Hoverspeed or Seacat are more expensive.

BY COACH

Eurolines coach and car ferry via Calais. Transchannel Away via Calais and Dover. P&O European Ferries Office (0181-575 8555). Hoverspeed, coach and hovercraft or

hydrofoil (01304 240241).

BY CHANNEL TUNNEL

The return fare for a car with any number of passengers ranges from £130 to £220. You can also take the Eurostar train from London's Waterloo Station for £195 first-class return, £155 standard class and £95 apex. Journey time is 3 hours to Paris, 3 ¼ hours to Brussels. (01233 617575)

BY UNDERGROUND

The official name of the London subway system is the Underground, but it is more colloquially called the "Tube" by Londoners. Opened on January 10, 1863, it is the oldest underground network in the world. It comprises nine lines, each of which has its own colorcode and name. The lines intersect and stop at 268 stations. To reach your destination, make a note of the name of the lines and connecting stations you will

the same platform; in this case, an illuminated platform indicator will flash up the destination of in-coming trains. The doors of carriages open automatically, except in certain carriages, where you must press a button. The Underground runs

from 5.30am to midnight, except on Sunday (7.30am–11.30pm). Rush hours: roughly 8–9am and 5–6.30pm. Each station displays a timetable with times of last trains. Certain stations are closed on the weekend or in the rush hour.

need to use, then follow the signs for east/westbound and north/southbound, depending on the direction you need. A word of warning: connecting trains sometimes leave from

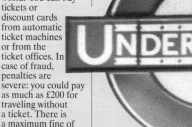

UNDERGROUND

Travel Information 071-222-1234
Travelcheck 071-222-1200

© Copyright London Regional Transport

For 24-hour information telephone (0171) 222 1234, or consult the various British Travel Centre offices or London Underground Ltd, 55 Broadway, SW1.

TICKETS.
The London Underground is one of the most expensive in the world. You can buy tickets or discount cards from automatic ticket machines or from the ticket offices. In case of fraud, penalties are severe: you could pay as much as £200 for traveling without a ticket. There is a maximum fine of

£1,000 for smoking.
◆ Single ticket 90p for one zone.
◆ Visitor's Travelcard This card includes transport between Heathrow Airport and London.

Key to lines

Bakerloo	
Central	Restricted service
Circle	
District	Restricted service
East London	Peak hours and Sunday mornings
Hammersmith & City	Peak hours only
Jubilee	
Metropolitan	Peak hours only
Northern	
Piccadilly	Peak hours only
Victoria	
Docklands Light Railway†	Under construction
Network SouthEast	Restricted service

○ Interchange stations
≋ Connections with British Rail
🚶 Connections with British Rail within walking distance
✕ Closed Sundays
✕ Closed Saturdays and Sundays
▲ Served by Piccadilly line all day Sundays and early morning and late evening Mondays to Saturdays
† For opening times see poster journey planners
Certain stations are closed during public holidays

Diary 1A 167mm x 110mm 2/92

Virtually unlimited use on BR trains, Underground and bus, as well as discount vouchers for certain tourist attractions. This can only be bought abroad at British Rail International offices.

◆ **Travelcards** Travel discount cards for Underground and bus, for 2, 4 or 6 zones, daily or weekly, can be bought at Underground stations. You will need a passport photo for the weekly card. One-day discount travelcards do not need a photograph, but can only be used after 9.30 am. They are sold in all Underground stations and from some ticket machines.

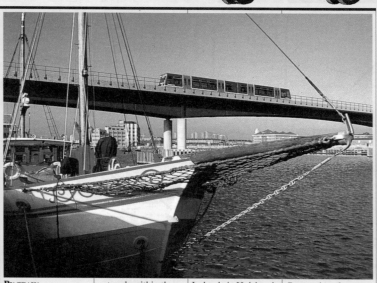

By train

◆ Docklands Light Railway (DLR)

Connects the Docklands with the City, Stratford and Greenwich. Docklands Light Railway Ltd (DLR) PO Box 154, Castor Lane, Poplar, London E14 0DX. (0171-918 4000) Trains run from 5.30am until 9.30pm, from Monday to Friday. Trains every 8 mins. 7am–8pm, every 10 mins. at other times. Tickets, travelcards and passes sold by DLR (ticket offices and machines in all DLR stations), London Transport, London Underground and British Rail. Valid on the entire DLR

network, within the relevant zones, and can be used on the London Underground system. Tickets cost 70p to £1.70 depending on the number of zones. Special "Docklander" discount card (only valid on DLR trains and buses) £2.20 (adult), £1.00 (child).

◆ Charing Cross Station

Strand, WC2
Tel. (0171) 928 5100
Connections for south London and the southeast of England.

◆ Euston Station

Euston Road, NW1
Tel. (0171) 387 7070
Connections for northwest London and northwest England, the Midlands, North Wales, Scotland and

Ireland via Holyhead.

◆ King's Cross Station

Euston Road, NW1
Tel. (0171) 278 2477
Connections for northeast London, the east and northeast of England, and the east coast of Scotland.

◆ Liverpool Street Station

Bishopsgate, EC2
Tel. (0171) 928 5100
Connects up east and northeast London, Essex and East Anglia.

◆ Paddington Station

Praed Street, W2
Tel. (0171) 262 6767
Connections for west London, Oxford, Bristol, Plymouth, the west of England, South Wales, Ireland via Fishguard.

◆ Victoria Station

Buckingham Palace Road, SW1
Tel. (0171) 928 5100
Connections for south London, Gatwick airport, southwest England and the Continent (Channel ports).

◆ Waterloo Station

Waterloo Road, SE1
Tel. (0171) 928 5100

Connections for south London and the south of England. Eurostar Channel Tunnel connection for journeys to Paris or Brussels.

By car

Road regulations:

drive on the left, speed limit 30 mph in town, 60 mph on single carriageways, and 70 mph on motorways and dual carriageways. Safety belts must be worn by all passengers. For further details, see the *Highway Code*, which can be obtained at Britain's ports of entry, from the Automobile Association (AA) or the Royal Automobile Club (RAC).
Car Rental:
– Avis Rent-a-Car

Heathrow Airport
Tel. (0181) 897 9321
Stanstead Airport
Tel. (01279) 663030
Gatwick Airport
Tel. (01293) 529721
Central London
Reservations
Tel. (0181) 848 8733
– Hertz Rent-a-Car
Central London
Reservations
Tel. (0181) 679 1799

BY TAXI
There are taxi ranks
in the stations, but
you can also find taxis
easily and quickly in
the street. You can
flag them down when
the "For Hire" or
"Taxi" sign is lit. In
general, taxis in
London are relatively
inexpensive and often
very comfortable.
You should allow
about £35 for the ride
from Heathrow
Airport–Piccadilly
Circus. It is
customary to give a
tip of about 10–15
percent of the cost of
the journey. Take one
of the famous
London black cabs at
least once.
Radio Taxicabs
(0171) 272 0272.
Computer-cab
(0171) 286 0286.

For nearest mini-cab
office, consult the
telephone directory
(*Yellow Pages*).
Mini-cabs are
generally cheaper
than traditional black
cabs, but often are
not so reliable – their
drivers don't have to
learn the extensive
"knowledge" of
London's back streets
tht black cab drivers
have, so may not take
the quickest route.
Only black cabs can
be hailed in the
street; mini-cabs have
to be called by phone.

BY RIVER
There are regular
pleasure boat services
downriver from
Westminster, Charing
Cross and Tower
Piers to Greenwich
and the Thames
Flood barrier. Boats
sail regularly every
20–30 mins. between
April and October,
and less frequently
during the winter.
– Westminster Tower
Boat Trips Ltd,
Tel. (0171) 930 4097,
or Tower Pier
Launches,
Tel. (0171) 488 0344.
– Westminster
Greenwich Thames

Passenger Boat
Services,
Tel. (0171) 930 4097,
or Greenwich Pier,
Te. (0181) 858 3996.
– London Launches,
Tel. (0171) 930 3373
– Catamaran Cruises
Ltd, Tel. (0171) 987
1185, or Greenwich
Pier, Tel. (0181) 858
3996.
– Campion Launches
Boat Services,
Tel. (0181) 305 0300.
– Thames Commuter
Services,
Tel. (0171) 537 4111.

– Circular Cruises
Westminster,
Tel. (0171) 936 2033.
– Festival South Bank
Cruises Ltd,
Tel. (0171) 278 6201.
– Upriver services
operate in the
summer, linking
Putney, Kew,
Richmond and
Hampton Court. For
details, contact
Westminster
Passenger Services
Association
(Upriver) Ltd,
Tel. (0171) 930 4721.

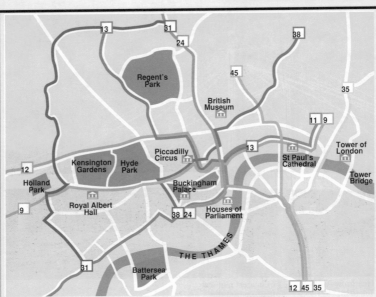

BY BUS

Traveling by bus is one of the nicest ways of discovering London. More picturesque than the Underground, London buses are also less expensive, although slower and less punctual. Don't miss your chance to

take one of these famous red double-decker buses, which are so characteristic of London: with the privatization of the network, they are becoming increasingly rare. The buses run from 5am to 11.30pm, and some run through the night.

◆ Catching buses

Be warned, some buses do not run the full length of the route, so check the destination displayed on the front. To stop the bus, ring the bell before you want to get off. You can obtain a comprehensive map of the routes at ticket offices in the Underground stations, but it is often easier to find your bearings using the posters at the bus stops. These display a list of buses and all the stops in the neighborhood.

◆ Bus stops

There are two types of bus stop: compulsory stops, indicated by signs with a white

background, and request stops, indicated by signs with a red background, which means you have to signal to the bus driver.

◆ Tickets

Either use a Travelcard (p. 369), or pay for the cost of your individual journey: the price will depend on how many zones you cross. In the new buses pay the driver on boarding; in the old buses, a conductor, who constantly does the rounds of the bus, will come over to inspect your ticket or take your money.

◆ Official London Transport sightseeing tours

London Transport offers a guided tour of the main tourist spots in a red double-decker bus. This lasts about 1 hr, and leaves every half hour from various pick-up points in the center. Price: £9. Tel: 0171-828 7395.

> "Even the addresses of friends in London tell you something of the city's secret corners, its rural past, its whims, its charms.
>
> Claude Roy

Terraces built around two triangular gardens.

"Fields": there were once meadows here.

"Place" may mean a square, but also a street.

Crescents were popular from the 18th century.

Wide road in the heart of "Theaterland".

"Mews": former stables.

Once a narrow lane, now a busy thoroughfare.

"Villas": road lined with detached houses.

Edgar Allan Poe once lived here.

A turning off Kensington High Street.

"Walk": once, no doubt, a path.

A prestigious area full of Victorian mansions.

"Gore": formerly a triangular piece of land.

"Terrace": row of adjoining houses.

London is the largest urban center in the United Kingdom, with an area of nearly 970 square miles and a population of 6.7 million. ("Greater London", with its thirty-two boroughs, exceeds 10 million inhabitants.) The capital city of Great Britain, it provides a home for the various political institutions: parliament, the government and the monarchy. The city is also the third-largest financial center in the world after New York and Tokyo. Airports, stations and telecommunication companies make it the key communications center in the country. Its press, which enjoys the widest circulation in Europe, has earned a worldwide reputation.

THE URBAN SCENE

THE CITY

To the north of London Bridge, the City is the hub of all financial activity: this is where you will find the Bank of England, the Stock Exchange and Lloyd's. This area, buzzing by day, is deserted at night: the number of inhabitants grows steadily smaller. It has been abandoned for the Greater London boroughs.

THE WEST END

This area around Westminster is home to the large parks, theaters and cinemas, as well as shops, and is linked to the City by the Strand.

Canary Wharf
(above left)
St Katharine's Dock
(above right).

THE EAST END

A working-class district near the ports.

THE NEW TOWNS

To cope with the number of Londoners moving out to the suburbs, several new towns were built after 1946: Crawley and Bracknell, south of the River Thames, Hemel Hempstead, Welwyn, Stevenage, Harlow to the north, and Basildon to the east. Today, new towns are being created more than 60 miles from the city center.

A FLAGGING ECONOMY

London's birthplace was near a ford on the Thames, in the middle of southeast England's sedimentary basin. So the economy naturally grew up around its port, which now extends for nearly 25 miles. England is no longer a major economic power. The capital's traditional branches of industry, such as the iron and steel,

chemical and motor industries, are in the grip of recession. The electronics industry has been hit by fierce competition from Japan, Europe and Southeast Asia. Oil mining in the North Sea has reduced the traffic of oil tankers through the port of London, which now handles no more than one-fifth of the national traffic.

William Boyd

AN INTERNATIONAL FOCUS FOR CULTURE AND THE MEDIA

THE CULTURAL SCENE
London owes its vital cultural life to the fact that the people who live there regularly go to the cinemas, concert halls, theaters (over three hundred) and libraries. English film-makers (Stephen Frears, Peter Greenaway, James Ivory) and pop stars (Elton John, Sting, Rod Stewart, Paul McCartney) have an international following.
British artistic output is stimulated by the cultural variety and huge market represented by the Commonwealth countries.

The city landscape makes it popular as the home of writers (William Boyd, Peter Ackroyd, Patricia Highsmith). The London literary scene includes such world-

THE BRITISH BROADCASTING CORPORATION

respected figures as Ian McEwan, Martin Amis and Anita Brookner.
EXPERTISE
London continues to enjoy a reputation for expertise in the field of creative education (professional recording studios, art schools, high quality drama schools and music colleges).

The late Anthony Burgess

My tailor is rich

The sectors of the economy that are still relatively buoyant include the leisure and tourism, banking and service industries.

LONDON, A MAJOR FINANCIAL CENTER
Today, London is still the leading stock market in Europe,

with £609 billion worth of shares and £973 billion worth of government bonds.

BOOKING FOR SHOWS
– At the theater box offices, usually open until 10pm. The same day unsold seats are offered at reduced prices.
– By telephone, if paying by credit card (this also applies to cinemas).

TICKET AGENTS
Be warned, there are hefty booking charges. Open 24 hours a day:
– First Call
Tel: (0171) 240 7200
– Ticketmaster
Tel: (0171) 379 4444
– Official Ticket Agency
Tel: (0181) 427 6566
– Theatre Booking Agents
Tel: (0171) 724 0747
– Ticket World
Tel: (0171) 702 9878
– Half-price ticket booth in Leicester Square (12–2pm for matinées; 2.30–4.30pm for evenings, except Sun.). Tickets half-price subject to availability on the day, limited to four per purchase. Payment in cash.

Royal Opera House, Covent Garden.

THEATER AND CINEMA
All shows are listed in the weekly publications *What's On* and *Time Out* and a shorter listing appears in the *Evening Standard*, published daily Monday to Friday. Theater listings are divided into West End and Fringe shows; the former are in larger, more central theaters and often feature star performers and the 'hit' shows. Fringe

performances can be more experimental and adventurous, taking place in smaller theaters, some of them simply rooms above pubs. Cinema listings are divided into the major central London cinemas showing current releases, local cinemas outside the city center, and a 'Repertory' section which features art movies and retrospectives.

LONDON'S PEARLY KING

THE MEDIA

◆ Press
Several daily newspapers: *The Times,* the *Independent, Daily Telegraph, Guardian* and *Financial Times.* The tabloids include the *Daily Mail,* the *Express,* the *Sun,* the *Mirror* and *Today.* On Sundays, choose from the *Observer, The Sunday Times,* the *Independent on Sunday, News of the World, Sunday Mirror, Sunday Express, The Mail on Sunday, Sunday Telegraph* and *People.*

◆ Radio
The BBC (five main channels and the World Service) has an audience of 120 million people all over the world and broadcasts 735 hours of programs in thirty-five languages every week.

The BBC headquarters, Portland Place.

BY APPOINTMENT
TO HER MAJESTY THE QUEEN
PATENT LOCK AND SAFE MAKERS

DIEU ET MON DROIT

◆ Television
British television is famous for its high quality all over the world. Many documentaries and drama programs are exported to Europe and the US. There are 4 main channels – BBC 1, BBC 2, ITV and Channel 4.

SHOPPING
The shops are open from around 9–9.30am until 5–6pm, some every day. Late-night shopping: Wednesdays in Knightsbridge and Kensington High Street until 7pm and in Sloane Square until 8pm; Thursdays in Oxford Street and Regent Street, until 7pm or 8pm. Traditionally, sales take place early in January and July.

MARKETS

London markets are very varied: you can unearth real finds and discover some very picturesque areas in the process.

ANTIQUES AND SECONDHAND GOODS
– Petticoat Lane and Brick Lane markets in the East End used to sell antiques and secondhand goods in the early 20th century. Now you will find they have everything from old computers to antique toys, not to mention 1960's clothes.
– The flea market in Portobello Road in west London, every Saturday, is similar to Brick Lane market. The goods on sale are of better quality, but more expensive.
– Camden Passage, in Islington, is the most

reputable market for antiques.
– Camden Lock, near the lock of an attractive canal, is one of the most popular markets in

London. Hundreds of little stalls selling all manner of things: jewelry, new and secondhand clothes, sculpture, paintings, crafts, records,

cassettes, etc. It is crowded and fairly expensive, but you will find some original gifts.

FLOWERS
– In Columbia Road, not far from Brick Lane, is a flower and plant market which can be visited very early on Sunday mornings.

ANTIQUARIAN BOOKS
– Paddington Road. People who love fine books can browse around this market which is a venue for a large number of booksellers.

MEAT MARKET
– Smithfield Market: this is where London butchers buy their meat. If you can stand the stench, go there between 5 and 8am, except on Sundays.

ACCOMMODATION

◆ Hotel reservation organizations

– Bed and Breakfast, PO Box 66, Henley-on-Thames, Oxon RG9 1XS
Tel: (01491) 578803
Fax. (01491) 410806
– British Hotel Reservation Centre
Victoria Station (at the exit from Platform 8)
Tel: (0171) 828 1027/1849
– Central London Accommodation Service
83 Addison Gardens W14 0DT

THE BISHOP
OUT OF RESIDENCE

Youngs

Tel (0171) 602 9668
– Hotel Booking Service Ltd
13–14 Golden Square W1R 3AG
Tel: (0171) 437 5052
Fax. (0171) 734 2124
– Hotel Finders
20 Bell Lane NW4 2AD
Tel: (0181) 202 7000
Fax. (0181) 202 3871
– Hotelguide
3 Crescent Stables
139 Upper Richmond Road
SW15 2TX
Tel: (0181) 780 1066
Fax. (0181) 780 2352
– London Accommodation Centre
22 Wardour St W1V 3HH
Tel: (0171) 287 6315
– Expotel
Kingsgate Place NW6 4HG
Tel: (0171) 328 1790
Fax. (0171) 328 8021.

◆ Hostels and student rooms

–Youth Hostels Association
Trevelyan House
8 St Stephen's Hill

St Albans, Herts AL1 2DY
Tel: (01727) 55215
–Imperial College Summer Accommodation Centre

My kingdom for a bed!

Room 170, Sherfield Building
Exhibition Road SW7 2AZ
Tel: (0171) 589 5111

◆ Camping

–Tent City
Old Oak Common Lane
W3 7DP
Tel: (0181) 749 9074
Open June– Sept.
No caravans
– Motorhome Rentals (Europe) Ltd
Lowood Garage
12 Kings Avenue
SW4 8BQ
Tel: (0181) 720 6492

ELECTRICAL APPLIANCES

The voltage most often used in Great Britain is 240V (alternating current). You will need an international adaptor for non-British appliances (razors, hairdriers, etc.). Such adaptors are some-times supplied by hotels.

377

As in many other European capitals, prices vary in London depending on the level of tourist activity in any given district and how select an area it is: a portion of fish and chips can double in price depending on whether it is eaten in Spitalfields or in Mayfair. The main problem remains that of accommodation: prices are usually high and can vary quite considerably for the same service within a fairly extensive range of establishments.

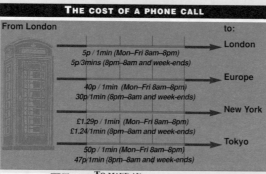

THE COST OF A PHONE CALL

From London		to:
5p / 1min (Mon–Fri 8am–8pm) 5p/3mins (8pm–8am and week-ends)	→	**London**
40p / 1min (Mon–Fri 8am–8pm) 30p/1min (8pm–8am and week-ends)	→	**Europe**
£1.29p / 1min (Mon–Fri 8am–8pm) £1.24/1min (8pm–8am and week-ends)	→	**New York**
50p / 1min (Mon–Fri 8am–8pm) 47p/1min (8pm–8am and week-ends)	→	**Tokyo**

MAKING A PHONE CALL IN LONDON

London is divided into two dialling code zones: 0171 for inner London and 0181 for outer London. You must dial this code if you are phoning from one zone to the other. Within a zone, dial only the seven digits of the number. National inquiries: 192. International directory inquiries: 153. Emergency services: 999. Operator: 100. International operator: 155.

TO MAKE AN INTERNATIONAL CALL

◆ Dial 00 followed by the country code (USA and Canada 1), the area code, and the number. From the US to London, dial 011 44 + the number you require.

PHONE BOXES

These take 10p, 20p, 50p and £1 coins or phonecards (which can be bought at post offices and shops displaying the "Phonecard" sign). Some phones accept credit cards.

Calls are cheaper after 6pm weekdays and at weekends.

Red phone boxes have nearly all been replaced.

TIME ZONES

Great Britain is five hours ahead of New York, and one hour behind Europe. The clocks are put back by one hour in late March, and return to Greenwich Mean Time at the end of October.

This 24 hour clock shows Greenwich Mean Time (GMT) basis of the International Time Zone System

British Summer Time (BST) is one hour fast on GMT

O: Midnight VI: 6am XII: Noon XVIII: 6pm

THE POSTAL SYSTEM

Post offices are usually open 9am–5.30pm Mon. to Fri., and 9am–1pm on Sat. The post office in William IV Street, near Charing Cross Station, is open on Sundays, 10am–5pm. Some newsagents now sell stamps. There are two postal tariffs: 1st class and 2nd class. First-class stamps can be used for letters to the EC.

EXCHANGE RATES

£1 = about $1.50. Currency and traveler's cheques can be changed in all banks on production of some means of identification (usually open Mon. to Fri. 9.30am–3.30pm. Some are open on Sat. mornings 10am–12.30pm.) There are also exchange facilities in many travel agencies, large stations, hotels and department stores, and airports offer a 24-hour service. The bureaus that open at night or weekends sometimes offer less favorable rates of exchange.

CURRENCY

The unit of currency is the pound sterling (£), which is divided into 100 pence (p). The notes in circulation are: £5, £10, £20, £50. The coins are: 1p, 2p, 5p, 10p, 20p, 50p, £1.

WHAT THINGS COST

1 PINT BEER: BETWEEN **£1.60** AND **£2.20**	**1 FISH & CHIPS:** **£1.80–£2.30**	**1 TEA WITH SCONES AND/OR SANDWICHES:** **£4–£5**	**1 TAXI:** **£4–£5** FOR 2 MILES
1 MUSEUM ADMISSION: **£3–£5**	**1 CLASSICAL CONCERT:** **£6–£30** OPERA : **£20–£150** (LESS FOR PROMS AND STANDBY)	**1 MEAL: £9–£25** OR MORE... (INDIAN OR CHINESE RESTAURANTS TEND TO BE CHEAP)	**1 DOUBLE ROOM** WITH BATH: **£40–£150** OR MORE...

FESTIVALS AND EVENTS

	JANUARY	FEBRUARY	MARCH	APRIL	MAY	JUNE	JULY	AUGUST	SEPTEMBER	OCTOBER	NOVEMBER	DECEMBER
• **CHINESE NEW YEAR** (DATE VARIES)	●	●										
• **LONDON BOOK FAIR**			●									
• **CHELSEA FLOWER SHOW**					23–26							
• **TROOPING THE COLOUR, HORSE GUARDS PARADE, FOR THE QUEEN'S BIRTHDAY**						11						
• **LAWN TENNIS CHAMPIONSHIPS AT WIMBLEDON**						19–3						
• **ROYAL TOURNAMENT**							●					
• **NOTTING HILL CARNIVAL**								●				
• **HALLOWEEN**										31		
• **GUY FAWKES NIGHT**											5	
• **LORD MAYOR'S PROCESSION AND SHOW**											●	

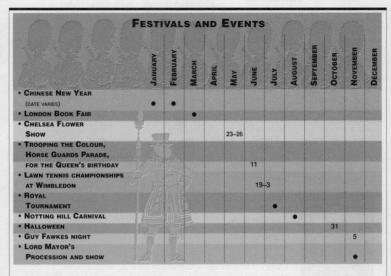

January 1, Good Friday, Easter Monday, first Monday in May (*May Day Holiday*), Whit Monday (*Spring Bank Holiday*), last Monday in August (*Summer Bank Holiday*), Christmas Day, December 26 (*Boxing Day*) are all public holidays.

LEVELS OF HUMIDITY AND RAINFALL

May, June, September and October are good months to visit London as the weather is usually fine and the city is not too busy. In July and August there are a lot of tourists and it can be very hot.

MINIMUM AND MAXIMUM TEMPERATURES

WESTMINSTER AND VICTORIA

CABINET WAR ROOMS
Clive Steps,
King Charles St, SW1
Tel: (0171) 930 6961.
Open 10am–5.15pm
daily.

WESTMINSTER ABBEY
Parliament Square,
SW1
Tel: (0171) 222 5152
Open Mon.–Fri.
8am–6pm, Sat. 8am–
2pm, 3.45–5pm, Sun.
between services.

INNS OF COURT

DR JOHNSON'S HOUSE
17 Gough Square, EC4
Tel: (0171) 353 3745
Open 11am–5pm
Closed Sun and public
holidays.

HUNTERIAN MUSEUM
Lincoln's Inn Fields,
WC2
Tel: (0171) 405 3474
Open 10am–5pm

PUBLIC RECORD OFFICE MUSEUM
Chancery Lane, WC2
Tel: (081) 876 3444
Open 9.30am–5pm
Closed Sat., Sun.

SIR JOHN SOANE'S MUSEUM
13 Lincoln's Inn Fields,
WC2
Tel: (0171) 405 2107
Open 10am–5pm
Closed Sun., Mon. and
public holidays.

CITY AND ST PAUL'S

BANK OF ENGLAND MUSEUM
Bartholomew Lane, EC2
Tel: (0171) 601 5545
Open Mon.–Fri.
10am–5pm. Sun. and
public holidays, 11am–
5pm in summer.

GUILDHALL
Off Gresham Street,
EC2
Tel: (0171) 606 3030
Open 10am–5pm
Closed Sun.

THE MONUMENT
Monument Street, EC3
Tel: (0171) 626 2717
Open 9am–6pm
Sat. and Sun. 2–6pm
From Oct. to Mar
9am–4pm, closed Sun.

MUSEUM OF LONDON
150 London Wall, EC2
Tel: (0171) 600 3699
Open Tue.–Sat.
10am–6pm, Sun.
noon–6pm. Closed
Mon. and Christmas.

NATIONAL POSTAL MUSEUM
King Edward St,
EC1
Tel: (0171) 239 5420
Open Mon.–Fri.
9.30am– 4.30pm.
Closed Sat., Sun and
public holidays.

THE TOWER

HMS BELFAST
Morgan's Lane,
Tooley Street, SE1
Tel: (0171) 407 6434
Open10am–6pm daily.

TOWER BRIDGE
Southwark, SE1
Tel: (0171) 407 0922
Open 10am–4pm
(winter); 10am-5.45pm
(summer).

TOWER OF LONDON
Tower Hill, EC3
Tel: (0171) 709 0765
Open Mar. to Oct.
9.30am–6.30pm, Sun.
2–6.15pm. Nov. to Feb.,
open 9.30am–5pm.
Sun 10am–5pm.

KENSINGTON

COMMONWEALTH INSTITUTE
230 Kensington High
Street, W8
Tel: (0171) 603 4535
Open 10am–5pm
Sun. 2–5pm.

NATURAL HISTORY MUSEUM
Cromwell Road
South Kensington,
SW7
Tel: (0171) 938 9123
Open 10am–5.50pm
Sun. 11am–5.50pm.

SCIENCE MUSEUM
Exhibition Road,
SW7
Tel: (0171) 938 8000
Open 10am–6pm. Sun.
11am–6pm.

VICTORIA & ALBERT MUSEUM
Cromwell Road
South Kensington, SW7
Tel: (0171) 938 8500
Open Tue.–Sun. 10am–
5.50pm, Mon.
noon–5.50pm.

HAMPSTEAD

FREUD MUSEUM
20 Maresfield Gardens,
NW3.
Tel: (0171) 435 2002
Open noon–5pm.
Closed Mon., Tues.

MARYLEBONE

MADAME TUSSAUD'S
Marylebone Road, NW1
Tel: (0171) 935 6861
Open Mon.–Fri. 10am–
5.30pm, Sat. and Sun.
9.30am–5.30pm

SHERLOCK HOLMES' MUSEUM
221b Baker Street, NW1
Tel: (0171) 935 8866
Open 9.30am–6pm.

COVENT GARDEN

LONDON TRANSPORT MUSEUM
The Piazza
Covent Garden, WC2
Tel: (0171) 379 6344
Open 10am–6pm

THEATRE MUSEUM
Covent Garden, WC2
Tel: (0171) 836 7891
Open 11am–7pm
Closed Mon.

SOHO

DESIGN CENTRE
28 Haymarket, SW1
Tel: (0171) 839 8000
Open 10am–6pm
Sun. 1–6pm.

BLOOMSBURY

BRITISH MUSEUM
Great Russell St, WC1
Tel: (0171) 636 1555
Open 10am–5pm
Sun. 2.30–6pm.

DICKENS' HOUSE
48 Doughty Street, WC1
Tel: (0171) 405 2127
Open 10am–4.30pm
Closed Sun.

SOUTH OF THE RIVER

DESIGN MUSEUM
Butler's Wharf
28 Shad Thames, SE1
Tel: (0171) 403 6933
Open 10.30am–5.30pm.

IMPERIAL WAR MUSEUM
Lambeth Road, SE1
Tel: (0171) 416 5000.
Open 10am–6pm daily.

LAMBETH PALACE
Lambeth Palace Road,
SE1
Tel: (0171) 928 8282.

LONDON DUNGEON
28 Tooley Street, SE1
Tel: (0171) 403 0606
Open 10am–5.30pm
daily. Last admission
4.30pm Oct. to Mar.

MUSEUM OF THE MOVING IMAGE (MOMI)
South Bank
Waterloo, SE1
Tel: (0171) 401 2636
Open 10am–6pm.
Closed at Christmas.

SHAKESPEARE GLOBE MUSEUM AND ROSE THEATRE EXHIBITION
Bear Gardens
Bankside, SE1
Tel: (0171) 928 6342
Open 10am–5pm
Sun. 2–5.30pm.
Closed public
holidays.

GREENWICH

CUTTY SARK & GIPSY MOTH IV
Greenwich Pier, SE10
Tel: (0181) 858 3445
Open 10am–6pm,
Sun. noon–6pm
Closed 4.30pm in
winter.

NATIONAL MARITIME MUSEUM
GREENWICh, SE10
Tel: (0181) 858 4422
Open 10am–6pm
Sun. noon–6pm
From Oct. to Mar. open
10am–5pm, Sun.
2–5pm.

OLD ROYAL OBSERVATORY
Flamsteed House
Greenwich Park, SE10
Tel: (0181) 858 1167
Open 10am–6pm
Closed 5pm in winter.

WEST ALONG THE THAMES

CHISWICK HOUSE
Burlington Lane, W4
Tel: (0181) 995 0508
Open 10am–1pm,
2–4pm.

SYON HOUSE
Park Road
Brentford, Middlesex
Tel: (0181) 560 0881
Open noon–4.15pm,
from Apr. to Oct. only.

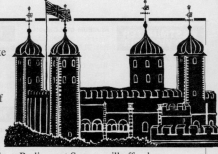

THE TOWER OF LONDON ▲ *182*
The four towers crowned by their Byzantine–style domes defend the White Tower, which dates from Norman times, and dominate the two walls that enclose the Tower.

NATIONAL GALLERY ▲ *287* Among many world-famous masterpieces, you will see works by Leonardo, Rembrandt, Constable and the Impressionists.

From Victoria Station, the best thing to do is take a double-decker bus into the political and religious heart of London: WESTMINSTER, ▲ *128*. Before you go into Westminster Abbey, Parliament Square will afford you a panoramic view of the HOUSES OF PARLIAMENT and BIG BEN, St Margaret's and the abbey itself. Then, from Westminster Bridge, you will be able to take in the neo-Gothic façades of the Palace of Westminster and a view of the Thames. In Westminster Abbey, the royal pantheon and burial place, you will find it easy to picture the elaborate coronation ceremonies. Do not miss the Henry VII Chapel and the Chapter House. Take the bus to TRAFALGAR SQUARE ▲ *284*, via WHITEHALL. A visit to the NATIONAL GALLERY ▲ *287* is essential, especially the rooms devoted to the English school of the 18th and 19th centuries. Also worth a look are Hogarth's *Marriage à la mode*, Gainsborough's *Mr and Mrs Andrews*, and the paintings by Constable and Turner.

HOUSES OF PARLIAMENT
"The Palladianism of the Adam brothers was abandoned for pointed arches, stained glass, vaulting, green rep curtains, nielloed spikes, and hooked ridge ornaments. The Perpendicular Style, now called 'radiator style', hides the polychromatic interior of a missal."
Paul Morand,
London

After a quick snack for lunch in the crypt of the nearby church, ST MARTIN-IN-THE-FIELDS ▲ *286*, built by James Gibbs, catch another bus, via Fleet Street, to ST PAUL'S CATHEDRAL ▲ *171*, Christopher Wren's masterpiece. From the dome you will be able to admire the interior of the sanctuary as well as, from the Golden Gallery, the city spread out below you. Then continue on, either by bus or on foot (to get a better feel of the City), to the stark fortress of the TOWER OF LONDON ▲ *182*, guarded by the famous Beefeaters and haunted by the memory of the people who were executed there. Having made your way through the two outer walls, go into the White Tower and the Jewel House. It is a short walk from the Tower to Tower Bridge, one of London's best-known sights. From the walkway of the bridge you will enjoy a superb view across the city. Finally, what could be nicer than dinner in one of the restaurants on the South Bank before a show?

DAY 1. Stay in one of the hotels in Russell Square, which will provide you with a convenient base for touring the city. Start your visit with the BRITISH MUSEUM ▲ *300*. In the Duveen Gallery you will see famous sections of the frieze from the Parthenon that Lord Elgin brought back to London from Athens. The Manuscript Room in the British Library has some Anglo-Saxon chronicles, charts, famous signatures, and musical scores on display. For lunch, order a "ploughman's" in a Bloomsbury pub. In LINCOLN'S INN FIELDS ▲ *165*, wander around one of the barristers' colleges and marvel at the eclectic collection put together by the well-known architect, Sir John Soane. Then head for the CITY ▲ *146* to discover Cheapside, Poultry and Lombard Street. Feel the atmosphere of a kingdom based on rumor and speculation, where communication is based on monetary symbols and fortunes are won and lost. If you like opera, the evening could begin with a performance at COVENT GARDEN ▲ *272* and continue with dinner at one of the restaurants in this lively area.

DAY 2. Spend the morning exploring "MUSEUM LAND" ▲ *228*. After a visit to the Science Museum, which is both educational and enjoyable, the VICTORIA AND ALBERT MUSEUM is a must. Be sure not to miss the Indian collections, some sketches by Raphael, and Constable's paintings. You can then have a good lunch (though rather expensive), in the museum restaurant. When you come out, go to the ROYAL ALBERT HALL ▲ *236* and, passing by the Albert Memorial, cross HYDE PARK ▲ *245* (perhaps hearing the renowned soap-box "preachers" on the way) to rejoin Oxford Street. A double-decker bus will take you to Tower Gateway, near the TOWER OF LONDON. From there the Docklands Light Railway will allow you to form a general impression of the new architectural developments in the Docklands including the monumental Canary Wharf tower. From ISLAND GARDENS ▲ *339*, you will have a breathtaking view of Greenwich and the Royal Naval College. Once you have negotiated the gloomy Thames tunnel, give yourself a well-earned rest in the *Trafalgar Tavern*. A passenger boat will take you from there back to LONDON BRIDGE. Finally, the *George Inn*, a picturesque 17th-century tavern in Southwark, south of the Thames, will make you very welcome.

VICTORIA AND ALBERT MUSEUM ▲ *229*
The "V&A" (left) was built at the instigation of Prince Albert, who wanted to keep alive the memory of the Universal Exhibition of 1851.

ST KATHARINE'S DOCK ▲ *334*
Wharves and docks alternate in the port of London. St Katharine's Dock dates from 1928.

BLOOMSBURY ▲ *298*
This residential district is renowned for its keen intellectual tradition.

THE ROYAL NAVAL COLLEGE ▲ *327*

BLAKE AND MORTIMER
In *The Affair of the Necklace*, Edgar P. Jacobs' two heroes pace the streets of London.

WESTMINSTER CATHEDRAL ▲ *145* (top right).

HAMPSTEAD ▲ *260*
In the 18th century this village attracted well-off Londoners as well as writers and artists.

THE "LA LUTINE" BELL, LLOYD'S MUSEUM ▲ *153*
This bell, captured by the English in 1793 from the French frigate *La Lutine*, was rung twice to announce good tidings and once for bad tidings.

MONDAY. It is not easy to find somewhere to stay at a reasonable price. Choose between a boarding house in Chelsea or Bloomsbury, and a bed-and-breakfast in a suburb such as Ealing, for example. Walk or catch a double-decker bus from Victoria Station in Victoria Street to WESTMINSTER CATHEDRAL ▲ *145*, London's Roman Catholic cathedral, in Italian Byzantine style. Then take a short walk through the narrow streets of the neighborhood to admire one of the last Victorian areas still intact. When you reach PARLIAMENT SQUARE, visit WESTMINSTER ABBEY, a real museum of English sculpture. Do

not neglect to visit ST MARGARET'S CHURCH as well, then continue on to the TATE GALLERY ▲ *208* to enjoy works by painters and sculptors from the 16th century to the present day. Spend the late afternoon and early evening in CHELSEA

▲ *194*: savor the tranquility of the Georgian squares and crescents before plunging into the clamor of the King's Road, where you can have dinner.
TUESDAY. Take a bus to HAMPSTEAD, and spend the morning at KENWOOD HOUSE ▲ *263*, an attractive country mansion designed by the Adam brothers for Lord Mansfield. The interior, which is very fine, provides a setting for the collection of paintings bequeathed by the last owner, E.C. Guinness, earl of Iveagh.
After a walk in the grounds and adjacent Heath and a bite to eat locally, head for the village. If you like Keats, visit the house where he lived from 1815 to 1820, then walk down Church Row and Frognal to Fenton House. If you are lucky, you may find your visit is accompanied by the strains of a sonata or a minuet played on the harpsichord. In the early evening go to TRAFALGAR SQUARE, and have a snack in the crypt of ST MARTIN-IN-THE-FIELDS before listening to a fine Baroque concert in the church. For dinner, you can take your pick of the many restaurants around Leicester Square.
WEDNESDAY. Devote the day to the CITY. In the morning, starting from the ALDWYCH, wander around the Inns of Court and the surrounding area, the heart of the world of litigation: visit the TEMPLE, in particular TEMPLE CHURCH; LINCOLN'S INN, which can be reached via Chancery Lane; and Lincoln's Inn Fields, where Sir John Soane built his home and kept the wonderful collections he accumulated. Then walk up Holborn to Smithfield, the meat market. The neighboring area of St Bartholomew is ideal for just wandering around: you will discover St Bartholomew-the-Great's church ▲ *176* and Cloth Fair. It is also worth spending some time at the Barbican Centre. Then take St-Martin's-le-Grand to ST PAUL'S CATHEDRAL ▲ *171*. Cheapside and Poultry will take you back to the heart of the City, the Bank of England, the STOCK EXCHANGE and the ROYAL EXCHANGE ▲ *151*, as well as Lloyd's, now housed in a striking building designed by Richard Rogers. THREADNEEDLE STREET, CORNHILL,

LOMBARD STREET, LEADENHALL STREET AND FENCHURCH STREET ▲ *156* all teem with men and women hurrying to and fro, briefcase in hand: have lunch at the same places they do, in or around Leadenhall Market. In the late afternoon you can cross the river at London Bridge, visit Southwark Cathedral ▲ *323* and have dinner at the *George Inn* in Borough High Street.

THURSDAY. Begin your day with a walk around BLOOMSBURY ▲ *298*, following in the footsteps of Virginia Woolf and her friends. Then pay a visit to the British Museum and the British Library. Do not miss the Egyptian and Greek galleries, as well as the Manuscript Room. Then discover Nash's London: from PICCADILLY CIRCUS ▲ *283*, walk up REGENT STREET ▲ *283* and PORTLAND PLACE to REGENT'S PARK ▲ *257*. Walk along the terraces in the Outer Circle and take a stroll in the gardens. If you like roses, do not miss Queen Mary's gardens in the center of the park. The walk back via Marylebone Road and Baker Street will give you the chance to discover one of the most elegant Georgian areas, around Portman Square, where you can visit Home House, built by Robert Adam, and, tucked away in Manchester Square, Hertford House, home of the Wallace Collection ▲ *254*.

FRIDAY. Spend your morning discovering GREENWICH ▲ *324*, which you can reach by the Docklands Light Railway and the Thames tunnel. After visiting the Royal Naval College and the National Maritime Museum, go to the Observatory. You can have lunch at the *Trafalgar Tavern*, then take a boat up-river to Charing Cross. Go into Somerset House and browse around the fine collection of the Courtauld Institute in the Royal Academy rooms. Start your evening off on a theatrical or

musical note in COVENT GARDEN, and then your table awaits in one of the restaurants around this former market.

SATURDAY. Devote your morning to "MUSEUM LAND" in Exhibition Road and Queen's Gate, with a detour to the VICTORIA AND ALBERT MUSEUM, where you will be amazed at the superb collection of furniture, ceramics, glass and jewelry. A quick bite to eat in the museum restaurant will recharge your batteries enough for you to explore Kensington Gardens, Paddington and Little Venice. A boat will take you down Regent's Canal to CAMDEN LOCK ▲ *259*. And after spending the afternoon browsing around the market in Camden, you can spend the evening in SOHO ▲ *296*.

SUNDAY. In the morning, go to WHITEHALL ▲ *142*, where you will see Inigo Jones' masterpiece and what remains of the former palace: the BANQUETING HOUSE ▲ *144*. In the main hall take a look at the ceiling decorated by Rubens for Charles I. Spend the afternoon at HAMPTON COURT ▲ *352*, which can be reached by boat, going up the Thames from Westminster. After visiting the palace, spend some time in the formal gardens created by Charles II in 1660 and by William III in 1689.

CUMBERLAND TERRACE, REGENT'S PARK ▲ *257* (below left) The elegant work of John Nash.

"THE BLACK FRIARS", BLACKFRIARS BRIDGE ● *87*. This pub sign depicts a monk in a black frock, revealing the origins of the name.

COVENT GARDEN ▲ *272* (above left).

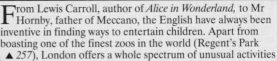

From Lewis Carroll, author of *Alice in Wonderland*, to Mr Hornby, father of Meccano, the English have always been inventive in finding ways to entertain children. Apart from boasting one of the finest zoos in the world (Regent's Park ▲ *257*), London offers a whole spectrum of unusual activities and attractions bound to delight youngsters.

ENTERTAINMENT AND TOYS

PUPPET THEATRE BARGE. Little Venice, Blomfield Road, W9. Tel: (0171) 249 6876. A puppet theater with seating for fifty children on board a barge that cruises up and down the Grand Union Canal. Shadow puppets and handmade marionettes provide shows that are full of imagination and poetry.

UNICORN THEATRE FOR CHILDREN. Great Newport Street, W2. Tel: (0171) 836 3334. The only theater in the West End exclusively for children (1–13 years old). It stages at least four plays every season, each designed for a particular age group, from modern puppet shows performed by real actors to mime and traditional theater, all of superlative quality.

MUSEUM OF THE MOVING IMAGE. South Bank Arts Centre, SE1. Tel: (0171) 401 2636. Opened in 1988 and acclaimed for its original concept, "Momi" retraces the history of cinema and other audiovisual media, from magic lanterns to the latest technology used in film studios today. Characters of the silver screen, played by actors, act as guides for the visitors (from Tuesday to Sunday, 10am–8pm).

BETHNAL GREEN MUSEUM OF CHILDHOOD. Cambridge Heath Road, E2. Tel: (0181) 980 2415. Exhibits include dolls in period costume from all over the world and fascinating doll's

BEEFEATERS
The halberdiers of the Tower wear a uniform that dates back to the time of Mary Tudor: blue with the sovereign's monogram, and the same in red and gold for ceremonies.

houses, ranging from miniature castles to rural cottages. Magic lanterns, model trains and troops of tin soldiers are among other delights of this unusual collection.

MADAME TUSSAUD'S. Marylebone Road, NW1. Tel: (0171) 935 6861 (adjoining the Planetarium). Very popular wax museum founded in 1835 by Mme Tussaud (1761–1850), who created her first wax figures at the age of seventeen in Paris. Life-size models, including important historical and contemporary figures, are exhibited here in realistic settings. The Chamber of Horrors may upset younger children.

GAMES AT "MOMI"
Children have the chance to demonstrate their acting abilities with drama tutors and to make their own animated films. They will love the interactive activities, such as the saloon bar straight out of a Western and the illusion of flying with Superman.

HAMLEY'S. 188–96 Regent Street, W1. Tel: (0171) 734 3161. Without question the largest toyshop in London. Its six floors boast a fantastic selection of cuddly animals, dolls, cars, models, electronic games, model-making kits and books: an Ali Baba's cave for children and parents alike.

HISTORY FOR CHILDREN

BUCKINGHAM PALACE. The Mall, SW1. London Tourist Board. Tel: (0171) 730 3488. Every morning in summer, at 11.27 am, a contingent of the Queen's Guard leaves Wellington

Barracks to march to Buckingham Palace and, at 11.30am, relieve the guards on duty there. This ceremony is based on a time-honored tradition symbolizing the durability of the monarchy, as St James's Palace is the oldest of the royal residences. The handing over of the palace keys and the changing of the guard is accompanied by a band and the loud clacking of boot heels. The guards in red uniforms, trained not to move a muscle, maintain their legendary impassive stare beneath their bearskins.

CROWN JEWELS. Tower of London, Tower Hill, EC3. Tel: (0171) 709 0765. A brooding atmosphere still emanates from this group of towers and ramparts, with its wheeling ravens, which served for centuries as a fortress and political prison. The oldest section dates back to William the Conqueror. The star attraction is undoubtedly the new Jewel House, where the Crown Jewels are kept: the largest cut diamond in the world, swords and crowns encrusted with sparkling gems, goblets and a huge gold incense burner, are watched over by a highly sophisticated electronic surveillance system.

"HMS BELFAST". Morgan's Lane, Tooley Street, SE1. This battleship from the Second World War played an important role in the Normandy landings. The tour takes in everything from the bridge and the machine room to the on-board bakery and theater, while an information booklet retraces the history of *H.M.S. Belfast* and the changing face of the Navy from 1914 to the present day (daily, 10am–6pm).

THE LONDON DUNGEON. 28 Tooley Street, SE1. Tel: (0171) 403 0606. This exhibition, tucked away under the arches of London Bridge Station, accurately conjures up (not without a certain sadistic pleasure) some of the darkest chapters in English history: the murder of Thomas à Becket in Canterbury Cathedral, the torture and execution of criminals, the Great Fire. This may upset sensitive children (daily, 10am–5.30pm; in winter 10am–4.30pm).

THE WORLD OF ANIMALS

LONDON ZOO. Regent's Park, NW1. Tel: (0171) 722 3333. One of the most varied zoological gardens in the world, with its eight thousand animals, sometimes very rare, including a giant panda, the incredible bird-eating spiders, and enormous lizards with their dragon-like heads. Above all, do not miss the *Twilight World*, where a simulated night habitat allows you to watch kiwis, which are extremely rare, and giant bats, at their nocturnal pursuits (daily, from 9am–6pm; in winter, from 10am–4pm).

NATURAL HISTORY MUSEUM. Cromwell Road, SW7. Tel: (0171) 938 9123. The dinosaur exhibition in the central hall is always popular with children, as is the earthquake simulator.

There is no lack of places in London for people who adore secondhand goods, for collectors of rare editions, for lovers of antique hallmarked silverware, to indulge their favorite vice. The trail starts in the classy West End shops and finishes with "car boot sales".

CURIOS AND RARE BOOKS

LONDON SILVER VAULTS. 53 Chancery Lane, WC2. Tel: (0171) 242 3844. These vaults, which are as well guarded as a bank, house thirty-five small stands selling antique and modern silverware, jewelry and porcelain. You can bargain.

ARTHUR MIDDLETON. 12 New Row, WC2. Tel: (0171) 836 7042. Lovers of antique scientific instruments will revel in this shop, which stocks everything from astrolabes to dentists' pliers.

JEAN SEWELL ANTIQUES LTD. 3 Campden Street, W8. Tel: (0171) 727 3122. English porcelain and china from the 18th and 19th centuries.

DAVID BLACK ORIENTAL CARPETS. 96 Portland Road, W11. Tel: (0171) 727 2566. The owner is a connoisseur of oriental carpets, and his shop is crammed with antique kilims.

HENRY SOTHERAN. 2–5 Sackville Street, W1. Tel: (0171) 439 6151. Charles Dickens and Winston Churchill were clients of this bookshop, the oldest in London (1761). There is an extensive selection of cards and engravings in the basement.

OTHER MAJOR SUPPLIERS OF RARE AND ANTIQUARIAN BOOKS INCLUDE:

MAGGS BROS LTD. 50 Berkeley Square, W1. Tel: (0171) 493 7160. **BERNARD QUARITCH.** 5 Lower John Street, W1. Tel: (0171) 734 2983. **E JOSEPH**. 1 Vere Street, W1. Tel: (0171) 493 8353. **JOHN THORNTON.** 455 Fulham Road, SW10. Tel: (0171) 352 8810. **HARRINGTON BROS.** Chelsea Antique Market, 253 Kings Road, Chelsea, SW3. Tel: (0171) 352 5689. **ULYSSES.** 40 Museum Street, WC1. Tel: (0171) 831 1600.

AUCTION ROOMS

SOTHEBY'S. 34 New Bond Street W1, Tel: (0171) 493 8080, is an institution that needs no further introduction: its fame is rivalled only by that of **CHRISTIE'S**, 8 King Street, SW1, Tel: (0171) 839 9060.

Other auction rooms sell items that are less expensive: **BONHAM'S**, Montpelier Street, SW7, Tel: (0171) 584 9161; **CHRISTIE'S SOUTH KENSINGTON**, 85 Old Brompton Road, SW7, Tel: (0171) 581 7611; **PHILLIPS**, 101 New Bond Street, W1, Tel: (0171) 629 6602; **LOTS ROAD GALLERIES**, 71 Lots Road, SW10, Tel: (0171) 351 7771.

> "THE SMALL SECONDHAND DEALERS ARE MORE LIKELY TO SELL THE UNEXPECTED, AND EVEN THOSE IN POOR DISTRICTS OR IN THE SUBURBS ARE FULL OF SURPRISES."
>
> PAUL MORAND

A TOUR OF THE MARKETS

PORTOBELLO ROAD. The conscientious devotee of antiques will not fail to visit this market (right), as famous now as the Tower of London, which is held every Saturday. Portobello has virtually everything, from wooden signs to Sheffield steel cutlery, and from old golf clubs to an antique dentist's chair, even if it is not the place to get the best bargains.

ALFIE'S ANTIQUE MARKET. 13–25 Church Street, NW8. Tel: (0171) 723 6066. Everything can be found in this covered market, the largest in England (open Tuesday to Saturday 10am–6pm). Do not hesitate to haggle. More than three hundred stalls.

CAMDEN PASSAGE ANTIQUES MARKET. Camden Passage, Islington, N1. Three hundred and fifty specialist secondhand dealers have stands here (right) every Wednesday and Saturday (silverware, jewelry, furniture), as well as Thursdays (books, prints and drawings).

ANTIQUARIUS. 131–41 King's Road, SW3. Tel: (0171) 351 5353. Although this market is primarily renowned for its antique clothes, it also has the ultimate in British china, 1920's jewelry, leather sporting goods and all manner of cheap bric-à-brac. In the King's Road at 181–3, CHENIL GALLERIES is a treasure trove of antique trinkets, prints, jewelry and hats (Mon.–Sat. 10am–6pm).

GRAYS ANTIQUE MARKET. 58 Davies Street and 1–7 Davies Mews, W1. Tel: (0171) 629 7034. Two more traditional antique markets where you can continue your quest; if you find your heart's desire, take advantage of a certificate of authenticity, which can often prove useful (open Mon.–Fri. 10am–6pm).

BERMONDSEY AND NEW CALEDONIAN MARKETS. At the corner of Long Lane and Bermondsey Street, SE1. These antique markets (right), south of the River Thames, are open every Friday from dawn to 1pm. Sacrifice your lie-in: to be successful you should be there, flashlight in hand if necessary, around 5am. You may unearth an engraving or a piece of silver at a much more competitive price than in Portobello.

GREENWICH ANTIQUES MARKET. There are different sections of this market along Greenwich High Road on Saturdays and Sundays. Good for furniture and bric-à-brac.

ANTIQUE FAIRS

Once a month you can get hold of some fine wooden kitchen utensils, lampshades or antique teapots in the attractive showroom of the HORTICULTURAL HALLS on Vincent Square, SW1. Another fair takes place four times a year in the elegant CHELSEA TOWN HALL on the King's Road, SW3. Some fairs only take place on public holidays. More often than not these are "car boot sales" where the sellers park their cars in huge carparks, like that of Wembley Stadium, and unload their trunks. To find out the exact dates, the best thing to do is consult the magazine *Time Out*.

"So many things had vanished from the London that Martin had loved! Sometimes, he would wander around Pimlico to explore the secondhand shops and head back to the center via Kensington...."
Michel Mohrt, *Un Soir, à Londres*

There are few cities that can take pride in five symphony orchestras of international status, as many prestigious chamber ensembles, two opera companies and a thriving record industry. The history of English music, which is primarily vocal, is dominated by such names as Henry Purcell (1659–95), George Frederick Handel (1685–1759) and Benjamin Britten (1913–76). Their genius was to take a rich religious vocal tradition and incorporate into it various external influences, especially Italian, to create genres that were new and unusual, such as the English oratorio. In the past few years English musical activity has been dominated by three trends: a liking for the vast frescoes of late Romanticism (Gustav Mahler, Richard Strauss, Dimitri Shostakovich); a keen interest in contemporary music, with orchestras such as the London Sinfonietta, the BBC Symphony Orchestra, Lontano and Music Projects; and the ever-growing success of authentic Baroque music promoted by ensembles such as the famous Academy of St Martin-in-the-Fields, founded by Sir Neville Marriner, the English Baroque Soloists, conducted by John Eliot Gardiner, and the Academy of Ancient Music under the baton of Christopher Hogwood.

THE MAJOR LONDON VENUES

ROYAL ALBERT HALL. Kensington Gore, SW7. Tel: (0171) 589 3203. Box office open daily, 9am–9pm. The Royal Philharmonic Orchestra plays here all the year round, but a typically British event, not to be missed, is the "Proms", the BBC season of promenade concerts held from mid-July to mid-September. On the last night of the season, musicians and audience join together to give a rousing performance of patriotic songs.

ROYAL ALBERT HALL (below) The flags are a sign that the "Proms" season has started ▲ 236.

ROYAL OPERA HOUSE (COVENT GARDEN). Bow Street, WC2. Tel: (0171) 240 1066 (box office) and (0171) 240 1911 (credit cards). Booking office open from Monday to Saturday, 10am–8pm. This theater, which everyone calls "Covent Garden", opened in 1858 with a performance of *Les Huguenots* by Giacomo Meyerbeer. It remains a platform for the great stars and the bastion of traditional repertoire, especially opera. Home of the Royal Opera and the Royal Ballet, it deserves its reputation as one of the foremost international venues.

ROYAL OPERA HOUSE Relaxing in a lounge at the Royal Opera House, above right ● 54, 55.

WIGMORE HALL. 36 Wigmore Street, W1. Tel: (0171) 935 2141. Booking office open daily, except Sunday, 10am–7pm. This venue was opened in 1901 as Bechstein Hall, after the name of its founder, the famous piano manufacturer. Many young artists have made their débuts in this beautiful hall, renowned for its

> "BEFORE THE PLAY BEGINS, TO PREVENT THE AUDIENCE FROM GETTING BORED OF WAITING, THE MOST DELIGHTFUL SYMPHONIES ARE PLAYED."
>
> COSIMO III, GRAND DUKE OF TUSCANY (ON A VISIT TO ENGLAND IN 1669)

acoustics. It is essential to book seats for song recitals four to six weeks in advance, as these are much in demand.

SOUTH BANK ARTS CENTRE. South Bank, SE1. Tel: (0171) 928 8800 (box office) and (0171) 928 3002 (information). Booking office open daily, 10am–9pm. This cultural center (opened in 1951) has three concert halls. The largest is the Royal Festival Hall, the size of which makes it ideal for accommodating symphony orchestras: the London Philharmonic is the resident orchestra here and the organ is renowned as much for use in Baroque music as in Romantic music. The Queen Elizabeth Hall (smaller, primarily used for chamber music concerts) and the Purcell Room (ideal for recitals), opened in 1967.

BARBICAN CENTRE. Silk Street, EC2. Tel: (0171) 638 8891 (box office) and (0171) 628 2295 (information). Booking office open daily, 9am–8pm. Do not be put off by the daunting appearance of the complex from the outside (Londoners insist that it is easier to escape from Alcatraz than from this concrete maze). The Barbican Centre (1981), home of the London Symphony Orchestra and the English Chamber Orchestra, has surprises in store for music-lovers.

KENWOOD HOUSE. Hampstead Lane, NW3. Open-air concerts in summer.

THE VOCAL TRADITION

If, by chance, you are walking in the vicinity of Westminster Abbey at lunchtime and you happen to hear the heavenly sound of choral music drifting out through the half-open door of a church, you are in communication with the very soul of English music. Dominique Fernandez describes this original tradition: "England did not produce *castrati*, but from the 15th century has possessed, and preserved intact, college and cathedral choir schools, made up entirely of men, an 'all-male cast', with the upper parts being taken by boys between eight and fourteen years old, and the alto parts by young adults, alongside the tenors and basses" (*La Rose des Tudors*).

ST JOHN'S. Smith Square, SW1. Tel: (0171) 222 1061. Booking office open Monday to Friday, 10am–5pm or until start of concert, weekends one hour before the performance. Come at lunchtime to hear choral and chamber music concerts in this beautiful 18th-century church right in the heart of Westminster. All major cities in England have choir schools (in London the one attached to Westminster Abbey is the most famous): the Friends of Cathedral Music publish a list of the cathedrals and colleges where each of these choirs can be heard.

ST MARTIN-IN-THE-FIELDS. Trafalgar Square, WC2. Tel: (0171) 930 0089. This church has given its name to the Academy of St Martin-in-the-Fields, the major exponent of English Baroque music today. Concerts on Mondays, Tuesdays, Wednesdays and Fridays at 1.05pm, and in the evenings.

HEAVENLY VOICES
"And on Good Friday afternoon [I attended] a heavenly concert of the St Matthew Passion by the St Paul's choir with full orchestra and a special service choir...."
Jack Kerouac, *The Lonesome Traveler*

ST JOHN'S CHURCH, SMITH SQUARE
The most Baroque of London's churches, built by Thomas Archer around 1720.

Even though the first tracking shot in history was filmed in Piccadilly Circus (by Robert William Paul, in 1900), today film-makers seem less drawn to London than before. However, the photogenic qualities of Tower Bridge looming out of the fog, and of Big Ben announcing the time of the crime should be enough to win it all the Oscars going for best film set.

LONDON THRILLERS

THE ROYAL ALBERT HALL AND "THE MAN WHO KNEW TOO MUCH", BY ALFRED HITCHCOCK (1956).
After countless twists, the American singer Jo Conway (Doris Day) arrives at the Albert Hall on the evening that the prime minister of a foreign country, on a visit to London, is to be assassinated. The killer is to shoot him at the very moment when the score calls for a crash of cymbals, but just before the fatal moment Jo cries out, the killer misses and leaps to his death from the balcony.

THE BRITISH MUSEUM AND "BLACKMAIL", BY ALFRED HITCHCOCK (1929).
A blackmailer, being followed by men from Scotland Yard, crosses several rooms and the British Library, scales the museum roof, which is dome-shaped, and falls to his death. The first talkie by Hitchcock and in British cinema.

SOHO AND "NIGHT AND THE CITY", BY JULES DASSIN (1950).
The narrow alleyways and labyrinthine backstreets of Soho provide the setting for the ventures of Fabian, a third-rate hoodlum (Richard Widmark). He wins the friendship of an old Greek boxer and sets up the fight of the century between his Greek protégé and a brute called the "Strangler". It all ends in tragedy for Fabian; he is ruined despite the luminous presence of Gene Tierney.

"BLACKMAIL"
Blackmail was conceived and made in a primitive silent version, but the British Film Industry requested that the last reel only be remade in a talking version. Hitchcock reworked more scenes than the producer expected. There are therefore two versions, one silent, with signboards for those cinemas that were not yet equipped to screen films with a soundtrack.

"STAGE FRIGHT"
Below, filming this classic by Alfred Hitchcock (1950) in England. One of the best scenes takes place in a London taxi.

HAMPSTEAD AND "BLOW UP", BY MICHELANGELO ANTONIONI (1967). In the "swinging" 1960's, a fashion photographer (David Hemmings) is preparing a story on London. But when he enlarges a photograph taken on Hampstead Heath, he can make out a hand pointing a revolver, as well as a body. On returning to the scene of the crime, he finds the corpse. Meanwhile, his studio has been searched...

WHITECHAPEL AND "A STUDY IN TERROR", BY JAMES HILL (1965). Sherlock Holmes versus Jack the Ripper. In a district where the faceless murderer commits his abominable crimes, two contrasting myths of Victorian times clash against a backdrop of wet pavements and the glow of streetlamps through the fog.

LONDON AND THE ROMANTIC COMEDIES

COVENT GARDEN AND "MY FAIR LADY", BY GEORGE CUKOR (1963). The steps of the Royal Opera House provided the location for the encounter between Professor Higgins (Rex Harrison) and the Cockney flower girl, Eliza (Audrey Hepburn), whom Higgins wagers he can pass off as an aristocrat after several lessons in elocution and deportment.

BELGRAVIA AND "INDISCREET", BY STANLEY DONEN (1958). An American diplomat (Cary Grant), posted to London, falls in love with an actress (Ingrid Bergman). A sparkling romantic comedy from the maker of *Singin' in the Rain*, which takes place in the neighborhood around the embassies.

ENGLISH COMEDIES

PIMLICO AND "PASSPORT TO PIMLICO", BY HENRY CORNELIUS (1949). This comedy classic, filmed in Pimlico, tells how, following an explosion, the inhabitants of this working-class borough, now a residential area, find a 15th-century edict proving that they are part of the duchy of Burgundy. They immediately declare their independence from the monarchy to avoid restrictions on pub opening hours and food rationing in post-war Britain.

DOCKLANDS AND "A FISH CALLED WANDA", BY JOHN CLEESE (1989). The London Docklands, when they were first being reconverted into luxury accommodation, provide the setting for a sequence in this zany comedy, in which a timid lawyer finds himself mixed up with a mob of gangsters, one of whom is the winsome Jamie Lee Curtis.

URBAN COMMENTARIES

CHELSEA AND "THE SERVANT", BY JOSEPH LOSEY (1963). In the elegant borough of Chelsea an idle gentleman (James Fox) takes on a manservant (Dirk Bogarde), who soon manipulates and debases him in an atmosphere fraught with latent homosexuality and class tensions.

SUBURBAN SOUTH LONDON AND "MY BEAUTIFUL LAUNDERETTE", BY STEPHEN FREARS (1985). A young homosexual Asian, whose family has been hard hit by racism, does everything humanly possible to escape from his poverty. He succeeds by transforming a run-down laundromat into a profitable business. Treated with humor, this black film tackles the problems faced by any minority.

"INDISCREET"
Ingrid Bergman and Cary Grant in a scene from *Indiscreet*, the film by Stanley Donen: a comedy of manners that takes place in the social milieu of the fashionable West End.

THE SCENE OF THE CRIME
"London's reputation as the capital of crime is firmly established throughout the world. And yet, there are fewer murders committed there than in Paris, New York or Chicago. Even Marseilles is much more dangerous. But London still retains a spine-chilling aura due to its past teeming with criminals and full of horror; is it the unexpected, thick darkness of fog which tempts the murderer, promising him impunity, or those legends of elusive wrong-doers, fostered by an entire genre of crime literature and by journalists in search of sensational stories? A halo of fog will transform even the most unassuming inhabitant of London into a Mr Hyde or a hound of the Baskervilles, and recreates, in the twentieth century, the setting of the Beggar's Opera, written by John Gay in the eighteenth century."

Paul Morand,
London

393

221 BAKER STREET, LONDON.

Sherlock Holmes tracked down criminals in London at the time of the Industrial Revolution. Now it is our turn to follow in the steps of this most famous of detectives: Elementary, my dear Watson!

BAKER STREET W1, SHERLOCK HOLMES' HOME. "Outside the wind swept Baker Street howling, and the rain lashed against our windows. It was strange how, right in the centre of the capital, surrounded by ten miles of human works, the iron fist of nature made itself felt as if London was no more than a molehill in the fields" (Arthur Conan Doyle, *The Adventure of the Abbey Grange*). "In the third week of November, in the year 1895, a dense yellow fog settled down upon London.... 'Look out of this window, Watson! See how the figures loom up, are dimly seen, and then blend once more into the cloud-bank. The thief or the murderer could roam London on such a day as the tiger does the jungle, unseen until he pounces, and then evident only to his victim.' " (Arthur Conan Doyle, *The Adventure of the Bruce-Partington Plans*).

WESTMINSTER: "MURDER IN WESTMINSTER". "A crime of mysterious character was committed last night at 16 Godolphin Street, one of the old-fashioned and secluded rows of eighteenth-century houses which lie between the river and the Abbey, almost in the shadow of the great Tower of the Houses of Parliament." (Arthur Conan Doyle, *The Adventure of the Second Stain*).

THE CITY. "It was one of the main arteries which conveyed the traffic of the City to the north and west. The roadway was

blocked with the immense stream of commerce flowing in a double tide inward and outward, while the footpaths were black with the hurrying swarm of pedestrians. It was difficult to realize as we looked at the line of fine shops and stately business premises that they really abutted on the other side upon the faded and stagnant square which we had just quitted." (Arthur Conan Doyle, *The Red-headed League*).

UPPER SWANDAM LANE. "But there was no great difficulty in the first stage of my adventure. Upper Swandam Lane is a vile alley, lurking behind the high wharves which line the north side of the river to the east of London Bridge. Between a slop-shop and a gin-shop ... I found the den of which I was in search." (Arthur Conan Doyle, *The Man with the Twisted Lip*).

THE EAST END, FROM WHITECHAPEL, E1, TO THE DOCKS. A large-scale building project has changed the appearance of this area, which was once one of the poorest districts in London: "In rapid succession we passed through the fringe of fashionable London, hotel London, theatrical London, literary London, commercial London, and, finally, maritime London, till we came to a riverside city of a hundred thousand souls, where the tenement houses swelter and reek with the outcasts of Europe." (Arthur Conan Doyle, *The Adventure of the Six Napoleons*).

More than one million of the seven million inhabitants of London now come from Pakistan, Bangladesh, the Caribbean and other distant countries. The first immigrants, who came from Hong Kong a century ago, were taken on as dockers before successfully turning to catering.

A TRIP TO CHINATOWN

The pedestrianized zone of Gerrard Street, below Soho, is the stronghold of the Chinese community, as can be seen by the Pagoda-shaped gateways and Chinese-style phone boxes.
DRAGON INN. 12 Gerrard Street, W1. Tel: (0171) 494 0870. Savor Cantonese specialities and excellent *dim sum* in elegant, modern surroundings.
LOON FUNG. 31 Gerrard Street. Discover an extensive range of goods from China, including fresh fruit and vegetables, in this supermarket.

A TASTE OF ASIA

If you have never tasted lamb masala or even tandoori chicken, this is your chance to do so. Indian restaurants are legion in London.
BOMBAY BRASSERIE. Courtfield Close, Courtfield Road, SW7. Tel: (0171) 370 4040. This is a must for its atmosphere and the excellent buffet lunch.
RAJDOOT. 49, Paddington Street, W1. Tel: (0171) 486 2055. Excellent cuisine in surroundings decorated with Mogul prints.
STAR OF INDIA. 154 Old Brompton Road, SW5. Tel: (0171) 373 2901. Theatrical setting and pleasant staff make this a fun place to eat.
KHAN'S. 13-15 Westbourne Grove, W2. Tel: (0171) 727 5420. Atmospheric bustling chaotic ambience, cheap and cheerful, variable food quality.
WHITTARDS. 81 Fulham Road, SW7. Tel: (0171) 589 4261. Inside the Conran Shop, Michelin House. There is nothing more exotic than a teashop where the air is perfumed by many varieties of tea imported from China, Ceylon and the Himalayan foothills.
FRONTIERS. 39 Pembridge Road, W11. Jewelry from Tibet and Asia, ceramics from North Africa and Asia.

ISLAND FEVER

NOTTING HILL FEVER. Notting Hill Gate, W11. Notting Hill (top left) is one of the trendiest areas in London. Avant-garde art galleries, secondhand dealers, hippy clothes shops, French bistros and Caribbean record shops thrive in the vicinity of Portobello Road.
SHEPHERD'S BUSH MARKET. Opposite Shepherd's Bush tube station, W12. The market and West Indian groceries offer an impressive array of fresh fruit and vegetables, spices, confectionery and tinned foods imported from Jamaica and Trinidad.

"I had had the man and his surroundings with me ever since my return from the eastern waters, some four years before the day of which I speak. It was in the front sittingroom of furnished apartments in a Pimlico square that they first began to live again with a vividness and poignancy quite foreign to our former real intercourse. ... Unknown to my respectable landlady, it was my practice directly after my breakfast to hold animated receptions of Malays, Arabs and half-castes."
Joseph Conrad,
A Personal Record

The city that once dominated a quarter of the planet has been transformed into an ethnic cauldron, where the smells of curry mingle with the aroma of glazed duck, and the pulse of Jamaican reggae blends with the delicate notes of the sitar.

Nightlife begins in Soho and Covent Garden, where there is a high concentration of cinemas, theaters, nightclubs and jazz clubs, and ends a long way from the center, in night-clubs where famous disc-jockeys put on a growing number of "theme" evenings based around music from Acid jazz to Raggamuffin (Jamaican version of rap). Buy *Time Out* or *What's On* for complete weekly listings of all events.

NIGHT ROUNDS

RONNIE SCOTT'S. 47 Frith Street, W1. Tel: (0171) 439 0747. This has been the London jazz Mecca for the past thirty years, and all the big names from the United States have performed here.

JAZZ CAFÉ. 5 Parkway, NW1. Tel: (0171) 916 6000. Small club with appearances by "big name" jazz musicians.

ROMANTIC REVERIE
"Certain feelings, nevertheless, without being more profound or passionate, are more moving than others; and often, when I am walking down Oxford Street in the light of the streetlamps, which is so conducive to dreaming, and when I hear a mouth organ playing melodies that, years ago, used to comfort us, me and my dear companion...."
Thomas de Quincey, *Confessions of an English Opium-Eater*

HARRY'S. 19 Kingly Street, W1. Tel: (0171) 434 0309. Until 6am. A very useful place if you want to allay those early morning hunger pangs with an English breakfast.

LIMELIGHT. 136 Shaftesbury Avenue, WC2. Tel: (0171) 434 0572. Superb interior, stark and simple. Let your hair down every Wednesday, dancing to the beat of rock and techno music.

HEAVEN. The Arches, Villiers Street, WC2. Tel: (0171) 839 3852. Until 3.30am. Theme evenings are often held at this trend-setting gay club where disc-jockeys alternate with the bands. Three dance floors, snack bar and several bars.

MINISTRY OF SOUND. 103 Gaunt Street, SE1. Tel: (0171) 378 6528. This club, which has the best sound system in the capital, attracts the most famous disc-jockeys as well as people who are keen to explore the latest sounds in house music.

MARQUEE. 105 Charing Cross Road, WC2. Tel: (0171) 437 6601. Live bands, different dance floors and industrial Techno music.

THE FRIDGE. Town Hall Parade, Brixton Hill, SW2. Tel: (0171) 326 5100. Until 2am. Each evening is badged differently (the first Wednesday of the month is devoted to single women) in this powerhouse of a club, which can accommodate 1,500 people and has its own restaurant.

THE GRAND. Clapham Junction, SW11. Tel: (0171) 738 9000, credit cards (0171) 284 2200. Wide variety of live music from 11pm.

THE CLUBS
"London's nightclubs date from 1912 and 1913. Then people used to go to Murray's (where I heard the first jazz music in the basement), which made its fortune from soldiers home on leave during the war...."
Paul Morand, *London*

BRIXTON ACADEMY. 211 Stockwell Road, SW9. Tel: (0171) 924 9999. Brixton, south of the river, is definitely the trendy place to be, with its wide range of nightclubs and bars. This is a music venue: the concerts at the Academy tend to be real crowd-pullers.

TURNMILLS. 63 Clerkenwell Road, EC1. Tel: (0171) 250 3409. Late-night house and dance music, sometimes running till the following day.

THE CAMDEN PALACE. 1a Camden High Street, NW1. Tel: (0171) 387 0428. Popular with a younger crowd.

Last order!

It is probably because the ghosts of Shakespeare, Dickens, Samuel Pepys and Wellington still raise their pint glasses at one end of the bar that London pubs (there are seven thousand of them) possess an undying charm. Most are now open from 11am to 10.30pm (on Sundays 12–3pm and 7–10.30pm) and you can compare the merits of pale ale, bitter or stout in peace until closing time. Wine bars are a different matter altogether: the Yuppies made them popular in the early 1980's and there is an escalating number of them in the center of London, attracting customers from the banking, law and business communities. Many pubs and wine bars in the City are closed at weekends.

PICTURESQUE PUBS

ANGEL. 101 Bermondsey Wall East, SE16. Tel: (0171) 237 3608. This former 15th-century seamen's tavern was frequented by, among others, Captain Cook and the omnipresent Samuel Pepys. Many artists have set up their easels on the balcony to paint the port of London. Very lively around mealtimes.

GEORGE INN. 77 Borough High Street, SE1. Tel: (0171) 407 2056. Dickens probably came here at times to relax after a stint of writing, because he describes the décor of an old coaching inn with galleries in his novel *Little Dorrit.* Another attraction is the picturesque layout of the bars.

GUINEA. 30 Bruton Place, W1. Tel: (0171) 499 1210. Another of London's excellent pubs, tucked away in the heart of Mayfair and yet almost always packed. Here you can savor the best bitter in the world, with food ranging from salads and sandwiches to roast meats.

YE OLDE CHESHIRE CHEESE. 145 Fleet Street, EC4. Tel: (0171) 353 6170. Formerly frequented by journalists, when newspapers were produced on Fleet Street, and before then by Samuel Johnson, William Thackeray and Charles Dickens.

CITY WINE BARS

EL VINO. 47 Fleet Street, EC4. Tel: (0171) 353 6786. Founded in 1879. Nothing but wine, and the best at that (bordeaux, sherry, moselle, vintage port) is served to smartly dressed customers, including City bankers and journalists, wearing ties (this is obligatory) and nibbling smoked salmon sandwiches.

OLDE WINE SHADES. 6 Martin Lane, EC4. Tel: (0171) 626 6876. This City wine bar is part of the El Vino chain, and dates from 1663. It has a restaurant (lunch only) in its vaulted cellars, and a less formal wine bar upstairs.

THE CITY, MEMORY'S LABYRINTH
"He only crossed the river to go to the theatre, to see a play by Shakespeare at the Old Vic.... But he had seen Scott's disappear in Piccadilly Circus; one by one the hat shops in Bond Street had shut up shop: there was only Lock left … . He still managed to forget himself around Blackfriars and drink a glass of dark ale on the worn wooden table of a tavern which dated from the time of Pepys...."
Michel Mohrt, *Un soir, à Londres*

WARMTH AND CONVIVIALITY
"Then passing a pub in the Charing Cross Road, I decided to go in and have something to drink to help me shake off my gloomy state of mind. After my snack, beer didn't appeal very much, so I ordered a whisky and, as I was not accustomed to alcohol, I was soon in a delightful mood. A young man with a beard came in shortly after me, escorting an artistic-looking girl who was wearing thick red stockings and a duffle-coat."
Colin Wilson, *Adrift in Soho*

THE "PRINCESS LOUISE"
Detail of a frieze.

397

"THE PUBS, WITH THEIR FROSTED WINDOWS, THEIR STRANGE
OPENING HOURS, FRIGHTENED ME IN THE SAME WAY AS BROTHELS
DID: I DIDN'T ONCE DARE TO VENTURE IN."

JULIEN GRACQ

USEFUL ADDRESSES

HONI
PENSE
DIEU ET
MON DROIT
BY APPOINTMENT
TO HER MAJESTY THE QUEEN
PATENT LOCK AND SAFE MAKERS

- VIEW
- CITY CENTER
- ISOLATED
- LUXURY RESTAURANT
- TYPICAL RESTAURANT
- BUDGET RESTAURANT
- LUXURY HOTEL
- TYPICAL HOTEL
- BUDGET HOTEL
- CAR PARK
- SUPERVISED GARAGE
- TELEVISION
- QUIET
- SWIMMING POOL
- CREDIT CARDS
- REDUCTION FOR CHILDREN
- NO ANIMALS
- MUSIC
- LIVE BAND

◆ CHOOSING A RESTAURANT

- ◆ Under £12
- ◆◆ £12 to 20
- ◆◆◆ Over £20

	PAGE	GARDEN/TERRACE	PRIVATE DINING-ROOM	CLIENTÈLE	SPECIALTIES	SPECIAL RATES FOR CHILDREN	CREDIT CARDS	PRICE
WESTMINSTER AND VICTORIA								
AUBERGE DE PROVENCE	404			LTC	FR		●	◆◆◆
TATE GALLERY RESTAURANT	404				NN	●	●	◆◆
INNS OF COURT								
EAGLE PUB	406	●		Y	I			◆
QUALITY CHOP HOUSE	406			L	N	●		◆◆
CITY AND ST PAUL'S								
AA TANDOORI	407			L	IN		●	◆
GEORGE AND VULTURE	407		●	L	N		●	◆◆
LOBSTER TRADING	407							
COMPANY			●	L	F		●	◆◆
LE POULBOT	407			L	FR		●	◆◆◆
VIC NAYLOR'S	407		●	T	N		●	◆◆
THE TOWER								
LE PONT DE LA TOUR	408	●	●	L			●	◆◆◆
KENSINGTON								
L'ACCENTO ITALIANO	408	●		L	IT		●	◆◆
THE ARK	409	●	●	L			●	◆◆
THE BELVEDERE	409	●	●	C		●	●	◆◆◆
BIBENDUM	409			L		●	●	◆◆◆
BOYD'S	410			L			●	◆◆
CLARKE'S	410				N		●	◆◆◆
ENGLISH HOUSE	410				N		●	◆◆◆
GEALES FISH RESTAURANT	410	●	●		F		●	◆
HARVEY'S CAFÉ	410		●			●		◆◆
KEN LO'S MEMORIES OF CHINA	410				C	●	●	◆◆◆
KENSINGTON PLACE	410			C			●	◆◆◆
LAUNCESTON PLACE	410		●	L		●	●	◆◆◆
LEITH'S	410		●	C	N		●	◆◆◆
RESTAURANT 192	410		●	L			●	◆◆◆
ST QUENTIN	410		●	L	FR		●	◆◆◆
WALTON'S	410		●		I		●	◆◆◆
WODKA	410		●		EE			◆
CHELSEA								
LA FAMIGLIA	411	●	●	I	IT	●	●	◆◆◆
GAVVERS	411				FR	●	●	◆◆
LA TANTE CLAIRE	411			TLC	FR		●	◆◆◆
HYDE PARK								
BOMBAY PALACE	411		●		IN		●	◆◆
NICO AT NINETY	412		●		FR		●	◆◆◆
REGENT'S PARK								
SEA SHELL FISH RESTAURANT	412			T	F	●	●	◆
STEPHEN BULL	412				I		●	◆◆◆
VILLANDRY DINING ROOM	412		●		FR	●	●	◆◆
HAMPSTEAD								
DIWANA	413		●	T	IN		●	◆
JAZZ CAFÉ	413				I		●	◆◆

401

Price categories:
- ♦ Under £40
- ♦♦ £40 to £80
- ♦♦♦ Over £80

	PAGE	GARDEN/TERRACE	TV IN ROOM	VIEW	QUIET	RESTAURANT	24-HOUR SERVICE	PARKING	No. OF ROOMS	PRICE
WESTMINSTER AND VICTORIA										
CORONA HOTEL	404		●						40	♦♦
ECCLESTON CHAMBERS	405		●						17	♦♦
ELIZABETH HOTEL	405	●	●		●				40	♦♦
GORING HOTEL	405	●	●		●		●	●	80	♦♦♦
HANOVER HOTEL	405		●						35	♦♦
KERWIN HOTEL	405		●						20	♦
ROMANO'S HOTEL	405		●						14	♦
SCANDIC CROWN HOTEL	405		●	●		●	●	●	210	♦♦♦
SIDNEY HOTEL	405		●						38	♦♦
STAKIS ST ERMIN'S LONDON HOTEL	405	●	●			●	●	●	290	♦♦♦
WINDERMERE HOTEL	405		●		●	●			23	♦♦
INNS OF COURT										
HOWARD HOTEL	406	●	●	●	●		●	●	135	♦♦♦
CITY AND ST PAUL'S										
CITY OF LONDON YOUTH HOTEL	407	●			●	●			46	♦
NEW BARBICAN HOTEL	407	●	●		●	●	●		470	♦♦♦
THE TOWER										
TOWER THISTLE HOTEL	408	●	●	●	●	●	●	●	826	♦♦♦
KENSINGTON										
ALISON HOUSE HOTEL	409		●						11	♦♦
ARLANDA HOTEL	410	●	●		●				16	♦
BEAVER HOTEL	410		●						38	♦♦
THE BERKELEY	410	●	●	●	●	●	●	●	160	♦♦♦
CLEARLAKE HOTEL	410	●	●						17	♦
CORONET HOTEL	410	●	●						23	♦♦
EBURY COURT HOTEL	410		●				●	●	45	♦♦♦
FENJA HOTEL	410	●	●		●			●	13	♦♦♦
GORE HOTEL	410	●	●		●		●	●	54	♦♦♦
HOLLAND HOUSE YHA	410	●		●	●	●			15	♦
HYATT CARLTON TOWER	410	●	●	●	●	●	●	●	224	♦♦♦
KENSINGTON PALACE HOTEL	410		●	●		●	●	●	299	♦♦♦
CHELSEA										
BLAIRHOUSE HOTEL	411		●						17	♦♦
LEYWARD HOUSE HOTEL			●						29	♦
HYDE PARK										
DELMERE HOTEL	412		●				●		40	♦♦
FOUR SEASONS INN ON THE PARK	412	●	●	●	●	●	●	●	227	♦♦♦
GROSVENOR HOUSE	412		●	●		●	●	●	454	♦♦♦
INTER CONTINENTAL HOTEL	412		●	●		●	●	●	467	♦♦♦
NAYLAND HOTEL	412	●	●		●		●	●	41	♦♦
RHODES HOUSE HOTEL	412	●	●		●				15	♦
WHITE'S HOTEL	412		●	●		●	●	●	54	♦♦♦
REGENT'S PARK										
BENTINCK HOUSE HOTEL	413	●	●		●		●		20	♦♦
BERNERS PARK PLAZA	413		●			●	●	●	229	♦♦♦
THE CHURCHILL	413		●	●		●	●	●	448	♦♦♦

	PAGE	GARDEN/TERRACE	TV IN ROOM	VIEW	QUIET	RESTAURANT	24-HOUR SERVICE	PARKING	No. OF ROOMS	PRICE
EDWARD LEAR HOTEL	413		●						31	♦♦
HOTEL LA PLACE	413	●	●				●	●	21	♦♦
INTERNATIONAL STUDENTS HOUSE	413					●	●		200	♦
MERRYFIELD HOUSE	413	●	●		●				7	♦♦
HAMPSTEAD										
BUCKLAND HOTEL	413	●	●		●				16	♦♦
CHARLOTTE COFFEE LOUNGE	413	●	●		●		●		40	♦
FIVE KINGS GUEST HOUSE	413	●			●				16	♦
FORTE POSTHOUSE HAMPSTEAD	414		●				●		140	♦♦
HAMPSTEAD HEATH YOUTH HOTEL (YHA)	414	●		●	●		●		15	♦
NONTAS	414		●				●		12	♦♦
REGENT'S PARK MARRIOTT HOTEL	414	●	●		●	●	●	●	303	♦♦♦
SANDRINGHAM HOTEL	414	●	●		●				19	♦♦
SWISS COTTAGE HOTEL	414	●	●		●		●	●	81	♦♦
COVENT GARDEN										
THE FIELDING HOTEL	415		●						26	♦♦
THE SAVOY	415		●	●		●	●	●	202	♦♦♦
HOTEL STRAND CONTINENTAL	415						●	●	22	♦
ROYAL ADELPHI HOTEL	415		●						50	♦♦
ST JAMES'S AND MAYFAIR										
CLARIDGE'S	416	●	●		●	●	●	●	196	♦♦♦
THE RITZ	416		●		●	●	●	●	129	♦♦♦
BLOOMSBURY										
ACADEMY HOTEL	419		●				●	●	35	♦♦♦
ARRAN HOUSE HOTEL	419	●	●		●		●		28	♦♦
CENTRAL CLUB	419		●			●	●		178	♦♦
CRESCENT HOSTEL	419	●	●	●	●		●		28	♦♦
GOWER HOUSE HOTEL	419		●						16	♦♦
HARLINGFORD HOTEL	419	●	●	●	●				44	♦♦
JOHN ADAM'S HALL	419	●			●		●		168	♦
KINGSLEY HOTEL	419	●	●		●		●	●	144	♦♦♦
LANGLEY HOTEL	419		●						16	♦
LONSDALE HOTEL	419	●	●		●				34	♦♦
MARLBOROUGH HOTEL	419		●			●	●	●	169	♦♦♦
RUSKIN HOTEL	419								33	♦♦
SALTERS HOTEL	419	●	●		●				60	♦
THANET HOTEL	419	●	●		●				12	♦♦
EAST END										
GREAT EASTERN HOTEL	420		●			●	●			♦♦♦
LAMBETH										
DRISCOLL HOUSE HOTEL	421								200	♦
LONDON PARK HOTEL	421		●			●			377	♦♦
GREENWICH										
BARDON LODGE HOTEL	422		●				●		67	♦♦
GREENWICH HOTEL	422	●	●		●	●			33	♦
STONEHALL HOUSE HOTEL	422	●	●	●	●				27	♦

403

GORING HOTEL   SCANDIC CROWN HOTEL   AUBERGE DE PROVENCE

UNITED STATES EMBASSY
24 Grosvenor Square, W1
Tel: (0171) 499 9000

LEGISLATION REGARDING ANIMALS
In order to protect the country from rabies, any animal brought into Great Britain must be placed in quarantine for six months.

There are Tourist Information Centres at Heathrow Airport, Victoria Station, and *Selfridges* department store on Oxford Street.

CITY OF LONDON INFORMATION CENTRE
St Paul's Churchyard, EC4
Tel: (0171) 606 3030

PRACTICAL INFORMATION

LONDON TOURIST BOARD
26 Grosvenor Gardens
SW1W 0DU
Tel: (0171) 730 3488
Open 9am–6pm
Closed Sat. and Sun.

POST OFFICE
24–8, William IV Street
Trafalgar Square
WC2N 4DL
Tel: (0171) 930 9580

HOSPITALS
MIDDLESEX HOSPITAL
Mortimer Street, W1
Tel: (0171) 636 8333
ST MARY'S HOSPITAL
Praed Street, W2
Tel: (0171) 725 6666
ST THOMAS' HOSPITAL
Lambeth Palace Road, SE1
Tel: (0171) 928 9292

CHEMISTS
BLISS CHEMIST
5 Marble Arch, W1
Tel: (0171) 723 6116
Open 9am–midnight.
BOOTS
Piccadilly Circus, W1
Tel: (0171) 734 6126
Open 8.30am–8pm
Sun. noon–6pm
Closed Christmas.

LOST PROPERTY
LONDON TRANSPORT
LOST PROPERTY OFFICE
200 Baker Street, NW1
METROPOLITAN POLICE
LOST PROPERTY & TAXI
LOST PROPERTY

15 Penton Street, N1
Tel: (0171) 833 0996
Open 9am–4pm.

WESTMINSTER AND VICTORIA

CULTURE

HOUSE OF LORDS
Palace of Westminster, SW1
Tel: (0171) 219 3107
The House sits Mon.–Wed. from 2.30pm and Thur. from 3pm.
Phone to check for particular debates, when queues will be longer.

TATE GALLERY
Millbank, SW1
Tel: (0171) 821 1313
Open 10am–5.50pm
Sun. 2pm–5.50pm.
British painters, sculpture and paintings from the 20th century. Don't miss the Turner exhibition in the Clore Gallery.

WESTMINSTER ABBEY
Parliament Square, SW1
Tel: (0171) 222 5152
Open 8am–6pm, Sun. between services.
The kings and queens of England have been crowned here since William the Conqueror. No groups.

WESTMINSTER CATHEDRAL
Victoria, SW1
Open 7am–8pm
From Apr. to Oct., open 10.30am–5.30pm.
The largest Roman Catholic church in England.

RESTAURANTS

AUBERGE DE PROVENCE
St James's Court Hotel
41 Buckingham Gate, SW1
Tel: (0171) 821 1899
Open 12.30–2.30pm, 7.30–11pm.
Closed Sat. lunch and Sun.
Typically Provençal. High quality dishes. Friendly atmosphere. For devotees of French cuisine. Specialties: lamb

charlotte, escalopes à l'orange, poulet fumé.
£30–£40.
🍷 💳 ✗

TATE GALLERY RESTAURANT
Tate Gallery
Millbank, SW1
Tel: (0171) 834 6754
Open noon–3pm
Closed Sun. and public holidays.
Murals by Whistler, fine, well-presented English cuisine. Unfortunately, though, the service leaves a great deal to be desired. Reservation required two days in advance. Specialties: traditional and modern.
£15–£25.
◑ 💳 ⚱ ✗

THE WELL
2 Eccleston Place, SW1
Tel: (0171) 730 7303
Open Mon.–Fri. 9am–6pm, Sat. 9am–5pm. Closed Sun.
Teashop well-known for its modest prices and homemade cakes. All proceeds go to St Michael's Church. There are religious debates in the afternoons.

ACCOMMODATION

CORONA HOTEL
87–9, Belgrave Road, SW1

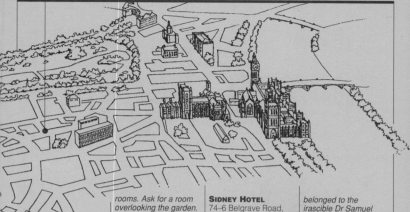

STAKIS LONDON HOTEL

Tel: (0171) 828 9279
Fax. (0171) 931 8576.
Good location (10 mins. on foot from Victoria Station and 2 mins. from Pimlico). "Bed & Breakfast" with 40 rooms, most with every comfort. Good value for money. Breakfast included. £52–£58.

ECCLESTON CHAMBERS
30 Eccleston Square, SW1
Tel: (0171) 828 7924
Fax. (0171) 828 7924
Received the 1990 award for the best "Bed & Breakfast". Competitive prices. Breakfast included. £45–£60.

ELIZABETH HOTEL
37 Eccleston Square, Victoria, SW1
Tel: (0171) 828 6812.
One of the best hotels near Victoria. Recently refurbished throughout. The print gallery is worth a look. Breakfast included. £77.

GORING HOTEL
Beeston Place Grosvenor Gardens, SW1
Tel: (0171) 396 9000
Fax. (0171) 834 4393.
Very pleasant atmosphere. Lovely rooms. Ask for a room overlooking the garden. Bathrooms with wood and marble fittings. £170.

HANOVER HOTEL
30–2 St George's Drive, Victoria, SW1
Tel: (0171) 834 0134
Fax. (0171) 834 7878.
Two Victorian houses built in 1859, facing a garden. Breakfast included. £56.

KERWIN HOTEL
20 St George's Drive, SW1
Tel: (0171) 834 1595.
Well-equipped rooms. Breakfast included. £28–£30.

ROMANO'S HOTEL
31 Charlwood Street, SW1
Tel: (0171) 834 3542.
In the process of being modernized. Friendly proprietors. Family rooms very economical. Rates negotiable. Breakfast included. £30–£45.

SCANDIC CROWN HOTEL
2 Bridge Place, SW1
Tel: (0171) 834 8123
Fax. (0171) 828 1099
Conference hotel very near to Victoria Station. Elegant, but lacking in originality. Breakfast only included in weekend rates. £135.

SIDNEY HOTEL
74–6 Belgrave Road, SW1
Tel: (0171) 834 2738
Fax. (0171) 630 0973.
Quality "Bed & Breakfast". About forty well-fitted rooms with every comfort. Some family rooms with up to six beds. Warm atmosphere. Breakfast included. £49–£58.

STAKIS ST ERMIN'S LONDON HOTEL
Caxton Street, SW1
Tel: (0171) 222 7888
Fax: (0171) 222 6914
Very good location. Warm atmosphere. Attractive rooms and opulent lounges. Buffet-style English breakfast extra. £139–£169.

WINDERMERE HOTEL
142–4 Warwick Way, Victoria, SW1
Tel: (0171) 834 5163
Fax: (0171) 630 8831.
Warm family atmosphere. Pleasant rooms. Breakfast included. £59–£67.

INNS OF COURT

CULTURE

DR JOHNSON'S HOUSE
17 Gough Square, EC4
Tel: (0171) 353 3745
Open 11am–5pm
Closed Sun. and public holidays.
Seventeenth-century brick house which belonged to the irascible Dr Samuel Johnson. Traditional English interior.

HUNTERIAN MUSEUM
Lincoln's Inn Fields, WC2
Tel: (0171) 405 3474
Open 10am–5pm
Closed to the public without authorization. Children under 16 years not allowed. Physiological and anatomical models made by the surgeon John Hunter (1728–93).

GRAY'S INN
Gray's Inn Road Holborn, WC1
Tel: (0171) 405 8164
Open 10am–4pm
Closed Sat., Sun., public holidays and Christmas week.
This is one of the four Inns of Court, a barristers' college since the 15th century. Beautiful gardens.

INNER TEMPLE
Crown Office Row, EC4
Tel: (0171) 797 8250
Open 10am–4pm
Closed Sat., Sun., public holidays and Christmas week.
Templar church attached to the Temple. 17th-century porch.

MIDDLE TEMPLE
Middle Temple Lane, EC4
Tel: (0171) 353 4355
Open 10am–4pm
Closed Sat., Sun. and public holidays.
The 15th-century hall is worth a look, especially for its vaulting.

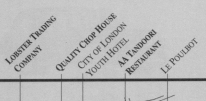

LOBSTER TRADING COMPANY — QUALITY CHOP HOUSE — CITY OF LONDON YOUTH HOTEL — AA TANDOORI RESTAURANT — LE POULBOT

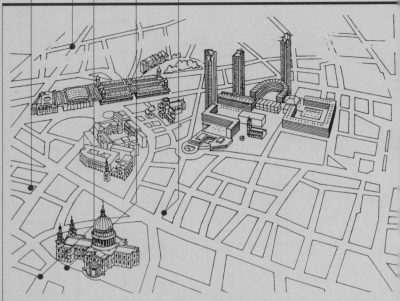

PUBLIC RECORD OFFICE MUSEUM
Chancery Lane, WC2
Tel: (0181) 876 3444
Open 9.30am–5pm
Closed Sat., Sun. and
public holidays.
*Documents illustrating
the history of England,
from the "Domesday
Book" (survey drawn up
in 1086) to modern
records.*

ROYAL COURTS OF JUSTICE
Strand, WC2
Tel: (0171) 936 6000
Open 10.30am–1pm,
2–4pm during hearings.
*The law courts. Gothic-
style building of the late
19th century.*

SIR JOHN SOANE'S MUSEUM
13 Lincoln's Inn Fields,
WC2
Tel: (0171) 405 2107
Open 10am–5pm
Closed Sun., Mon. and
public holidays.
*Sir John Soane's
collection: paintings by
Hogarth, Turner and
Watteau.*

RESTAURANTS

EAGLE PUB
159 Farringdon Road,
EC1
Tel: (0171) 837 1353

Open noon–midnight,
Closed Sat., Sun. and
public holidays.
*Pub with a particularly
warm atmosphere.
Varied range of
delicious Italian
dishes. Specialty:
crostini.*
£8–£15.
○ ⌘

QUALITY CHOP HOUSE
94 Farringdon Road,
EC1
Tel: (0171) 837 5093
Open Mon.-Sat. noon–
3pm, 6.30–midnight,
Sun. noon–4pm,
7pm–11.30pm.
*The Victorian décor of
the dining room adds a
finishing touch to the
presentation of the food.
Reservation essential.
English cuisine.*
£12–£20.
◑ ⌘ ⌘

ACCOMMODATION

HOWARD HOTEL
Temple Place
Strand, WC2
Tel: (0171) 836 3555
Fax:. (0171) 379 4547
*Very "British" luxury
hotel. Magnificent view
over the well-
kept gardens.*
£226.
⌘ ⌘ ⌘ ⌦ □ ⌘
⌘ ⌦

NIGHT LIFE

BLACK FRIAR
174 Queen Victoria
Street, EC4
Tel: (0171) 236 5650
Open 11.30am–10pm
Closed Sat., Sun. and
public holidays.
*A famous 19th-century
pub, right in the heart of
the City. Superb Art
Nouveau mosaics.
Pleasant atmosphere.*

CITY AND ST PAUL'S

CULTURE

BANK OF ENGLAND MUSEUM
Bartholomew Lane, EC2
Tel: (0171) 601 5545
Open Mon.–Fri.
10am–5pm, Sun. and
public holidays,
11am–5pm in summer.
*This is housed in the
same building as the
Bank of England and
retraces its history from
its creation in 1694.*

BARBICAN ART GALLERY
Barbican Centre, 8th
floor. Silk Street, EC2
Tel: (0171) 638 4141
Open 10am–6.45pm
Tues. 10am–5.45pm
Sun. and public

holidays noon–6.45pm.
*Numerous art
exhibitions.*

BARBICAN CENTRE
Silk Street, EC2
Tel: (0171) 638 8891
Open 9am–8pm
Closed Christmas.
*The largest cultural
complex in Europe.
It boasts concert halls
and conference rooms,
theaters, cinemas, an
art gallery, library,
restaurants, etc.
24-hour information and
program on (0171) 628
2295 /(0171) 628 9760.*

GUILDHALL
Off Gresham Street, EC2
Tel: (0171) 606 3030
Open 9.30am–5pm
Closed Sun. and public
holidays.
*Official home of the
"Corporation of the City
of London", the city's
administrative center for
centuries. Great
historical and
architectural interest.*

THE MONUMENT
Monument Street, EC3
Tel: (0171) 626 2717
Open 9am–6pm
Sat. and Sun. 2–6pm
From Oct. to Mar
9am–4pm, closed Sun.
*An unimpeded view
from the top of the*

311 steps. Wren built this to commemorate the rebirth of London after the Great Fire.

MUSEUM OF LONDON

150 London Wall, EC2
Tel: (0171) 600 3699
Open Tues.-Sat.
10am–6pm, Sun.
noon–6pm. Closed
Mon. and Christmas.
History of London and its inhabitants since prehistory. Exhibitions, reconstructions.

NATIONAL POSTAL MUSEUM

King Edward Building
King Edward Street,
EC1
Tel: (0171) 239 5420
Open 9.30am–4.30pm.
Closed Sat., Sun. and
public holidays.
Large collection of stamps including the "Penny Black", and bank notes.

ST PAUL'S CATHEDRAL

Ludgate Hill, EC4
Open for sightseeing
8.30am–4.15pm.
Closed Sun. Crypt and
galleries: open
9.45am–4.15pm.
Sat. 11am–4.15pm.
Guided tours at 11am,
11.30am, 1.30pm and
2pm.
Cathedral built by Wren.

MARKETS

LEADENHALL MARKET

Between Gracechurch
Street and the Lloyd's
Building, EC3
Stalls open 6am–4pm,
shops 9am-5.30pm.
Closed Sat., Sun. and
public holidays.
An architectural gem in the heart of the City. A market has been on the site since 80 AD. The current land was given to the City of London by its major Richard (Dick) Whittington in 1411. Poultry, game, meat, fish, fruit and vegetables, etc. Good little restaurants.

RESTAURANTS

AA TANDOORI RESTAURANT

5, Deans Court, EC4
Tel: (0171) 489 1847
Open noon–10.30pm.
Closed Sat. and Sun.
Top-quality Indian restaurant in the heart of the City. Very attractive surroundings and bright dining room.
£9–£15.
❶ ▭ ✇

GEORGE AND VULTURE

3 Castle Court
Cornhill, EC3
Tel: (0171) 626 9710
Open noon–2.45pm.
Closed Sat., Sun. and
public holidays.
Traditional restaurant where the City business community mixes with

tourists. Don't miss
Dickens' books upstairs.
English cuisine.
£12–£18.
❶ ▭ ✇

LE POULBOT

45 Cheapside, EC2
Tel: (0171) 236 4379
Open noon–2.30pm.
Closed Sat., Sun. and
public holidays.
Typically French atmosphere. Speedy service which has ensured its success in the City. Reservation advised. The wine is reasonably priced. Specialties: ballottine de foie gras, mousse de langoustine
£31.
⓶ ▭ ✇

LOBSTER TRADING COMPANY

32 Old Bailey, EC4
Tel: (0171) 236 7931
Upstairs Tapas Bar
open 11am-8pm Mon.-
Fri., downstairs
restaurant and
brasserie open noon-
3pm. Closed Sat., Sun.
and public holidays.
Seafood specialties.
£20–£25.
⓶ ▭ ✇

VIC NAYLOR'S

38–40 St John Street,
EC1
Tel: (0171) 608 2181
Open noon–midnight
Mon.-Fri., Sat. 7pm–
1am. Closed Sun. and
public holidays.
Popular City brasserie.

◆ **NEW BARBICAN HOTEL** ◆

This hotel is situated in the center of the modern Barbican district, which some people consider to be an anonymous concrete jungle.

Decorated throughout in
dark wood. Great
variety of dishes.
Prestigious wines and
beers. Specialties:
*monkfish mysterioso,
fish in general.*
£12–£15.
❶ ▭ ✇

ANTIQUES

CAMDEN PASSAGE

Islington High Street, N1
Open Sat. 8am–5pm,
Wed. 6.45am–4pm,
Thur. 7am–4pm.
Most prestigious of the antique markets in London; books, silverware, jewelry, furtniture etc

ACCOMMODATION

CITY OF LONDON YOUTH HOSTEL

36 Carter Lane, EC4
Tel: (0171) 236 4965
Fax:. (0171) 236 7681
Well-placed youth hostel. Friendly atmosphere.
Large English breakfast included. Room reservation 7am–11pm.
£20.
⌂ ▣ ⌂ ✇ ▭ ⚲

NEW BARBICAN HOTEL

120 Central Street
Clerkenwell, EC1
Tel: (0171) 251 1565
Fax. (0171) 253 1005.
Large City hotel. Weekend rates. Book through an agency for the best prices
£85.
⌂ ▣ ⌂ ▢ ✇ ▭ ⚲

NIGHT LIFE

YE OLDE WATLING

29 Watling Street, EC4
Tel: (0171) 248 6252
Open 11am–9pm
Closed Sat., Sun. and
public holidays.
*Very close to St Paul's.
Old wooden pub,
reconstructed by Wren
after the Great Fire of
1666. You can now eat
and drink here, basking
in the warm
atmosphere.*

CULTURE

TOWER BRIDGE

Southwark, SE1
Tel: (0171) 403 3761

Open 10am–4pm (winter) 5.45pm (summer)
An extraordinary view from the top of the bridge. Don't miss the "Engine Room Museum" containing the steam-powered machinery that has worked the bridge since 1894.

TOWER HILL PAGEANT
1 Tower Hill Terrace, EC3
Tel: (0171) 709 00181
Open 9.30am–5.30pm
From Nov. to Mar., open 9.30am–4.30pm.
Closed at Christmas.
Automated vehicles take visitors on a ride around reconstructed London of the last two centuries. Also archeological finds.

TOWER OF LONDON
Tower Hill, EC3
Tel: (0171) 709 0765
Open Mar. to Oct.
9.30am–6.30pm
Sun. 2–6.15pm.
Nov.-Feb. open 9.30am-5pm, Sun. 10am-5pm
Former royal residence. The Tower is one of the major historical monuments in England. Don't miss the Crown Jewels.

RESTAURANTS

LE PONT DE LA TOUR
Butler's Wharf Building
36d Shad Thames
Butler's Wharf, SE1
Tel: (0171) 403 8403
restaurant
Tel: (0171) 403 9303
bar and grill
Open noon–3pm daily, 6–midnight Mon.–Sat.; 6–11pm Sun.
Terence Conran's latest venture. 1930's décor with view of the river.
£40–50.

ACCOMMODATION

TOWER THISTLE HOTEL
St Katharine's Way, E1
Tel: (0171) 481 2575
Fax: (0171) 488 4106.
Huge hotel with restaurant and discotheque. View of the Thames. Discount rates through the High Life Value Breaks agency.

£135.
🏨 📶 ⌂ ⚜ 🖳 🐕
🚗 ▭

KENSINGTON
CULTURE

BROMPTON ORATORY
Brompton Road, SW7
Tel: (0171) 589 4811
Open 6.30am–8pm
Catholic church in Italian Renaissance style, renowned for its organ.
Times of services on (0171) 589 4811.
Latin Mass Sun. at 8am and 11am.

COMMONWEALTH INSTITUTE
230 Kensington High Street, W8
Tel: (0171) 603 4535
Open 10am–5pm
Sun. 2–5pm.
Everything there is to know about the history, countryside, fauna and arts of Commonwealth countries.

HOLLAND PARK
Off Kensington High Street, W8
Closed at nightfall.
Probably the nicest park in London. Don't miss the Japanese Garden, the exhibitions in the Orangery and the Ice House.

NATURAL HISTORY MUSEUM
Cromwell Road
South Kensington, SW7

Tel: (0171) 938 9123
Open 10am–5.30pm
Sun. 11am–5.30pm
Closed at Christmas and New Year.
Fossils, minerals, animals... Exhibitions on human biology, ecology. Earthquake simulator.

SCIENCE MUSEUM
Exhibition Road, SW7
Tel: (0171) 938 8000
Open 10am–6pm. Sun. 11am–6pm.
The history and evolution of science and industry. Do not miss the interactive children's gallery and the "Launch Pad".

SERPENTINE GALLERY
Kensington Gardens, W2
Tel: (0171) 402 6075
Open 10am–6pm
Closed public holidays.
Modern and contemporary art exhibitions. Recorded information on (0171) 723 9072.

VICTORIA & ALBERT MUSEUM
Cromwell Road
South Kensington, SW7
Tel: (0171) 938 8500
Open Tues.-Sun. 10am–5.50pm, Mon. noon–5.50pm
Closed at Christmas.
Outstanding art museum covering all countries, all periods and all styles. Includes the National Art Library.

◆ FENJA HOTEL ◆
An attractive red-brick hotel near the expensive terraces of the district of Kensington.

RESTAURANTS

L'ACCENTO ITALIANO
16 Garway Road, W2
Tel: (0171) 243 2201
Open 12.30–2.30pm; 6.30–11.30pm
New, busy restaurant with exciting Italian food: stuffed sardines, tagliatelle with walnut sauce, ravioli filled with pumpkin purée and flavored with sage, gnocchi with saffron and courgettes, fried calamari and aubergine strips. Italian wines. Reservation recommended.
£20–30.
▭

THE ARK
122 Palace Gardens Terrace, W8
Tel: (0171) 229 4024
Open noon–3pm, 6.30–11.15pm
Closed Sun. lunch and public holidays.
Behind its wooden façade, this establishment is always crowded. Friendly service and excellent dishes. Another restaurant at 135 Kensington High Street. Specialties: lamb, chicken pilaf, crème brulée.
£12–£15.
◑ ▭ ✖

THE BELVEDERE
Holland House, Off Abbotsbury Road, W8
Tel: (0171) 602 1238
Open noon–3pm Mon.-Sat., noon–4pm Sun.
Dinner Mon.-Sat. 6–11pm summer, 7–11pm winter.
Elegant surroundings in the heart of Holland Park. First-class "modern British" cuisine. Magnificent terrace. Reservation required. Specialties: French, English.
£19–£30.
◑ ▭ ⚲ ✖ 🅿

BIBENDUM
Michelin Building
81 Fulham Rd, SW3
Tel: (0171) 581 5817
Open 12.30–2.30pm
Mon.–Fri., 12.30–3pm
Sat.–Sun and 7–11pm
evenings. Oyster bar open noon–10pm daily (no alcohol served on Sun. afternoon).

Traditional French café favorites. Book fifteen days in advance. Sample food at oyster bar with the shortened seafood menu.
£40–50.
Ⓜ 🗋 👤

BOYD'S
135 Kensington Church Street, W8
Tel: (0171) 727 5452
Open 12.30–2.30pm, 7–11pm
Closed Sun. and public holidays.
Romantic surroundings for first-class "modern British" cuisine. The clientèle tend to be regulars. Reservation required. Specialties: salmon, Scottish beef.
£12–£25
◑ 🗋 ✼

CLARKE'S
124 Kensington Church Street, W8
Tel: (0171) 221 9225
Open 12.30–2pm, 7–10pm
Closed Sat., Sun. and public holidays.
The choice is taken out of the customer's hands: there is one set menu, but it is changed every day. Liberal helpings and delicious food; the restaurant is never empty. Various influences, use of natural ingredients. Reservation required.
£22–£37
Ⓜ 🗋 ✼

ENGLISH HOUSE
3 Milner Street, SW3
Tel: (0171) 584 3002
Open 12.30–2.30pm, 7.30–11.15pm
Sun. 12.30–2pm, 7.30–10pm.
Absolutely delightful. The welcome leaves nothing to be desired, and the cuisine is in the best English tradition.
£15–£35.
Ⓜ 🗋 ✼

GEALES FISH RESTAURANT
2 Farmer Street, W8
Tel: (0171) 727 7969
Open noon–3pm, 6–11pm.
Closed Sun., Mon., Easter and Christmas.
Decorated in the style of an old-fashioned English teashop. Reputedly the best

"Fish & chips" restaurant in London, extremely popular with Elton John, as can be seen from the photos on display. Specialties: fish, apple crumble.
£8–£12.
◯ 🗋 ✼

HARVEY'S CAFÉ
358 Fulham Road, SW10
Tel: (0171) 352 0625
Open 12.30–3pm; 7.30–11pm.
Closed Sun. night, Mon.
Café above a pub. Simple surroundings full of fresh flowers.
£10–£15.
👤

KEN LO'S MEMORIES OF CHINA
67–9 Ebury Street, SW1
Tel: (0171) 730 7734
Open Mon.-Sat. noon-2.30pm, 7–11.15pm, Sun. 7-10.30pm.
Closed public holidays.
Huge Chinese restaurant, patronized by the royal family. Modern surroundings. First-rate dishes that occasionally court Western tastes a little too much. Reservation required.
£21–£29.
Ⓜ 🗋 👤 ✼

KENSINGTON PLACE
201–5 Kensington Church Street, W8
Tel: (0171) 727 3184
Open noon–3pm, Mon–Fri; noon–3.30pm

Sat, Sun; 6.30–11.45pm Mon–Sat; 6.30–10.15pm Sun. *Glamorous place where diners are on show through vast plate-glass windows.*
£20–£30.
Ⓜ 🗋

LAUNCESTON PLACE
1a Launceston Place, W8
Tel: (0171) 937 6912
Open Mon.–Fri. 12.30-2.30pm, Sun. 12.30-3pm; Mon.–Sat. 7–11.30pm.
Closed Sat. lunch, Sun. evenings.
Comfortable and luxurious décor. Modern British food. Reservations required.
£45
Ⓜ 🗋

LEITH'S
92, Kensington Park Road W11
Tel: (0171) 229 4481
Open 7.30–11.30pm.
Closed 28–29 August and Christmas.
Delicious dishes, well-presented, many from original recipes; the portions are generous. Services is professional and prices reflect the high standards. Reservation required. Specialties: vegetarian cuisine, monkfish.
£42–£47.
Ⓜ 🗋 ✼

RESTAURANT 192
192 Kensington Park Road, W11

Tel: (0171) 229 0482
Open 12.30pm–3pm Mon.-Fri., 12.30–3.30pm Sat, Sun., 5.30–11.30pm Mon.–Sat., 5.30–10.30pm Sun.
Closed Mon. afternoon.
One of the first places to serve warm salads, which are as delicious as ever. Wide choice of varied dishes on a menu that changes daily. Excellent wine list at attractive prices. Specialties: nouvelle cuisine, warm salads.
£19–£25.
◑ 🗋 ✼

ST QUENTIN
243 Brompton Road, SW3
Tel (0171) 589 8005
Open noon–3pm, 7–11pm Mon.–Sat.; noon–3.30pm, 6.30–11.00pm Sun.
Décor of Parisian brasserie. Classic French cooking in classic French setting.
£20–30.
Ⓜ 🗋

WALTON'S
121 Walton Street, SW3
Tel: (0171) 584 0204
Open 12.30pm–2.30pm, 7.30–11.30pm
Sun. 12.30pm–2pm, 7–10pm.
English cuisine with a French influence, in a stylish atmosphere. Marvelous presentation of dishes. Reservation required at the weekend. Specialties: seafood, guineafowl.
£15–£35.
Ⓜ 🗋 ✼

WODKA
12 St Albans Grove, W8
Tel: (0171) 937 6513
Open noon–2.30pm Mon.–Fri., 7.15–11.15pm Mon.–Sat.
Closed Sat. lunch, Sun.
Authentic modern Polish food. Thirteen kinds of home-flavored vodka (among them plum, pepper and bison grass flavor). Good value.
£15.
Ⓜ 🗋

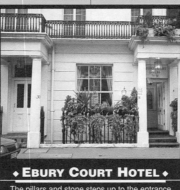

◆ **EBURY COURT HOTEL** ◆
The pillars and stone steps up to the entrance of this hotel are evocative of the neo-classical style of Belgravia.

ACCOMMODATION

ALISON HOUSE HOTEL
82 Ebury Street
Belgravia, SW1

CLEARLAKE HOTEL
KENSINGTON PALACE HOTEL
GORE HOTEL

Tel: (0171) 730 9529
Fax: (0171) 730 5494
Modest hotel, shared bathroom facilities, except for one room. Children are welcome. Extremely good value for money. Breakfast included.
£48.

ARLANDA HOTEL
17 Longridge Road, SW5
Tel: (0171) 370 5213.
Small hotel, 16 rooms with shared bathroom facilities. Breakfast included. Discounts for long stays.
£25.

BEAVER HOTEL
57–9 Philbeach Gardens, SW5
Tel: (0171) 373 4553
Fax: (0171) 373 4555
Well-served by public transport and conveniently placed. Ask for a room with a view over the gardens. English breakfast included. Garage (£3).
£58.

THE BERKELEY
Wilton Place
Knightsbridge, SW1
Tel: (0171) 235 6000
Fax: (0171) 235 4330
Superb view over Hyde Park. Sumptuous rooms and suites. Particularly friendly service with a personal touch. Health and fitness center.
£250.

CLEARLAKE HOTEL
18–19 Prince of Wales Terrace, W8
Tel: (0171) 937 3274
Fax: (0171) 376 0604.
Average status. Breakfast included. Cooking facilities in all rooms. Studios and apartments to rent.
£40–£50.

CORONET HOTEL
59 Nevern Square, SW5
Tel: (0171) 373 6396
Fax: (0171) 370 0034
Warm atmosphere and pleasant rooms. Competitive prices. Breakfast included. Catering available. Discounts for cash payment and long stays.
£49.

EBURY COURT HOTEL
28 Ebury Street
Belgravia, SW1
Tel: (0171) 730 8147
Fax: (0171) 823 5966.
Family hotel. Numerous rooms. The "Honeymoon" suite is delightful. Breakfast included.
£95.

FENJA HOTEL
69 Cadogan Gardens, SW3
Tel: (0171) 589 7333
Fax: (0171) 581 4958
Quiet hotel. The rooms, tastefully decorated, are named after famous painters.
£130.

GORE HOTEL
189 Queen's Gate, SW7
Tel: (0171) 584 6601
Fax: (0171) 589 812
Pleasant atmosphere. Good value for money.

Special rates for weekends and long stays.
£128.

HOLLAND HOUSE YHA
King George VI,
Holland Park
Kensington, W8
Tel: (0171) 937 0748
Fax: (0171) 376 0667.
Magnificent setting for this youth hostel in Holland Park. Friendly atmosphere. Reasonably priced restaurant, open to everyone. Breakfast included.
£36.

HYATT CARLTON TOWER
2 Cadogan Place, SW1
Tel: (0171) 235 5411
Fax: (0171) 235 9129
Opulent rooms, health and fitness center. Breakfast is extra but worth it. Weekend rates.
£285.

KENSINGTON PALACE HOTEL
De Vere Gardens, W8
Tel: (0171) 937 8121
Fax: (0171) 937 2816
Luxury hotel, fine view

over the gardens. Polite reception. Breakfast not included, except in the special weekend rates.
£110.

NIGHT LIFE

GRENADIER
18 Wilton Row, SW1
Tel: (0171) 235 3074
Open noon–3pm, 5–11pm, Sun. noon–3pm, 7–10.30pm.
Very near Hyde Park Corner, in a quiet little street, this pub, which was highly valued by Wellington's officers, is a must for its incredible ceiling. A good restaurant but somewhat expensive.

ANTIQUES

PORTOBELLO ROAD
Portobello Road, W11
Open 7am–5pm, Sat. 8am–5pm Fri.
Flea market where antiques are very over-priced.

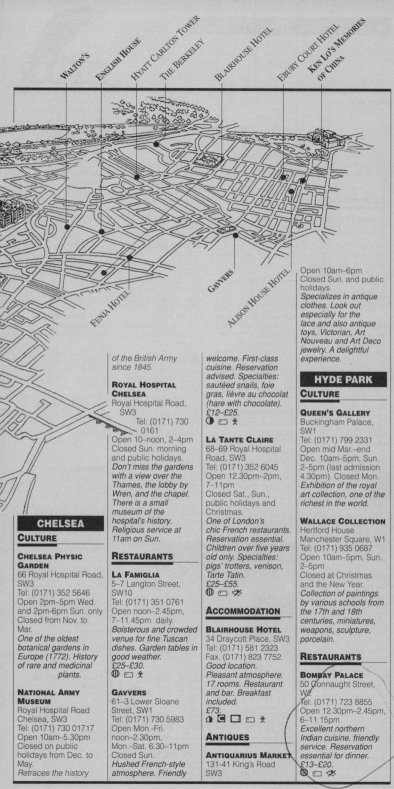

WALTON'S
ENGLISH HOUSE
HYATT CARLTON TOWER
THE BERKELEY
BLAIRHOUSE HOTEL
EBURY COURT HOTEL
KEN LO'S MEMORIES OF CHINA

GAVVERS
FENJA HOTEL
ALISON HOUSE HOTEL

of the British Army since 1845.

ROYAL HOSPITAL CHELSEA
Royal Hospital Road, SW3
Tel: (0171) 730 0161
Open 10–noon, 2–4pm
Closed Sun. morning and public holidays.
Don't miss the gardens with a view over the Thames, the lobby by Wren, and the chapel. There is a small museum of the hospital's history. Religious service at 11am on Sun.

CHELSEA

CULTURE

CHELSEA PHYSIC GARDEN
66 Royal Hospital Road, SW3
Tel: (0171) 352 5646
Open 2pm–5pm Wed. and 2pm–6pm Sun. only
Closed from Nov. to Mar.
One of the oldest botanical gardens in Europe (1772). History of rare and medicinal plants.

NATIONAL ARMY MUSEUM
Royal Hospital Road Chelsea, SW3
Tel: (0171) 730 01717
Open 10am–5.30pm
Closed on public holidays from Dec. to May.
Retraces the history

RESTAURANTS

LA FAMIGLIA
5–7 Langton Street, SW10
Tel: (0171) 351 0761
Open noon–2.45pm, 7–11.45pm daily.
Boisterous and crowded venue for fine Tuscan dishes. Garden tables in good weather.
£25–£30.

GAVVERS
61–3 Lower Sloane Street, SW1
Tel: (0171) 730 5983
Open Mon.-Fri. noon–2.30pm, Mon.–Sat. 6.30–11pm
Closed Sun.
Hushed French-style atmosphere. Friendly

welcome. First-class cuisine. Reservation advised. Specialties: sautéed snails, foie gras, lièvre au chocolat (hare with chocolate).
£12–£25.

LA TANTE CLAIRE
68–69 Royal Hospital Road, SW3
Tel: (0171) 352 6045
Open 12.30pm–2pm, 7–11pm
Closed Sat., Sun., public holidays and Christmas.
One of London's chic French restaurants. Reservation essential. Children over five years old only. Specialties: pigs' trotters, venison, Tarte Tatin.
£25–£55.

ACCOMMODATION

BLAIRHOUSE HOTEL
34 Draycott Place, SW3
Tel: (0171) 581 2323
Fax. (0171) 823 7752.
Good location. Pleasant atmosphere. 17 rooms. Restaurant and bar. Breakfast included.
£73.

ANTIQUES

ANTIQUARIUS MARKET
131-41 King's Road
SW3

Open 10am–6pm
Closed Sun. and public holidays.
Specializes in antique clothes. Look out especially for the lace and also antique toys, Victorian, Art Nouveau and Art Deco jewelry. A delightful experience.

HYDE PARK

CULTURE

QUEEN'S GALLERY
Buckingham Palace, SW1
Tel: (0171) 799 2331
Open mid Mar.–end Dec. 10am–5pm, Sun. 2–5pm (last admission 4.30pm). Closed Mon.
Exhibition of the royal art collection, one of the richest in the world.

WALLACE COLLECTION
Hertford House
Manchester Square, W1
Tel: (0171) 935 0687
Open 10am–5pm, Sun. 2–5pm
Closed at Christmas and the New Year.
Collection of paintings by various schools from the 17th and 18th centuries, miniatures, weapons, sculpture, porcelain.

RESTAURANTS

BOMBAY PALACE
50 Connaught Street, W2
Tel: (0171) 723 8855
Open 12.30pm–2.45pm, 6–11.15pm
Excellent northern Indian cuisine. friendly service. Reservation essential for dinner.
£13–£20.

411

NICO AT NINETY
90 Park Lane, W1
Tel: (0171) 409 1290
Open Mon.-Fri. noon–
2pm, 7–11pm, Mon.–
Sat.Closed Sun.
*Classic French food in
luxurious setting.*
£40–£50 or more.

ACCOMMODATION

DELMERE HOTEL
130 Sussex Gardens,
W2
Tel: (0171) 706 3344
Fax: (0171) 262 1863.
*Attractive rooms. Very
friendly atmosphere.
English breakfast.
Weekend rates.*
£72–£91.

FOUR SEASONS INN ON THE PARK
Hamilton Place
Park Lane, W1
Tel: (0171) 499 0888
Fax: (0171) 493 6629
*Handsome luxury hotel
frequented primarily by
the business
community. Fax and
safes in the rooms.*
£288.

GROSVENOR HOUSE
Park Lane, W1
Tel: (0171) 499 6363
Fax: (0171) 493 3341
*Huge hotel, dating from
the start of the century,
in the heart of Mayfair.
Claims to be a "way of
life" rather than a hotel.*
£229.

INTER CONTINENTAL HOTEL
1 Hamilton Place, W1
Tel: (0171) 409 3131
Fax: (0171) 730 5494.
*Luxury American-style
hotel. Lovely suites.
Breakfast included at
the weekend.*
£145–£284.

NAYLAND HOTEL
132–4 Sussex Gardens,
W2
Tel: (0171) 723 4615
Fax: (0171) 402 3292
*Good location.
Attractive rooms.
Good value for
money. Breakfast
included. Business*

*clientèle during the
week.*
£44–£58.

RHODES HOUSE HOTEL
195 Sussex Gardens,
W2
Tel: (0171) 262 5617
Fax: (0171) 723 4054
*Easy-going atmosphere.
Rooms with shower or
bath. Breakfast
included. Free parking.*
£40.

WHITE'S HOTEL
Lancaster Gate, W2
Tel: (0171) 262 2711
Fax: (0171) 262 2147.
*Unimpeded view over
Hyde Park, from the
other side of the road.
Polite reception.
Fairly attractive rooms.
Restaurant with
veranda.*
£170.

REGENT'S PARK
CULTURE

LONDON PLANETARIUM
Marylebone Road, NW1
Tel: (0171) 486 1121
Open 10am–5.30pm.
Public holidays
9.30am–5.30pm.
*Sound and light shows,
talks on constellations
and space travel, every
hour.*

◆ GROSVENOR HOUSE ◆
This well-known modern hotel is named
after the Grosvenor family who are major
landowners in London.

LONDON ZOO
Regent's Park,
NW1
Tel: (0171) 722 3333
Open 10am–4pm
(winter), 10am–6am
(summer).
*One of the largest zoos
in the world. You can
watch the animals
being fed at specific
times (phone for
details). Special
events organized in
the summer.*

LORD'S CRICKET GROUND
St John's Wood,
NW8
Tel: (0171) 289 1611.
*Lord's is one of the
grounds where England
and Australia compete
for the Ashes.
Reservation required
for guided tours of the
cricket ground.*

MADAME TUSSAUD'S
Marylebone Road, NW1
Tel: (0171) 935 6861
Open Mon.-Fri.
10am–5.30pm, Sat. and
Sun. 9.30am–5.30pm
Closed at Christmas.
*Famous waxworks
museum. A joint ticket
for this and the
Planetarium saves
money. Photos allowed.*

SAATCHI GALLERY
98A Boundary Road
St John's Wood, NW8
Tel: (0171) 624 8299
Open noon–6pm
Fri.(free), Sat. and Sun.
only.

*The main part of
the Saatchi brothers'
collection has modern
British works, Pop Art,
new expressionists.*

RESTAURANTS

AMBALA SWEET CENTRE
112 Drummond Street,
NW1
Tel: (0171) 387 3521
Open 10am–8.30pm.
Closed Christmas.
*Very popular patisserie,
selling delicious Indian
cakes (£25 per pound).
Specialties: rusmali,
habshihalvwe.*
£2–£3.

SEA SHELL FISH RESTAURANT
49–51 Lisson Grove,
NW1
Tel: (0171) 723 8703
Open noon–2.15pm,
5.15–10.30pm, Sat.
noon–10.30pm. Closed
Sun.
*Restaurant famed for its
fish. Dishes to take
away. Specialty: fish
and chips.*
£9–£12.

STEPHEN BULL
5–7 Blandford Street,
W1
Tel: (0171) 486 9696
Open 12.30–2.30pm
Mon.–Fri., 6.30–
10.30pm Mon.–Sat.
Closed Sat., Sun.
*Austere and functional
décor but excellent
food, especially fish
dishes: fillet of brill with
oyster mushrooms and
rosemary, home-salted
cod with clams, and
delicious desserts.
Nearly ninety different
wines under £20 a
bottle.*
£25–£30.

VILLANDRY DINING ROOM
89 Marylebone High
Street, W1
Tel: (0171) 224 3799
Open 12.30–2.30pm
Mon.–Sat.
*Dinner served once a
month, or for parties of
fifteen or more.
Closed Sun.
Excellent food and*

attractive prices.
£17.

ACCOMMODATION

BENTINCK HOUSE HOTEL
20 Bentinck Street, W1
Tel: (0171) 935 9141
Fax: (0171) 224 5903
Pleasant hotel, close to Hyde Park. Breakfast included. Competitive weekend rates.
£65.

BERNERS PARK PLAZA
10 Berners Street, W1
Tel: (0171) 636 1629
Fax: (0171) 580 3972
Well-positioned hotel. Very attractive rooms. Competitive weekend rates.
£130.

CHURCHILL HOTEL
Portman Square, W1
Tel: (0171) 486 5800
Fax: (0171) 486 1255
Conveniently located and elegant. Warm atmosphere. Lovely rooms. View over the square. Tennis. Weekend rates.
£185.

EDWARD LEAR HOTEL
28–30 Seymour Street, W1
Tel: (0171) 402 5401
Fax: (0171) 706 3766
A pleasant Georgian house decorated with illustrations from "The Book of Nonsense" (1848) by Edward Lear. Attractive rooms. Breakfast included.
£62.

HOTEL LA PLACE
17 Nottingham Place, W1
Tel: (0171) 486 2323
Fax: (0171) 486 4335
Good location, near Oxford Street. Breakfast included.
£70.

INTERNATIONAL STUDENTS HOUSE
229 Great Portland Street, W1
Tel: (0171) 631 3223
Fax: (0171) 636 5565
Huge youth hostel

(restaurant, bar, discotheque, gym...). Breakfast included. Discounts for long stays.
£38–£46.

MERRYFIELD HOUSE
42 York Street, W1
Tel: (0171) 935 8326.
Tiny hotel in the heart of the West End. Family atmosphere. Breakfast included, served in the room.
£47.

MARKETS

ALFIE'S MARKET
13-25 Church Street, NW8
Open 10am–6pm
Closed Sun. and Mon.
Fascinating, lively market. Everything from antique lace to cameras.

HAMPSTEAD
CULTURE

FENTON HOUSE
Hampstead Grove, NW3
Tel: (0171) 435 3471
Open Sat., Sun. 2–5pm
Mar., Apr.–end Oct.
Sat., Sun. 11am–5.30pm., Mon.–Wed
1–5.30pm. Closed
Thurs., Fri. and winter.
Seventeenth-century house. Superb collection of porcelain and musical instruments.

FREUD MUSEUM
20 Maresfield Gardens, NW3
Tel: (0171) 435 2002
Open noon–5pm
Closed Mon., Tues., Christmas and New Year.
House where Sigmund Freud lived until his death in 1939. You can see where he worked, especially his famous couch, brought over from Vienna in 1938.

HIGHGATE CEMETERY
Swains Lane, N6
Tel: (0181) 340 1834
Open 10am–5pm,
Sat. and Sun. 11am–5pm. Closed at 4pm in winter.
You can only visit the western side with a

guide. Unaccompanied visits to the eastern side when there is no funeral taking place.

KEATS MEMORIAL HOUSE
Wentworth Place
Keats Grove, NW3
Tel: (0171) 435 2062
Open 10am–1pm, 2–6pm
Sat. 10am–1pm, 2–5pm
Closed Sun. morning and public holidays
From Nov. to Mar., closed in the morning except on Sat.
The poet John Keats lived in this semi-detached house from 1818 to 1820. Don't miss the library.

KENWOOD HOUSE
Hampstead Lane, NW3
Tel: (0181) 348 1286
Open 10am–4pm
Closed at Christmas.
Seventeenth-century country house built by Adam. Paintings by Rembrandt, Vermeer, Gainsborough, Turner. Large grounds. Admission free.

RESTAURANTS

DIWANA
121 Drummond Street, NW1
Tel: (0171) 387 5556
Open noon–12pm.
Closed at Christmas.
This restaurant, built entirely of wood, could not enjoy a higher reputation. A reservation is absolutely essential. Specialties: Indian vegetarian.
£7–£10.

JAZZ CAFÉ
5–7 Parkway, NW1
Tel: (0171) 916 6000
Open noon–3pm, 9pm–midnight.
Very popular. First-class restaurant, reasonable prices. Send an SAE for their monthly jazz program. Reservation essential for dinner.
£8–£15.

N.B.
17 Princess Road
Camden Town, NW1
Tel: (0171) 722 9665
Open noon–2.30pm
Mon.–Fri., 7–10.30pm
Mon.–Sat.

Picturesque with patio garden. Informal service.

NONTAS
14–16 Camden High Street, NW1
Tel: (0171) 387 4579
Open noon–2.45pm, 6–11.30pm. Closed
Sun. and public holidays.
Highly reputable Greek restaurant. Warm atmosphere. Portions not over-generous. Reservation required for tables in the garden when the weather is fine.
£8–£12.

ZEN
83 Hampstead High Street, NW3
Tel: (0171) 794 7863
Open noon–11.30pm
Closed at Christmas.
This restaurant, which is part of the "Now and Zen" chain, offers an extensive range of Chinese specialties. Modern décor. Warm atmosphere.
£19–£30.

ACCOMMODATION

BUCKLAND HOTEL
6 Buckland Crescent, NW3
Tel: (0171) 722 5574
Fax: (0171) 722 5594
Family atmosphere. Spacious rooms. Breakfast included.
£45–£50.

CHARLOTTE COFFEE LOUNGE
221 West End Lane, NW6
Tel: (0171) 794 6476
Fax: (0171) 431 3584
Well-served by all forms of transport and situated 10 mins. from Piccadilly. Certain rooms have kitchen facilities. Breakfast included.
£35–£40.

FIVE KINGS GUEST HOUSE
59 Anson Road, N7
Tel: (0171) 607 3996
"Bed & Breakfast" with family atmosphere. Friendly welcome.

Shared bathroom facilities. Parking.
£30–£32.

FORTE POSTHOUSE HAMPSTEAD
215 Haverstock Hill, NW3
Tel: (0171) 794 8121
Fax: (0171) 435 5586
Attractive, comfortable rooms. Excellent value for money. Breakfast £6. Meals also available (£8).
£39–£53.

HAMPSTEAD HEATH YOUTH HOSTEL (YHA)
4 Wellgarth Road, NW11
Tel: (0181) 458 9054
Fax: (0181) 209 0546.
Pleasant youth hostel. 14 double rooms. Meals available at reasonable prices. Breakfast £2.30.
£28.

NONTAS
14–16 Camden High Street, NW1
Tel: (0171) 387 1380
Fax: (0171) 383 0335
Conveniently located hotel. Stylish rooms. Well-known Greek restaurant. Bar with fireplace. Continental breakfast included.
£47–£51.

REGENT'S PARK MARRIOTT HOTEL
128 King Henry's Road, NW3
Tel: (0171) 722 7711
Fax: (0171) 586 5822
Large, traditional luxury hotel, good location, near Regent's Park, with swimming pool, sauna, hairdresser, etc.
£128–£154.

SANDRINGHAM HOTEL
3 Holford Road, NW3
Tel: (0171) 435 1569
Fax: (0171) 431 5932
Very friendly atmosphere. A nice hotel frequented by many regulars (conference delegates, among others). Lavish English breakfast.
£61.

SWISS COTTAGE HOTEL
4 Adamson Road, NW3
Tel: (0171) 722 2281
Fax: (0171) 483 4588.
Large, luxurious Victorian house. Warm and welcoming atmosphere. Lovely rooms with original furniture and that personal touch. English breakfast included.
£75–£85.

NIGHT LIFE

JACK STRAW'S CASTLE
North End Way Hampstead, NW3
Tel: (0171) 435 8885
Open 11am–11pm.
This pub was built around the time of the first "poll tax" imposed in 1381. Superb view over London. Gardens for outdoor drinking in summer.

OLD BULL AND BUSH
North End Way Hampstead, NW3
Tel: (0181) 455 3685
Open 11am–11pm, Sun. noon–3pm, 7–10.30pm.
Immortalized by Florrie Forde, this popular pub has sold beer since 1721 and was a favorite watering hole of Hogarth and Dickens. Situated right on the edge of Hampstead Heath.

THE FLASK
Flask Walk, NW3
Tel: (0171) 435 4580
Open 11am–11pm, Sun. noon–3pm, 7–10.30pm.
Traditional English pub tucked away in a typical Hampstead side street. Darts and "real ale". It is also a wine bar. Live music on Thur. evenings.

ANTIQUES

CAMDEN LOCK
Chalk Farm Road, NW1
Open 9am–6pm Sat. and Sun. only.
Canal-side market on a lock. Very mixed crowd of customers. Crafts, secondhand goods, clothes, health products and antiques.

COVENT GARDEN

CULTURE

COURTAULD INSTITUTE GALLERIES
Somerset House Strand, WC2
Tel: (0171) 873 2526
Open 10am–6pm Sun. 2–6pm
Closed at Christmas and New Year.
Gallery of Impressionist and Post-Impressionist paintings, works of art from the Renaissance, the Baroque and the 20th century.

LONDON TRANSPORT MUSEUM
The Piazza
Covent Garden, WC2
Tel: (0171) 379 6344
Open 10am–6pm
Closed public holidays.
London transport over the past two centuries.

NATIONAL GALLERY
Trafalgar Square, WC2
Tel: (0171) 839 3321
Open 10am–6pm, Sun. 2–6pm
Closed public holidays.
Fabulous collection of paintings from the 13th to the 20th centuries. Admission free for the gallery. Recorded information on (0171) 839 3526.

NATIONAL PORTRAIT GALLERY
2 St Martin's Place, WC2
Tel: (0171) 306 0055
Open 10am–5pm, Sat. 10am–6pm, Sun. 2–6pm.
Closed public holidays.
Portraits of famous men and women of Great Britain from the Tudor period to the present day.

ST-MARTIN-IN-THE-FIELDS CHURCH
Trafalgar Square, WC2
Tel: (0171) 930 0089
Open 10am–9pm
Sun. noon–6pm.
Café, bookshop and brass-rubbing center in the crypt. Services at 7.30am and 7.30pm. Lunchtime concerts Mon., Tues., Wed., Fri.

THEATRE MUSEUM
Covent Garden, WC2
Tel: (0171) 836 7891
Open 11am–7pm
Closed Mon.
In the old flower market of Covent Garden. National collection of theater (since the time of Shakespeare), opera and pantomime memorabilia.

RESTAURANTS

AJIMURA JAPANESE
51–53 Shelton Street, WC2
Tel: (0171) 379 0626
Open noon–3pm, 6–11.30pm. Closed Sat. afternoon, Sun. and public holidays.
Japanese restaurant with 1970's décor intact. Friendly atmosphere. Reservation is essential.
£10–£25.

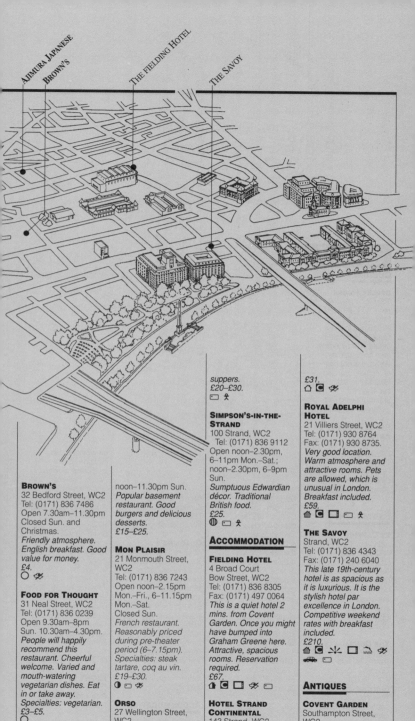

AJIMURA JAPANESE
BROWN'S
THE FIELDING HOTEL
THE SAVOY

BROWN'S
32 Bedford Street, WC2
Tel: (0171) 836 7486
Open 7.30am–11.30pm
Closed Sun. and
Christmas.
*Friendly atmosphere.
English breakfast. Good
value for money.*
£4.
○ ✗

FOOD FOR THOUGHT
31 Neal Street, WC2
Tel: (0171) 836 0239
Open 9.30am–8pm
Sun. 10.30am–4.30pm.
*People will happily
recommend this
restaurant. Cheerful
welcome. Varied and
mouth-watering
vegetarian dishes. Eat
in or take away.
Specialties: vegetarian.*
£3–£5.
○

JOE ALLEN
13 Exeter Street, WC2
Tel: (0171) 836 0651
Open noon–11.45pm
Mon.–Sat.;

noon–11.30pm Sun.
*Popular basement
restaurant. Good
burgers and delicious
desserts.*
£15–£25.

MON PLAISIR
21 Monmouth Street,
WC2
Tel: (0171) 836 7243
Open noon–2.15pm
Mon.–Fri., 6–11.15pm
Mon.–Sat.
Closed Sun.
*French restaurant.
Reasonably priced
during pre-theater
period (6–7.15pm).
Specialties: steak
tartare, coq au vin.*
£19–£30.
➊ ▭ ✗

ORSO
27 Wellington Street,
WC2
Tel: (0171) 240 5269
Open noon–midnight
daily.
*Elegant and fashionable.
Ideal for pre-theater
dinners and after-theater*

suppers.
£20–£30.
▭ ✗

SIMPSON'S-IN-THE-STRAND
100 Strand, WC2
Tel: (0171) 836 9112
Open noon–2.30pm,
6–11pm Mon.–Sat.;
noon–2.30pm, 6–9pm
Sun.
*Sumptuous Edwardian
décor. Traditional
British food.*
£25.
➊ ▭ ✗

ACCOMMODATION

FIELDING HOTEL
4 Broad Court
Bow Street, WC2
Tel: (0171) 836 8305
Fax: (0171) 497 0064
*This is a quiet hotel 2
mins. from Covent
Garden. Once you might
have bumped into
Graham Greene here.
Attractive, spacious
rooms. Reservation
required.*
£67.
⌂ ⦿ ▢ ✗ ▭

HOTEL STRAND CONTINENTAL
143 Strand, WC2
Tel: (0171) 836 4880.
*Good location (near
Theaterland) and
simple. Indian
restaurant. Bar.
Breakfast included.*

£31.
⌂ ⦿ ✗

ROYAL ADELPHI HOTEL
21 Villiers Street, WC2
Tel: (0171) 930 8764
Fax: (0171) 930 8735.
*Very good location.
Warm atmosphere and
attractive rooms. Pets
are allowed, which is
unusual in London.
Breakfast included.*
£59.
⌂ ⦿ ▢ ▭ ✗

THE SAVOY
Strand, WC2
Tel: (0171) 836 4343
Fax: (0171) 240 6040
*This late 19th-century
hotel is as spacious as
it is luxurious. It is the
stylish hotel par
excellence in London.
Competitive weekend
rates with breakfast
included.*
£210.
⌂ ⦿ ≈ ▢ ⊿ ✗
🚗 ▭

ANTIQUES

COVENT GARDEN
Southampton Street,
WC2
Open daily 9am-7pm.
*Famous craft market.
Rather pricey but there
are also countless
street entertainers to
watch.*

415

ST JAMES'S AND MAYFAIR

CULTURE

APSLEY HOUSE
149 Piccadilly, W1
Tel: (0171) 499 5676
Closed until 1995 for
reconstruction.
*Duke of Wellington's
house built by Adam,
then converted by
Wyatt. It is not only
of architectural and
historic interest
but also of
artistic interest (art
gallery on upper floor).*

**ROYAL ACADEMY OF
ARTS**
Burlington House
Piccadilly, W1
Tel: (0171) 439 7438
Open 10am–6pm
Closed at Christmas.
*Outstanding temporary
exhibitions.*

RESTAURANTS

LE CAPRICE
Arlington House
Arlington Square
St James, SW1
Tel: (0171) 629 2239
Open noon–3pm,
6pm–midnight daily.
*Impeccable, slick and
understated.*
£25–£40.
Ⓜ ▭ ⚡

THE CONNAUGHT
Carlos Place, W1
Tel: (0171) 499 7070
Open 12.30–2pm,
6.30–10.30pm daily.
*Grand setting for
French classic dishes
and traditional British
cooking.*
£50–£60
Ⓜ ▭ ⚡

LE GAVROCHE
43 Upper Brook Street,
W1
Tel: (0171) 408 0881

Open noon–2pm,
7–11pm
Closed Sat., Sun.,
public holidays and
Christmas week.
*A converted basement.
Excellent French
cuisine. The service
lives up to its
reputation. Reservation
required in advance.
Specialties: soufflé
à la suissesse, meat
platter, omelette
Rothschild.*
£36–£80.
Ⓜ ▭ ⚡

THE GREENHOUSE
27A Hay's Mews, W1
Tel: (0171) 499 3331
Open Mon.-Fri.
noon–2.30pm, 7–11pm
Sat. 7.30–11pm, Sun.
12.30–3pm, 6–10pm.
*Friendly atmosphere.
Fine English cuisine
with French and
Italian touches.
Reservation essential.
Specialties: carpaccio,
veal with smoked*

bacon, confit de
canard.
£20–£30.
Ⓜ ▭ ⚡ ⚡

QUAGLINO'S
16 Bury Street, SW1
Tel: (0171) 930 6767
Open noon–2.45pm
daily, 5.45–11.45pm
Mon.–Thur., 5.45pm–
12.30am Fri.-Sat.,
6–10.45pm Sun.
*Used to be a nightclub
in the 1950's. Rebuilt,
redesigned, refurbished
by Terence Conran.
Book 2 months in
advance. Impressive
architecture and good
food.*
£20–£30.

ACCOMMODATION

CLARIDGE'S
Brook Street, W1
Tel: (0171) 629 8860
Fax: (0171) 499 2210
*Hotel as charming as it
is luxurious with a
delightful old-fashioned*

*air. For over two
centuries it has
welcomed crowned
heads, politicians and
diplomats visiting
London. The welcome
leaves nothing to be
desired.*
£255.
🏛 Ⓒ ⌂ ▢ ⚡ ▭

RITZ
Piccadilly, W1
Tel: (0171) 493 8181
Fax: (0171) 493 2687.
*This Ritz is very similar
to its Parisian
counterpart: it was built
by the same architects.
Reservation required in
advance for the famous
afternoon tea.*
£220.
🏛 Ⓒ ⚡ ▢ ⚡ ▭

NIGHT LIFE

RED LION PUB
2 Duke of York Street
St James's Square, SW1
Tel: (0171) 930 2030
Open 11.30am–11pm
Closed Sun. and
Christmas.
*The customers of this
little pub, with its
original ceiling and*

THE RITZ

cuisine. Talented
pianist.
Specialties: Irish.
£10–£16.

GAY HUSSAR
2 Greek Street, W1
Tel: (0171) 437 0973
Open 12.30–2.30pm,
5.30–11pm Mon.–Sat.

Closed Sun.
*Hungarian restaurant
where the literary world
of Soho gathers for
lunch. Very welcoming.
The décor is grand and
there are delicious meat
dishes from all Middle
European countries.
£20–£30.*

mirrors, are mainly
artists and sporting
personalities. Genuinely
warm atmosphere. In
the evenings you can
drink "real ale" outside.

SHEPHERD'S TAVERN
50 Hertford Street
Shepherd Market,
W1
Tel: (0171) 499 3017
Open 11am–11pm,
Sat. and Sun.
11am–3pm, 6–11pm
Closed at 7pm on
public holidays.
*This 18th-century
pub was a shop
before becoming a
favorite spot for RAF
pilots in the Second
World War. Don't miss
the "Sedan chair".*

**WALKERS OF ST
JAMES'S**
32A Duke Street
St James's, SW1
Tel: (0171) 930 0278
Open 11.30am–11pm
Mon.–Fri.
Closed Sat., Sun. and
public holidays.
*This pub is in a
basement, near
Piccadilly. Its wooden*

paneling makes for a
very picturesque décor.
Popular with the
business community.
Large selection of wines
and beers, snacks until
3pm.

ANTIQUES

**GRAY'S MEW'S
ANTIQUE MARKET**
1–7 Davies Street, W1
Open 10am–6pm
Closed Sat. and Sun.
*Three hundred stands
in a disused factory.
Antiques, modern art
and Art Deco.*

SOHO

CULTURE

DESIGN CENTRE
28 Haymarket, SW1
Tel: (0171) 839 8000
Open 10am–6pm
Sun. 1–6pm
Closed public holidays.
*A display on three
floors of a thousand
utilitarian objects,
selected for their
advanced technology
and well-designed
forms.*

RESTAURANTS

ALASTAIR LITTLE
49 Frith Street, W1
Tel: (0171) 734 5183
Open noon–3pm,
6–11.30pm
Closed Sat. lunch, Sun.
*Modern British food.
Unpretentious cooking
though remarkably high
standard and constantly
innovative. Credit cards.*
£30–£40.

CHUEN CHENG KU
17 Wardour Street, W1V
Tel: (0171) 437 1398
Open 11am–11.30pm
daily.Dim sum
11am–5.30pm daily.
*Cantonese specialties
in lively bustle of
Chinatown.*
£13.

FLANAGAN'S
14 Rupert Street, W1
Tel: (0171) 434 9201
Open noon–2.30pm,
5.30–11pm
Sun. noon–2.30pm,
5.30–10pm.
*Near Piccadilly Circus.
Original décor. Good*

GOPAL'S OF SOHO
12 Bateman Street, W1
Tel: (0171) 434 1621
Open noon–3pm daily,
6–11.30pm Mon.–Sat.,
6–11pm Sun.
*High quality food in this
quite recently opened
Indian restaurant. Very
good prices.*
£20–30.

THE IVY
1 West Street, WC2
Tel: (0171) 836 4751
Open noon–3pm,
5.30–midnight.
*Stained-glass windows
create a traditional,
attractive décor. Fine
English cuisine.
Reservation essential.
Specialties: chicken
bang bang, Caesar
salad.*
£20–£30.

MELATI
21 Great Windmill
Street, W1
Tel: (0171) 437 2745
Open noon–11.30pm
Sun.–Thur., Fri. and Sat.
noon–12.30am.
The Indonesian décor is

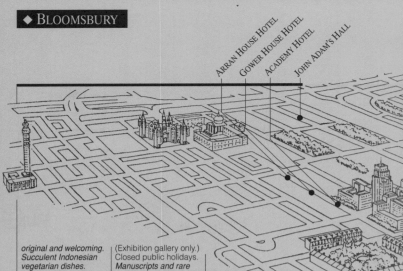

ARRAN HOUSE HOTEL
GOWER HOUSE HOTEL
ACADEMY HOTEL
JOHN ADAM'S HALL

original and welcoming. Succulent Indonesian vegetarian dishes. Reservation required for the evening. Specialties: acar Melati, mee goreng, sago. £12–£15.

NIGHT LIFE

100 CLUB
100 Oxford Street, W1
Tel: (0171) 636 0933
Open 7.30pm–1am
Fri. 8.30pm–3am.
One of the best discotheques: jazz, rock and blues.

RONNIE SCOTT'S
47 Frith Street, W1
Tel: (0171) 439 0747
Open 8.30pm–3am
Closed Sun. and Christmas.
Famous Soho jazz club, which has been running for thirty-three years. First-class entertainment.

FRENCH HOUSE
49 Dean Street, W1
Tel: (0171) 437 2799
Open noon–11pm
Sun. noon–3pm, 7–10.30pm.
Frequented by French Resistance workers during World War Two, it is now a congenial piano-bar. French wines and champagne. This is the haunt of artists and actors.

BLOOMSBURY

CULTURE

BRITISH LIBRARY
British Museum
Great Russell Street, WC1
Tel: (0171) 323 7111
Open 10am–5pm
Sun. 2.30–6pm

(Exhibition gallery only.) Closed public holidays. Manuscripts and rare books (Gutenberg bible, Shakespeare's first work) on display. Tours of famous reading room.

BRITISH MUSEUM
Great Russell Street, WC1
Tel: (0171) 636 1555
Open 10am–5pm
Sun. 2.30–6pm
Closed public holidays. National collection of archeology, Greek and Oriental art, Egyptian sculptures. Admission free. Temporary exhibitions. Information on (0171) 580 1788.

CRAFTS COUNCIL GALLERY
44A Pentonville Road Islington, N1
Tel: (0171) 278 7700
Open 11am–6pm
Sun. 2–6pm
Closed Mon.
Contemporary and antique crafts. Reference library and information on all aspects of the craft industry.

THOMAS CORAM FOUNDATION
40 Brunswick Square, WC1
Tel: (0171) 278 2424
Open 9.30am–4pm.
Closed Sat., Sun., public holidays and Christmas week.
Offices of the foundling foundation. Exhibition of works by artists (Reynolds, Gainsborough) to raise funds.

DICKENS' HOUSE
48 Doughty Street, WC1
Tel: (0171) 405 2127
Open 10am–4.30pm

Closed Sun., public holidays and Christmas week.
This is where Dickens lived between 1837 and 1839. He wrote many novels here. Portraits, letters and manuscripts on display.

RESTAURANTS

CHAMBALI
146 Southampton Row, WC1
Tel: (0171) 837 3925
Open noon–3pm, 6–12pm.
Very popular Indian restaurant. Friendly atmosphere. First-class cuisine.
£10–£15.

THE HERMITAGE
19 Leigh Street, WC1
Tel: (0171) 387 8034
Open 10am–10.30pm.
You will feel completely at home in this rather "bohemian" setting. Excellent sandwiches. Reservation required. Specialties: French.
£8–£15.

THE MUSEUM TAVERN
49 Great Russell Street, WC1
Tel: (0171) 242 8987
Open 11am–10pm (food), 11pm (drinks).
Really friendly atmosphere in this pub opposite the British Museum. Bona fide English snacks at very reasonable prices.
£5–£8.

PIED-À-TERRE
34 Charlotte Street, W1

Tel: (0171) 636 1178
Open 12.15–2pm, 7.15–10.30pm.
Closed Sat. lunch, Sun.
Impressive French cooking in pleasant surroundings. Extremely friendly service. Amuse-gueules often offered while you're waiting for your food. Set lunch £19.50 three courses. Set dinner £38 three courses.

POONS OF RUSSELL SQUARE
50 Woburn Place, WC1
Tel: (0171) 580 1188
Open noon–3pm, 5.30–11.30pm
Closed at Christmas.
Chinese restaurant which is enormous, elegant but, notwithstanding, very welcoming. All the old favorites in Chinese cuisine, but also some new dishes.
£15–£18.

WAGAMAMA
4 Streatham St
Off Coptic St, WC1
Tel: (0171) 323 9223
Open noon–2.30pm
Mon.–Fri., 1–3pm Sat., 6-11pm Mon.-Sat.
Very popular among students, this cheap Japanese noodle bar has good food and generous portions. Very busy at night – be prepared to queue. Non-smoking.
£6–£10.

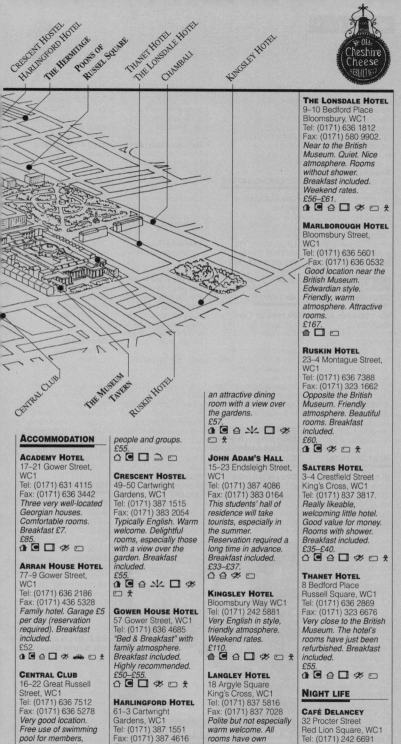

CRESCENT HOSTEL
HARLINGFORD HOTEL
THE HERMITAGE
POONS OF RUSSEL SQUARE
THANET HOTEL
THE LONSDALE HOTEL
CHAMBALI
KINGSLEY HOTEL

Ye Olde Cheshire Cheese REBUILT 1667

CENTRAL CLUB
THE MUSEUM TAVERN
RUSKIN HOTEL

ACCOMMODATION

ACADEMY HOTEL
17–21 Gower Street, WC1
Tel: (0171) 631 4115
Fax: (0171) 636 3442
Three very well-located Georgian houses. Comfortable rooms. Breakfast £7.
£85.

ARRAN HOUSE HOTEL
77–9 Gower Street, WC1
Tel: (0171) 636 2186
Fax: (0171) 436 5328
Family hotel. Garage £5 per day (reservation required). Breakfast included.
£52.

CENTRAL CLUB
16–22 Great Russell Street, WC1
Tel: (0171) 636 7512
Fax: (0171) 636 5278
Very good location. Free use of swimming pool for members, hairdresser, coffee shop. Attractive prices for long stays, rooms for several

people and groups.
£55.

CRESCENT HOSTEL
49–50 Cartwright Gardens, WC1
Tel: (0171) 387 1515
Fax: (0171) 383 2054
Typically English. Warm welcome. Delightful rooms, especially those with a view over the garden. Breakfast included.
£55.

GOWER HOUSE HOTEL
57 Gower Street, WC1
Tel: (0171) 636 4685
"Bed & Breakfast" with family atmosphere. Breakfast included. Highly recommended.
£50–£55.

HARLINGFORD HOTEL
61–3 Cartwright Gardens, WC1
Tel: (0171) 387 1551
Fax: (0171) 387 4616
Typically English and delightful with it. Very friendly atmosphere. Breakfast is served in

an attractive dining room with a view over the gardens.
£57.

JOHN ADAM'S HALL
15–23 Endsleigh Street, WC1
Tel: (0171) 387 4086
Fax: (0171) 383 0164
This students' hall of residence will take tourists, especially in the summer. Reservation required a long time in advance. Breakfast included.
£33–£37.

KINGSLEY HOTEL
Bloomsbury Way WC1
Tel: (0171) 242 5881
Very English in style, friendly atmosphere. Weekend rates.
£110.

LANGLEY HOTEL
18 Argyle Square
King's Cross, WC1
Tel: (0171) 837 5816
Fax: (0171) 837 7028
Polite but not especially warm welcome. All rooms have own shower. English breakfast included.
£25.

THE LONSDALE HOTEL
9–10 Bedford Place
Bloomsbury, WC1
Tel: (0171) 636 1812
Fax: (0171) 580 9902.
Near to the British Museum. Quiet. Nice atmosphere. Rooms without shower. Breakfast included. Weekend rates.
£56–£61.

MARLBOROUGH HOTEL
Bloomsbury Street, WC1
Tel: (0171) 636 5601
Fax: (0171) 636 0532
Good location near the British Museum. Edwardian style. Friendly, warm atmosphere. Attractive rooms.
£167.

RUSKIN HOTEL
23–4 Montague Street, WC1
Tel: (0171) 636 7388
Fax: (0171) 323 1662
Opposite the British Museum. Friendly atmosphere. Beautiful rooms. Breakfast included.
£60.

SALTERS HOTEL
3–4 Crestfield Street
King's Cross, WC1
Tel: (0171) 837 3817.
Really likeable, welcoming little hotel. Good value for money. Rooms with shower. Breakfast included.
£35–£40.

THANET HOTEL
8 Bedford Place
Russell Square, WC1
Tel: (0171) 636 2869
Fax: (0171) 323 6676
Very close to the British Museum. The hotel's rooms have just been refurbished. Breakfast included.
£55.

NIGHT LIFE

CAFÉ DELANCEY
32 Procter Street
Red Lion Square, WC1
Tel: (0171) 242 6691
Open 8am–11pm
Closed Sat., Sun. and public holidays.
A very French café

419

where you can listen to Aznavour and Piaf. Very friendly atmosphere. Rub shoulders here with the business world and the occasional tourist.

PRINCESS LOUISE
208–9 High Holborn, WC1
Tel: (0171) 405 8816
Open 11am–11pm
Sat. 3–6pm
Sun. 2–7pm.
Decorated by Arthur Chitty, this pub is worth a detour. Sandwiches. Music on Saturdays.

EAST END

CULTURE

WHITECHAPEL ART GALLERY
80 Whitechapel High Street, E1
Tel: (0171) 377 0107
Open Tues.-Sun.
11am–5pm, open until 8pm Wed.
Closed Mon. and Christmas.
Art Nouveau gallery designed by Townsend. Temporary exhibitions of modern and contemporary art.

RESTAURANTS

BLOOM'S
90 Whitechapel High Street, E1
Tel: (0171) 247 6001
Open 11am–9.30pm
Closed Fri. after 2.30pm, Sat. and Jewish festivals.
The most famous Jewish restaurant in London. Lavish helpings of food. Not to be missed.
£10–£15.
○ ▭ ⚑ ✾

CITY BUTTERY
85 Aldgate High Street, EC3
Tel: (0171) 480 7287
Open 6.30am–3pm
Closed Sat., Sun. and public holidays.
Cafeteria-style. Quality food for very reasonable prices.
£9–£11.
○ ✾

LAHORE KEBAB HOUSE
2 Umberston Street, EC1
Tel: (0171) 481 9737

Open noon–midnight daily.
Plain setting but excellent value. Authentic Indian cooking.
£8
○ ▭

ACCOMMODATION

GREAT EASTERN HOTEL
Liverpool Street, EC2
Tel: (0171) 283 4363
Fax: (0171) 283 4897.
Large hotel in the center of the City. Breakfast included.
£102
🏛 ▣ ▢ ✾ ▭ ⚑

ANTIQUES

PETTICOAT LANE
Middlesex Street, E1
Open 9am–2pm Sun. only.
One of the most famous flea markets in London, now specializing in clothes and cheap household goods. Brick Lane market is nearby, also on Sun. Bargains to be had. Very popular.

SOUTH OF THE RIVER

CULTURE

DESIGN MUSEUM
Butler's Wharf
Shad Thames, SE1
Tel: (0171) 403 6933
Open 10.30am–5.30pm
Closed Christmas and New Year.

Temporary and permanent exhibitions of the best from the design world.

HAYWARD GALLERY
South Bank Centre, SE1
Tel: (0171) 928 3144
Open 10am–6pm
Open Tues., Wed. till 8pm.
Contemporary and historical art exhibitions. Recorded information on (0171) 261 0127.

LAMBETH PALACE
Lambeth Palace Road, SE1
Tel: (0171) 928 8282.
One of the last stately homes on the banks of the Thames. Owned by the archbishops of Canterbury. Don't miss the Guard Chamber and the Tower. Open to groups only.

LONDON DUNGEON
28 Tooley Street, SE1
Tel: (0171) 403 0606
Open 10am–5.30pm daily
Last admission 4.30pm from Oct. to Mar.
Museum of horrors (instruments of torture) and exhibits, including a recreation of the Great Fire.

MUSEUM OF THE MOVING IMAGE (MOMI)
South Bank
Waterloo, SE1
Tel: (0171) 401 2636
Open 10am–6pm

Closed at Christmas.
Museum of cinema and television. Act out the role of a star or a producer here, or simply watch some old films again.

SHAKESPEARE GLOBE MUSEUM AND ROSE THEATRE EXHIBITION
Bear Gardens
Bankside, SE1
Tel: (0171) 928 6342
Open 10am–5pm
Sun. 2–5pm
Closed public holidays.
On the site of a 15th-century playhouse. Permanent exhibition dealing with Shakespeare's theater and its history.

SOUTHWARK CATHEDRAL
Borough High Street
London Bridge, SE1
Tel: (0171) 407 2939
Open 8.30am–5.30pm
Public holidays 9am–4pm.
Collegiate churches of St Saviour and St Mary. Cathedral on the South Bank. Early Gothic style, restored in the 19th century.

RESTAURANTS

COOKES' EEL AND PIE SHOP
84 The Cut, SE1
Tel: (0171) 928 5931
Open 10.30am–2.30pm
Closed Sun. and Mon.
Excellent "Pies & Mash" in the old London tradition. Only non-alcoholic drinks. Drop in for a quick bite of lunch.
£2–£4.
○

RSJ (RESTAURANT ON THE SOUTH BANK)
13A Coin Street, SE1
Tel: (0171) 928 4554
Open noon–2pm, 6–11pm. Closed Sat. afternoon and Sun.
Restaurant renowned for its selection of wines from the Loire, and also for its original French cuisine. Pre-theater menus. Reservation required for lunch.
£16–£30.
⬓ ▭ ✾

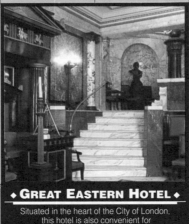

◆ **GREAT EASTERN HOTEL** ◆
Situated in the heart of the City of London, this hotel is also convenient for Liverpool Street station.

ACCOMMODATION

DRISCOLL HOUSE HOTEL
172–180 New Kent Road, SE1
Tel: (0171) 703 4175
Fax: (0171) 703 8013
This boarding house is eighty years old. Warm atmosphere. Simple rooms, shared shower facilities. Breakfast included. Competitive rates for full board (£130 per week). Over eighteen-year-olds only.
£50.
⌂ ✿ 🚗 �

LONDON PARK HOTEL
Brook Drive
Elephant and Castle, SE11
Tel: (0171) 735 9191
Fax: (0171) 582 7688
All the advantages of a large hotel (restaurant, bar). Very close to the Underground. Breakfast included.
£70.
⌂ 🅲 ▢ ✿ 🚗 ▭ �

NIGHT LIFE

GEORGE INN
77 Borough High Street, SE1
Tel: (0171) 407 2056
Open 11am–11pm
An old coaching-inn with open galleries overlooking a cobbled courtyard, this is a very popular haven of peace. Several bars completely fitted out in wood. Sometimes, in the summer, Shakespeare is performed. The restaurant is fairly expensive.

GOOSE AND FIRKIN
47–48 Borough Road, SE1
Tel: (0171) 403 3590
Open noon–11pm Mon.–Fri., Sat. noon–3pm, 7–11pm, Sun. noon–3pm, 7–10.30pm
This pub welcomes both the business community and footballers. It was the first establishment to brew its own beer.
🍺

ANTIQUES

BERMONDSEY MARKET
Bermondsey Street, SE1

Open 4am–2pm Fri. only.
Secondhand goods, clothes, and also antiques.

GREENWICH

CULTURE

CUTTY SARK & GIPSY MOTH IV
Greenwich Pier, SE10
Tel: (0181) 858 3445
Open 10am–6pm
Sun. noon–6pm
Closed 4.30pm in winter.
Naval museum. The Cutty Sark was the last of the tea clippers, and the most famous.

NATIONAL MARITIME MUSEUM
Greenwich, SE10
Tel: (0181) 858 4422
Open 10am–6pm. Sun. noon–6pm.
From Oct. to Mar. open 10am–5pm, Sun. 2–5pm.
Naval museum housing some of the finest exhibits in the world: royal barges and sailing ships, models and other objects of naval interest.

OLD ROYAL OBSERVATORY
Flamsteed House
Greenwich Park, SE10
Tel: (0181) 858 1167
Open 10am–6pm
Closed 5pm in winter.
Former observatory of King Charles II.

It houses the longest telescope in the United Kingdom, a collection of astronomical instruments and watches.

QUEEN'S HOUSE
Greenwich, SE10
Tel: (0181) 858 4422
Opening hours as for National Maritime Museum (above)
The work of architect Inigo Jones, this house is in the style of a Venetian villa. Particular points of interest are the spiral staircase and the loggia. This is also the home of the National Maritime Museum.

ROYAL NAVAL COLLEGE
King William Walk
Greenwich, SE10
Tel: (0181) 858 2154
Open 2.30–4.45pm
Closed Thur..
Former naval hospital designed by the famous architect Sir Christopher Wren. Do not miss the painted dining hall and the chapel which is often used for concerts. Admission free.

RESTAURANTS

GREEN VILLAGE RESTAURANT
11–13 Greenwich Church Street, SE10
Tel: (0181) 858 2348
Open 11am–midnight.
Many of Greenwich's

inhabitants eat in this attractively decorated restaurant. English cuisine.
£7–£12.
○ ▭ ♱ ✿

MEAN TIME RESTAURANT
47–9 Greenwich Church Street, SE10
Tel: (0181) 858 8705
Open noon–2.30pm, 6.30–10pm
Closed Sun. evening and Mon.
Welcoming proprietor, warm atmosphere in very "British" surroundings. Mouth-watering cakes. Tea rooms (10am–5pm). Specialty: jacket potatoes.
£3–£15.
○ ▭ ✿

PLUME OF FEATHERS
19 Park Vista
Greenwich, SE10
Tel: (0181) 858 1661
Open 11am–11pm.
Sun. noon–2.30pm, 7–10.30pm.
Three-hundred-year-old pub (its historical pedigree is on display in the bar). Local clientèle. View of Greenwich Park. English dishes. Specializies in barbecues.
£5–£8.
○ ♱ ✿

ROYAL TEAS
76 Royal Hill
Greenwich, SE10
Tel: (0181) 691 7240
Open 10am–6.30pm.
This tiny, very friendly restaurant-bar serves an incredible range of teas and coffees, as well as meals and homemade cakes. Specialties: vegetarian meals, tea and coffee.
£5–£7.
○

SPREAD EAGLE
1–2 Stockwell Street, SE10
Tel: (0181) 853 2333
Open noon–3pm, 6.30–10.30pm
Closed at Christmas.
The menu, mainly composed of French dishes, changes every month. Friendly atmosphere and service. Pre-theater menus. Reservation

FIRKIN BREWERY
GOOSE & FIRKIN
ESTABLISHED 1979
USQUE AD MORTEM BIBENDUM
SOUTHWARK

47-48 Borough Road, London SE1
Tel: 071-403 3590

required. Specialties:
Scottish grouse,
marquise au chocolat.
£13–£20.
◑ ▭ ☆ ✵

ACCOMMODATION

BARDON LODGE HOTEL
15–17 Stratheden Road
Blackheath, SE3
Tel: (0181) 853 4051
Fax: (0181) 858 7387
*Large Victorian house
with garden and bar.
Very pleasant
surroundings. Warm
atmosphere.
Comfortable rooms.
Breakfast included.
Restaurant in the
evening.*
£65.
⌂ ⊡ ▭ ✵ ⇆
▭ ☆

GREENWICH HOTEL
2 Tunnel Avenue
Greenwich, SE10
Tel: (0181) 293 5566
Fax: (0181) 293 5566
*Delightful hotel, a
typical example of
domestic architecture in
Greenwich. Breakfast
included.*
£39.
⌂ ⌂ ▭ ✵ ⇆ ▭
☆

STONEHALL HOUSE HOTEL
35–7 Westcombe Park
Road, SE3
Tel: (0181) 858 8706
Fax: (089) 525 1948
*Family hotel.
Particularly friendly
atmosphere. Delightful
landscaped garden.
Lovely rooms. Breakfast
included.*
£37.
⌂ ⌂ ⊡ ☼ ▭ ✵
▭ ☆

NIGHT LIFE

CUTTY SARK
Lassell Street
Tel: (0181) 858 3146
Open 11am–11pm,
Sat. and Sun. noon–
3pm, 7–10.30pm.
*The oldest pub in
Greenwich. View over
the Thames. Friendly
atmosphere. Jazz band.*
☼

ANTIQUES

GREENWICH ANTIQUES MARKET
Greenwich High Road,
SE10
Open 8am–4pm
Sat. and Sun. only.
Antiques

GREENWICH ARTS AND CRAFTS COVERED MARKET
Nelson Road, SE10
Open 9am–5pm Sat.
and Sun.
*Broad selection of arts
and crafts, clothing,
jewelry, ceramics,
paintings and
photographs, all
produced by local
artists.*

DOCKLANDS
CULTURE

THAMES BARRIER VISITORS' CENTRE
Unity Way
Woolwich, SE18
Tel: (0181) 854 1373
Open 10am–5pm,
Sat. and Sun. 10.30am–
5.30pm
*Exhibitions focusing on
the barrier designed to
protect London from
floods.*
NIGHT LIFE

MAYFLOWER
117 Rotherhithe Street,
SE16
Tel: (0171) 237 4088
Open noon–3pm,
6–11pm, Sat. 6.30–
11pm, Sun. 7–10.30pm.
*This Tudor inn changed
its name when the
"Pilgrim Fathers" set off
for the New World.
Food is served here.*

PROSPECT OF WHITBY
57 Wapping Wall, E1
Tel: (0171) 481 1095
Open 11.30am–3pm,
5–11pm.
*The oldest pub in the
Docklands (16th
century) with a view
over the Thames. Live
music on Fri. evenings
and Sun.*
☼ ⊭ ▭

TOWN OF RAMSGATE
62 Wapping High
Street, E1
Tel: (0171) 488 2685
Open 11.30am–11pm.
*This is a pub with a
great deal of historical
interest, just by the
Wapping Old Stairs.*
☼

WEST ALONG THE THAMES
CULTURE

CHISWICK HOUSE
Burlington Lane, W4
Tel: (0181) 995 0508
Open 10am–1pm,
2–4pm
Closed at Christmas.
*Set in a garden filled
with classical
monuments, this
prestigious private
residence was
commissioned by the
Earl of Burlington in
1725. Interior designed
by William Kent.*

KEW GARDENS
Kew, Richmond, Surrey
Tel: (0181) 940 1171
Open 9.30am–4pm daily
(glasshouses close at
3.30pm)
*The Royal Botanic
Gardens at Kew house
a vast number of plants,
together with exotic hot
houses.*

SYON HOUSE
Park Road
Brentford, Middlesex
Tel: (0181) 560 0881
Open noon–4.15pm,
from Apr. to Oct. only.
*Sixteenth-century
furnished residence,
redecorated in 1762 by
Robert Adam.
Magnificent gardens.*

RESTAURANTS

OSTERIA ANTICA BOLOGNA
23 Northcote Road,
SW11
Tel: (0171) 978 4771
Open 6–11pm Mon.;
noon–11pm Tues.–Sat.;
12.30–10.30pm Sun.
*Excellent Italian food
in lively setting.*
£15–£20.
◑ ▭ ☆

RIVER CAFÉ
Thames Wharf
Rainville Road, W6
Tel: (0171) 381 8824
Open 12.30–3pm;
7.30–9.15pm Mon.–Sat.,
Sun. 1–3pm
Closed Sat. Sun. night.
*Expensive, but worth
the trek for superb
modern Italian food.*
£30–£40.
◐ ▭ ☆

◆ BARDON LODGE HOTEL ◆
Greenwich is famous for its meridian and
for its monumental architecture, but it is also a
charming village with narrow lanes.

APPENDICES

ESSENTIAL ◆ READING ◆

◆ ACKROYD (P.): *Dickens' London*, Headline Books, 1989.
◆ BARKER (F.): *London: Two Thousand Years of a City and its People*, Macmillan, 1984.
◆ BURKHARDT (W.): *A Guide to the Architecture of London*, Weidenfeld & Nicolson, 1983.
◆ HALSEY (A.H.): *Trends in British Society Since 1900*, London, 1972.
◆ HIBBERT (C.): *London, The Biography of a City*, Longman, 1969.
◆ KITCHEN (P.): *Poets' London*, Longman, 1980.
◆ LAWSON (A.): *Discover Unexpected London*, Phaidon, 1979.
◆ LEBRECHT (N.): *Music in London: a History and Handbook*, Aurum Press, 1991.
◆ LLOYD (T.O.): *Empire to Welfare State, 1906–76*, 2nd ed., Oxford University Press, 1979.
◆ MITCHELL (R.J.): *A History of London Life*, Penguin, 1969.
◆ PALIS (L.M.): *The Blue Plaques of London*, Equation, Wellingborough, 1989.
◆ PEVSNER (N.): *London*, Penguin, 1973.
◆ PIPER (D.): *Artists' London*, Weidenfeld & Nicolson, 1982.
◆ WEINREB (B.) and HIBBERT (C.): *The London Encyclopaedia*, Dictionary of London Ltd, Macmillan, 1983.

◆ GENERAL ◆

◆ ALFRY (S.): *London Life*, Wayland, Hove, 1978.
◆ BETJEMAN (J.): *Victorian and Edwardian London from Old Photographs*, Batsford, 1969.
◆ BUSH (G.), DIXEN (H.) BOOL (A.) and BOOL (J.): *Old London*, Academy Editions, 1975.
◆ CAMERON (R.): *Above London*, Bodley Head, 1980.
◆ CLAYTON (R.): *Portrait of London*, Robert Hale (Portrait Books), 1980.
◆ *A Cockney Camera* (Compiled by G. Winter), Penguin, 1975.
◆ CRACKNELL (B.): *Portrait of London's River*, 2nd edn, Hale, 1980.
◆ FITZGIBBON (T.): *A Taste of London*, Pan Books, 1976.
◆ FRIEDMAN (J.), photographer: Aprahamian (P.): *Inside London: Discovering London's Period Interiors*, Phaidon, 1988.
◆ GENTLEMAN (D.): *London*, Weidenfeld & Nicolson, 1986.
◆ GIROUARD (M.): *Victorian Pubs*, Studio Vista and Yale University Press, 1975.
◆ GREEN (Benny.): *London*, Oxford University Press, 1984.
◆ JACOBS (M.): *Art in London*, Jarrold, Norwich 1980.
◆ LEJEUNE (A.): *The Gentlemen's Clubs of London*, Macdonald & Jane's, 1979.
◆ NELSON (W.H.): *The Londoners*, Hutchinson, 1975.
◆ NORRIE (I.): *A Celebration of London*, André Deutsch, 1984.
◆ PEARLMUTTER (K.): *London Street Markets*, Wildwood, 1983.
◆ UNDERWOOD (P.): *Haunted London*, Fontana, 1975.
◆ WITCHOUSE (R.): *A London Album: Early Photographs Recording the History of the City and its People from 1840 to 1915*, Secker & Warburg, 1980.
◆ WITTICH (J.): *London Villages*, Shire Publications, Aylesbury, reprinted 1992.

URBAN ◆ DEVELOPMENT◆

◆ BETJEMAN (J.): *London's Historic Railway Stations*, John Murray, 1978.
◆ BIGNELL (J.): *Chelsea Seen from its Earliest Days*, 2nd ed., Robert Hale, 1987.
◆ DAY (J.R.): *The Story of London's Underground*, London Transport Executive, 1974.
◆ DROGHEDA (C.G.P.M.): *The Covent Garden Album: 250 Years of Theatre, Opera and Ballet*, Routledge & Kegan Paul, 1981.
◆ DYOS (H.J.) and WOLFF (M.): *The Victorian City: Images and Realities*, 2 vols., Routledge & Kegan Paul, 1973.
◆ HARRISON (M.): *The London that was Rome. The Imperial City Recreated by the New Archeology: the Remapping of Londinium Augusta, Capital of Maxima Caesariensis. Chief of the Four Provinces of Britain*, Allen & Unwin, 1971.
◆ LOBEL (M.D.): *The City of London from Prehistoric Times to c. 1520*, Oxford University Press, 1989.
◆ *London 1500–1700: The Making of the Metropolis*, (ed. A.L. Barir, R. Finlay), Longman, 1986.
◆ *London Docklands: Past, Present and Future*, (edited by S.K. al Naib), Thames & Hudson, 1990.
◆ *The Making of Modern London*, 4 vols.: *1815–1914* by G. Weightman and S. Humphries; *1914–39*, by G. Weightman and S. Humphries; *1939–45*, by G. Weightman and J. Taylor; *1945–85*, by J. Mack and S. Humphries, Sidgwick and Jackson, *1984–6*
◆ MARSDEN (P.): *Roman London*, Thames & Hudson, 1986.
◆ MEARS (K.J.): *The Tower of London: Nine Hundred Years of English History*, Phaidon, 1988.
◆ OLSEN (D.J.): *Town Planning in London: the 18th and 19th Centuries*, Yale University Press, 1964; *The Growth of Victorian London*, Batsford, 1976.
◆ ROSE (M.): *The East End of London*, C. Chivers, 1973.
◆ STAMP (G.): *The Changing Metropolis: Earliest Photographs of London, 1839–79*, Viking, 1984.
◆ THOMPSON (F.M.L.): *The Rise of Suburbia*, Leicester University Press, 1982.
◆ TRENT (C.): *Greater London: its Growth and Development through Two Thousand Years*, Phoenix House, 1965.
◆ YOUNG (K.) and GARSIDE (P.L.): *Metropolitan London: Politics and Urban Change, 1837–1981*, Edward Arnold, 1982.

◆ HISTORY ◆

◆ BARKER (F.) and JACKSON (P.): *The History of London in Maps*, Barrie & Jenkins, 1990.
◆ BARKER (T.C.) and ROBBINS (M.): *A History of London Transport*, 2 vols., Allen & Unwin, 1974.
◆ BARTLETT (C.J.): *A History of Post-war Britain, 1945–74*, London, 1977.
◆ BOLTON (J.L.): *The Medieval English Economy 1150–1500*, London, 1980.
◆ BUSHELL (P.): *London's Secret History*, Constable, 1983.
◆ *The Cambridge Historical Encyclopaedia of Great Britain and Northern Ireland*, (Edited by C. Haigh), Cambridge University Press, 1985.
◆ CAMPBELL (J.): *The Anglo-Saxons*, Penguin, 1991.
◆ CHURCHILL (Winston.): *A History of the English-speaking Peoples*, first publ. 1951–6, Cassell, 1991.
◆ COWARD (B.): *The Stuart Age*, Longman, 1980.
◆ DAVIS (J.): *Reforming London: the London Government Problem 1855–1900*, Clarendon Press, 1990.
◆ *The English Parliament in the Middle Ages* (edited by R.G. Davies and J.H. Denton, Manchester, 1981.
◆ MARGRETSON (S.): *Regency London*, Cassell, 1971.
◆ MERRIFIELD (R.): *London: City of the Romans*, Batsford, 1983.
◆ MOSLEY (L.): *London under Fire: 1939–45*, Pan Books, 1971.
◆ OWEN (J.B.): *The Eighteenth Century, 1714–1815*, London, 1974.
◆ *The Oxford Illustrated History of Britain* (edited by K.O. Morgan), Oxford University Press, 1984.
◆ ROSEN (A.): *Rise Up Women*, London, 1974.
◆ RUDÉ (G.): *Hanoverian London 1714–80*, Secker and Warburg, 1971.
◆ RUSSEL (C.): *The Crisis of Parliaments 1509–1660*, Oxford, 1971.
◆ STRONG (R.): *The Cult of Elizabeth: Elizabethan Portraiture and Pageantry*, Thames & Hudson, 1977.
◆ THOMPSON (E.P.): *The Making of the English Working Class*, London, 1963.
◆ TRENCH (R.): *London under London*, John Murray, 1984.

◆ WHITE (H.P.): *London Railways History*, David & Charles, 1971.
◆ WILLIAMS (G.A.): *Medieval London: from Commune to Capital*, London, 1963

◆ GEOGRAPHY ◆

◆ *Atlas of London and the Region* (edited by E. Jones and D.J. Sinclair), Pergamon Press, 1969.
◆ DYOS (H.J.): *Collins's Illustrated Atlas of London*, Leicester University Press, 1973.
◆ *The Geography of Greater London* (edited by R. Clayton), G. Philip & Son, 1964.
◆ HOWGEGO (J.): *Printed Maps of London circa 1553–1850*, Dawson & Son, Folkestone, 1978.
◆ RAYNS (A.W.): *The London Region*, G. Bell, 1971.

◆ NATURE ◆

◆ CROWE (A.): *The Parks and Woodlands of London*, Fourth Estate, 1987.
◆ FITTER (R.S.R.): *London's Natural History*, Collins, 1945; reprinted Bloomsbury, 1990.
◆ McLEOD (D.): *The Gardener's London: Four Centuries of Gardening, Gardeners and Garden Usage*, Duckworth, 1972.

◆ TRADITIONS ◆

◆ COLLOWAY (S.): *The House of Liberty: Masters of Style and Decoration*, Thames & Hudson, 1992.
◆ *The Criers and Hawkers of London* (edited by S. Shesgreen, with engravings and drawings by M. Laroon), Stanford University Press, 1990.
◆ FRANKLIN (J.): *The Cockney. A survey of London Life and Language*, André Deutsch, 1953.

◆ SOCIETY ◆

◆ ALDERMAN (G.): *London Jewry and London Politics: 1889–1986*, Routledge, 1989.
◆ ALEXANDER (S.): *Women's Work in Nineteenth Century London*, Journeyman, 1983.

◆ ANDREW (D.T.): *Philanthropy and Police: London Charity in the 18th Century*, Princeton University Press, 1989.
◆ ARCHER (I.W.): *The Pursuit of Stability: Social Relations in Elizabethan London*, Cambridge University Press, 1991.
◆ AUBREY (J.): *Brief Lives*, Penguin, 1962.
◆ BISHOP (J.): *Social History of the First World War*, Angus & Robertson, 1982.
◆ BRANDT (B.): *London in the Thirties*, Gordon Fraser, 1983.
◆ BRIGGS (A.): *The Age of Improvement*, London, 1959.
◆ CRUICKSHANK (D.): *Life in the Georgian City*, Viking, 1990.
◆ DEKREY (G.S.): *A Fractured Society: the Politics of London in the First Age of Party 1688–1715*, Clarendon Press, 1985.
◆ *Development of English Society* (edited by D. Marshall), 4 vols., Charles Scribner's 1973–9.
◆ DU BOULAY (F.R.H.): *An Age of Ambition*, London, 1970.
◆ FOSTER (J.): *The Class Struggle in the Industrial Revolution*, London, 1974.
◆ GEORGE (M.D.): *London Life in the Eighteenth Century*, London, 1925.
◆ HARRIS (T.): *London Crowds in the Reign of Charles II: Propaganda and Politics from the Restoration until the Exclusion*, Cambridge University Press, 1987.
◆ *The History of British Society 1832–1939*, 7 vols. (edited by E.J. Hobsbawn), Weidenfeld & Nicolson, 1971
◆ HOOK (J.): *The Baroque Age in England*, Thames & Hudson, 1976.
◆ JONES (G.S.): *Outcast London*, Penguin, 1976.
◆ JORDAN (W.K.): *The Charities of London 1480–1660. The Aspirations and the Achievements of the Urban Society*, Allen & Unwin, 1960.
◆ LANDES (D.): *The Unbound Prometheus: Technological Change 1750 to the Present*, Cambridge, 1969.
◆ LASLETT (P.): *The World we Have Lost*, London, 1971.

◆ LEES LYNN (H.): *Exiles of Erin, Irish Migrants in Victorian London*, Manchester University Press, 1979.
◆ MALCOMSON (R.W.): *Life and Labour in England, 1700–80*, Hutchinson, 1981.
◆ MARWICK (A.): *The Explosion of British Society, 1914–70*, Macmillan, 1971.
◆ MOWAT (C.L.): *Britain Between the Wars*, London, 1955.
◆ NEEDHAM (L.W.): *Fifty Years of Fleet Street*, Michael Joseph, 1973.
◆ PALLISER (D.M.): *The Age of Elizabeth*, London, 1983.
◆ PELLING (H.): *A History of British Trade Unionism*, 2nd ed., London 1971.
◆ PERKIN (H.): *The Origins of Modern English Society, 1780–1880*, Routledge & Kegan Paul, 1969; *The Rise of Professional Society. England since 1880*. Routledge & Kegan Paul, 1989.
◆ PORTER (R.): *English Society in the Eighteenth Century*, Penguin, 1984.
◆ SEAMAN (L.C.B.): *Life in Victorian London*, Batsford, 1973.
◆ SHEPHERD (J.): *A Social Atlas of London*, Clarendon Press, 1974.
◆ SMITH (C.M.): *Curiosity of London Life or Phases, Physiological and Social, of the Great Metropolis*, F. Cass, 1972.
◆ *Society and Industry in the 19th Century: a Documentary Approach*, 6 vols. (edited by K. Dawson and P. Wall), Oxford University Press, 1968–70.
◆ STEDMAN (J.): *Outcast London: a Study in Relationship between Classes in Victorian Society*, Oxford University Press, 1971.
◆ STENTON (D.M.): *English Society in the Early Middle Ages 1066–1307*, 2nd ed., Penguin, 1952.
◆ STONE (L.): *The Crisis of the Aristocracy*, Oxford University Press, 1965; *The Family, Sex and Marriage, 1500–1800*, Weidenfeld & Nicolson, 1977.
◆ THOMPSON (F.M.L.): *The Cambridge Social History of Britain*, Cambridge University

Press, 1990
◆ *The Victorian City* (edited by H.J. Dyos and M. Wolff), 2 vols., London 1973.
◆ WALKOWITZ (J.R.): *City of Dreadful Delight: Narrative of Sexual Danger in Late Victorian London*, Virago, 1992.
◆ WHITE (J.): *The Worst Street in North London, Campbell Bunk, Islington between the Wars*, Routledge & Kegan Paul, 1986.
◆ WILKES (J.): *The London Police in the 19th Century*, Cambridge University Press, 1977.
◆ WRIGHTSON (K.): *English Society 1580–1680*, Hutchinson, 1983.
◆ YOUNG (G.M.): *Victorian England: the Portrait of an Age*, Oxford, 1936.
◆ YOUNG (M.) and WILLMOTT (P.): *Family and Kinship in East London*, Routledge, 1957; *Family and Clan in a London Suburb*, Routledge, 1960.

◆ RELIGION ◆

◆ BARLOW (F.): *The English Church 1066–1154*, Longman, 1979
◆ BEDE: *Ecclesiastical History of the English People*, trans. L. Sherley-Price, rev. ed., Penguin, 1968.
◆ BOOTH (C.): *Life and Labour of the People in London. Third Series: Religious Influence*, 7 vols., Macmillan, 1902–1904: Ams Press, New York 1970.
◆ CHADWICK (O.): *The Victorian Church*, 2 vols., 3rd ed., London, 1973
◆ COBB (G.): *London City Churches*, Batsford, 1977.
◆ GAY (J.D.): *The Geography of Religion in Britain*, Duckworth, 1971.
◆ HARVEY (B.): *Westminster Abbey and its Estate in the Middle Ages*, Oxford University Press, 1977.
◆ HIBBERT (C.): *London's Churches*, Queen Anne Press, 1988.
◆ KENYON (J.P.): *The Popish Plot*, London, 1972.
◆ LAMONT (W.N.): *Godly Rules: Politics and Religion 1603–60*, Macmillan, 1969.

◆ BIBLIOGRAPHY

◆ LIU (T.): *Puritan London: a Study of Religion and Society in the City Parishes*, University of Delaware Press, Associated Uni Corp., 1986.

◆ MCGRATH (P.): *Papists and Puritans under Elizabeth I*, London, 1967.

◆ PETTIGREW (A.): *Foreign Protestant Communities in 16th-Century London*, Clarendon Press, 1986.

◆ *Radical Religion in the English Revolution* (edited by J.F. McGregor and B. Reay), Oxford University Press, 1986.

◆ REARDON (B.M.G.): *From Coleridge to Gore. A Century of Religious Thought in Britain*, Longman, 1971.

◆ THOMAS (K.): *Religion and the Decline of Magic*, London, 1971.

◆ Young (E.): *Old London Churches*, Faber & Faber, 1956.

ARCHITECTURE AND ◆ SCULPTURE ◆

◆ ASTAIRE (L.), photographer BOYS (M.): *Living in London*, Thames and Hudson, 1990.

◆ BAKER (M.): *London Statues and Monuments*, Shire Publications, reprinted 1992.

◆ BYRON (A.): *London Statues: a Guide to London's Outdoor Statues and Sculptures*, Constable, 1981.

◆ CAMPBELL (K.): *Home Sweet Home: Housing Designed by the London County Council and Greater London Council Architects: 1888–1975*, Academy Editions, 1976.

◆ CROOK (J.M.): *The British Museum: a Case Study in Architectural Politics*, Penguin, 1972.

◆ CRUICKSHANK (D.): *London: the Art of Georgian Building*, Architectural Press, 1975.

◆ DOWNES (K.): *Hawksmoor*, rev. ed., Thames & Hudson, 1987.

◆ HEAL (A.): *The London Furniture Makers from the Restoration to the Victorian Era: 1660–1840*, Dover, 1972.

◆ *A History of English Architecture* (edited by

P. Kidson, P. Murray and P. Thompson), London 1979.

◆ MORDAUNT COOK (J.): *Victorian Architecture: a Visual Anthology*, Johnson Reprint Corp., New York, 1971.

◆ NELLIST (J.B.): *British Architecture and its Background*, Macmillan, London, St Martin's Press, New York, 1967.

◆ OLSEN (D.J.): *The City as a Work of Art: London, Paris, Vienna*, Yale University Press, 1986.

◆ PEARCE (D.): *London's Mansions: the Palatial Houses of the Nobility*, Batsford, 1986

◆ PEVSNER (N) and CHERRY (B.): *The Buildings of England: London*, vol. 1: *The Cities of London and Westminster*, vol. 2: *South*, vol. 3: *North West*, Penguin, 1973, 1983, 1991.

◆ PORT (M.H.): *The Houses of Parliament*, Yale University Press, 1976.

◆ ROSENEAU (H.): *Social Purpose in Architecture. Paris and London 1760–1800*, Studio Vista, 1970.

◆ SAUNDERS (A.): *The Art and Architecture of London: an Illustrated Guide*, Phaidon, 1984.

◆ SCHOFIELD (J.): *The Building of London from the Conquest to the Great Fire*, British Museum Publications, 1984.

◆ SERVICE (A.): *The Architects of London and their Buildings: from 1066 to the Present Day*, Architectural Press, 1979. *London: 1900*, Granada, 1979.

◆ SUMMERSON (J.N.): *The London Building World of the Eighteen-sixties*, Thames & Hudson, 1974; *The Architecture of Victorian London*, University Press of Virginia, 1976; *Architecture in Britain: 1530 to 1830*, Penguin, 1977; *Georgian London*, rev. ed., Penguin, 1978. *The Life and Works of John Nash, Architect*, Allen & Unwin, 1981.

◆ THACKRAH (J.R.): *The Royal Albert Hall*, T. Dalton, 1983.

◆ *Victorian London*, Victorian Society/London

Transport Executive, 1975.

◆ WHINNEY (M.): *Wren*, Thames & Hudson, 1985.

◆ LITERATURE ◆

◆ ACKROYD (P.): *Hawksmoor*, Abacus Books, 1986

◆ CONAN DOYLE (A.): *The Penguin Complete Adventures of Sherlock Holmes*, Penguin, 1984.

◆ *A Personal Record*, J.M. Dent & Sons, 1975.

◆ CONRAD (J.): *The Secret Agent* (edited by R. Tennant), Oxford University Press, 1983.

◆ DICKENS (C.): *Oliver Twist*, (edited by K. Tillotson), Oxford University Press, 1982; *A Tale of Two Cities* (edited by G. Woodcock), Penguin, 1970; *The Old Curiosity Shop* (edited by A. Basson), Penguin, 1972.

◆ FORSTER (E.M): *Howard's End*, Penguin, 1989.

◆ JAMES (H.): *Washington Square*, Penguin, 1984.

◆ JAMES (P.D.): *A Mind to Murder*, Penguin, 1963.

◆ KEROUAC (J.): *The Lonesome Traveler*, Paladin, 1990.

◆ *London in Verse* (edited by C Logue), Secker & Warburg, 1982.

◆ STEVENSON (R.L.): *Dr Jekyll and Mr Hyde*, Dover Publications, 1991.

◆ UPDIKE (J.): *Bech: a Book*, Penguin, 1972.

◆ WILDE (O.): *The Picture of Dorian Gray*, Oxford University Press, 1981.

FIRST-HAND ◆ ACCOUNTS ◆

◆ HANFF (H.): *84 Charing Cross Road*, Futura Publications, 1979.

◆ *The Illustrated Pepys* (edited by R.C. Latham), London, 1978.

◆ ORWELL (G.): *Down and Out in Paris and London* (edited by D. Murphy), Penguin, 1989.

◆ TRENCH (S.): *Bury Me in my Boots*, Hodder & Stoughton, 1983.

◆ WOOLF (V.): *The London Scene*, Hogarth Press, 1982.

CRITICAL ◆ WORKS ◆

◆ BAER (M.): *Theatre and Disorder in Late Georgian London*, Clarendon Press, 1992.

◆ BRADBROOK (M.C.): *The Living Monument: Shakespeare and the Theatre of his Time*,, Cambridge University Press, 1977.

◆ BYRD (M.): *London Transformed: Images of the City in the 18th Century*, Yale University Press, 1978.

◆ CHALFANT (F.C.): *Ben Jonson's London*, University of Georgia Press, 1978.

◆ COLLINS (P.): *Trollope's London*, University of Leicester, 1982.

◆ GARDNER (J.): *Yeats and the Rhymer's Club: a Nineties' Perspective*, P. Lang, 1989.

◆ GROSS (J.): *Rise and Fall of the English Man of Letters*, London, 1969.

◆ HARRISON (M.): *The London of Sherlock Holmes*, David & Charles, 1972.

◆ HEWISON (R.): *Under Siege: Literary Life in London 1939–45*, Weidenfeld & Nicolson, 1977.

◆ HODGES (W.C.): *Shakespeare's Second Globe: the Missing Monument*, Oxford University Press, 1973.

◆ KIMMEY (J.L.): *Henry James and London: the City in his Fiction*, P. Lang, 1991.

◆ *Literature and the Social Order in Eighteenth-Century England* (edited by S. Copley), Croom Helm, 1984.

◆ LUCAS (V.): *Tolstoy in London*, Evans Bros., 1979.

◆ *The Pelican Guide to English Literature* (Edited by B. Ford), Penguin, 1973.

◆ SCHWARZBACH (F.S.): *Dickens and the City*, Athlone Press, 1979.

◆ WEINTRAUB (S.): *The London Yankees*, W.H. Allen, 1979.

◆ MUSIC ◆

◆ HOGWOOD (C.): *Handel*, Thames & Hudson, 1988.

◆ MACKERNESS (E.D.): *A Social History of English Music*, Routledge & Kegan Paul, 1964.

◆ MILLIGAN (T.B.): *The Concerto and London's*

Musical CUuture in the Late Eighteenth Century, UMI Research Press, 1983.
◆ ORGA (A.): *The Proms*, David & Charles, 1974.
◆ POHL (C.F.) *Mozart and Haydn in London*, Da Capo Press, 1970.
◆ WEBER (W.): *Music and the Middle class: the Social Structure of Concert Life in London, Paris and Vienna*, 1975.
◆ YOUNG (P.): *A History of British Music*, London, 1967.

PAINTING AND DECORATIVE ◆ ARTS ◆

◆ ANSCOMBE (I.): *Omega and After: Bloomsbury and the Decorative Arts*, Thames & Hudson, 1985.
◆ ARCHER (M.): *Indian Painting for the British: 1770–1880*, Oxford University Press., 1955.
◆ BINDMAN (D.): *Hogarth*, Thames & Hudson, 1981.
◆ BLAYNEY BROWN (D.): *The Art of J.M.W. Turner*, Headline, 1990.
◆ *British Art and the Modern Movement, 1930–40*, exh. cat. Arts Council, 1962.
◆ COOPER (J.): *Victorian and Edwardian Furniture and Interiors: from the Gothic Revival to Art Nouveau*, Thames & Hudson, 1987.
◆ DE MARÉ (E.): *The London Doré Saw: a Victorian Evocation*, Saint Martin's Press, 1973.
FARR (D.): *English Art 1870–1940*, Oxford, 1978.
◆ GAUNT (W.): *English Painting: a Concise History*, Thames & Hudson, 1985.
◆ HARRIS (M.): *The Artist and the Country House*, 1979.
◆ HILTON (T.): *The Pre-Raphaelites*, Thames & Hudson, 1970.
◆ HUTCHISON (H.C.): *The History of the Royal Academy, 1768–1968*, 1968.
◆ MURDOCH (J.), MURRELL (J.), NOON (P.) and STRONG (R.): *The English Miniature*, 1981.
◆ PIPER (D.): *The English Face*, 1957; *The Genius of British Painting*, Weidenfeld & Nicolson, 1975.
◆ PRESTON (H.): *London and the Thames: Paintings of Three Centuries*, exh. cat.,

National Maritime Museum, undated.
◆ ROSENTHAL (M.): *British Landscape Painting*, 1982; *Constable*, Thames & Hudson, 1987.
◆ SHONE (R.): *Bloomsbury Portraits: Vanessa Bell, Duncan Grant and their Circle*, Phaidon, 1976
◆ SUNDERLAND (J.):*Painting in Britain: 1525–1975*, Phaidon, 1976.
◆ *The Thames & Hudson Encyclopaedia of British Art* (edited by D. Bindman), Thames & Hudson, 1985.
◆ TREVHERZ (J.): *Victorian Painting*, Thames & Hudson, 1993.
◆ WALPOLE (H.): *Anecdotes of Painting in England, 1762–80*, Penguin, 1954.
◆ WATERHOUSE (E.): *Painting in Britain 1530 to 1790*, Penguin, 1954.
◆ *William Morris: Selected Writings and Designs*, (edited by A. Briggs), London, 1962.

◆ GUIDES ◆

◆ ADBURGHAM (A.): *Shopping in Style*, Thames & Hudson, 1979.
◆ BAILEY (C.): *Harrap's Guide to Famous London Graves*, Harraps, 1975.
◆ BANKS (F.R.): *The Penguin Guide to London*, 7th ed., Penguin, 1977.
◆ BARKER (F.) and SILVESTER CARR (D.): *The Black Plague Guide to London*, Constable, 1987.
◆ BLACKWOOD (A.): *London: a Times Bartholomew Guide*, Times Books, 1987.
◆ BORER (M.C.): *London Walks and Legends*, Granada, 1981.
◆ BUSHELL (P.): *London's Secret History*, Constable, 1983.
◆ CLARKE (J.): *In our Grandmothers' Footsteps*, Virago, 1984.
◆ DAVIES (A.) and HAZELTON (F.): *Walk in London: Forty Selected Walks in Central London*, John Bartholomew & Son (A Bartholomew Map and Guide), Edinburgh, 1988.
◆ DOWNIE (R.A.): *Murder in London: a Topological Guide to*

Famous Crimes, A. Barker, 1973.
◆ DUNCAN (F.), GLASS (L.) AND SHARPE (C.): *London up Close*, Passport Books, Lincolnwood (Chicago), 1992.
◆ FAIRFAX (B.): *Walking London's Waterways*, David & Charles, 1985.
◆ *Fodor's London*, Hodder & Stoughton, 1979.
◆ GIBSON (P.): *The Capital Companion: a Street-by-street Guide to London and its Inhabitants*, Webb & Bower, 1985.
◆ GREEN (M.): *A Guide to London's Best Pubs*, Virgin, 1982.
◆ KAY (F.G.): *London*, rev. ed., Collins, 1984.
◆ LANE (E.): *A Guide to Literary London*, Hippocrene Books, undated.
◆ *London*, Michelin Guide, 1990.
◆ *London*, Blue Guide, 1990.
◆ PEARSON (M.M.): *Discovering London for Children*, 6th ed., Shire Publications, Aylesbury, 1983.
◆ PEPLOW (M.): *London for Free*, Panther, 1984.
◆ SAUNDERS (N.): *Alternative London*, 5th ed., WIldwood House, 1977.
◆ TWORT (D.): *London (Guide in Jeans)*, Octopus, 1980.
◆ WILLIAMS (G.): *Guide to Literary London*, Batsford, 1973.
◆ WITTICH (J.): *Discovering London Street Names*, Shire Publications, Aylesbury, reprinted 1990.

◆ MUSEUMS ◆

◆ DANTO (E.): *Undiscovered Museums of London*, Surrey Books, Chicago, 1991.
◆ FARR (D.) and NEWMAN (J.): *Guide to the Courtauld Institute Galleries at Somerset House*, Courtauld Institute of Art, 1990.
◆ GRAVES (A.): *Treasures of the Royal Academy*, 1963.
◆ *Guide to London Museums and Galleries*, Her Majesty's Stationery Office, 1974.
◆ INGAMELLS (J.): *The Wallace Collection*, Scala, 1990.
◆ *The National Gallery, London* (intro. by M. Wilson), Letts, 1978.

◆ *The National Maritime Museum* (edited by B. Greenhill), Philip Wilson, 1982.
◆ NICOLSON (B.): *The Treasures of the Foundling Hospital*, 1972.
◆ *The Tate Gallery: an Illustrated Companion to the National Collections of British and Foreign Modern Art*, Tate Gallery Publications, 1979.
◆ *The Victoria and Albert Museum*, Scala, 1991.

ACKNOWLEDGEMENTS

We would like to thank the following publishers or copyright-holders for permission to reproduce the quotations on pages 105–20.

◆ HARCOURT BRACE & COMPANY and FABER AND FABER LTD: Excerpt from "The Waste Land" in *Collected Poems 1909–1962* by T.S. Eliot, copyright © 1963, 1964 by T.S. Eliot. Rights outside the U.S. administered by Faber and Faber Ltd., London. Reprinted by permission of the publishers.

◆ HARCOURT BRACE & COMPANY and A.M. HEATH & COMPANY LTD: Excerpt from *Down and Out in Paris and London* by George Orwell, copyright © 1933 by George Orwell, copyright renewed 1961 by Sonia Pitt-Rivers. Rights outisde the U.S. administered by A.M. Heath & Company Ltd, London on behalf of the Estate of the late Sonia Brownell Orwell and Martin Secker & Warburg Ltd. Reprinted by permission of the publishers.

◆ VIKING PENGUIN and PETERS FRASER & DUNLOP: Excerpt from *Money* by Martin Amis, copyright © 1984 by Martin Amis. Rights outside the U.S. administered by Peters Fraser & Dunlop Group Ltd. Reprinted by permission of Viking Penguin, a division of Penguin Books U.S.A. Inc., and the Peters Fraser & Dunlop Group Ltd.

◆ LIST OF ILLUSTRATIONS

◆ LIST OF ILLUSTRATIONS

◆ LIST OF ILLUSTRATIONS

We have not been able to trace the heirs or publishers of certain documents. An account is being held open for them at our offices.

INDEX

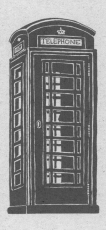

STREET MAPS
OF
CENTRAL LONDON

LONDON STREET MAP KEY

KEY TO SYMBOLS ON THE STREET MAPS

Main through road

Main street

Other street

Pedestrian zone

Steps

Road under construction

Train station and railway line

O BARBICAN   Underground station

Place of outstanding interest

Important sight or place of interest

Other sight or place of interest

Catholic church

Protestant church

△   Public office

▫   Hotel

•   Restaurant

Youth hostel

Å   Campsite

✚   Hospital

Garden or park

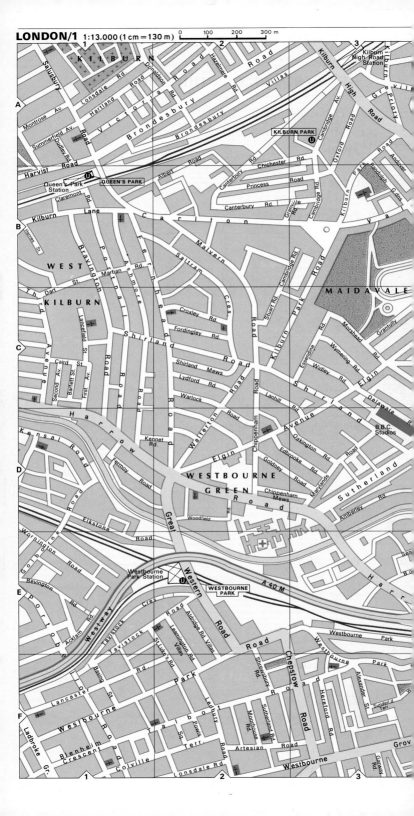

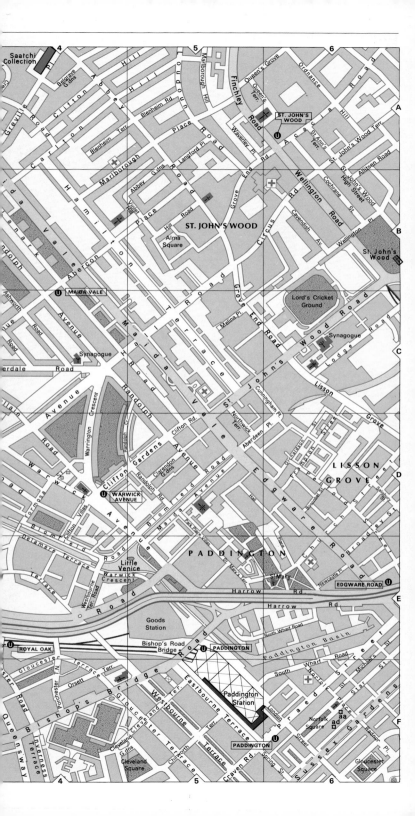

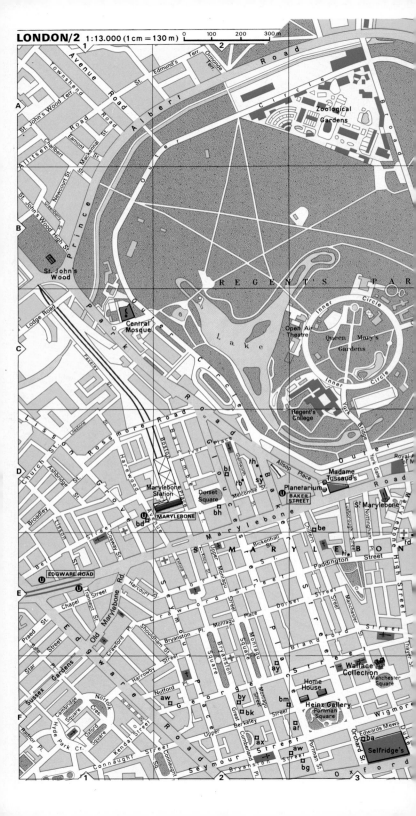

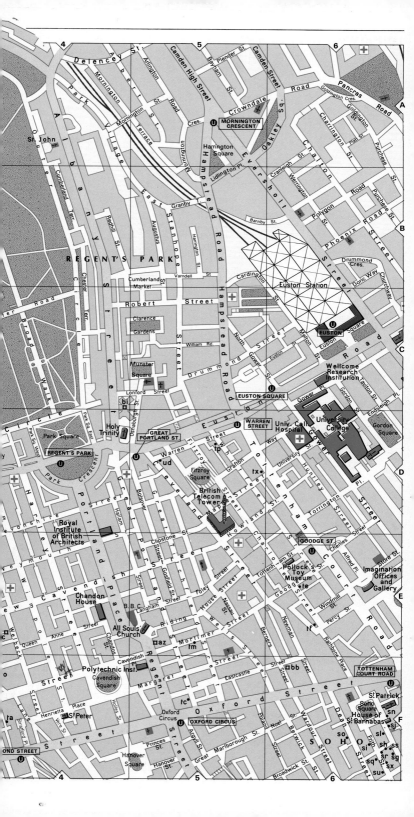

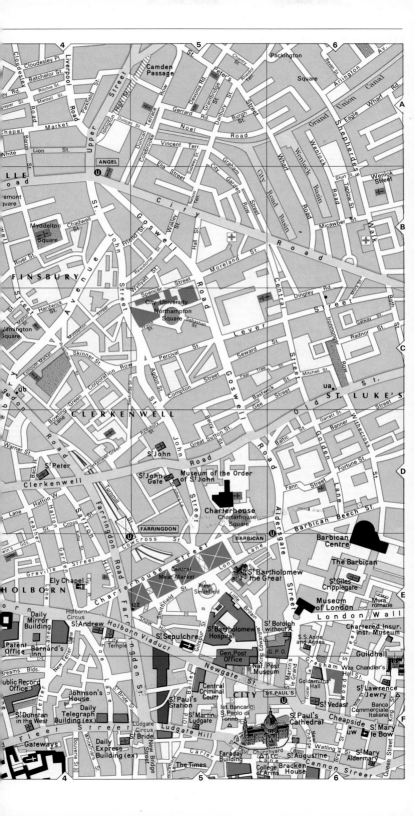

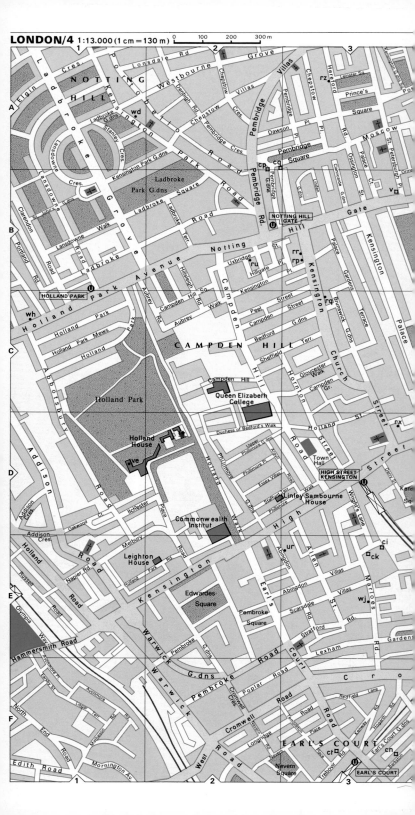

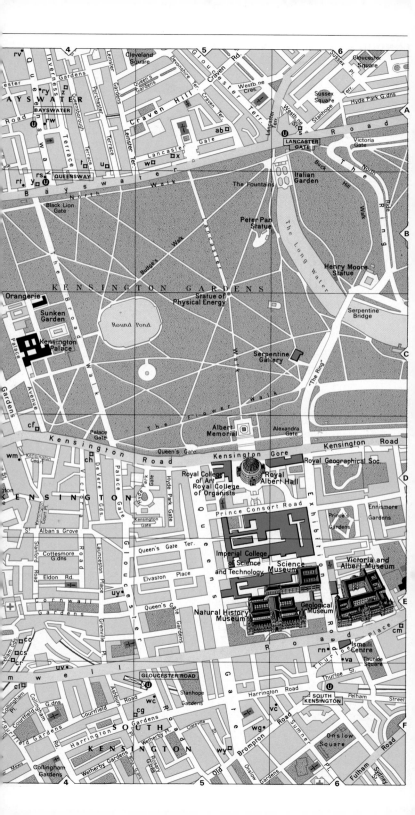

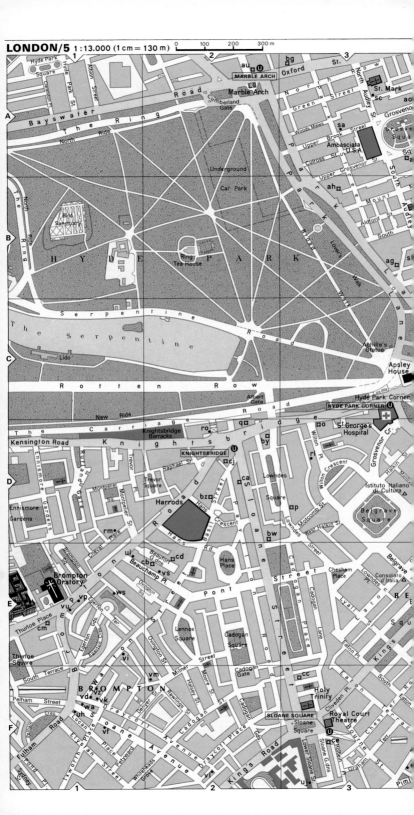

0   100   200   300 m

1   2   3

Hyde Park
Square

Hyde Park St.

Albion Street

Bayswater

The Ring

North Ride

bg

au U

MARBLE ARCH

Oxford   St.

Marble Arch

Cumberland
Gate

North Row

Green   Street

North Audley St.

St. Mark

sc

ao

A

Woods Mews

Upper   Brook   Street

sa

Grosveno

Grosve
Squa

Ambasciata
U.S.A

Cutross St.

Upper Grosvenor St.

South   Audley   St.

Sq

The North Ride

Underground
Car Park

ah

Mount

Audley

B

Bird
Sanctuary

H   Y   D   E   P   A   R   K

Ring
Tea House

Aldford   St.

ag

South

Lover's

Walk

Lane

sl

The Serpentine

Serpentine   Road

The   Serpentine

Lido

Achille's
Statue

Apsley
House

C

R   o   t   t   e   n   R   o   w

New   Ride

Albert
Gate

Hyde Park Corner

HYDE PARK CORNER U

Hyde Park   Corner

S! George's
Hospital

Grosvenor Cr.

Halkin

Montc

The   Carriage

Knightsbridge
Barracks

ro

q

ri   d   g   e

do

Wilton

Pl

Kensington Road   K   n   i   g   h   t   s   b

by

Istituto Italiano
di Cultura

KNIGHTSBRIDGE U

cj

Raphael St.

Trevor
Square

Montpelier Pl.

Montpelier St.

Sloane
Street

ca

Lowndes

Square

Wilton Crescent

p

West Halkin St.

Motcomb St.

Belgrave
Square

D

Ennismore

Rutland   Gate

Montpelier
Sq.

b

bz

Harrods

Hans Crescent

Hans

Rd.

Lowndes

Street

Belgrave

Ennismore
Gardens

rm

Cheval   Place

Hans

Place

bw

Cadogan

Place

Chesham
Place

Consolato
d'Italia

Belgra

BE

E

ul

Beauchamp
Gdns.

cb

cd

vs

Beauchamp Pl.

Brompton   Oratory

vu

vp

Egerton   Gds.

Egerton   Ter.

vo

ws

Walton   Street

Ovington   Sq.

Pont   Street

Lennex
Square

Cadogan
Lane

Eaton Pl.

Lyall   St.

S   g   u

Kings

Eaton

Thurloe Place

cm

Egerton Gdns.

Egerton Pl.

vi

BROMPTON

vm

Milner St.

Moore St.

Halsey St.

Cadogan
Square

Cadogan
Gate

Sloane

Street

Cadogan

Cadogan   Place

cc

Holy
Trinity

Chesham Pl.

Eaton Ter.

South

Eaton

Chester   Terr.

F

Thurloe
Square

South   Terrace

Pelham   Street

Fulham   Road

Elystan   Pl.

Sydney   Pl.

vd

vk

wa

uh

S

vf

Denyer   St.

Rawlings St.

Draycott   Avenue

Cadogan   Place

Sloane   Avenue

Whiteheads   Grove

Draycott   Place

Draycott   Gds.

Cadogan

Kings

Road

SLOANE SQUARE U

Sloane
Square

Royal Court
Theatre

ce

Lower   Sloane   St.

Sloane Gdns.

uj

Cliveden Pl.

Holbein

Graham   Terr.

Pim

1   2   3

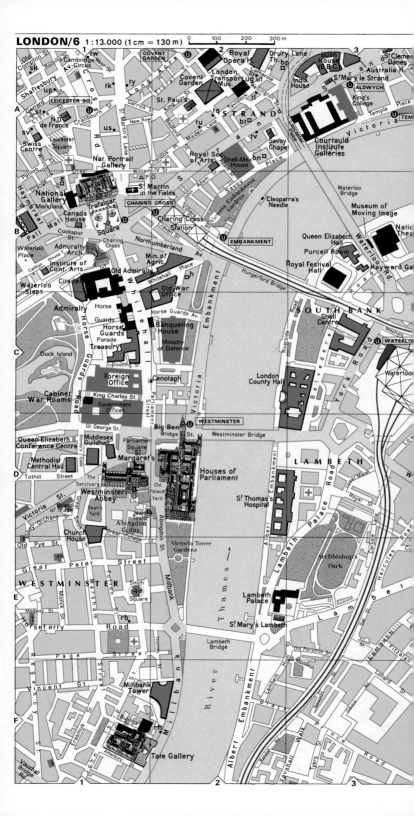

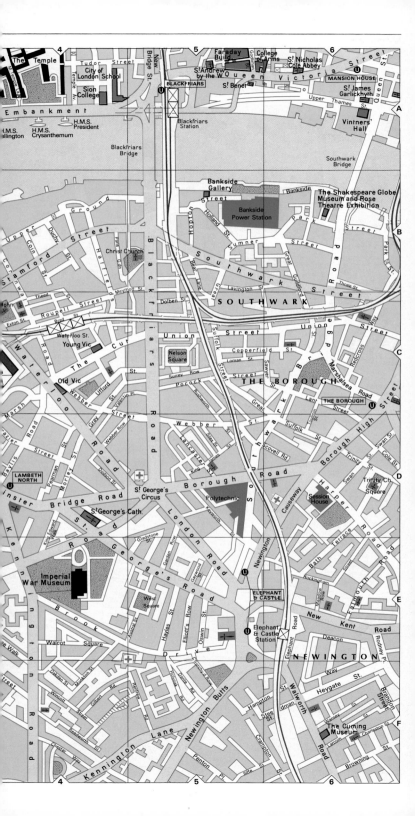

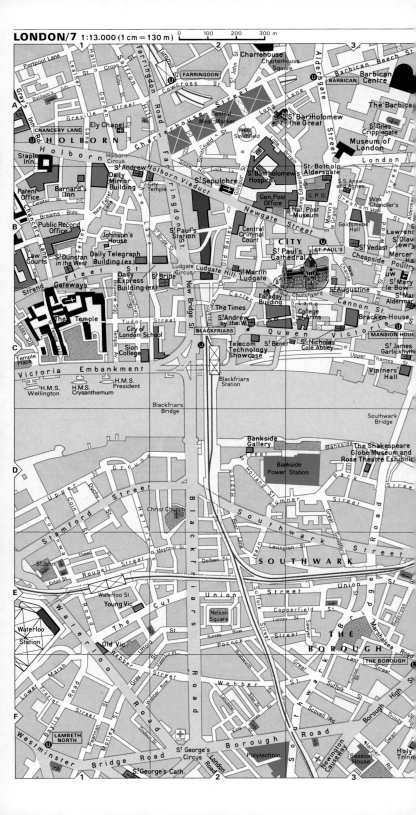

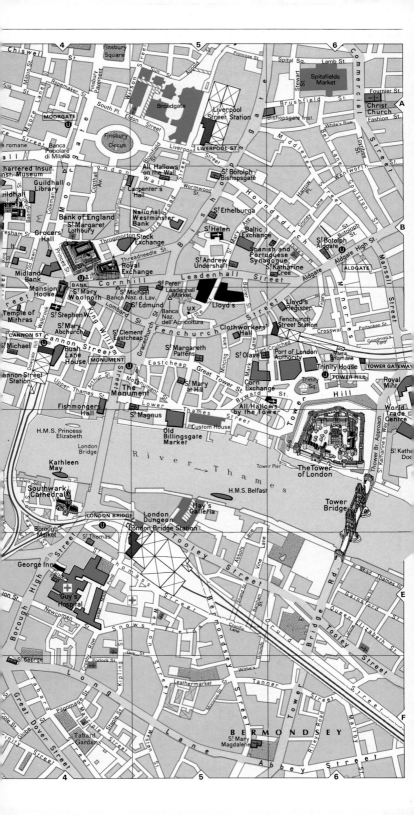

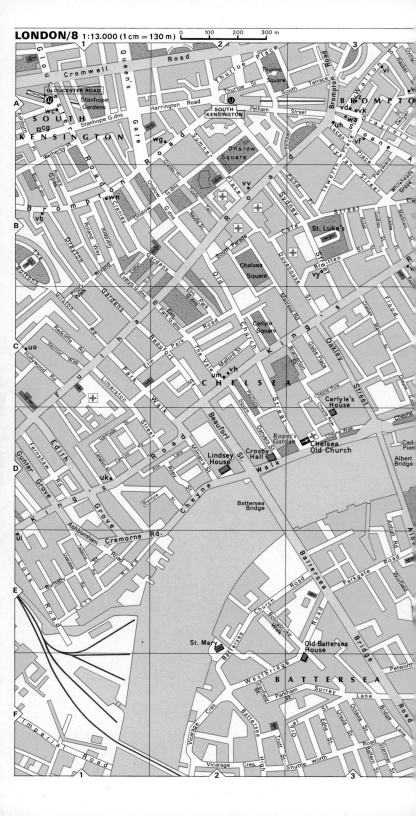

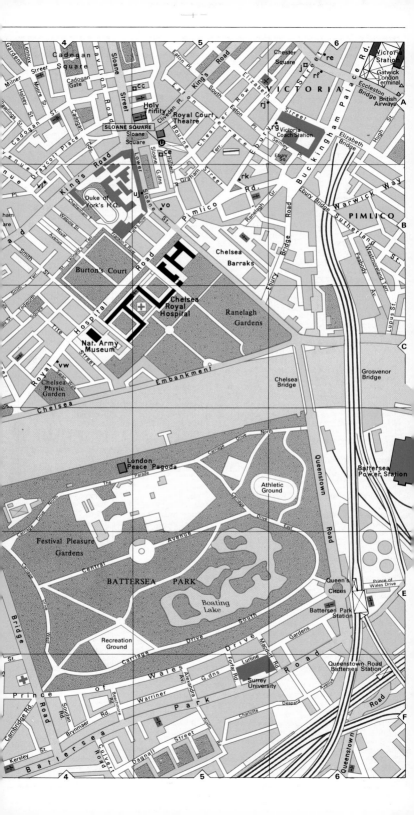

◆ MAP INDEX

465